MARK GIROUARD

THE RETURN TO CAMELOT

Chivalry and the English Gentleman

Yale University Press
New Haven and London 1981

TO MARJORIE VILLIERS

Designed by Dorothy Girouard
Calligraphy by Anne Moring

Typesetting and monochrome origination by
BAS Printers Limited, Over Wallop, Hampshire.
Printed in Italy by
Amilcare Pizzi s.p.a., Milan.

Published in Great Britain, Europe, Africa, and Asia (except Japan) by Yale University Press Limited, London. Distributed in Australia and New Zealand by Book & Film Services, Artarmon, N.S.W., Australia; and in Japan by Harper & Row, Publishers, Tokyo Office.

Library of Congress Cataloging in Publication Data

Girouard, Mark, 1931–
    The Return to Camelot.

    Bibliography: p.
    Includes index.
    1. Great Britain—Social life and customs—18th century.
2. Great Britain—Social life and customs—19th century.
3. Great Britain—Social life and customs—20th century.
4. Upper classes—Great Britain—History—18th century.
5. Upper classes—Great Britain—History—19th century.
6. Upper classes—Great Britain—History—20th century.
I. Title.   II. Title: Chivalry and the English gentleman.
DA533.G5   941   81-51343
ISBN 0-300-02739-7   AACR2

PREFACE

This book describes how the code of mediaeval chivalry, and the knights, castles, armour, heraldry, art and literature that it produced, were revived and adapted in Britain from the late eighteenth century until the 1914–18 war. Once one starts looking for the influence of chivalry in this period one finds it in almost embarrassingly large quantities. Knights in armour by the thousand are described in literature, depicted in painting, sculpture or stained glass, or actually appear live, jousting (or attempting to joust) at the Eglinton Tournament. Modern castles are everywhere, and so is the heraldry to go with them. Less obvious, but of equal if not greater interest is the part which the revival of chivalry played in creating ideals of behaviour, by which all gentlemen were influenced , even if they did not consciously realise it. In this respect chivalry had, in fact, a continuous if waning history from the Middle Ages; but from the late eighteenth century onwards it acquired a new intensity and new characteristics. The result was the chivalrous gentleman of Victorian and Edwardian days, who can be watched at work from the public schools to the Boy Scouts, and from Toynbee Hall to the outposts of the British Empire.

It is with this aspect of chivalry that the book is especially concerned; it is not an art-historical or literary study, and pictures, works of literature, and buildings are brought in only in so far as they express or helped to form ideals of conduct. Even when limited in this way the subject is dauntingly large, and also dauntingly hard to define; it has often been difficult to know where to draw the line. Two major limitations have been made, in order to produce a manageable result. In the first place, tempting though it would have been to examine the chivalric elements in, for instance, Waugh and Wodehouse, the story has been brought to a close with the 1914–18 war; since the war both brought Victorian chivalry to its climax and helped to destroy it, it forms a natural termination. Secondly, the book confines itself to the influence of chivalry in the British Isles and virtually excludes Europe and America.

This is not because chivalry was not at work there. It would have been fascinating, for instance, to have traced the influence of chivalry on German attitudes before and during the Great War or on the kind of American gentleman who died with such style on the *Titanic*. The Kaiser talked about putting on 'shining armour', and the war posters of Germany and her allies contain far more chivalric images than the English ones. America at this period had a flourishing boys' movement called the Knights of King Arthur; most of the popular editions of Malory in circulation in late Victorian and Edwardian England were written by Americans; England had nothing as ambitious as Abbey's great sequence of Arthurian paintings in the Boston Public Library; and chivalry was sufficiently strong for Mark Twain to deliver a vicious attack on it in *A Yankee at the Court of King Arthur*, a book which is by no means the light-hearted piece of fooling that most people presume it to be.

Mark Twain attacked mediaeval knights as superstitious, snobbish and ignorant exploiters of the rest of society. In England, too, sympathy for chivalry was by no means universal; it is worth stressing how many people and organisations, including many sympathetic and creative ones, remained indifferent to its ideals, and in some cases actively hostile to them. A concentrated study of its influence inevitably tends to make it loom too large.

None the less, its influence was very great, and trying to trace it has been a fascinating task. Among those who have helped me I would like to thank Ursula, Countess of Eglinton and Winton, Mrs Pryce, Richard Pryce, and above all Ian Anstruther for help and loans of material concerning the Eglinton Tournament; Michael Dormer for showing me the surviving papers of Kenelm Henry Digby; Viscount Boyne for help in working out the nineteenth-century history of Brancepeth Castle; Lord Dufferin, Lord Ferrier, and Nancy Hore-Ruthven for information and loans; Veronica Tritton and Lord Revelstoke for welcoming me at Parham and Lambay; Mrs Ella W. Wetherill and Marshall Haseltine for hospitality at the Château de Drouilly; and Jill Howell and John Harris for giving me the run of their Great War collections. Many organisations have dealt patiently with visits and requests, especially the Royal Library and Archives at Windsor Castle, the Lord Chamberlain's Office, the Guildhall Library, the Fitzwilliam Museum, the County Record Office, Lincoln, the Watts Gallery, the Fine Arts Society and the Scout Association. I would also like to thank Mrs Aldridge, Helen Bennett, Mark Bence-Jones, Anne Black, Maurice Bond, David Cheshire, Mary Cosh, Geoffrey de Bellaigue, Peter Ferriday, Desmond FitzGerald, Lord and Lady Gage, Stephen Green, Francis Haskell, William Hillcourt, Lord Howe, Emma James, Jane Langton, Patrick Lindsay, Elizabeth Longford, James Macaulay, Mrs McRory, Raymond Mander, Diana Martin, Sir Oliver and Lady Millar, David Milinaric, Joe Mitchenson, Lady Mulholland, David Muspratt, M. H. Noel Paton, Valerie Pakenham, Nicholas Penny, Daphne Pollen, David Reed, Sir James Richards, J. Martin Robinson, Mary Rous, Sidney Sabine, Sarah Stevenson, Jim and Mary Stirling, Patrick Strong, Christopher S. Sykes, Roger Sylvester, and Hugh Weldon; and finally Claudia Elliott, Faith Hart, John Nicoll, Michael Shaw and my wife for help in rough times and smooth.

Contents

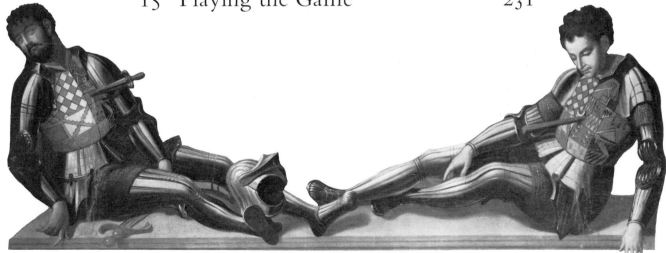

1. (previous page) A. T. Hudson. *John and Thomas Fitzwilliam*
2. Captain Oates walks out to his death, from the painting by J. C. Dollman, 1913

CHAPTER 1

1912

DURING THE FIRST FEW MONTHS OF 1912 A NEW PLAY, *Where the Rainbow Ends*, was running to packed audiences of parents and children at the Savoy Theatre in London.[1] It had had its first performance on 21 December, and was soon to rival *Peter Pan* and be repeated every Christmas until the 1950s. The play is about two children, Rosamund and Crispian Carey. They and two friends escape by magic carpet from Riversdale, Maidenhead, the home of their wicked aunt and uncle, and go to look for their shipwrecked parents in the Land where the Rainbow Ends. To get there they have to pass through the realm of the Dragon King, but they are protected by St George, whom Rosamund calls to their aid: 'We are starting on a journey of perils and dangers. Oh, it's too lovely! Well, I'm going to wish for a knight to fight for us.'

St George's first appearance in the library of Riversdale is a disappointment; he is just a grey-haired, soldierly man in a long grey cloak. But on Rosamund's doubtfully saying, 'I am an English maiden in danger, and I ask for your aid', there is a blinding flash, the cloak vanishes and St George is revealed in shining armour, complete with sword and red cross. After a little chat about Agincourt he sends the children on their way: 'Dear English maid, remember though you see me not that I am ever with you—your faithful guardian knight.' He kisses his sword and swears himself once more to England's cause: 'God for George, England and the Right.'

The children are pursued by the Dragon King, their Aunt Matilda and their Uncle Joseph—the latter a sadistic buffoon, wearing a top hat and carrying a whip. They have various adventures, but St George comes to their aid and finally fights and conquers the Dragon King in his own castle. He is only just in time, for the children are about to be thrown from the ramparts. 'And in a very small unfamous way,' says Rosamund, 'this will be dying for England, won't it?'

The play is full of patriotism and the Empire. Crispian is a smart young naval cadet from Dartmouth. He has a pet lion cub, 'Cubs', who wears a red, white and blue ribbon and is fed on 'Commonwealth Mixture for British Lion. Equal parts of Canadian, Australian, and New Zealand Iron, mixed with South African Steel.' The bottle is marked 'Poison to Traitors', and chokes Uncle Joseph when he takes a sip, just after he has been making fun of the British flag, 'that little bit of bumptious bunting'. The Dragon King is fighting against St George and trying to corrupt the English. 'Almost had I worked the downfall of his land—I flung my gold dust in the people's eyes and lulled them into false security.' But St George calls them back to their true destiny, which is to join the nations of the world and 'fight aggression and foul tyranny'. At the end of the play he cries out to the audience:

> Rise, Youth of England, let your voices ring
> For God, for Britain, and for Britain's King.

Audience and cast sing the National Anthem together.

While *Where the Rainbow Ends* was running, Captain Robert Falcon Scott and his four companions were travelling on the last stages of their journey to the

3. Reginald Owen as St George plights his troth in the first production of *Where the Rainbow Ends*

South Pole. Scott was what Crispian might have become, an ex-Dartmouth cadet fighting through snow and ice to win glory for his king and country. The expedition reached the Pole on 17 January, only to find that a Norwegian team led by R. E. G. Amundsen had been there just over a month before. Despondently they started on the eight hundred mile journey back to their base camp. They were short of food and had to drag their heavy sledges on half rations. Most of them were already in poor physical condition. On 16 February Petty Officer Evans collapsed, and died the next night. Captain Oates's feet turned gangrenous from frost-bite and it became clear that he could not go on much longer. In the early morning of 17 March he limped out of the tent in which they were all sleeping, walked into the falling snow and did not return. Scott wrote in his journal: 'We know that poor Oates was walking to his death . . . it was the act of a brave man and an English gentleman. We all hope to meet the end in the same spirit and assuredly the end is not far.'[2]

The bodies of Scott and his two remaining companions, Dr Edward Wilson and Lieutenant B. H. R. Bowers, were found in November 1912. They were lying frozen in their tent at the point where they had given up a few days after Oates's death. With them were Scott's journals and the letters which he had written while he was waiting to die. To Mrs Bowers he wrote that 'We are very near the end of our journey and I am finishing it in company with two gallant, noble gentlemen. One of these is your son.' To Sir Edgar Speyer, 'But we have been to the Pole and we shall die like gentlemen.' To Admiral Bridgeman, 'After all we are setting a good example to our countrymen, if not by getting into a tight place, by facing it like men when we were there. We could have come through had we neglected the sick.'[3]

Oates's body was never found, but a cairn was put up in his memory; its inscription reads, 'Hereabouts died a very gallant gentleman, Capt. L. E. G. Oates, of the Inniskilling Fusiliers.' When the news reached England, and the journal and letters were published, the dead men became national heroes. A memorial service was held in their memory at St Paul's; the cathedral was packed and George V was among the congregation. Especial honour was given to Oates, who had sacrificed his life in order not to be a burden to his friends, and to Scott, leader and inspirer of the expedition, 'firm in his friendship and chivalrous in his conduct', as *The Times* put it. They had entered that pantheon of Polar heroes of whom Sir Clements Markham, Scott's first patron, had written, 'the thrilling narratives of their exploits team with deeds of devotion unequalled in all the deeds of knight-errantry'.[4]

Ten months before the memorial service for Scott and his companions, St Paul's had been the scene of another service in memory of those drowned in the *Titanic*. The *Titanic* was the biggest and most luxurious liner in the world. She was on her maiden voyage, and her passenger list was studded with millionaires and famous names. She ripped her hull open on an iceberg at 11.40 p.m. on the night of 14 April 1912 and sank two hours and forty minutes later (Plate I). The scene in those hours, as described by the survivors, was an extraordinary one. It was a calm and clear night, the huge liner was blazing with light, the band was playing rag-time at the head of the grand staircase, and except for a slight tilt in the hull and the stillness of the engines there was little surface sign that the ship was doomed until the very end. The lifeboats were gradually filled; the inevitable order went out: 'Women and children first.' Gentlemen escorted ladies to the boats as though to their carriages, and helped them courteously in. Colonel John Jacob Astor handed in his new young bride, 'smiled, touched his cap and . . . turned back to his place among the men'. Mrs William T. Graham, having been helped into her boat by Howard Case, London manager of Vacuum Oil and 'one of the chivalrous young heroes of the Titanic', watched him lean against the rail, light a cigarette and wave goodbye as her boat was rowed away. 'Walter, you must come with me', begged Mrs Walter D. Douglas. 'No,' replied Mr Douglas, turning away, 'I must be a gentleman.' Miss Marie Young, who had taught music to President Taft's children in the White House, described her treatment by Major Archibald Butt, the President's Military Aide. 'Archie himself put me into the boat, wrapped blankets about me, and tucked me in as carefully as if we were starting on a motor ride . . . performing the little courtesies as calmly and with as

smiling a face as if death were far away . . . When he had carefully wrapped me up he stepped upon the gunwale of the boat, and lifting his hat, smiled down at me. "Good-bye, Miss Young," he said, "Good luck to you and don't forget to remember me to the folks back home."'[5]

Major Butt, 'one of God's own noblemen', was described as having acted equally well towards 'those poor frightened steerage people'; his tenderness combined with manly firmness prevented the loss of many lives from panic. None the less there were some who did panic. 'There were various men passengers,' according to one of the stewards, 'probably Italians, or some foreign nationality other than English or American, who attempted to rush the boats.'[6] J. Bruce Ismay, managing director of the White Star Line, which owned the *Titanic*, dropped quietly into a lifeboat just as it was leaving; he was never able to hold his head up again.

When the last boat had gone the men who were left behind waited calmly for the end. W. T. Stead, the great English journalist, had sat reading in the first class smoking room until the last possible moment. Samuel Guggenheim appeared with his valet, both in evening dress. 'We've dressed in our best,' he explained, 'and are prepared to go down like gentlemen.'[7] All were agreed that the crew behaved wonderfully. They remained at their posts to the very last minute. The stewards were unfailingly courteous and helpful. The physical-training instructor continued to instruct passengers on the horse and parallel bars. The engineers stayed by their engines. The band went on playing rag-time; just before the boat

5

4, 5. Illustrations from Logan Marshall's *Sinking of the Titanic*, 1912: (left) Major Archibald Butt, who went down with the *Titanic*; (right) 'Heart-Breaking Farewells', as seen by a contemporary artist

MISS VIOLET KEPPEL
As a Wayting Ladye

COUNTESS
PAULINE PAPPENHEIM
As a Wayting Ladye

VISCOUNTESS CURZON
As Queen of Beauty

EARL WINTERTON
As one of the Knights

PRINCESS PLESS
As the Princess Errant

6. Viscountess Curzon, the Queen of Beauty, and other participants in the Elizabethan Triumph of 1912, as shown in the *Bystander*, 17 July

went down it changed to the Episcopal hymn 'Autumn'—or, according to some witnesses, 'Nearer, my God, to Thee'.

About fifteen hundred people were drowned; only six hundred and fifty-one were saved. The redeeming feature of the disaster, it was generally agreed, was the chivalry shown by the men, both passengers and crew. *Punch* published a full-page cartoon of a mourning Britannia, with appropriate verses:

> What courage yielded place to other's need,
> Patient of discipline's supreme decree,
> Well may we guess, who knew that gallant breed
> Schooled in the ancient chivalry of the sea.

The American Logan Marshall thought that '"Chivalry" is a mild appellation for their conduct. Some of the vaunted knights of old were desperate cowards by comparison. A fight in the open field, or jousting in the tournament, did not call out the manhood in a man as did the waiting till the great ship took the final plunge.'[8]

The year 1912 could offer 'jousting in the tournament' as well. A tournament took place in the Empress Hall at Earl's Court on 11 July. It was part of an 'Elizabethan Triumph', itself part of the tri-centenary 'Shakespeare's England' celebrations organised by Lady Randolph Churchill—or Mrs George Cornwallis-West, as she had become. The Queen of Beauty, Viscountess Curzon, was carried to her pavilion in a purple-plumed litter. Attendant ladies rode after her on rose-wreathed palfreys, among them Lady Diana Manners, Mrs Raymond Asquith, Vita Sackville-West and Violet Keppel. Next came Princess Pless, as 'Princess Errant', all pale blue and silver on a huge grey horse. Her escort of 'stranger knights' included the Duke of Berwick and Alba, Prince Kinsky (who had been Lady Randolph Churchill's lover), the future King of Greece and the Grand

6

7. Lord Crichton (in armour) rehearsing with Lord Compton

Duke of Mecklenberg-Strelitz. Among the audience (not as large as had been hoped for, owing, it was thought, to the high price of the tickets) were Queen Alexandra, Lord Curzon of Kedleston, Lord Rosebery, Sir Ernest Cassel, Winston Churchill and Mr Pierpont Morgan.[9]

Six knights jousted in pairs: they were the Duke of Marlborough, Lord Craven, Lord Compton, Lord Crichton, Lord Tweedmouth and Lord Ashby St Legers. As they fought, the herald intoned, 'Fight on, brave Knights, man dies but Glory lives; fight on, Death is better than defeat, fight on, Brave Knights, for bright eyes behold your deeds.' Then they joined battle with six more knights in a mêlée. Finally, the judges announced that 'The Duke of Marlborough had well jousted, but Lord Ashby St Legers had jousted best', and the latter was presented with a gold cup by the Queen of Beauty.[10]

★   ★   ★

Knights in armour, St George, the Empire, knights rescuing maidens in distress, chivalrous and gallant gentlemen, dying like gentlemen, women and children first—the occurrence of all these themes in different contexts within the same year is more than coincidence. A thin but genuine thread connects the Duke of Marlborough in his suit of armour to Samuel Guggenheim in his dinner-jacket. The latter was dying like a gentleman, and how gentlemen lived and died was partly determined by the way in which they believed knights had lived and died. All gentlemen knew that they must be brave, show no sign of panic or cowardice, be courteous and protective to women and children, be loyal to their comrades and meet death without flinching. They knew it because they had learnt the code of the gentleman in a multitude of different ways, through advice, through example, through what they had been taught at school or by their parents, and through endless stories of chivalry, daring, knights, gentlemen and gallantry which they had read or been told by way of history books, ballads, poems, plays, pictures and novels.

Those with the right background knew how they were expected to behave, in shipwreck or blizzard, or in other situations. Both the wreck of the *Titanic* and Scott's expedition take their place in a roll-call of similar stories. The *Titanic*, for instance, comes in a sequence of heroic shipwrecks of which the most famous was the wreck of the *Birkenhead* in 1852. The *Birkenhead* was a troop ship which split on the rocks off the west coast of Africa. There were only enough boats to take off the women and children, all of whom were saved through the exertions of soldiers and crew. There was no panic, and no attempt on the part of any of the men to rush the boats. Sir William Napier, veteran of the Peninsular War, wrote to *The Times* asking for national recognition of 'the matchless chivalry' of the officers in charge and the 'responding generous devotion' of their men.[11] The wreck was celebrated in at least three poems, recounted in school history books, and told by Sir Robert Baden-Powell to his boys in the section of his *Scouting for Boys* (1908) headed 'Chivalry of the Knights'.

Scott and his companions were fully conscious of the many stories of Polar heroism and disaster which had preceded their expedition. One of Scott's inspirations had been the famous but ill-fated Franklin expedition in 1845, which finally discovered the North-West Passage, but only at the cost of the death of Sir John Franklin and all his one hundred and twenty-eight men. Franklin was described by a contemporary as a modern Chevalier Bayard, 'in all things and under all circumstances . . . "sans peur et sans reproche" . . . Thus, in this prosaic age, went forth again John Franklin, in true knightly mood, to endure, labour and accomplish much.'[12] His Arctic expeditions encouraged Scott's rival, Amundsen, as a young man 'to see myself as a kind of Crusader in Arctic exploration. I wanted to suffer for a cause—not in the burning desert on the way to Jerusalem—but in the frosty North.'[13]

The Earl's Court Tournament and *Where the Rainbow Ends* also take their place in chivalric sequences. The former derived of course from mediaeval tournaments, but the lords and ladies who took part in it saw it more in terms of the famous and even more aristocratic Eglinton Tournament of 1839. It was referred to as the 'revived Eglinton tournament',[14] at least four of the knights descended from people who had played a part at Eglinton, and one of them, the Earl of Craven, was actually wearing the armour worn by his grandfather when he fought at Eglinton as the Knight of the Griffin.[15] In between came a mini-tournament at Parham in Sussex in 1875; a projected but abortive tournament at Taymouth Castle in Perthshire in 1880; and a tournament at Budapest in 1902, in which the Hungarian aristocracy jousted before the Emperor of Austria, and were presented with wreaths by the archduchesses Augusta and Elizabeth.[16]

By 1912 St George had had a long and illustrious history as patron saint both of the Garter and of England; but (besides having just been adopted as patron saint of the Boy Scouts) he had come into increasing prominence since the late nineteenth century as a symbol of imperialism. Reginald Owen, who played St George in the original production of *Where The Rainbow Ends* (and had actually collaborated in writing it under the pseudonym of John Ramsey), had acted a few years earlier in an extremely successful stage-version of Anthony Hope's *Prisoner*

8

I. (right) The sinking of the *Titanic*, from a contemporary needlework picture

II. (following page) Robert Adam. Design for the East Window, the Chapel, Alnwick Castle, 1777

R. Adam Archt. 1777.

Scale of

Feet

8. The Wreck of the *Birkenhead*, from the picture by Napier Hemy

of Zenda. The hero of this and its companion novel *Rupert of Hentzau* was Rudolf Rassendyll, the true but pure lover of Queen Flavia of Ruritania. 'God be with you, Rudolf, my knight', she says to him. He dies tragically, and his friends call him a 'most gallant gentleman' and 'the noblest gentleman I have known'.

Similar phrases were to be applied to Captain Oates and his companions. Gentlemen in fact not only knew how gentlemen should behave, but how to describe that behaviour. Particular situations produced a particular kind of language. They had all read the right books as children. A contemporary school history book describes the wreck of the *Birkenhead* as follows: 'The roll of the drum called the soldiers to arms on the upper deck. The call was promptly obeyed, though every man knew that it was his death summons. There they stood, as if on parade, no man showing restlessness or fear, though the ship was every moment going down, down.' A popular painting re-created the scene, with the men standing quietly in ranks while a drummer-boy rolled his drum.[17]

In fact there was no drummer-boy, no rolling drum; the men were not called on parade, and did not stand in ranks. The event, inspiring enough in itself, was improved in the telling. It and similar events, similarly dramatised, joined with a mass of similar scenes in history books or fiction to provide a composite manual of language as well as behaviour. As a result descriptions of heroic events, even those

III. (preceding page) Benjamin West. *Edward III and the Black Prince after the Battle of Crecy*, 1788 (detail)

IV. (left) The King's Champion at the Westminster Hall banquet, 1821. Detail from the illustration, after George Jones, in Whittaker's *Coronation of George IV*, 1823

of eye-witnesses, are often so stylised that the event loses all reality; it is sometimes hard, when reading Scott's journal or, even more, the accounts of the end of the *Titanic*, to realise that these were actual and terrible tragedies, not episodes in a bad novel. Moreover, as in the case of the *Birkenhead*, the descriptions tended to improve on the event, in order to put it in line with the literary tradition. Many of the eye-witness accounts of the wreck of the *Titanic* certainly or almost certainly bear little relation to what happened. The heroism of Major Archibald Butt, 'God's own nobleman', for instance, depends on two possibly unreliable witnesses; it is doubtful whether he helped Miss Young or anyone else into a lifeboat.[18] The almost unanimous tendency of Anglo-Saxon witnesses to assume that anyone who behaved badly was an Italian, or some other form of foreigner, needs to be treated with caution.

In fact Victorian and Edwardian chivalry produced its own world of myth and legend, just as much as mediaeval chivalry. And, as in the case of mediaeval chivalry, the inspiring images are sometimes out of touch with the reality. Proportionately fewer steerage children, for instance, survived from the *Titanic* than men travelling first or second class; the figures are somewhat disconcerting, even if they reflect the unconscious operation of the class structure rather than any deliberate decision. Moreover, the whole disaster need never have happened if proper precautions had been taken. The *Titanic* had 2,340 aboard and lifeboats for 1,100. What lifeboats there were only managed to take off 651 people in spite of the calm sea; four were wrecked on launching, and most went off without a full load. There had been no boat-drill, no crews or passengers allotted to particular lifeboats. (Similarly, not only did the *Birkenhead* have pathetically few boats, but half of those which she did have had rusted to their supports and were unusable.) Amundsen's expedition went smoothly and successfully to the South Pole and back largely because its members were carefully trained professionals whereas Scott and his men were, by comparison, hopelessly and in some aspects culpably amateurish. Scott's last message, 'we are setting a good example to our countrymen, if not by getting into a tight place, by facing it like men when we were there', suggests an attitude in which heroism becomes more important than the intelligent forethought which would make heroism unnecessary. In the code of the gentleman intelligence was a little suspect.

And yet something surely remains. Even when the *Titanic* story is reduced to size, it is still an impressive and moving one. They don't, one feels, thinking of Colonel Astor and the rest, make them like that any more. In such feelings there are, for most people, elements of affection, admiration and regret. Many will remember that particular mixture of gentleness, courtesy, sweetness, lack of guile and unbending sense of honour which characterised old-fashioned gentlemen of a certain kind. One says old-fashioned, because the type scarcely survives; it was the product of a particular set of circumstances which no longer exist. What those circumstances were, how it happened that Bayard, the Black Prince, King Arthur and their companions came back from the days of chivalry to crowd into literature and painting, and influence the lives and characters of officers, gentlemen, schoolboys, lovers and Boy Scouts, is at least an interesting story.

14

9. (right) The Earl of Cumberland dressed for tilting, from the miniature by Nicholas Hilliard

CHAPTER 2

Survival
and
Revival

WHAT IS MEANT BY CHIVALRY? CLEARLY SOME SORT OF DEFINITION HAS TO BE attempted, in a book which treats of its revival. It is sure to be inadequate, because chivalry is not a simple phenomenon; its origin, meaning and early development call for a book, not a few paragraphs.[1] Chivalry is not the same as feudalism, although the two concepts are clearly related; it concerned itself with one particular class, not the structure of society. It was the code of conduct evolved for the knights of the Middle Ages, that is to say for an élite and increasingly hereditary class of warriors; it accepted fighting as a necessary and indeed glorious activity, but set out to soften its potential barbarity by putting it into the hands of men committed to high standards of behaviour. These derived from an amalgamation of Christianity with the pre-Christian traditions of the warrior bands of Northern Europe; they were adapted to the social structure of feudalism and· amended by the cult of courtly love as it developed in the rich and sophisticated courts of Southern France. The ideal knight was brave, loyal, true to his word, courteous, generous and merciful. He defended the Church and the wrongfully oppressed but respected and honoured his enemies in war, as long as they obeyed the same code as he did. Failure to keep to accepted standards meant dishonour, to which death was preferable. Many knights dedicated themselves to the service of one particular woman, not necessarily or even usually their wives, and vied with each other in performing deeds of valour in her honour and under her inspiration. In its purest form courtly love, as this type of service came to be called, did not imply sexual relationships; but sex had a way of creeping in.

From time to time attempts were made to write down the code of chivalry, either in treatises or in the form of vows to be taken by those initiated into the order of knighthood. But works such as the *Chanson de Roland*, the *Niebelungenlied*, the poems of the troubadours and the minnesingers, the stories of Parsifal, Gawain, Tristram and Iseult, and all the endless other episodes in the epic of King Arthur and his knights were more important source material for chivalrous behaviour. Many of these were based on much earlier legends, but were always being adapted and amplified for knightly audiences. Between them they presented a world of splendid fights and heroic deaths, of loyal and courteous lovers, of expeditions to rescue damsels from dragons, sorcerers or false knights. The real world bore little enough relationship to this; all too often mediaeval knights were brutal, quarrelsome and self-seeking. But none the less the ideal existed and was recognised.

Chivalry as a code of conduct can be distinguished from the armour which the knights wore, the castles in which they lived, the tournaments in which they fought, the heraldry which distinguished one fighting knight from another, the individual Orders to which many of them belonged, and the ceremonies with which they were installed. But the blanket term of chivalry has always been applied both to the code and to its mediaeval trappings. In the sixteenth, seventeenth and eighteenth centuries one can watch the code gradually developing until it becomes one element of the accepted code of conduct for gentlemen, and the trappings gradually losing their practical function, but sometimes surviving because put to new uses or used for symbolic purposes.

16

In England, mediaeval chivalry had an Indian summer during the reign of Elizabeth—a summer which lasted on into the early seventeenth century, and more or less ended in the 1620s. It centred round the cult of Elizabeth herself, who could demand the loyalty of her knights as a monarch, and their devotion as a mistress. Elizabethan chivalry has an exotic and unreal quality, because the apparatus of chivalry is all still there, but has been increasingly injected with fantasy and has almost entirely lost any relationship to contemporary warfare. Elizabeth's knights vowed extravagant devotion to her, and jousted before her in elaborate armour; but jousting was no longer a form of training for the battlefield, and half the point of the jousts lay in the allegorical pageantry, half Gothic, half Renaissance, which accompanied them.[2] Castles were still being built, or at least houses with a castle air about them, but their tangled and exotic skylines of domed turrets and pierced battlements had nothing to do with the squat bastions and carefully calculated sight-lines of Renaissance military engineering. The early seventeenth-century Bolsover Castle in Derbyshire, with its mock fortifications, vaulted rooms, carved chimney-pieces and statue of Venus at the centre of a crenellated garden enclosure, is essentially a more solid version of the pasteboard castles that were erected as part of the entertainments put on to celebrate royal events, or of the allegorical castles of Spenser's *Faerie Queene*.[3]

Spenser's epic is full of castles, monsters, knights, queens and ladies, but behind them all lies an elaborate moral and political allegory, in which Gloriana, the Faerie Queene, is Elizabeth herself. Elizabethan chivalry in general, however out of touch with reality it may seem, was in fact a genuine reaction to a real situation, one way of stimulating loyalty and service to the queen of a Protestant nation fighting for power, prestige and survival. The mimic battles of Elizabethan tournaments took place in the same years as real battles against the Spaniards on sea and land, accompanied by real acts of chivalry and heroism. Sir Philip Sidney, whose *Arcadia* is full of knights and tournaments, and whom Elizabeth had watched when he donned superb blue and gold armour and took part in a mock attack on a mock Castle of Perfect Beauty, died as a result of being wounded in a real battle at Zutphen in 1586; and by giving up his water-bottle to a dying soldier, when in desperate need of it himself, he entered the pantheon of chivalrous heroes.

If one moves from Elizabethan chivalry and its Jacobean aftermath to England of the early eighteenth century, one finds that in the interval it has gone almost entirely underground. Certain of its elements as a code of behaviour survive, absorbed into contemporary manners; the language in which a gentleman addresses a woman, or writes poetry or love letters to his mistress, or challenges another gentleman to a duel, or toasts his king, is likely to be conditioned by the chivalric tradition, whether he is aware of it or not. The small professional armies and navies, to whom the conduct of war is now almost entirely entrusted, follow an agreed code of conduct, as regards paroles, or the treatment of prisoners or of women and children, which ultimately derives from the code of chivalry.

But the last tournament had probably taken place in 1624;[4] Malory's *Morte d'Arthur*, the main English version of the Arthurian legend, which had come out

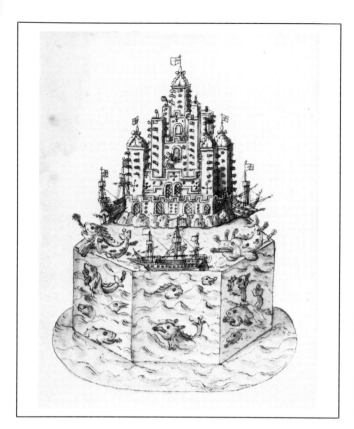

in regular new editions since its first printing in 1485, had not been reprinted since 1634. Occasional castles or castellated houses were still being built, especially in Scotland, where the feeling that a great territorial magnate should live in a castle had never quite died. In England the architect Sir John Vanbrugh had a weakness for castles, and even built a little one for himself at Greenwich. Around 1700 Lord Coningsby restored Hampton Court in Herefordshire in castle style, and commissioned a portrait of Henry IV on horseback and in armour to hang in it.[5]

The science of heraldry survived and flourished, but its chivalric origins had been largely forgotten; a coat of arms was evidence of gentle birth or illustrious ancestry, not a means of identification in battle. The two great mediaeval Orders of knighthood, the Garter and the Bath, maintained their prestige; but the Knights of the Garter were no longer warriors, and held their traditional feasts in St George's Hall at Windsor against a background of Baroque frescoes in which their founder, the Black Prince, was depicted in Roman dress.[6] At the great banquet held in Westminster Hall to celebrate each coronation, the King's Champion still rode into the hall in armour, escorted by the Lord High Constable and the Earl Marshal, also on horseback, threw down his gauntlet three times, and challenged anyone to dispute the king's right to the throne. The annual Lord Mayor's Procession in the City of London still included the Lord Mayor's Champion, a solitary knight in armour carrying a drawn sword.[7]

It did not amount to very much. So much else had happened to overshadow the chivalric tradition, or make it seem barbarous and absurd. The literature, art and architecture of classical Greece and Rome and of Renaissance Italy had provided

10. (left) A pageant castle erected as part of the fireworks display given in honour of the marriage of Princess Elizabeth to the Elector Palatine, 1613

11. (right) Henry IV, as painted for Hampton Court, Herefordshire, in the early eighteenth century

an alternative culture which dominated most aspects of European civilisation. New discoveries in science or movements in thought had upset the structures of belief on which the Middle Ages had rested. Chivalry had little relevance to ordinary gentlemen living in security and comfort and leaving war to professionals. What meaning could it have for an average Georgian landowner busily planting parks or turnips, building temples, enclosing commons, looking for an heiress, or cementing political alliances? He might be proud of mediaeval ancestors, in so far as they contributed to the status of his family, but that he should in any way imitate them would have seemed absurd to him. Many of the most important elements of chivalry now conflicted with the conviction of the upper and most of the middle classes that anything that savoured of 'enthusiasm' should be avoided, and the belief of progressive people that society could and should be remodelled according to the dictates of reason. Loyalty to a king or leader, however disastrous the result, faithful love, however little requited, readiness to fight for one's honour, however slight the slur on it, or truth to one's word, however rashly given, were qualities which the literature of chivalry singled out for praise, but which eighteenth-century opinion tended to consider stupid rather than noble. Chivalry had no more typical or famous expression than the Crusades; but Hume, in his *History of Great Britain* (1761), wrote them off in a much-quoted phrase as 'the most signal and durable monument of human folly that has yet appeared in any age or nation'.[8]

Thirty years later, in his *Reflections on the Revolution in France* (1790) Edmund Burke talked of chivalry as dead, but in a very different mood to that of Hume. In a moving and memorable passage he described his only meeting with Marie Antoinette and lamented her fall. 'Surely,' he wrote, 'never alighted on this orb, which she hardly seemed to touch, a more delightful vision. I saw her just above the horizon, decorating and cheering the elevated sphere she just began to move in, — glittering like the morning star, full of life, and splendour, and joy . . . Little did I dream that I should have lived to see disasters fallen upon her in a nation of gallant men, in a nation of men of honour, and of cavaliers. I thought ten thousand swords must have leaped from their scabbards to avenge even a look that threatened her with insult. But the age of chivalry is gone. That of sophisters, economists, and calculators, has succeeded; and the glory of England is extinguished for ever.'[9]

In fact, even as he lamented, the age of chivalry was on the way back. The signs of its return were numerous, but one of the most striking can be used to stand for the rest. In 1788 Benjamin West had painted a huge and panoramic picture depicting Edward III's meeting with the Black Prince after the Battle of Crecy. Bareheaded, modest, with eyes downcast, the Black Prince (Plate III) is shown as the epitome of the chivalrous young knight, whose sword would surely have leapt from his scabbard to avenge any wrong to a beautiful woman in distress. All around him swirls the panoply of chivalry: standards wave, war-horses rear, the crests and helmets of the knights are silhouetted against a stormy sky. The picture is one of a series of seven episodes in the reign of Edward III, which West painted in 1787–9 for the King's Audience Chamber at Windsor Castle. Three of these are

battle scenes; two more, *The Black Prince receiving King John of France after Poitiers* and *Edward II entertaining his Prisoners*, illustrate one of the archetypal virtues of chivalry, courteous consideration of the vanquished by the victors; another, the *Burghers of Calais*, shows mercy being given at the intercession of a beautiful queen; the *Institution of the Order of the Garter* celebrates the foundation of one of the most famous of the chivalric Orders, and one closely connected with Windsor Castle. The series was completed by an overmantel picture of *St George and the Dragon*: the patron saint of England and the Order of the Garter, at once defeating the forces of evil and rescuing a damsel in distress.[10]

West's pictures did not occur in a vacuum. In the thirty-odd years between Hume's *History* and Burke's *Reflections* the Middle Ages had slowly begun to come back into favour, bringing chivalry with them. Curiously enough, eighteenth-century glorification of reason and intellect had helped bring this about. It had led to a new attitude to history, based on a critical study of original documents, monuments and artefacts, undertaken in an attempt to work out a coherent and accurate account of what had actually happened. The Middle Ages benefited from this new approach. Antiquaries began to study mediaeval buildings. Bishop Percy published mediaeval ballads and poems in his *Reliques of Ancient English Poetry* (1765), and mediaeval literature was seriously discussed in Thomas Warton's three-volume *History of English Poetry* (1774–81). Grose's *Treatise of Ancient Armour and Weapons* (1786) and the various works published by the able antiquarian Joseph Strutt between 1773 and 1801 produced a flood of new evidence as to the impedimenta of mediaeval life. As a result the armour and other chivalric trappings in West's pictures are far more convincing as re-creations of the Middle Ages than, for instance, the knights designed only twelve years earlier by Robert Adam for the chapel of Alnwick Castle (Plate II)

But the fact that a historic castle such as Alnwick was being lavishly redecorated and restored in the Gothic style was in itself significant, however gaily inaccurate the results. Alnwick was in fact one of a sizeable group of new castles being built, or old ones being restored, in the mid and late eighteenth century. Some,

20

12. John and James Adam. Douglas Castle, Lanarkshire, 1757, from *Vitruvius Scoticus*

especially in Scotland or the North of England, were the work of landowners who were proud of their mediaeval lineage, or had inherited a historic castle. Others expressed the antiquarian enthusiasms of their owners. The castle which Richard Payne Knight began to build for himself at Downton in Herefordshire in 1773 introduced yet another movement which was to help bring castle-building back to England. Knight was a pioneer in applying to architecture the new concept of the Picturesque which had been developed in landscape gardening. There was no castle tradition at Downton, and Knight himself belonged to a new family. He chose the castle style because it allowed him to combine an octagonal, a circular and a square tower in one picturesquely irregular composition.[11]

Building a castle because it was picturesque did not necessarily imply sympathy with the Middle Ages, but building a castle for antiquarian or neo-feudal reasons did. As tends to happen, studies which may have been embarked on in a neutral, merely curious or even hostile spirit tended to end with those engaged in them becoming attached to, and finally enthusiastic for, their period. Thomas Warton moved on from studying mediaeval poetry to composing poems in honour of Arthur and his Round Table. Horace Walpole both read old romances and wrote a modern one, *The Castle of Otranto*; he collected ancient armour and portraits and built Strawberry Hill to put them in, adapting mediaeval tombs and screens to make chimney-pieces for living-rooms and alcoves for bedrooms. By the second half of the eighteenth century there was a sizeable group of country gentlemen with antiquarian tastes, or antiquarians with friends among the gentry, all busy studying the Middle Ages, publishing the results of their researches and building Gothic buildings.

Interest in the Middle Ages inevitably led to an interest in chivalry. As early as 1759 Richard Hurd, later to become Bishop of Worcester, spoke up for chivalry in the third of his *Moral and Political Dialogues*. The tilt-yard was a 'school of fortitude and honour to our generous forefathers'. 'Affability, courtesy, generosity, veracity, these were the qualifications most pretended to by the men of arms, in the days of pure and uncorrupted chivalry.' Moreover, chivalry had

13. Benjamin West. *Edward III and the Black Prince after the Battle of Crecy*, 1788

helped inspire wit and poetry 'amidst the assemblies of noble dames and courteous knights'.[12] Hurd greatly expanded the last point three years later in his *Letters on Chivalry and Romance*. Chivalry and the old romances, he argued, were especially suited to inspire poetry. He cited Spenser, Shakespeare and Milton as examples; the rejection of chivalry was ascribed to the growing ascendancy of reason over imagination. Hurd was one of the first writers to suggest that this was not entirely a good thing; he was also one of the first to draw parallels between chivalric romances and the epics of Homer, and to suggest that they resembled each other because both were the product of war-like and primitive societies.[13]

In 1759, the same year as that in which Hurd published his *Moral and Political Dialogues*, the first two volumes of J. B. de la Curne de Sainte-Palaye's *Mémoires de l'ancienne chevalerie* were published in Paris. An additional third volume appeared in 1781. In 1774 he published his *Histoire littéraire des troubadours*. Horace Walpole owned a copy of the French edition; an English translation by Susan Dobson appeared in 1779, and a translation of his work on chivalry, also by Susan Dobson, came out in 1784. The translation of de Sainte-Palaye's books was significant, because not only did they provide English readers with a mass of information about the age of chivalry, but de Sainte-Palaye was unreservedly enthusiastic about chivalry and all that it stood for.

Hurd was later to be taken up by George III, who appointed him tutor to the Prince of Wales, made him a bishop (and offered him an archbishopric, which he refused), visited him in Worcestershire, and frequently invited him to Windsor or Kew. Hurd may have encouraged, and even suggested, West's Garter series at Windsor, for he was seeing the King regularly both immediately before and while it was being painted.[14]

Indeed the importance of the series lies less in its high quality, impressive though that is, than in the fact that George III had commissioned it. A taste for mediaevalism was now no longer the preserve of a comparatively small circle of antiquarians and a scattering of Northern peers. It, and chivalry with it, had been given royal approval. Similarly, the fact that a politician as eminent as Burke had reached the state of mind where he could lament the decay of chivalry was a symptom of its revival. Burke's swing from progressive Whiggery in the 1770s to nostalgic conservatism in the 1790s, George III's commissioning of the pictures at Windsor and the attitude to politics and society that lay behind the commission, the French Revolution and the revulsions and reactions inspired by it, were related signs or causes of a change in climate.

George III was a natural conservative. He instinctively revered ancient institutions, above all the Church and the monarchy; he disliked and distrusted change. He resisted any increase in democracy and the freedom of the press at home, and any degree of self-government for the colonies abroad. In the first half of his reign the absurdities of the John Wilkes affair and the disasters of the American War of Independence made him very unpopular, especially among those who thought that English institutions were in need of reform.

The French Revolution, and all that resulted from it, brought about a great change, not to his own character or views, but to the way in which these were regarded by his subjects. The overthrow of the whole traditional structure of society in France, the violence that resulted from it, above all the execution of Louis XVI and Marie Antoinette, produced a revulsion against change and reform, in favour of authority and existing institutions. Politicians like Burke and Pitt, who had started their careers as advocates of reform, moved rapidly to the right. Burke's *Reflections on the Revolution in France* worked out a new philosophy of organic growth in politics and society: existing institutions were the end product of the collective wisdom of the centuries and any change in them should only be gradual. The Church, the Crown and the Constitution ceased either to be taken for granted or to be seen as a piece of machinery which could be scrapped or improved according to the dictates of reason. The war against France, once it started in 1793, gave the impetus towards strong central government that is the usual result of wars. Among the upper and middle classes the small number of people who still fought for democracy and the freedom of the press were attacked and persecuted; disaffection among the working classes was ruthlessly suppressed. Traditional Tories combined with rightwards-moving Whigs under the leadership of Pitt to form what was to develop into the nineteenth-century Conservative party. Good, serious, conservative Farmer George, who trusted Pitt and hated democracy, became the focus of a new affection and loyalty.

All these changes affected attitudes to the Middle Ages. An age based on the social structure of feudalism, when kingship was reverenced and the Church at its most powerful, became increasingly attractive to peers, gentlemen and clergymen whose counterparts were having their heads cut off across the channel. It was tempting to romanticise it as an age of simple faith and loyalties and the source of much that now appeared both sacred and threatened. Castles ceased to be considered as at best picturesque relics, at worst products of ignorance and violence; they began to be seen as symbols of authority and tradition.

As a young man George III had been taught architecture by Sir William Chambers, and had almost certainly learned from him to reverence the classical tradition and despise Gothic. It seems likely that his mediaevalism was less the result of personal interest than of appreciation of its value as a buttress to the monarchy. Not surprisingly, in view of the close connection between chivalry and kingship, it was the chivalric aspects of the Middle Ages which he chose to revive. His first modest move was in 1772. In that year Benjamin West, his new favourite among painters, was commissioned to paint a picture of the *Death of the Chevalier Bayard*. This was to be one of a set of three, designed to hang at Buckingham House alongside West's *Death of Wolfe* and *Death of Epaminondas*.[15] The three between them were intended to show how heroes died in the classic, Gothic and modern ages. The Windsor paintings followed in 1787–9.

In 1800 George III appointed James Wyatt his own personal architect, paid from his Privy Purse. It was a prelude to his embarking on a second and more ambitious bout of mediaeval patronage. Wyatt's work for William Beckford at Fonthill had already given him the reputation of someone who knew more about Gothic than anyone else. Everything that he designed for the King was Gothic. In September 1803 George III wrote rather apologetically to his daughter, the

Duchess of Wurtemburg: 'I never thought I should have adopted Gothic instead of Grecian architecture, but the bad taste of the last fifty years has so entirely corrupted the professors of the latter, I have taken to the former from thinking Wyatt perfect in that style.'[16]

West's Edward III pictures had been inserted into the late seventeenth-century decor of the King's Audience Chamber; no attempt was made to Gothicise their setting. But between 1800 and 1814, £150,000 were spent on Gothicising the state apartments at Windsor, inside and out. 'His Majesty plans all the alterations himself,' wrote Mrs Kennedy, a Windsor resident, in 1804; 'it is his great amusement.'[17] In 1805 he extended his interest to the Order of the Garter. On St George's Day, 1805, twenty-five Knights of the Garter were installed at Windsor with a magnificence such as had not been seen since the seventeenth century. After the ceremony superb banquets were given, not only to the knights in St George's Hall, but to separate gatherings of lords and ladies in other parts of the castle. A baron of beef was roasted and served on a silver dish specially made for the occasion; as one contemporary source put it, 'It was his majesty's particular wish, that as many of the old customs should be kept up as possible.' According to the same source, no ceremony could have been 'so well calculated to cherish that chivalrous spirit . . . which burned in the breasts of our ancestors', and its revival at the height of the Napoleonic Wars was an act of sound policy calculated 'to fan the flame of loyalty and patriotism'.[18]

At about the same time work started on the unfinished mediaeval chapel at the east end of St George's Chapel, with the object of converting it into a combination of royal burial-vault and chapter house for the Order of the Garter. James Wyatt's nephew Matthew started work on twenty-eight pictures of the founding Knights of the Garter, which were to form part of its decoration, as well as producing a series of paintings of the story of St George for the King's Closet and the King's and Queen's State Dressing Rooms.[19]

But Wyatt's most remarkable work for the King was at Kew.[20] Windsor was rich in mediaeval and chivalric associations; there was a good case for new Gothic work or for re-Gothicising those parts of it which had been made classical. But at Kew and Richmond the eighteenth-century tradition had been to build or project royal lodges and palaces in the classical style. By commissioning a new castle on the banks of the Thames in Kew Gardens, George III deliberately reversed this policy.

24

14. James Wyatt's Kew Palace, built in 1802–11, but never completed

The new building was modestly called at the time the 'new lodge in Richmond Gardens'. It was in fact bigger than many mediaeval castles. A great square block embellished with corner towers and numerous turrets, rose up beyond a forecourt lined with subsidiary buildings and entered through a battlemented gatehouse.

Little if any evidence survives as to George III's own reasons for building as he did at Kew. A castle may or may not have appealed to him as an expression of authority; but that was certainly the way it appeared to radicals at the time. They nicknamed it the 'Bastille'. 'The rascally Democrats', the architect George Dance wrote to Sir John Soane on 2 August 1802, 'have lately made it their stalking horse.'[21] To others it suggested chivalry rather than oppression. Sir Nathaniel Wraxall compared it to a castle 'in which Ariosto or Spenser depicted captive Princesses detained by Giants or Enchanters'. But Wraxall and others at the time were not prepared to accept so flamboyantly mediaeval a building, even from the King; Wraxall called it a 'most singular monument of eccentricity and expense', an 'image of distempered reason'.[22]

Wraxall wrote this in his memoirs, and was being wise after the event. There is in fact no reason to suppose that George III's mind was affected when he commissioned the castle at Kew. But his madness in 1810, followed by the death of Wyatt in 1813, brought his work at Kew and Windsor to a halt, and left much of it incomplete. The unfinished shell of Kew Castle was blown up in 1827–8; whatever had been done in the proposed Garter chapter house disappeared when the building was converted into a memorial chapel for Prince Albert in the 1860s. Wyatt's work on the state apartments disappeared almost entirely as a result of Wyatville's far more extensive remodelling for George IV; the same remodelling removed West's Edward III series from the Audience Chamber.

George IV had never got on with his father. As a young man he had expressed his dislike, in the traditional way of heirs-apparent, by turning violently Whig in opposition to his father's Toryism. There may have been an element of getting his own back in the way in which he effaced almost all his father's work at Windsor, Kew and Buckingham House. But politically, as soon as he became Prince

15. The Guard Chamber, Windsor Castle, as shown in Nash's *Windsor Castle*, 1848

16. The King's Herbwomen and her maids, from Sir George Nayler's *Coronation of King George IV*, 1825–7

Regent, he rapidly deserted his Whig friends and ended up an extreme conservative. His politics expressed themselves in his buildings. Like his father he seems to have had little personal interest in the Middle Ages; his own taste was for the age of Louis XIV. The reason why Louis XIV's absolute monarchy, and the gilding and glitter that went with it, appealed to him was obvious enough; but he was also well aware of the value of mediaevalism as an alternative symbol of tradition and authority. As early as 1811–13 he had himself painted as the Black Prince, in a vanished portrait by P. E. Stroehling.[23] But the two most important expressions of his mediaevalism were his coronation and his remodelling of Windsor Castle.

The coronation took place on 19 July 1821. It was far more magnificent than George III's coronation had been, or than any English coronation has been since.[24] As with George III's Garter installation in 1805, the greatest care was taken that 'as many of the old customs should be kept up as possible'. The coronation banquet in Westminster Hall took place for the last time, complete with the ceremony of the Challenge (Plate IV). Westminster Hall was equipped with tempory Gothic galleries for the spectators. More than three hundred guests were at the banquet; nearly two thousand others, who had taken part in the coronation procession, were fed in the adjacent buildings. At one end of Westminster Hall George IV sat at the high table, under a superb canopy; at the other a great Gothic archway was built, through which the King's Champion rode on horseback at the appropriate moment.

But the most extraordinary and unique feature of the coronation was that almost everyone who took part in it wore clothes especially designed for the occasion. All the innumerable members of the King's Household, the Privy Councillors and Clerks of the Privy Council, the trainbearers of the King and the royal dukes, the Barons of the Cinque Ports, the Knights of the Bath, the pages, waiters and ushers, wore pseudo-Elizabethan cloaks, ruffs, slashed–doublets, hose, and plumed caps of carefully contrasted colours.[25] The King was preceded by a band of herbwomen, wearing a decorative combination of ruffs and high–

26

17. George IV in his coronation procession, as depicted by George Nayler

waisted Regency dresses, and scattering rose-petals as they went. The whole
ceremony must have assumed the character of a gigantic fancy-dress pageant on
the theme of the Faerie Queene, in which George IV played the part of a male
Gloriana.

Foreigners, according to Walter Scott, were 'utterly astonished and delighted
to see the revival of feudal dresses and feudal grandeur when the occasion
demanded it, and that in a degree of splendour which, they averred, they had
never seen paralleled in Europe'.[26] Three years later feudal grandeur of an equally
unparalleled and more permanent nature began to take shape as George IV
embarked on the remodelling of Windsor Castle, at an ultimate cost of more than
a million pounds.[27] The architect was Jeffry Wyatt, who changed his name to
Wyatville to be in keeping with the grandeur of the commission. Sir Charles
Long, who was the King's aesthetic *eminence grise* and had helped direct the
coronation, exerted a powerful influence; the best features of the remodelling
owe more to him than to Wyatville, who was a very competent rather than
interesting architect. Externally the upper ward was entirely remodelled and the
Round Tower doubled in height; inside new private and state apartments were
provided on a scale previously unequalled in any royal palace. The bulk of the
private and some of the state apartments were decorated in the King's favourite
Louis Quatorze style, but the state sequence of grand staircase, armoury,
Waterloo Chamber and St George's Hall, embellished with arms, armour and
heraldry without end, was suitably chivalric and feudal.

St George's Hall, the traditional setting for the dinners of the Garter knights,
was nearly doubled in length. Its new and equally large neighbour, the Waterloo
Chamber, was designed for the annual dinner held to celebrate the battle of
Waterloo, and was hung with Lawrence's portraits of the potentates, warriors and
statesmen who had led the fight against Napoleon. The juxtaposition expressed
the spirit in which the castle was remodelled. Edward III, the founder of the
Garter, was linked to George IV, Crecy and Poitiers to Waterloo; the feudal
glories of Windsor were restored and enhanced to make it worthy of a nation

27

whose modern paladins had once again conquered France. The resulting magical silhouette and splendid interiors exactly suited national pride; of all George IV's many extravagances his work at Windsor was the only one which was never seriously criticised.

George IV's visit to Edinburgh in 1822 was accompanied by celebrations almost as lavish as those of his coronation. They had nothing to do with knights or chivalry, but a great deal with their nearest modern equivalent, clans and chieftains.[28] These played so large a part that to begin with there was much criticism from the resentful Lowlanders. As Lockhart put it, 'it appeared to be very generally thought, when the first programmes were issued, that the Highlanders, their kilts, and their bagpipes, were to occupy a great deal too much space in every scene of public ceremony'.[29] But as the festivities got under way, a wave of romantic enthusiasm for the Highlands enveloped the Lowland city, until people with little or no Highland connections were appearing by the dozen draped in tartans and sporrans. Highland dress, proscribed in 1745 and only re-allowed since 1783, had come back into fashion with a vengeance.

Bagpipes and clansmen featured prominently in the procession up from the royal yacht at Leith to Holyrood; the King was offered the keys of the palace by the Duke of Hamilton, and welcomed by the Master of the Household, the Duke of Argyll, both in full Highland dress. But the supreme moment of the visit came when the King himself, at his opening levée in Holyrood, appeared as a Highland chieftain, resplendent in Royal Stewart tartan. The dress was said to have 'displayed his manly and graceful figure to great advantage'.[30] It was somewhat unfortunate that a very fat alderman, Sir William Curtis, had loyally clothed himself in an almost identical get-up.

Apart from this minor contretemps, the visit was a triumphant success. In addition to the Highland elements, the royal regalia, the keys of Holyrood and the Royal Company of Archers in their picturesque dress were all made to play an appropriate part. George IV had a gift for finding a good impresario. His coronation and his new setting at Windsor had been stage-managed by Sir George Nayler and Sir Charles Long. His visit to Edinburgh was brilliantly directed by Sir Walter Scott. But Scott is a figure of such importance in the revival of chivalry that he must be considered separately.

28

18. David Wilkie. *The Entrance of George IV into Holyrood*

19. (right) Frontispiece to the Abbotsford edition of the Waverley Novels, 1841–6

CHAPTER 3
Sir Walter Scott

ONE SUMMER EVENING IN 1814 A PARTY OF YOUNG MEN WERE DRINKING noisily together in a house in George Street in Edinburgh. One of them, William Menzies, grew less and less cheerful; and when his friends asked him why, he burst out: 'There is a confounded hand in sight of me here, which has often bothered me before, and now it won't let me fill my glass with a good will.' He pointed to a house across the way, in the window of which were the hand and pen that 'like the writing on Belshazzar's wall, disturbed his hour of hilarity'. 'Since we sat down', he said, 'I have been watching it—it fascinates my eye—it never stops . . .'[1]

The hand belonged to Walter Scott. It was to continue to write for another twenty-eight years, until it made its owner the world's most famous living author. By his writing Scott encouraged aristocrats and country gentlemen to build castles and cram their halls with weapons and armour; he made young girls thrill to the thought of gallant knights, loyal chieftains and faithful lovers; he spurred young men on to romantic gestures and dashing deeds in both love and war. He so glamourised the clans and the Jacobites that he virtually created the tourist industry of the Highlands, and flooded the whole of Scotland with tartans and Scottish Baronial mansions. As early as 1811 a travelling Frenchman compared Windsor Castle as remodelled by Wyatt for George III to 'a castle of Walter Scott's own building'.[2] The poet William Johnson Cory described how he started to read Scott's novels as a little boy of six or seven in the late 1820s: 'As they came out, before Scott died, I used to read them, sometimes I half-spoilt them with my childish cutting of the pages: sometimes I hid the volumes under the old horsehair sofa cushion in the drawing room when my Father came in, for fear of being scolded for reading novels all day. What else was I to do? That was my life: all else was dim and dull.'[3]

Scott's genius was based on almost inexhaustible creative energy, combined with remarkably wide reading and research. His friendships and acquaintances included writers in the same vein, such as 'Monk' Lewis and Robert Southey, and antiquarians such as George Ellis, whose versions of early poems and romances put into contemporary English brought huge chunks of mediaeval literature back into general circulation, and Samuel Rush Meyrick, whose *Critical Enquiry into Antient Armour* (1824) placed the study of armour on a new footing of expertise. Scott dealt with such friends on equal terms as a fellow antiquarian, who had probably read as much early literature as Ellis, and to whom Meyrick acknowledged 'the valuable communications in all that relates to Scotch armour from one no less to be admired for his private virtues than his boundless talents, his good friend Sir Walter Scott, Bart.'[4] The extent of his researches ranged, like his novels, far beyond the Middle Ages. It was shown in the extensive and often fascinating footnotes attached to his poems and novels, in his separate editing of subjects as varied as Border ballads, the complete works of Swift and Dryden, the mediaeval ballad of *Sir Tristram*, and the Civil War memoirs of Sir Henry Slingsby and others; in his biographies or sketches of Swift, Dryden and Napoleon; and in the long articles on chivalry and romance which he wrote for the *Encyclopaedia Britannica*. He learnt German to read the German Romantics, and was amongst the first to translate Goethe, Bürger and others into English verse. But unlike his fellow historians and antiquarians, he could transmute his reading and research into stories and ballads that were avidly read in drawing-rooms all over the world.

What was it that drew Scott both to the past, and to certain virtues and ways of life which he found especially vividly embodied in the past? To some extent he seems to have been born an instinctive conservative, royalist, romantic and story-teller; as he himself put it, 'Show me an old castle or a field of battle, and I was at home at once, filled it with its combatants in their proper costume, and overwhelmed my hearers by the enthusiasm of my description.'[5] But he was also pushed that way by the circumstances of his birth, background and early years.

Scott belonged to a younger branch of a younger branch of the Scotts of Raeburn, themselves a younger branch of the Scotts of Harden, who were a younger branch of the Scotts of Buccleuch, the chief line of the great Border family of Scott. Any landed property had long since passed out of his branch of the Scotts; but his father's mother was a Haliburton, and the ownership of the Haliburton estate, including the ruins of Dryburgh Abbey, would have come through her to his father, if her brother had not gone bankrupt and left nothing to Walter Scott's family except the right to be buried in the Abbey ruins.

In a country as pedigree-conscious as Scotland, Scott's ancestry was sufficient for him to be, in his own words, 'esteemed gentle'.[6] Throughout his life he was proud to be, and extremely conscious of being, a gentleman. Families which are distantly allied to the great, or conscious of landed property which should, but for mischance or misfortune, have been theirs, or who live in a city but have roots in the country, tend to be especially romantic about their ancestry and connections; and Scott, to whom all three conditions applied, was no exception. It was not surprising that he had more feeling for his sixteenth-century forebear 'Wat of Harden', who was one of the heroes of Border legend, or his Jacobite great-grandfather 'Beardie', who refused to cut his beard until the Stuarts returned, than for his grandfather, who was a Whig cattle-dealer and farmer, or his father, who was a respectable Edinburgh solicitor. His feelings for the Duke of Buccleuch, the head of the Scott family, and his Duchess were expressed in his couplet

Health to the chieftain from his clansman true
From her true minstrel, health to fair Buccleuch.[7]

Although he grew into terms of familiar friendship with them, he always kept something of the attitude of a loyal subject to his sovereign. In general, any relationship that could be described as feudal, or involved personal loyalty, was immediately attractive to him. He enjoyed the company of people of all types and classes, and was unfailingly courteous to everyone; but he got a particular romantic kick out of meeting or knowing anyone who inherited a historic name or ancient traditions—from George IV downwards.

Scott was taken ill at the age of eighteen months, and left with a withered leg. Even though he otherwise developed into a man of considerable strength, there were many things which he could not do. His boundless admiration for physical prowess or bravery must to some extent have been caused by his lameness; so must his fascination with battles, soldiers and deeds of arms. He could not become a soldier himself, but he came as near to it as possible. In 1797, when local bodies of yeomanry were starting up all over Britain in answer to the threat of invasion from France, he was one of the founders of the Edinburgh troop of the Volunteer Light Horse. Scott's lameness did not prevent him from riding, and yeomanry cavalry enabled him to become at least a part-time home-based soldier. Over the next fifteen years or more the amount of Scott's time which the yeomanry involved, and the enjoyment which he got out of it, can scarcely be exaggerated. Several months each year were spent on duty at Musselburgh. In 1802 he wrote that a cavalry charge (even with no enemy at the end of it) 'appears to me to partake highly of the sublime'.[8] In the year 1805 the volunteers were especially active and 'to the end of his life, Scott delighted to recall the details of their counter-marches, ambuscades, charges and pursuits'.[9] His military life was closely tied up with his poetry, large portions of which were composed when he was on duty. In 1802, when in camp at Musselburgh, a kick from a horse kept him to his lodgings for three days, in which he wrote the draft of *The Lay of the Last Minstrel*.[10] In 1807, when he was once more in camp, many of the stanzas of *Marmion* were composed as he galloped on his black charger through waves and flying spray along the edge of the beach.[11]

> To horse! To horse! the standard flies,
> The bugles sound the call;
> The Gallic navy stems the seas,
> The voice of battle's on the breeze,
> Arouse ye, one and all!

So ran the opening stanza of Scott's 'war-song' written in 1802 for his 'band of brothers' in the Edinburgh Light Dragoons. Soldiering in Scotland never distracted him from the real fighting across the sea. He travelled everywhere with a map of Spain and Portugal, studded with black and white pins to mark the progress of Wellington's campaigns.[12] Only his wife's expostulations kept him from going out to the Peninsula in person, and he was one of the thousands of tourists who crossed the channel to walk or ride over the battlefield of Waterloo. Two of his longer poems, *The Vision of Don Roderick* and *The Field of Waterloo*, celebrate contemporary battles, as do a number of shorter ones. To a considerable extent all his most famous poems, even though set in the Middle Ages, were war-poems, written in time of war and under stress of its excitement, at once inspired by the deeds being performed by contemporary soldiers, and intended to inspire them. The battle description in Canto VI of *The Lady of the Lake* was read by Scott's friend Adam Fergusson to encourage his company of soldiers when pinned down by enemy artillery in the lines of Torres Vedras.[13] His 'Bard's Incantation', written 'under threat of an invasion' in 1804, called up the 'minstrels and bards of other days' to inspire a war-like spirit in the present. One of the closing stanzas of *The Field of Waterloo* triumphantly associates mediaeval and modern chivalry:

> Now, Island Empress, wave thy crest on high,
> And bid the banner of thy patron flow,
> Gallant St George, the flower of Chivalry,
> For thou hast faced, like him, a dragon foe,
> And rescued innocence from overthrow,
> And trampled down, like him, tyrannic might,
> And to the gazing world mayst proudly show
> The chosen emblem of thy sainted Knight,
> Who quelled devouring pride, and vindicated right.

Scott's romantic inclinations and military enthusiasms combined to make him a dedicated Tory. Gratified though he was that Charles James Fox expressed enthusiasm for his *Lay of the Last Minstrel* all his loyalty went to Pitt:

> Ah, woe!
> Weep to his memory
> Low lies the pilot that weather'd the storm.[14]

For Wellington, a duke, a Tory and a military genius, he reserved his greatest measure of hero-worship; he once told his son-in-law that he 'had never felt awed or abashed except in the presence of one man—the Duke of Wellington'.[15]

Given Scott's character and background it was inevitable that the Middle Ages in general, and chivalry in particular, should appeal to him. In this respect he was in notable contrast to Byron, who wrote off chivalry curtly in 1813: 'I fear a little investigation will teach us not to regret these monstrous mummeries of the Middle Ages.'[16] Even so, Scott was by no means uncritical. In 1818, when he wrote his essay on chivalry for the *Encyclopaedia Britannica*, he criticised it for numerous defects: its fanaticism which made killing Moslems by the thousand 'an indifferent or rather meritorious action'; its superstition; the extravagance to which it pushed both religious and amorous devotion; the way in which, under the influence of courtly love, 'the marriage tie ceased to be respected'; the fact that 'enterprises the most extravagant in conception, the most difficult in execution, the most useless when achieved, were those by which an adventurous knight chose to distinguish himself'. Nevertheless 'nothing could be more beautiful and praiseworthy than the theory on which it was grounded'. It softened and dignified the conduct of war; it gave women an honourable place in society; it provided an education for young men which was calculated to give them physical strength, bravery, grace, courtesy, and respect for women.

But Scott wrote of chivalry as a thing of the past. 'We can only now look back on it as a beautiful and fantastic piece of frostwork, which has dissolved in the beams of the sun.' It survived only in so far as the best elements in it had been absorbed into the code of the gentleman: 'From the wild and overstrained courtesies of Chivalry has been derived our present system of manners.'[17]

Scott had been brought up in Edinburgh, in a predominantly Whig society of lawyers, academics and professionals, whose education was based on the classics and most of whom accepted the current eighteenth-century view of chivalry as an absurd and overstrained system. Emotionally he responded instinctively to the Middle Ages; intellectually he was always apologising for them. One can see him being pulled in two ways all through his essay. In fact Scott's ideal of a gentleman corresponded only approximately to contemporary practice; it was an ideal of his own making, based partly on what he admired in his contemporaries, partly on what he admired in the past. One of Scott's greatest achievements was to bring chivalry up to date, and popularise a type of character which could reasonably be called chivalrous, but was acceptable as a model both by himself and his contemporaries.

As a child Scott learnt Jacobite sympathies, and the traditions and ballads of the Scottish Borders, from his mother and grandmother. As a child, when he should have been in bed in his aunt's house in Kelso, he sat up reading Shakespeare by the light of the fire; at the age of thirteen he forgot his dinner because he was so absorbed in his first reading of Percy's *Reliques*. He and his school-friend John Irving wandered over Arthur's Seat and Salisbury Crags making up romances and telling them to each other. On leaving school he trained to become, and ultimately became, a barrister; but his enthusiasm went into reading, writing and translating poetry, ballads and black-letter books.

In 1792 he began to make annual expeditions to Liddesdale, in one of the remotest parts of the Borders, in order to collect and write down the Border ballads that had been handed down verbally among the crofters and shepherds. His *Minstrelsy of the Scottish Border* was published in three volumes in 1802–3, and did for the ballads of the Borders what Bishop Percy's *Reliques* had done for early English poetry. In 1805 he published his first important original poem, *The Lay of the Last Minstrel*. It and its successor *Marmion* (1808) dealt with the Borders at the time of Flodden; *The Lady of the Lake* (1809) and *The Lord of the Isles* (1814) moved up to the Highlands in the days of Bruce and James V respectively; *Rokeby* (1813) was set in the Civil Wars.

These poems made Scott famous, and sold in very large numbers. But the later poems sold less well than the earlier ones, partly because the novelty of Scott's verse was wearing off, partly because his sales were affected by those of Byron. In 1814 Scott published his first novel, *Waverley*, anonymously. It was an instantaneous success, as were nearly all of Scott's many novels until the end of his life. They ranged through many centuries and countries; fewer than a third, including *Ivanhoe* (1820), *The Talisman* (1825) and *Quentin Durward* (1823), were set in the Middle Ages, but of these *Ivanhoe* was the most successful, especially in England. The identity of 'the author of Waverley' was soon an open secret. In 1820 George IV created Scott a baronet; as early as 1812 he told Byron that he preferred Scott 'to every Bard past and present'.[18]

Scott gave his thousands of readers a Walter-Scott version of the Middle Ages that captured their imagination because it was presented so vividly, was so different from the life they themselves lived, and yet seemed to express certain virtues and characteristics which they felt their own age was in need of. This world was at its most stylised and simplified in the poems, in which, in imitation of mediaeval ballads,

> Strength was gigantic, valour high
> And wisdom soared beyond the sky
> And beauty had such matchless beam
> As lights not now a lover's dream.[19]

In a setting of lakes, mountains, forests, islands, castles and towers, passions were violent, feuds relentless, battles frequent, loyalties unbreakable, and loves lasted for ever. Everything was depicted in high contrast. Even the sounds were strong and simple; armour clanged, teeth gnashed, maids shrieked, spirits groaned, hounds howled, and every knight lived in imminent expectation of

> The bursting crash of a foeman's spear
> As it shivered against his mail.[20]

Readers thrilled when they read in *The Lady of the Lake* of the meeting of the lost and exhausted Fitzjames with his enemy Roderick Dhu; of the latter's refusal to take advantage of his condition:

> But not for clan nor kindred's cause
> Will I depart from honour's laws;[21]

of his feeding and looking after him, and of the two men's lying down to sleep side by side, preparatory to fighting each other in the morning.

Scott described castles complete with drawbridges, iron-studded gates, and portcullises; smoke-blackened armour-hung halls, with a high table on the dais

35

20, 21. Scenes from *Ivanhoe* (1830 ed.) and *Marmion* (1809 ed.), engraved from drawings by John Martin and Richard Westall

and mastiffs rooting in the rushes; Christmas feasting, with Yule logs and Lords of Misrule; morris dancing, maypoles, and the whole concept of Merry England; tilts, tournaments and knights with ladies' favours pinned to their helmets; Richard Coeur de Lion, Robin Hood and his merry men, Arthur and the Knights of the Round Table. Scenes and characters such as these, once set in circulation by Scott, were copied and adapted *ad nauseam* in novels, poems and pictures all through the nineteenth century and beyond, so that now it is almost impossible to recapture the vividness of their impact when Scott first presented them. They influenced manners as well as people's imaginations. Christmas, for instance, as it came to be celebrated in the nineteenth century, especially in country houses, was heavily indebted to Scott's description of a mediaeval Christmas in the introduction to the sixth canto of *Marmion*:

> Then open'd wide the Baron's Hall
> To vassal, tenant, serf and all. . .
>
> Then the grim boar's head framed on high,
> Crested with bays and rosemary. . .
>
> Then came the merry maskers in
> And carols roared with blithesome din. . .
>
> England was merry England, when
> Old Christmas brought his spark again.

The world of Scott's novels was much less stylised than that of his poems, and had much more of everyday life in it. In particular, he used his own recollections and reminiscences of old people to whom he talked to give his Scottish novels a vividness which makes them the most attractive of his works. But even in them Scott's mediaeval enthusiasms keep breaking through; there are many references to Arthur and his knights, chivalry, and knight-errantry; the castles and feudal families are still there, but given an extra degree of romantic melancholy by being in decay. More generally both novels and poems, whatever the period they cover, celebrate virtues especially associated with feudal, chivalric or old-fashioned societies. They are full of examples of bravery, loyalty, hospitality, consideration towards women and inferiors, truth to a given word, respect for rank combined with a warm relationship between different ranks, and refusal to take advantage of an enemy except in fair fight.

Scott's heroes tend to conform to a common type. Quentin Durward, for instance, is brave, dashing, honourable, proud of his birth, pure-minded, gentle to women and loyal to his master, Louis XI, even though the latter is not worthy of him. His impetuous idealism cannot help attracting tough old soldiers like Crèvecoeur, or cynics like King Louis, however much they make fun of him. Louis called him 'that wandering Paladin . . . like a young knight who had set out upon his first adventures'; Crèvecoeur feared his 'happy journey through fairy-land—all full of heroic adventure, and high hope, and wild minstrel-like delusion, like the gardens of Morgaine la Fée'.[22] Harry Bertram in *Guy Mannering*, Lovel in

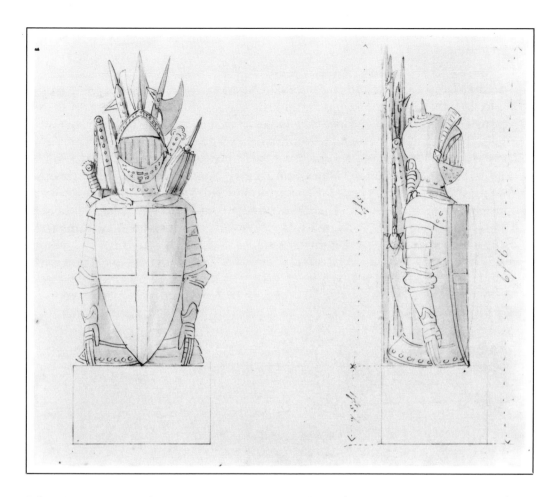

The Antiquary, and Darsie Latimer in *Redgauntlet* are Quentin Durwards in eighteenth-century dress; or alternatively, Quentin Durward is a mediaeval Bertram, Lovel or Latimer. Scott had created a type of character which not only was to be imitated in innumerable later novels, but was to become a model for young men in real life. The type was the result of amalgamating a mediaeval knight-errant with a modern gentleman, and adding something which was not necessarily part of either: Scott's heroes never say, do or think anything which could embarrass a contemporary young lady. A cynic might say that they were like this because Scott was thinking of his sales. But, if Lockhart is to be relied on, in this respect Scott's 'high sense of honour' and 'instinctive delicacy' made him remarkably like his own heroes.[23]

Scott's novels suggested desirable standards, not just for young gentlemen but for gentlemen of all ages. Moreover, his influence was extended by example as well as by his novels. Perhaps the most influential and successful character created by him was himself. Most people assume one or more roles at some stage in their lives, with varying degrees of success; novelists, not surprisingly, tend to be especially good at doing so. Scott's role was completely successful, because he believed in it. Failing the profession of a soldier, which was barred to him, he thought that there was no better life than that of a Scottish laird living on his estates; and that is what he became. He bought the property which he renamed Abbotsford in 1811. He started with a cottage and a small farm, but by the 1820s

22. Design for the hall stove at Bentley Priory, Middlesex, made by John Soane in 1799 for Scott's friend the first Marquess of Abercorn

he was Sir Walter Scott, Bart., owner of a full-blown country house on an estate of fourteen hundred acres.

Scott's life at Abbotsford became known to a very large audience, partly because he entertained a stream of visitors there, many of whom wrote about their visits, and even more because of Lockhart's life of him. He rode, hunted, shot and fished with the enthusiasm of a born country gentleman, and encouraged his sons to do the same; the proudest moment of his life, he professed, was when his eldest son shot his first blackcock. He was devoted to his many dogs, and talked to them as to old friends. He worked side by side with his foresters at cutting down trees in his woods, and never seemed happier than when chatting and joking with his tenants and workpeople. Every summer he entertained the local gentry to an outdoor salmon banquet by the banks of the Tweed; every autumn he gave a convivial autumn dinner for the gentry and farmers who followed the Abbotsford hunt; every November he invited his own workers and the local peasantry to a Harvest Home at Abbotsford, at which he and his wife distributed whisky-punch, and his children joined in dancing reels and hornpipes.

But Scott's role as a country gentleman imposed considerable strains on him. The novels which paid for it had no recognised part in it. From the beginning of his career he had played down his position as a writer. 'Author as I am,' he once whispered in Lockhart's ear, 'I wish these good people would recollect that I began with being a gentleman, and don't mean to give up the character.'[24] The anonymity with which the novels were published was partly due to the fact that he thought writing novels was not quite a suitable occupation for a gentleman. Visitors to Abbotsford commented with amazement on the fact that he seemed to do no writing at all; in fact he got up at five every morning and did the bulk of it before breakfast. Even his children, when they were young, did not realise that their father was an author.[25]

Scott spent more on buying land and building Abbotsford than he could really afford, even with his considerable earned income. In 1805 he had entered into partnership with John (and later his brother James) Ballantyne, the printers, in an attempt to increase his income. The Ballantynes printed all his books, but the partnership was kept a secret; being a printer was even less of a job for a gentleman than being a novelist. Scott's treatment of the situation was an unhappy compromise; he drew his profits (when there were any) but was too gentlemanly to examine the accounts. The Ballantynes got into difficulties, and signed bills with Constable, the publisher, and the banking house of Hurst and Robinson; when both of these crashed in 1826 the firm of Ballantyne crashed with them.

The liabilities of the firm were about £130,000; the Ballantynes had no assets to speak of. They went bankrupt, but to Scott the right course for an honourable gentleman was clear. He refused to retreat into bankruptcy and assumed responsibility for the whole debt. He came to an arrangement with his creditors and spent the rest of his life writing to pay what he owed. The disaster probably precipitated Lady Scott's death in 1826; it certainly shortened Scott's life. He had paid off some £76,000 of the debt when he died in 1832; the remainder was paid out of his royalties in the years after his death.

23. (right) Abbotsford, from the title-page of Lockhart's *Life of Scott*, 1839, Vol. VI

CHAPTER 4

The Age of Abbotsford

'WALTER SCOTT,' THOMAS CARLYLE WROTE, 'ONE OF THE MOST GIFTED OF the world, whom his admirers call the most gifted, must kill himself that he may be a country gentleman, the founder of a race of Scottish lairds.'[1] One can see what he was getting at, yet he was missing the point; the romanticism which produced Scott's novels and the romanticism which turned him into a Scottish laird were essential to each other. Abbotsford, for which in the end he suffered so much, survives today as a fascinating document of his taste and character. Scott the gentleman of good family and connections, Scott the antiquary and collector of armour, Scott the lover of dogs, soldiers and Border castles, are all represented in it. Moreover, since Scott's tastes were shared, and had helped to form those of his contemporaries, the house is a microcosm of its age as well as of Scott.[2]

The hall at Abbotsford (Plate V) is full of heraldry. The arms of the leading Border families run round the cornice; the arms of Scott's ancestors run along the crest of the vault. It was scarcely surprising that the reviving interest in chivalry led to a revival of heraldry. It had been invented for the knights; and now that people were increasingly anxious to show that they were connected with the Middle Ages, there was no better way of doing it than by heraldic display. King Edward's Gallery in William Beckford's Fonthill was decorated with seventy-two coats of arms, representing Edward III and seventy-one Knights of the Garter, from all of whom Beckford claimed descent. Such a display helped to conceal the fact that the Beckfords themselves, whatever their connections through marriage, were West Indian sugar planters of very dubious origin. Coats of arms tended to be divided into more and more quarterings, each showing the arms of a separate family with the heiress of which the family displaying the coat claimed alliance. Such multiple quarterings, often adopted on very dubious grounds, became extremely popular and could be carried to extraordinary lengths. In 1825 Sir Samuel Brydges, one of the most indefatigable of early nineteenth-century genealogists, published a book called *Stemmata Illustria* in which the supposed glories of his ancestry were illustrated by a shield containing no fewer than three hundred and sixty quarterings.

Brydges also wasted many years on abortive attempts to have the mediaeval barony of Chandos called out of abeyance in his favour. This method of at once acquiring a title and demonstrating the antiquity of one's lineage was understandably popular.[3] The pioneer in the field had been Norborne Berkeley, who managed to call the barony of Botetourt out of abeyance in 1764. Baronies were being revived in this manner all through the nineteenth century; the most successful decade was the 1830s. Those without the right connections to achieve such a barony (and pay the genealogists and lawyers for the extensive work involved) could at least aim for a new title with a good mediaeval sound. Mr Morris, an Irish M.P., for instance, graduated to becoming Viscount Frankfurt de Montmorency in 1816, having changed his surname to de Montmorency in the previous year. The Anglo-Irish were especially addicted to gestures of this kind; but many county families in both England and Ireland added 'de' to their surnames, sometimes on reasonable genealogical grounds, and sometimes just because they liked the sound.

40

Change of name could be accompanied by a suitable change of habitat, or vice versa. Sir George Jerningham of Costessey Hall, near Norwich, having managed to get the barony of Stafford revived in his favour in 1824, completely remodelled his house in ultra-Gothic style in 1826. Walter Wilkins, having made a fortune in India, built Maesllwych Castle in Radnorshire in 1829–40 and changed his name to de Winton to go with it.

The heraldry at Abbotsford has obvious connections with chivalry; but so, less obviously, have Walter Scott's yeomanry sword and pistols, which hang in the armoury off the hall, and Sir William Allan's dashing portrait of Scott's son as a cornet in the Eighteenth Hussars, which dominates the library. (Scott was delighted that he chose to become a regular soldier.) Military glory was very much in the air, acclaimed during the French wars, and remembered with nostalgia after them. Scott was not alone in being proud to have lived in a heroic age, and in linking it to other heroic ages in the past. The heroes themselves were, in some cases at any rate, fully aware of their predecessors in the age of chivalry. Nelson, for instance, soaked himself in Shakespeare; his favourite Shakespearian play was, predictably, *Henry V*. In 1799 he quoted from Henry V's speech before Agincourt, and called the officers serving under him at the Battle of the Nile a 'band of brothers'.[4] The phrase was to be re-used over and over again in the nineteenth century; in 1802 Scott applied it to his volunteer friends in the Edinburgh Light Dragoons.[5]

The brothers Charles and William Napier, who made their names as especially gallant and honourable soldiers in the Peninsular War, were also very much aware of the traditions of chivalry. As boys in Ireland they had devoured Froissart's chronicles of the Hundred Years' War, Malory's *Morte d'Arthur* and any other mediaeval romance they could lay their hands on; Charles Napier was later to christen his brother officer Outram the 'Bayard of India'.[6] His brother's great *History of the Peninsular War* was written in the spirit of a modern Froissart's *Chronicles*, and chivalrously gave as much honour to French heroism as to

41

24. Charles Lamb's coat of arms, as drawn by himself in 1839

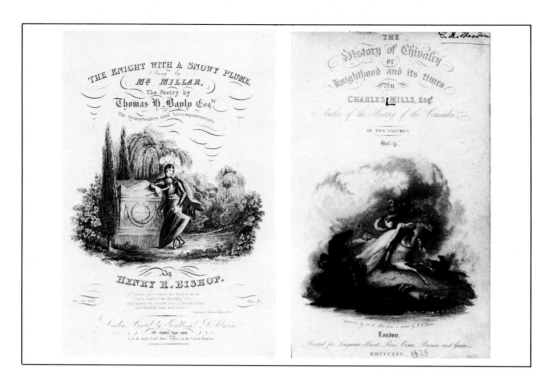

English. Both brothers had something of Wordsworth's 'Character of the Happy Warrior'. This famous poem, written in 1805 or 1806 and published in 1807, epitomized the pride and hero-worship which British victories evoked at home. Wordsworth's warrior was strong, brave, compassionate, gentle, selfless and able to transmute the horrors of war to 'glorious gain':

> But who, if he be called upon to face
> Some awful moment to which Heaven has joined
> Great issues, good or bad for human kind,
> Is happy as a Lover; and attired
> With sudden brightness, like a Man inspired.

The phrase 'happy warrior' was to become as popular, and in the end as hackneyed, as 'band of brothers'.

It is surely more than coincidence that the years of the French wars saw an outbreak of translations or editions of mediaeval romances, ballads, and chronicles. Scott's own *Border Minstrelsy* came out in 1802–3, and his edition of Thomas of Erceldoune's *Sir Tristram* in 1804. His friend Ellis's *Specimens of Early English Metrical Romance* was published in 1805. Thomas Johnes went on from translating de Sainte-Palaye's life of Froissart (1801) to translate Froissart's *Chronicles* themselves; the three handsome quarto volumes in which these came out between 1803 and 1805 were so successful that they were immediately republished in a pocket-size edition. Johnes also translated the chronicles of de Joinville (1807), de la Brocquière (1807) and de Monstrelet (1809). Southey's translations of the three great Spanish romances *Amadis of Gaul, Palmerin of England* and *Chronicles of the Cid* came out in 1803, 1807 and 1808.

Editions of Malory came out in 1816 and 1817, the latter edited by Southey. Charles Mills published his *History of the Crusades* in 1820 (fourth edition 1828),

42

25. (left) An early nineteenth-century music cover

26. (right) Title-page from Charles Mill's *History of Chivalry*, 1825

and his *History of Chivalry* in 1825 (second edition 1826). Mills was an enthusiastic admirer of chivalry in all its aspects; his work was followed in 1830 by the equally enthusiastic *History of Chivalry* by the historical novelist G. P. R. James, and by H. Stebbing's *History of Chivalry and the Crusades*. In addition to such historical works, or editions of chivalric literature, a mass of modern prose and poetry dealt with chivalric themes ranging from Southey's *Roderick, the Last of the Goths* (1814) or 'L.E.L.'s' best-selling *The Troubadour* (1825) to the interminable novels of G. P. R. James and sentimental songs written for performance in fashionable drawing-rooms.

The illustrations which accompanied the songs and novels, and indeed the chivalric pictures which were occasionally bought to hang in the drawing-rooms, can have considerable charm; but, oddly enough, none of them approached the power or the verisimilitude of West's Edward III series. The dominant painter and illustrator of mediaeval subjects in the period was Thomas Stothard. His son, Charles Alfred, was the author of *The Monumental Effigies of Great Britain* (1811–33) a superbly illustrated folio published in many parts, and packed with accurate depictions of mediaeval dress. C. A. Stothard was well aware of the help which 'these Monumental effigies would render the Historical Painter'. But his father, even though he made use of this and other publications, managed to impart a feeling of quite extraordinary unreality to his delicately boneless figures.

To a lesser extent the same can be said of the work of other painters and illustrators such as Richard Westall and George Cattermole. The castles of the period are a much more impressive group. The rate of production quickened noticeably after 1800, and perhaps reached its peak in the 1820s. In England John Nash's great sequence of castles starts in 1798, Smirke's in 1806, Lugar's in 1808; in Ireland the first of a remarkable group by Francis Johnson dates from about 1800, and the Morrisons started their own tireless sequence in about 1810; in Scotland

43

27. Thomas Stothard. *The Tournament*

28. Lowther Castle, Westmorland, designed by Robert Smirke in 1806

Gillespie Graham and Archibald Elliot designed their first castles in 1802 and 1804. Scott's main building at Abbotsford was one of a large group of castles and castellated buildings in England, Ireland and Scotland designed by William Atkinson between 1803 and 1824. All over the British Isles brand-new castles were rising above the trees, and battlemented lodges, bridges and stables were being built to go with them.[7]

There were many motives for choosing to build a castle. Castles were picturesque; they were romantic; they stood for tradition, authority or military glory. Picturesque castles, in spite of Payne Knight's pioneering work at Downton, only really got under way when Humphrey Repton started selling the idea of building them to his clients in around 1800, and brought in John Nash to design them. In 1799 he persuaded a rich banker to build a castle at Luscombe in Devon by arguing that a castle would 'have infinitely more picturesque effect' than a conventional classical building 'by blending a chaste correctness of proportion with bold irregularity of outline, its deep recesses and projections producing broad masses of light and shadow, while its roof is enriched by turrets, battlements, corbels and lofty chimneys'.[8] Repton and others sometimes wrote as though such visual arguments were the only ones for building castles, but questions of association could scarcely be avoided, especially once Scott's poems were in every drawing-room. Castles suggested romance, dashing deeds, ancient lineage, and lavish hospitality in baronial halls; as the architect P. F. Robinson wrote in 1827 of his design for a castle in Yorkshire, it led the mind 'back to the days of our feudal system, and in wandering among the neighbouring hills we almost expect to see the ancient Baron, surrounded by his followers ascending the valley, or to hear the bugle announce the arrival of some new comer at the Warder's gate'.[9] Such associations were especially suitable for old families, but often tempted new ones.

A castle designed by an admirer of the picturesque was almost by definition asymmetrical. But symmetrical castles, in the tradition of Adam's Scottish castles or Wyatt's royal castle at Kew, continued to be built well into the nineteenth

V. (right) Abbotsford, Roxburghshire. The Hall

VI. (following page) 'Sir John Cornwell, Lord Fanhope' from Meyrick's *Critical Inquiry into Antient Armour*, 1824

29. Eastnor Castle, Herefordshire, designed by Robert Smirke in about 1810

century; sometimes they were given a degree of asymmetry by having a servants' wing to one side of a symmetrical main block. A formidably symmetrical facade was perhaps especially suggestive of authority and power; this may have been one reason (in addition to obvious associations of dungeons and security) why this type of design was especially popular for gaols and court-houses. Fear of democracy, of disaffection in the lower classes and of the effects of the French Revolution loomed large in upper-class consciousness. It was probably more than coincidence that Francis Johnson's sequence of castles in Ireland started so soon after the suppression of the 1798 rebellion. In 1833 Wordsworth apostrophised Lowther Castle in Westmorland as follows:

> Lowther! in thy majestic pile are seen
> Cathedral pomp and grace, in apt accord
> With the baronial castle's sterner mien;
> Union significant of God adored,
> And charters won and guarded by the sword
> Of ancient honour; whence that godly state
> Of polity which wise men venerate,
> And will maintain, if God his help afford.
> Hourly the democratic torrent swells;
> For airy promises and hopes suborned
> The strength of backward-looking thought is scorned. . .
>
> Fall if ye must, ye Towers and Pinnacles,
> With what ye symbolise; authentic Story
> Will say, Ye disappeared with England's Glory![10]

Lowther Castle had been designed by Robert Smirke in 1806 for Wordsworth's patron, the arch-Tory magnate Lord Lonsdale. It was closely based on George III's castle or 'Bastille' at Kew. Smirke followed it in about 1810 with a castle on the same model at Eastnor, designed for Lord Somers, a moderate

49

Whig who developed into a Tory, and was an ardent supporter of the war with France.[11] Somers's hatred of the French Revolution and all it stood for is the dominating feature of the pamphlet which he published in 1817, *A defence of the constitution of Great Britain and Ireland, as by law established, against the innovating and levelling attempts of the friends to Annual Parliaments and Universal Suffrage*. 'It is Equality', he wrote, 'which jars with Liberty.' The gentlemen, nobility and clergy gave employment to the poor, dispensed justice to them, and protected them from oppression. 'Any mad and wicked cry against this deserving, useful and most respectable class of the community' was 'actually injurious to the lower classes.'[12] The battlements and towers of Eastnor helped to suggest ideas of protection to the right kind of working classes and correction to the wrong.

The building of new castles was accompanied by the recording of old ones, whether in the form of romantic watercolours by artists such as Turner or Francis Towne, or the more detailed representations published by antiquaries and architectural draughtsmen such as John Britten and the elder Pugin. The battlements, towers and gateways of most early nineteenth-century castles are, as a result, more correct, in an archaeological sense, than those of eighteenth-century ones. But on the whole no attempt was made to imitate the planning or arrangement of mediaeval castles. Penrhyn Castle in North Wales, which was started in about 1827, was probably the first castle to attempt at least a degree of verisimilitude: the Norman keep at one end, and the main block straggling round courtyards to one side of it, are suggestive of the arrangement of a genuine castle of motte-and-bailey type.[13] Most clients, however, wanted no more than a symbolic and picturesque veneer of castellation applied to a comfortable modern house. At Abbotsford Scott pioneered the revival of Scottish castellated architecture of the sixteenth century, which in its own day had been a compromise between castle and domestic architecture; the resulting style, soon to be named 'Scottish Baronial' became immensely popular north of the Border, and even occasionally penetrated south of it.

Inside, comfort and modern upholstery usually reigned supreme, and chivalric symbols seldom got much further than the halls and staircase. Here heraldry, of course, was always acceptable; so was a scattering of knights in armour, either in the form of stained glass or statues, or alternatively a scattering, and often more than a scattering, of armour without the knights.

It had been a common practise to hang arms and armour in mediaeval halls, ready for use. The practice continued until the seventeenth century, and by the late eighteenth century there were still a number of old houses which had arms and armour of some kind in their halls, although these were more likely to date from the seventeenth century than the Middle Ages. More often, however, such collections had been banished to the attics, if they survived at all. Around 1800 a few sympathetic owners began to refurbish their armour and make a consciously chivalric or antiquarian display of it. The walls of the hall at Browsholme Hall in Lancashire were described in 1804 as covered with arms, armour, antlers and stained glass, all said to have been found elsewhere in the house, and by 1812 there was a similar display in the hall at Cotehele in Cornwall.[14]

By then, inevitably, people were beginning to collect armour. The first recorded sale of it in England was held at Christie's in 1789. To begin with, the buyers were mostly antiquarians or artists; the latter (who included Zoffany and Cosway) presumably bought it to make use of in their paintings. Horace Walpole was a pioneer among collectors; by 1784 a suit of armour which he believed had belonged to Francis I was the main feature of the staircase at Strawberry Hill, and an armoury off the staircase contained a miscellaneous collection of arms of all dates and countries.[15]

By 1817 the three biggest and best-known collections of armour in England, outside the royal collections, were all in London; two of them were unashamedly commercial, and regularly open to the public. These were the collections of Thomas Gwennap, on show first at the 'Oplotheca' in Lower Brook Street, and then in the Gothic Hall in Pall Mall; and the collection of William Bullock, a Liverpool goldsmith who brought his armour down to London and put it on show in the Egyptian Hall in Piccadilly.[16] The third collection belonged to Samuel Rush Meyrick, a London solicitor turned antiquary who was a serious student of armour as well as a collector of it.

In 1824 Meyrick published in three splendid folio volumes *A Critical Inquiry into Antient Armour as it existed in Europe but particularly in England from the Norman Conquest to the reign of Charles II* (Plate VI). This immediately replaced Grose's *Treatise on Ancient Armour and Weapons* as the standard English work on the

51

30. (left) Drawing by Edward Blore for Goodrich Court, Herefordshire

31. (right) The grand armoury at Goodrich Court

subject. It was dedicated to George IV and acknowledged the help of Walter Scott. Suitably enough, both Abbotsford and Windsor were, on their very different scales, about to become show-places for armour in the year in which it was published. Scott had just completed his new additions to Abbotsford, in which the hall and adjacent armoury were to be lined with the collection of arms and armour which he had begun to form in 1813.[17] Wyatville's new armoury and extended St George's Hall at Windsor were ready to take a selection of the royal collection of armour, arranged by Meyrick.[18] Meanwhile in 1821 the armour in both the Gothic and the Egyptian Halls had been put up for sale, and a substantial proportion of it had gone to form the nucleus of the great armour collection in the newly built Brancepeth Castle.[19] In 1826–8 Meyrick supervised the erection and arrangement of a new gallery to contain the main part of the superb but long-neglected collection of armour in the Tower of London. In 1828–31 he built a whole new castle (Plate 30), designed by Edward Blore, to contain his own collection. It was modestly called Goodrich Court, but less modestly looked straight across the valley of the Wye at the ruins of the genuinely mediaeval Goodrich Castle. Although Goodrich Court was built to be lived in, its extraordinary interiors were more suggestive of Madame Tussaud's than a country house; they included a 'hastiltude chamber', which contained a tableau of a tournament, and above all the Great Armoury, eighty-six feet long, in which a formidable enfilade of mounted or standing knights led the eye to where a regal figure under a canopy presided over the still and chilly assembly.[20]

The armoury created in the 1830s by the sixteenth Earl of Shrewsbury at Alton Towers in Staffordshire was one hundred and twenty feet long and contained

52

32. Armour originally in the hall at Parham, Sussex

twenty-four figures in full armour, holding lances, swords or battleaxes and surveying a mounted and armoured figure representing the first Earl of Shrewsbury, the 'Great Talbot', which dominated the centre of the room.[21] The country-house craze for armour was now well under way, and Europe as well as England was being ransacked to satisfy it. One of the most famous of mid-century collections, that formed at Parham in Sussex (Plate 138) by Lord Zouche (better known as Robert Curzon, the author of *Monasteries in the Levant*), was based on armour which came from the Imperial Armoury in Constantinople by way of an Italian dealer or dealers who bought it in about 1840.[22] Armouries or halls full of armour (Plates 58, 78) were fast becoming the mid-nineteenth-century equivalent of the sculpture galleries of Georgian country houses;[23] and, as in the sculpture galleries, the contents were not always as genuine as their proud owners believed.

A curious side product of the armour cult appeared in 1824, in the form of a little book titled *A Suit of Armour for Youth*. It was written by Stacey Grimaldi, an English antiquary who claimed descent from a seventeenth-century Doge Grimaldi of Genoa; its introduction ends 'Farewell, dear English Boys! for your advantage has this little Book been made.' It uses the different portions of a suit of armour and its appurtenances to symbolise different virtues; each virtue is given a page of text with an engraving of the relevant portion of armour opposite, which can be lifted up to reveal an example of the virtue in action. The virtues chosen were mainly the obviously chivalric ones, such as loyalty, valour, mercy, gallantry (toward women), modesty, friendship and honour. They are exemplified by chivalrous figures which include the Black Prince at Poitiers and Crecy, Lord Cavendish offering to take his friend Lord Russell's place in prison in

53

33. (left) The armour of the 'Great Talbot', originally in the armoury at Alton Towers, Staffordshire

34. (right) A knight in the hall at Parham

35. Frontispiece of Stacey Grimaldi's *A Suit of Armour for Youth*, 1824

36. Illustration from *A Suit of Armour* shown with flap down and raised

the seventeenth century, and a wounded ensign at Waterloo, refusing to let go of the regimental colours.

The interest of the book, apart from its considerable charm as a curiosity, lies in the fact that instead of treating chivalry as something belonging to the past, as Scott did, it effectively treated it as a living code, still relevant to modern life, and expressed as a continuous tradition from the Middle Ages. Two years before its publication the relevance of chivalry to modern life had been expressed much more explicitly, and at much greater length, in a book that was to become famous, *The Broad Stone of Honour*.

54

37. (right) Frontispiece of the Tancredus volume of *The Broad Stone of Honour*, 1844

CHAPTER 5

The Broad Stone of Honour

IN THE YEARS AROUND 1820 A STRANGE YOUNG MAN SPENT HIS SUMMER vacations roaming around Europe. Those who met and talked with him in the remoter inns of France, Germany or Switzerland must have wondered who on earth he was. He tended to be travelling on foot, in rough, torn and dirty clothes, but his great height and the black eyes flashing from his darkly handsome features would have made him remarkable anywhere; the maids in all the inns were mad about him. His talk was as remarkable as his looks. The Middle Ages seemed more vivid to him than the present, and a great deal preferable. As he grew more excited knights, castles, King Arthur, Charlemagne, honour, loyalty, quests, monsters and tournaments came tumbling into his conversation; there seemed to be nothing even remotely connected with chivalry that he had not read. Did, he would ask, they know Malory? or the Faerie Queene? or Amadis of Gaul? or the history of Huon de Bordeaux? or Michaud on the Crusades? or de Sainte-Palaye? Had they heard how Steward, the famous Duke of Northumberland, met his last illness, sitting upright on a chair in a full suit of armour, waiting for death with a spear in his hand? Did they know about Beatrice of Cleves? A mysterious young man had appeared below her castle one day, in a golden boat drawn by swans; he said the fairies had given it to him. She married him of course. And what about the wonderful cake served at Philip of Burgundy's banquet at Lille? It represented the castle of Lusignan, complete with towers and moat; Mellusine, the famous sorceress, was shown coming out of the top tower, in the form of a serpent. Had they been to the castle of Sigismundsburg? It was a ruin now, on an island in a lake. He himself had swum across to it by moonlight; the only sound to be heard was the splash of the ripples as he slid through the water. He loved swimming; he had swum across the Rhine once, and the current had carried him three miles before he could get to the opposite shore; he had thought he was done for. How he would love to do deeds of daring; he had, it was true, once sat on the back of a lion, in a travelling zoo at Cambridge—but that was nothing. What splendid fellows Sir Lancelot and Godfrey of Boulogne were—or Homer's old Greeks, for that matter. How dare the Utilitarians and all such wretched modern sophists pretend that the age of chivalry had gone for ever! Chivalry could never die. So he would go on; and in the end his audience would climb up to bed, their heads spinning with Perceval, Tancred, Garcilass of Toledo, Gyron le Courtois, Ottocar, Vladislaus, Hector, Palmerin de Oliva, and dozens of others, convinced, perhaps, that they had never met a greater nut, or a nicer one.[1]

Or perhaps they would end up as excited as the young man, for it was an impressionable age, and the soil was ripe for chivalry, as the young man himself was to discover when he published his first book. His name was Kenelm Henry Digby, and the book was called *The Broad Stone of Honour*. The first and second editions appeared anonymously in 1822 and 1823, with the subtitle of 'Rules for the Gentlemen of England'. An expanded edition, subtitled 'The True Sense and Practice of Chivalry', appeared under Digby's name in four volumes in 1828–9 and 1844–8, and was enlarged to five volumes in 1877. Scott, however much he was drawn to chivalry, had always been a little apologetic about it. Inevitably, however, he prepared the way for the next generation to go further.

Digby was born in Ireland, probably in 1797.[2] His ancestor Everard Digby had fought in the Wars of the Roses; Sir Kenelm Digby, the seventeenth-century writer and natural philosopher, was his kinsman; his great-grandfather Simon Digby, Bishop of Elphin, had visited James II at St Germain; and his cousin, the Abbé Edgeworth, had attended Louis XVI on the scaffold. But proud as he became of these connections, essentially he was born into the heart of the Irish Protestant establishment. His branch of the Digbys had gone to Ireland in the sixteenth century, and married the FitzGerald heiress of Geashill, in County Offaly; his father, a cousin of Lord Digby, of Geashill and Sherborne Castle in Dorset, was Rector of Geashill and Dean of Clonfert.

In the curious world of late Georgian Ireland the landowning classes, although usually divided from the peasantry by both race and religion, still tended to have a semi-feudal relationship with them, especially when, as in the case of the Digbys, property came to them by descent through an ancient line such as that of the FitzGeralds. Digby later described how 'at my father's gate there were never less than eight or more poor people fed daily, and at stated hours'.[3] Nearby, frequent visits to two castles, one new and one old, helped to feed his imagination. He clambered over the ruins of Geashill Castle, which his ancestress Lettice FitzGerald, Lady Offaly, had refused to surrender to the Irish Catholic army in 1642; 'I have been, and still am, desirous to avoid the shedding of Christian blood,' she declared to her besiegers, 'yet being provoked, your threats shall no whit dismay me.' He visited Charleville Castle, the most splendid of all modern Irish castles, and found the owner's stepdaughter, Catharine Tisdall, 'a vision in the sky'.[4]

It only needed Scott's poems, as they came out in succession between 1805 and 1813, to push him firmly into the Middle Ages. He became chivalry-mad, first in Ireland (where his father's carpenter built a four-foot-high model of an abbey, as a mausoleum for his pets)[5] and even more in England. He moved there after his father's death in 1812, was educated at a school at Petersham, near London, went up to Trinity, Cambridge, in 1816, and graduated in 1819. At Cambridge in his day the liveliest undergraduates tended to be enthusiastic for republicanism and reform; but Digby moved in the contrary direction, and was ardent for monarchy, the Church and chivalry.

Many years later he described the progress of his chivalric studies:

> From reading Scott and Southey's Cid
> (The truth exact must not be hid),
> Favyn and Barbazan's 'Ordene,'
> Lord Berners' Arthur's knightly strain,
> The Palmerin of England too;
> What was done there he thought he'd do.
> Don Quixote pass'd not through his brain,
> But still a Knight he would remain;
> Though all the world should recreant prove,
> That was the type that he would love . . .

Well later, famed Sainte Palaye read,
Of Knights continued full his head.[6]

After Digby graduated he kept rooms in Cambridge until about 1829 and made it his main base in England. Undergraduates of those later years whom he may have met included Frederick Maurice, John Sterling, Alfred Tennyson and Arthur Hallam; his main friends among the dons were Julius Hare, William Whewell and Adam Sedgwick. Edward FitzGerald (who was up from 1826 to 1830) knew him by sight only, and later described his appearance as: 'A grand, swarthy fellow, who might have stepped out of the canvas of some knightly portrait in his Father's house—perhaps the living image of one sleeping under some cross-legg'd effigies in the church.'[7]

His best friend while he was still an undergraduate was George Darby, who lived at Marklye in Sussex but whose family came from County Offaly, like Digby's. He fired Darby (whom he later described as 'the model of a knight') with his own chivalric enthusiasms. He and Darby held mock tournaments at Marklye, riding on ponies and using hop-poles instead of spears, and made abortive plans to ride by night to Hurstmonceux Castle, in emulation of Walter of Deloraine's night-time gallop to Melrose in *The Lay of the Last Minstrel*. One evening Digby got into King's College Chapel and kept vigil there until dawn; on another occasion, while he was riding near Hastings, he rescued a seventeen-year-old girl from the threat of assault by a 'felon on the road' and escorted her home with the gallantry of a true knight-errant.[8]

In the summers Digby, alone or with friends, wandered all over England and Europe. His European tours can be traced in some detail, by means of his writings, and his surviving sketch-books.[9] In France, he visited the castle of Pierrefonds, not yet restored by Viollet-le-duc, and the Chevalier Bayard's castle at Bayard; in Switzerland, Chillon, Wildenstein and Hapsburg; in Austria, Sigismundsberg, Gravenstein and Durrenstein, where Richard Coeur de Lion had been imprisoned; in Germany, the castles of the Rhine, including Ehrenbreitstein, which was later to give him the title of his book.[10] Near Vienna he was delighted by the modern castle which the Emperor Francis II had built at Laxenburg, had filled with old furniture and paintings of coronations and tournaments, and equipped with figures of knights in armour and a prisoner in a dungeon who 'lifts up his hands as you enter, and his chains clash as they resume their former

38. (left) The castle at Laxenburg, as drawn by Kenelm Henry Digby

39. Pierrefonds, as drawn by Digby (from a sketch-book damaged by fire in the nineteenth century)

40. Another drawing from the same sketch-book

41. Digby's drawing of Gravenstein in Austria

position'.[11] In later years he loved to remember his continental travels, 'the midnight ride over the mountains, the dismounting at the castle gate, the stride along the sounding cloister . . . adventures of his youth, when the heart was full of fancy's dream'.[12]

In 1825 Digby became a Catholic; his friends at Cambridge seemed to have considered it an amiable aberration, but the whole of the rest of his life was conditioned by it. He enlarged and partly rewrote *The Broad Stone of Honour*, largely in order to show that true chivalry and the Catholic Church were essentially bound up together, and that the Reformation, the decay of chivalry and the degeneration of his own time were all connected. The new version, which first appeared in 1828–9, was divided into four parts: *Godefridus* and *Tancredus*, named after Godfrey of Boulogne and Tancred de Hauteville, heroes of the Crusades; *Morus* (which had already been issued separately in 1826), named after Sir Thomas More; and *Orlandus*, named after Ariosto's Orlando Furioso. *Godefridus* contained a general introduction; *Tancredus* discussed 'the religion and the discipline which belonged to chivalry in the heroic age of Christianity'; *Morus* was largely filled with an attack on the Reformation, and greatly offended many of Digby's former admirers; *Orlandus* gave 'a more detailed view of the virtues of the chivalrous character'.

Digby had none of Scott's reservations. Even admirers of the Middle Ages criticised his refusal to see anything but good in them. Everything that had been said against mediaeval chivalry he either minimised, or explained away, or even accepted as a virtue rather than a defect. The religious zeal of the Crusades might have been extravagant, but he contended that it was better than the 'easy indifference' practised in his day 'under the name of toleration and liberality'.[13] As for that over-scrupulosity on points of honour, which was to survive after the Middle Ages in the form of duelling, it had nothing to do with true chivalry at all, but was an aberration introduced by the Arabs.[14]

But Digby was not writing a history of chivalry; he was encouraging his readers to be chivalrous. 'The object in view', he wrote, 'is not knowledge but practice.'[15] He brought chivalry up to date, as a code of behaviour for all men, not just for soldiers; he enabled modern gentlemen who had never been near a battlefield to think of themselves as knights. To Walter Scott chivalry was a purely mediaeval phenomenon, some elements of which had been adapted and improved over the centuries until they formed part of the code of conduct of the modern gentleman. To Digby it was a permanently valid code, which expressed itself in different ways in different centuries, but remained essentially the same. Scott saw the knight ultimately developing into the gentleman, Digby used 'knight' and 'gentleman' as virtually interchangeable terms. It might be argued that they were saying the same thing in different ways. But Digby's approach did in fact express a different attitude. Scott saw the world from a basically eighteenth-century standpoint as, by and large, in a state of improvement; he was fascinated by mediaeval knights, and admired many aspects of them, but he still thought that nineteenth-century gentlemen were a superior article. To Digby mankind was in a permanent state of conflict between good and evil in which good was not necessarily advancing. Chivalry, in his view, had had two especially heroic periods, the Homeric and the mediaeval. The mediaeval was the superior of these, because chivalry was then infused with Christianity; but however much modern 'sophists' might boast that 'the world is hastening under their influence to a period of increased light and sophistication',[16] both periods were in many ways superior to the modern age. The forces of evil were, if anything, on the increase, and the true knights fighting against them could be excused for having moments of despondency when 'even the heart of the brave will fail'.[17] But Digby's final message was one of hope: 'The noble fellowship of the round table cannot be broken for ever; but fresh aspirants will again appear to revive the generous lists, to keep ahead of the degraded world, and to bear the palm alone.'[18]

The Broad Stone of Honour is full of enemies. They include atheists, deists, rationalists, Radicals, Americans, Utilitarians, and supporters of both dictatorship and democracy. If there is one major villain in the book, it is Utilitarianism. Digby was one of the first of a long line of nineteenth-century writers to launch a counter-attack on the Utilitarians. In doing so he was taking on a formidable set of opponents. In the 1820s the Utilitarians dominated intellectual life in England, and were rapidly making their way into the confidence of politicians. They believed in reshaping society on the basis of intelligent analysis, and had constructed a system the logic and clarity of which was irresistibly attractive to many of Digby's generation. Happiness was caused by the presence of pleasure and the absence of pain. The only criterion by which the rightness of actions could be judged was whether they contributed to 'the greatest happiness of the greatest number'. It was possible (so Jeremy Bentham, at least, believed) to calculate the total sum of pleasure or pain which any given action would cause with, at any rate, sufficient accuracy to make it possible to decide between alternatives.

Digby refused to accept that pleasure and pain were the basis of right and wrong; to him this was a system of 'refined selfishness'. He saw himself as a Platonist who believed in absolute standards of good, right and beauty. But he was not a philosopher, and made little attempt to take on the Utilitarians on their own ground. His method of attack was simple. The Utilitarians prided themselves on refusing to let their intellects be clouded by emotion; as John Stuart Mill said of his father James, 'for passionate emotions he expressed the greatest contempt'.[19] Digby took an exactly opposite line and asserted that the heart was more important than the head. He attacked 'that principle, the curse of modern times, which leads men to idolise the reason and understanding, and to neglect and even despise the virtues of the heart'.[20] True knights and honourable gentlemen instinctively recognised what was right through 'the wisdom of the heart'[21] and pursued it regardless of self-interest. A chivalrous atheist or democrat was an impossibility, because the truly chivalrous man would instinctively recognise that atheism and democracy were evil. Digby set out less to argue than to state and exemplify certain ideals of conduct, confident that the reader whose heart was in the right place would respond.

The distinctive virtues of the chivalrous man, according to Digby, were belief and trust in God, generosity, high honour, independence, truthfulness, loyalty to friends and leaders, hardihood and contempt of luxury, courtesy, modesty, humanity, and respect for women. Generosity could be displayed in refusing money as well as dispensing it; the Chevalier Bayard had despised riches all his life. High honour included refusal to break a promise, tell a lie, act the spy or beg for mercy. Independence included refusal to push oneself, truthfulness included openness; gentlemen did not conceal their feelings, and always gave fair warning of their intentions. Loyalty to friends involved perfect confidence in them.[22]

Anyone who possessed or acquired these qualities was chivalrous, and therefore a gentleman; chivalry had no essential connection with birth. On the other hand it was easier for men of good birth to be chivalrous, because they were encouraged to maintain their standards through pride in the example of their ancestors and because public opinion expected it of them. A mainly hereditary governing class ruling wisely under a king was the best and most natural order of society; democracy was 'utterly opposed to all the principles of the ancient as well as of the Christian chivalry'.[23]

The Broad Stone of Honour is very far from concise, even in its original one-volume form. Digby's method was to teach by example and quotation, and new examples and new quotations were constantly occurring to him. As he himself disarmingly put it, his reader 'must be willing frequently to wander on with me without being confined to any strait rules or fixed directions . . . like a knight of the round table, who rides through adventurous forests'.[24] Numerous examples are drawn from mediaeval chronicles and romances; there is a great deal from Froissart and rather less from Malory; there are massive chunks of untranslated Greek, especially from Homer and Plato, and of Latin, especially from Cicero. Of more recent writers he was especially fond of Friedrich Schlegel, the German literary critic, and Julius Hare, who had been his tutor at Trinity; he quotes (among others) Wordsworth, Chateaubriand, Coleridge's *Lay Sermon*, Gibbon's defence of aristocracy, and the opening paragraph of La Motte Fouqué's *Sintram*.[25] There are charming passages of reminiscence, and his own argument is always enthusiastic, and sometimes infectiously so. It takes him eighty-six pages to get to a definition of chivalry, but in the end it is worth it: 'Chivalry is only a name for that general spirit or state of mind which disposes men to heroic and generous actions, and keeps them conversant with all that is beautiful and sublime in the intellectual and moral world. It will be found that, in the absence of conservative principles, this spirit more generally prevails in youth than in the later periods of men's lives; and, as the heroic is always the earliest age in the history of nations, so youth, the first period of human life, may be considered as the heroic or chivalrous age of each separate man: and there are few so unhappy as to have grown up without having derived the advantage of being able to enrich their imagination and to soothe hours of sorrow with its romantic recollections . . . Every boy and youth is, in his minds and sentiments, a knight, and essentially a son of chivalry. Nature is fine in him . . . As long as there has been or shall be, young men to grow up to maturity, and until all youthful life shall be dead, and its source withered for ever, so long must there have been, and must there continue to be, the spirit of noble chivalry.'[26]

And then off he goes again, telling one about Amyntas, and Telamon, and Alexander, and Oliver de Clisson, and Antalcidas, and Lord Bacon, and how Perceforest kissed his squire Lionnel, and Cleanbrotus threw himself into the sea. A modern reader working through the *Broad Stone* may sometimes feel as though he is pulling out pieces of interminable spaghetti, or having a telephone conversation with someone who is constitutionally incapable of hanging up. But one can see how young men of those days, already ripe for chivalry and more inured to prolixity than we are, could have been roused to a furore of excitement.

Excited they were, and not just young men. Admittedly Macaulay said that Digby 'seemed to be of the opinion that the world was made exclusively for gentlemen',[27] and Southey considered the *Broad Stone* 'a book full of exaggerated admiration of chivalry' by an author who 'was determined not to see the evils connected with it'.[28] But Julius Hare called it 'that volume which, had I a son, I would place in his hands, charging him, though such prompting would be needless, to love it next to his Bible'.[29] Wordsworth dedicated a poem to Digby 'as an acknowledgment, however unworthy, of pleasure and instruction derived from his numerous and valuable writings, illustrative of the piety and chivalry of the older time'.[30] Ruskin wrote that 'the reader will find . . . every phase of nobleness illustrated in Sir Kenelm Digby's "Broad Stone of Honour."'[31] Copleston, who was Provost of Oriel in the great days of Keble and Newman, spoke of it approvingly as designed 'to revive the principles of loyalty and generosity and honour that were almost extinct amongst mankind'.[32] Edward FitzGerald made it the basis of his dialogue on education, *Euphranor*. William Johnson Cory, William Morris and Edward Burne-Jones were all excited by it as

63

42. Digby's drawing of Ehrenbreitstein, the 'Broad Stone of Honour'

young men, and Burne-Jones later kept it and Digby's *Mores Catholici* next to his bed.[33] 'Sillyish books both,' he once said, 'but I can't help it, I like them.' (His wife commented, 'And no wonder, for his youth lay enclosed in them.') Baden-Powell probably read the *Broad Stone* in youth, and certainly went to it for ideas when he was forming the Boy Scouts.[34]

There are various aspects of Digby's arguments which are worth looking at in a little more detail, because of their subsequent influence. Perhaps the most important of these is the belief that character is more important than intellect. It may have been the fact that most of the clever men of his generation were Utilitarians that made him so suspicious of the 'vain pride of mere intellectual ability'.[35] He admits, for instance, that mediaeval knights were ignorant, but (while pointing out that ignorance is not an essential element of chivalry) suggests that this did not matter too much: 'The scholar may instruct the world with his learning, the philosopher may astonish and benefit it by his researches, the man of letters may give a polish and a charm to society, but he who is possessed of simple faith and of high honour, is, beyond all comparison, the more proper object of our affection and reverence.'[36] How many rugger-playing Victorian prefects are implicit in that sentence.

When he deals with the education of gentlemen in mediaeval times, it is its character-building aspects which he especially admires, among them the training of the body as a means towards strengthening the character; he found a similar value in the games played at public schools and universities. 'The effects of exercise and activity, and even of the violent amusements of ancient chivalry and of our modern youth are, I conceive, unquestionable, in warming the heart and in exciting the love of virtue.'[37] He commends the system of education in Sparta because it was mainly designed to teach children 'how to obey and how to command'.[38] He refers with approval to the lack of luxury in mediaeval households, to Henri Quatre's training as a child of being made to walk barefooted and bareheaded across snow-covered mountains, and to the habit of some unspecified modern (possibly himself) of 'swimming daily three times across the Tiber, in winter'.[39]

Digby had in fact a claim to be considered one of the founding fathers of the cold bath and cold dip, so enthusiastically advocated by Victorian gentlemen and schoolmasters. He was not educated at a public school and seems never to have played football or cricket. The two sports in which he delighted were swimming and rowing. One of his fellow undergraduates described how 'his habits were as far as possible in conformity to his sturdy views of self discipline and moral hardihood, as well as courteous bearing. At 6 a.m. he would daily swim across the Cam, unless the ice was sufficiently strong to obstruct his passage.'[40]

Digby himself claimed to be 'founder of boating on the Cam'. As a schoolboy at Petersham he used to race on the Thames in wherries and four-oared boats. At Cambridge he and some friends from Petersham despised 'the tubs that then did serve for boats', and had their own model constructed, with the final result that

> . . . their eight-oar'd races proved
> A school for art they long had loved.

64

And then observe to him was given
The task of pulling number seven
In Trinity's first famous boat.[41]

Digby helped popularise another belief, one which was to become a favourite among the upper classes. 'So far', he wrote, 'from intending any reproach upon the lower classes of society, I pronounce that there is ever a peculiar connection, a sympathy of feeling and affection, a kind of fellowship, which is instantly felt and recognised by both, between these and the highest order, that of gentlemen. In society, as in the atmosphere of the world, it is the middle which is the region of disorder and confusion and tempest.'[42] One result of this was that 'the lower orders of people in England are generally, if not always, desirous of serving gentlemen instead of persons of inferior rank'.[43]

A corollary to this was the idea of the 'natural gentleman'. Digby quotes with approval the opinion of Bartholomew Arnigio, that 'the greatest nobility is that which is natural or divine, which may belong to him who walks barefooted in rags'.[44] There is many a shepherd, peasant or mountaineer who is as much, if not more, of a gentleman than the greatest aristocrat. Such examples of the 'chivalry of nature' have a natural dignity but they have no desire to rise in the social scale; they accept the existing order, and their place in it. There is, however, a different but equally admirable type, the young man of humble birth who combines natural nobility with ardour and great ability. Such a man can rise in society and be welcomed into the ranks of those who are gentlemen by birth.

The presupposition is that it is much harder, if not virtually impossible, for a man of prosperous middle-class origin to become a gentleman. The money-making middle class was, in Digby's view, the origin of nearly all that was wrong with England. It was because of it that England had abandoned its 'ancient spirit', had 'looked for happiness, and found riches and commercial prosperity, in neither of which does chivalry any more than religion take any great interest'.[45] From the middle classes came that supreme enemy of the gentleman, what Digby called the 'churl', the man who very often had made a fortune and established a worldly position, but was 'the savage envious hater of all superiority either of virtue or of rank'.[46]

Digby despised money and money-making with all the happy innocence of a man who had inherited a comfortable income and married a wife with money of her own. The Victorian belief that a gentleman should not be interested in money owed much to him. He believed that any gentleman who was born poor must expect to remain so because 'the merit which can have made you noble, has nothing to do with avarice, or with the pursuit of wealth'. But for such a man 'the absence of affluence is no misfortune, and . . . the inheritance of a virtuous name is of more value than all the treasures of the East'. 'If you will endeavour to arrive at distinction,' he said, 'the prize must be, not riches, but virtue.'[47] His suspicion of wealth made him a little ambivalent about great aristocrats; he accepted and respected their existence as a class, but noted how easy it was for them to be corrupted by their wealth. Primogeniture had been sanctioned by the Bible and confirmed by the general judgement of mankind; but in many ways the lot of the younger son was the better one.[48]

Digby's contempt of money-making, dislike of the middle classes and suspicion of cleverness made it difficult for him to recommend a career to his readers.[49] Any occupation 'chiefly directed toward the attainment of wealth' was of course out of the question. Going into Parliament was an honourable career, but unfortunately too many men of the middle classes had found their way there; as a result an M.P. had 'to sit down with men who are disloyal to their King and traitors to their religion' and 'be fronted with the vain insolence of new-made wealth'. The Law was acceptable, but tended to corrupt all but the strongest character because 'subtilty is soon mistaken for wisdom'. That left the Church and the army. The Church was of course admirable, as long as it was entered for the right reasons. So was the army, which offered an ideal career for gentlemen. 'The soldier is religious and brave, humane and merciful, open-hearted and just, frank, sincere, faithful, and firm.'[50]

Another of Digby's achievements was to extend the concept of chivalry to classical times. The idea did not of course originate with him; the comparison, for instance, had been drawn by Bishop Hurd as early as 1762. But he extended it, and helped set it in general circulation. The *Broad Stone* contained more quotations from Homer than from almost anyone else. But Digby did not confine himself to the Homeric age. He pointed out, for instance, that 'the oath which used to be taken by the Athenian youths might well have been proposed by the chivalry of a Christian land';[51] above all, he argued that 'there is hardly a virtue belonging to the chivalrous character which is not enforced and illustrated in the life-breathing philosophy of Plato'.[52] The point was made visually by two of the few engravings which accompanied the *Broad Stone*. Most editions start with an engraving of Athenian youths on horseback (taken from the frieze of the Parthenon) and end with one of the effigy of a Crusader. Under the Athenian youths is painted the motto 'Semper fuit idem.'

The Broad Stone of Honour was to continue to exert an influence through the century and beyond, but Digby himself had been largely forgotten long before his death.[53] His Catholicism, his character and his private means combined to take him out of the mainstream of Victorian life. His *Mores Catholici*, an exposition of the Catholic virtues which appeared in eleven enormous volumes between 1831 and 1842, did, it is true, attract a certain amount of attention. But the rest of his life was spent in publishing, at his own expense, volumes of memories or reflections which very few people read. Many are not without interest or charm; but his tendency to diffuseness got steadily worse. In the 1860s and 1870s he moved from prose to verse, and poured out indifferent heroic couplets apparently without end or effort. In old age he painted religious pictures with equal facility and distributed them free to Catholic churches all over England. It was as a gentle, courteous, slightly melancholy old man, living with his daughter in a comfortable house set in a large garden in Kensington, spending his days in writing, painting or wandering across London parks and commons (where he loved watching young lovers or children at play), that he passed the last years before his death in 1880.

66

43. (right) Contemporary cartoon of the Brass Founders' procession, 1821 (detail)

CHAPTER 6

Radical Chivalry

ON 12 JANUARY 1821 A PROCESSION OF ABOUT EIGHTEEN HUNDRED PEOPLE marched four abreast through the centre of London; the crowds which turned out to watch them were so great that the Strand was impassable for seven hours. The procession included eight knights on horseback in full armour, spaced out at intervals through the procession. All wore white plumes, and were accompanied by squires or attendants on foot, wearing half-suits of armour. Some of the knights were very splendid; the newspapers noted especially the first knight, who was preceded by three trumpeters on horseback, accompanied by six esquires, and wore 'a compleat and very splendid suit of brass scale armour', and an 'Ancient Knight on horseback' in the centre of the procession 'attired in a most superb suit of silver-plated steel cuirass Armour, attended by four armed esquires'. Apart from the knights, their attendants and a selection of brass bands, all taking part in the procession held brass rods, and many wore brass hats; in addition they carried a weird variety of objects and devices, including a royal crown, a George and Dragon, battleaxes, tea kettles and warming-pans.

Although Kenelm Digby believed that 'tournaments and steel panoply' were not essential to chivalry, one cannot help feeling that, had he seen or heard of this procession (there is no evidence that he did either), his heart would have warmed at the thought of so many knights in armour riding once more through the streets of London. Even the rest of the procession had an air of mediaeval fantasy about it that might have appealed to him. But its objective and background could only have filled him with disgust. The procession was made up of brass founders and coppersmiths, and was one of the many deputations of London artisans which marched to present a loyal address to Queen Caroline, in defiance of her husband George IV.[1] It was a demonstration, not of naturally noble peasants, but of what Digby would have considered the London equivalent of the Jacquerie, city artisans stirred up against authority by the kind of people he most disliked and distrusted: middle-class agitators and gentlemen who had betrayed their class by supporting democracy.

It was easy enough for Digby, Walter Scott and others to conjure up modern knights; it was less easy to control the direction in which they charged. Throughout the nineteenth century (and indeed in the twentieth century as well) individuals or groups who were proud to call themselves gentlemen set out, with what may reasonably be described as chivalrous enthusiasm, not to support the existing order, but to make radical changes in it. Admittedly sometimes these changes were in directions of which Scott or Digby might have approved; but all too often they were in support of everything that was expressed in the word 'democracy': trades unions, votes for all, cheap newspapers and education without religion. For what, after all, could be more chivalrous than for a gentleman to disregard his own self-interest and the interests of his class, and fight for the rights of working men?

Did anyone stage-manage the brass founders' procession? The Brass Founders' Company traditionally provided the knight in armour who rode in the Lord Mayor's Procession, but the deputation to Queen Caroline was far more elaborate than anything they had previously put on.[2] Did Lord Brougham (then still plain

Henry Brougham) have anything to do with it? The Whigs had taken up Queen Caroline's cause, largely in order to embarrass the Tories, who were in office, but Brougham was her chief protagonist. He was officially a Whig, but was distrusted by many of his own party owing to his Radical sympathies. He tends to be thought of as middle class, because he was brought up in Edinburgh professional circles by a middle-class mother, but he himself was very conscious of being Brougham of Brougham Hall, heir of a line of Westmorland squires and descended, as he (but not many others) believed, from crusading Broughams of the Middle Ages. In sympathy with his ancestry he remodelled Brougham Hall until it 'had the aspect of a feudal castle', and created a baronial hall inside it known as the Armour Hall from the collection which it contained.[3]

Another figure who has a possible link with the procession was Charles Tennyson, the uncle of the poet. The 'superb suit of silver-plated steel cuirass Armour' which featured in it was about to be purchased by him on behalf of his brother-in-law Matthew Russell of Brancepeth Castle.[4] Tennyson resembled Brougham in being a Whig M.P. with Radical leanings, an ardent supporter of Queen Caroline, and intensely proud of his ancestry, as the modern representative of the mediaeval family of d'Eyncourt.[5]

Charles Tennyson, Matthew and William Russell, and Colonel Thomas Wildman of Newstead Abbey form a close-knit group. Charles Tennyson was the only one of them who carried any political weight; but they had links with three men who caused more stir in the world, Lord Brougham, Lord Durham and Edward Bulwer-Lytton. All seven had characteristics in common. They were, or became, substantial landowners. They combined belief in the need for a land-owning upper class with support of advanced political causes; they tended to be called Radicals even if they did not admit to the name. And they all fought for the people from elaborately feudal castles or Gothic mansions. Between 1818 and 1829 the Russells spent (it is said) at least £120,000 on restoring Brancepeth Castle. In the 1820s Lord Durham turned Lambton Hall into Lambton Castle, Lord Brougham castellated and Gothicised Brougham Hall, and Colonel Wildman remodelled

69

44. Lord Brougham tilting at the ring, in the cartoon *Practising for the Tournament* by H. B., 1838

and restored Newstead. As soon as Tennyson inherited Bayons in 1835, and Lytton inherited Knebworth in 1844, they began to inundate them with battlements, pinnacles, and fortifications; they would almost certainly have done so earlier, if they had had the chance.

Politically, something of the atmosphere of upper-class Radicalism in which they moved is suggested by the character of the Duke of St Aldegonde in Disraeli's novel *Lothair*: 'St Aldegonde held extreme opinions, especially on political affairs, being a republican of the reddest dye. He was opposed to all privileges, and indeed to all orders of men, except dukes, who were a necessity. He was also strongly in favour of the equal division of all property, except land. Liberty depended on land, and the greater the landowners, the greater the liberty of a country. He would hold forth on this topic even with energy, amazed at any one differing from him; "as if a fellow could have too much land," he would urge, with a voice and glance which defied contradiction.'[6] Disraeli exaggerated, and (having a weakness for dukes) made St Aldegonde grander than he should have done; but he was writing from personal experience.

But what was a Radical in the 1820s and 1830s? The Radical party of the 1840s was a coherent political group, but earlier in the nineteenth century the Radicals were far from coherent. There were political Radicals, many of whom were not on speaking terms with each other, and philosophic Radicals, who wanted some of the same things as the political Radicals but for different reasons. One group descended from Thomas Paine, the other was the political wing of the Utilitarians. The political Radicals believed in justice for the people, and the rights of individuals; the philosophic Radicals believed in analysis, and the 'greatest happiness of the greatest number'. The political Radicals supported universal suffrage because they thought that everyone had a right to vote; the philosophic Radicals supported it because, since all men were basically selfish, giving everyone a vote would make it harder for them to exploit one another. The political Radicals attacked the aristocracy because it oppressed the people; the philosophic Radicals, because its vested interests stood in the way of logical reform. The political Radicals wanted Factory Regulations and a limit to hours of work because people had a right to decent working conditions; the philosophic Radicals opposed them, because they believed that 'the greatest happiness' could best be obtained by allowing free play to market forces.

Many political Radicals were republicans, but by no means all of them were; and some of those who were, were prepared to accept a republic in which there was a role for gentry and even aristocracy. English Radicalism at this period contained a strong vein of romantic nostalgia for a pre-industrial, or pre-Hanoverian (or even, in some cases, a pre-Norman) England in which a beneficent monarch had protected the rights of Parliament and people, and benevolent landowners had looked after their dependants. The wide variety in their attitudes was one reason why the political Radicals of the 1820s and 1830s were so disunited. But it also meant that members of the upper classes with popular sympathies could be accepted as being 'for the people' and yet retain a belief in the necessity of an upper class. This was the attitude taken up by the upper-class Radicals with whom this chapter is concerned. Some of them, without being whole-hearted Utilitarians, were also attracted to reforms supported by the philosophic Radicals; this was not always logical of them, but on the whole logic was not their strong point.

Lord Brougham was much the closest to the Utilitarians, and also much the cleverest. He was a personal friend as well as a political associate of Lord Durham for many years, until they quarrelled violently in the early 1830s. But Durham never had much sympathy with the Utilitarians, and resisted the advances made to him by the philosophic Radicals. It was his links with the political Radicals which gained him his nickname of 'Radical Jack'. His radicalism did not prevent him from being inordinately proud both of his ancient lineage and of his new title. Socially he was a cut above Tennyson and the Russells but politically they were associates. Brancepeth and Lambton Castles were both in Durham, about ten miles apart. The Russells supported Lord Durham's political interests in the county. Their money, like his, came from coal. Lord Durham's family, the Lambtons, had been gentry in Durham since at least the twelfth century, but their money (of which there was a great deal) was almost as new as their title, which was not created until 1828. Matthew Russell's father was a self-made man, a Sunderland banker who had had the good fortune to foreclose on a coal mine which suddenly became extremely profitable.[7] Charles Tennyson made great play of his undoubted, if remote, connections with the mediaeval d'Eyncourts, but almost all the Tennyson money had been made by his father, who started life as a solicitor in Grimsby.[8] Thomas Wildman was the son of a sugar-factor, who had managed the Beckford sugar plantations in the West Indies, and grossly milked them to his own advantage.[9] To some extent the combination of radicalism and feudalism in all three families (and even in the case of Lord Durham) may have expressed different ways of reacting to county neighbours envious or scornful of new money.

Charles Tennyson's Radical enthusiasms sent him on three chivalrous quests in the 1820s, to rescue Queen Caroline from her husband, the working classes from man traps, and Birmingham from non-representation in Parliament. His bill to make all kinds of traps and spring-guns illegal became law in 1826, in spite of bitter opposition from most of the landed classes. His fight to give Birmingham a Member of Parliament lasted through four sessions, and in the end brought down Wellington's administration in 1828. During the same year he became founder of an English branch and provincial Grand Master of the revived Order of the Templars.[10] This was an international organisation which combined an elaborate apparatus of robes, titles and decorations with championing Bolivar in South America and opposing the Holy Alliance in Europe. At one stage the Grand Prior of the Order was the Duke of Sussex, the only one of George IV's brothers to hold anything approaching Radical views. Both Tennyson and Wildman became friendly with the Duke (who was also a supporter of Lord Durham) and seem to have served as his equerries.[11] Tennyson also mysteriously acquired the title of Count Palatine, and played with the idea of becoming a Knight of Malta, but rejected it on learning that the Order 'could not be had without paying far too dear for the whistle'.[12]

Until his father died in 1835 he was in no position to build anything himself. Instead, he concerned himself with the building operations of his brother-in-law at Brancepeth and his friend at Newstead. Matthew Russell greatly enlarged and substantially remodelled Brancepeth Castle between 1818 and his death in 1822.[13] His architect was John Paterson of Edinburgh, but Russell was constantly asking for advice and suggestions from Charles Tennyson, who clearly thought he knew more about Gothic architecture than Paterson; not surprisingly the two did not get on. One of the elements of Brancepeth with which Tennyson was especially involved was the Baron's Hall. This was a vaulted room newly created in one of the old towers. Its main feature was a large stained-glass window showing the Battle of Neville's Cross. The battle had taken place near Brancepeth in 1346; Thomas Lord Neville (the then owner of Brancepeth) and other English lords had defeated and taken prisoner King David Bruce of Scotland. Tennyson was responsible for commissioning this window, and all the other stained glass at Brancepeth. It was made in 1820–1 by William Collins of London, but the Neville's Cross window seems to have been based on a design by Thomas Stothard.[14] Between 1818 and 1821 Tennyson bought at least four groups of arms and armour with which to embellish the Baron's Hall, the entrance hall and the armour gallery, including substantial purchases from Gwennap's collection in the Gothic Hall in Pall Mall and Bullock's in the Egyptian Hall in Piccadilly.[15] When the collection was catalogued in 1888 it contained over four hundred items.

72

45. Matthew Russell lying in state in the Baron's Hall, Brancepeth Castle, 1822

46. (above) Brancepeth Castle as restored for Matthew Russell, 1818–22

47. (right) The Battle of Neville's Cross. Drawing for the window in the Baron's Hall, Brancepeth

Tennyson probably also made the arrangements for Matthew Russell's elaborate lying-in-state in the Baron's Hall, after his death on 8 May 1822.[16]

The years 1830–2 were ones of great activity for the group, as they took part in the campaigns which culminated in the Reform Bill. In both 1830 and 1831 Tennyson stood for Stamford, in deliberate opposition to the Cecils, Marquesses of Exeter, great Tory magnates who had long considered Stamford their perquisite. He failed in 1830 but succeeded in 1831; his success resulted in a duel with Lord Thomas Cecil and a letter of congratulation from Lord Durham.[17] Thomas Wildman never stood for Parliament himself, but on 7 November 1832 he wrote in high excitement to Tennyson to tell him that he was chairing the committee for the local Reform candidate, 'having undertaken the task of opposing aristocratic usurpation in this Country . . . in opposition to all the grandees of the North . . . I trust however that we shall *beat the Dukeries*'.[18] Tennyson himself was standing for one of the new seats produced by Reform, representing the notably Radical borough of Lambeth. At the end of November he went up to Lincolnshire to chair a Reform dinner at Gainsborough. 'We bear the stamp of freedom on our brow', he told his audience, 'and scorn the recognition of the proudest peer who ever bore a coronet upon his. The aristocracy at large must be taught their proper places.'[19]

Another Reform candidate was Edward Bulwer-Lytton, who stood for Lincoln in 1832 with Tennyson's support.[20] They had been friends for some years. Lytton (who was to be created Lord Lytton in 1866) was a dandy, and had more of a taste for smart London society than Tennyson; but the two had much in common. 'I do not call myself a Radical,' Lytton wrote to Lord Durham in 1835, 'though I am generally called so.'[21] But, like Lord Durham, he was too much of a reformer to feel really at home with the Whigs. Lytton was also intensely proud of his lineage and a firm believer in the necessity of the landed classes. His father's family, the Bulwers, claimed Norman blood, and had owned land in Norfolk since the Conquest; his mother was a Lytton, heiress of a family which had been seated at Knebworth in Hertfordshire since the time of Henry VIII. He himself was to inherit Knebworth when his mother died. S. C. Hall, who worked under him when he edited the Radical *New Monthly Magazine* in 1831–3, described him as 'thoroughly an aristocrat: all his affinities were with his "order", although he sought, and thought, to connect himself with the hard-handed men of the working classes. I could fancy him scrupulously washing his hands after a meeting with his constituents.'[22] In supporting the Reform Bill in the House of Commons he assured members that it would not affect 'the wholesome power of the aristocracy' but only their 'illegitimate influence'.[23] He chose to sit for Lincoln because it was one of the few places where he could combine support of a Reform programme with opposition to the repeal of the Corn Laws; he was opposed to the latter because of the effect it would have on the position of the landed classes.

In the years immediately after the Reform Bill neither Lytton nor Tennyson was happy with Lord Grey's government; it was not sufficiently reforming for their tastes. In the early 1830s Charles Tennyson made a violent attack on Lord Grey in Parliament; his father, who had always been unhappy about Charles's Radical leanings, was in despair over what he called 'that dreadful speech'.[24] In 1835 his father died, and Charles Tennyson inherited his father's house and very considerable property in Lincolnshire. He immediately changed his name to Tennyson d'Eyncourt, that of the house from Bayons Hall to Bayons Manor, and started to rebuild.

For the next ten years his building operations occupied much of his time and energy. His executive architect was W. A. Nicholson of Lincoln; elements of an alternative design produced by Anthony Salvin were also incorporated; but Tennyson d'Eyncourt himself bombarded his architects and craftsmen with sketches, orders and suggestions. The first stage was to transform what had been a modest Regency house to the most convincing re-creation yet put up in England of the manor house of a late-mediaeval gentleman. But after a few years Tennyson's chivalric enthusiasms became too much for him, and the house assumed more and more the air of a castle. In 1837 a battlemented central tower rose above the manorial roofs. In 1839 Tennyson decided to surround the building with a complete fortified *enceinte*, studded with towers, and approached by a bridge, drawbridge and fortified gatehouse. Finally, sometime in the 1840s, an artificially ruined keep appeared on a hill within the fortifications, to the rear of the house.[25]

One of the most important and interesting features of Bayons was its great hall. This was re-creation of a mediaeval great hall, complete with screens,

74

50. (bottom left) Newstead Abbey, Nottinghamshire. The Hall, as shown in 1892

51. (bottom right) Design by Pugin for the hall at Scarisbrick, 1837

48. Charles Tennyson's election poster

49. Bayon's Manor, Lincolnshire, as depicted in Charles Tennyson's *Eustace: An Elegy*, 1851

minstrels' gallery, and open-timber roof. Radical gentlemen have at least as much claim to be considered the revivers of the great hall as Tory ones. It formed an important part of their philosophy: a great hall, in which all classes of society were, from time to time, entertained together symbolised the approach to life which would keep gentlemen in existence, as the natural leaders of a democratic society. There had been baronial halls of some kind at Lambton and Brougham, but both have been demolished without record.[26] The most notable feature of Thomas Wildman's extensive work at Newstead in the 1820s was his re-creation of the original mediaeval great hall, which had been marred by later alterations.[27] The result is probably the first convincing revived great hall of the nineteenth century (Plate 50). It not only has screens and an exposed-timber roof, but a vaulted kitchen in the style of the Abbot's Kitchen at Glastonbury to go with it. The architect at Newstead was John Shaw, but Charles Tennyson gave advice and made suggestions—and later surpassed the hall by his own at Bayons.

★　　　★　　　★

Up till 1830, the revival of chivalry had had a strong upper-class flavour. In spite of Kenelm Digby's contention that chivalry was not 'exclusively attached to aristocratical institutions', a modern knight still seemed to need the setting of a modern castle—or at least something approaching to it. But the 1830s saw the appearance of a group of journalists and novelists, almost all of middle-class origin, whose vigorous incursions into life, literature and politics were noticeably conditioned by the spirit of chivalry. These were the lively and sometimes brilliant contributors to *Fraser's Magazine*, which had started publication in 1830 under the editorship of a boisterous, drunken but extremely gifted Protestant from Cork called William Maginn.[28]

Superficially, the Fraserians had many of the characteristics of what Digby distastefully labelled the 'churl': 'the savage envious hater of all superiority'. Not only were they often scurrilous, abusive and obscene, but for a time they directed their most violent abuse against the Tory party and its leaders, especially Sir Robert Peel and the Duke of Wellington. But in fact, even if their method of controversy was too often unacceptable to gentlemen, there were no more ardent supporters of the monarch, the Church and the landed classes. They went into the attack because, as Maginn put it, of 'the disgraceful pusillanimity and desertion by the Tories of their own principles'.[29]

Fraser's claimed to have 'the counsel of Coleridge and the countenance of Scott'.[30] Its friends and contributors included Scott's son-in-law, Lockhart, and his old friends Hogg and Southey. But the most important figures in the evolution of its political philosophy were Carlyle and Maginn. Like Digby in *The Broad Stone of Honour*, both men rejected the doctrine of progress. They thought that England was on the whole a worse place than it had been two hundred years before; they hated Utilitarianism and the laissez-faire economics which had developed out of it. Carlyle had already put his point of view in *Signs of the Times* (1829) and developed it in articles written by him for *Fraser's*, some of which were published in book form as *Sartor Resartus*. These and his later works are

52. The Fraserians seated at their Round Table, after the drawing by Maclise

remembered, even if seldom read; Maginn's articles have been largely, and unfairly, forgotten.

By 1830 it was becoming increasingly hard to ignore the underside to the wealth created by the Industrial Revolution. Slums, disease, child-labour, over-long hours, pollution and poverty of the most appalling description were only too apparent for anyone who took the trouble to look for them. According to the laissez-faire analysis, first formulated by the Utilitarian economists and accepted by most factory-owners and landowners, there was little to be done about this. It was the result of surplus of labour, and surplus of labour was due to God and Nature; if the situation was left to itself (with a little help from the new Poor Law) God and Nature would adjust it again. As long as the wealth of the nation was increasing, there was nothing to worry about.

Fraser's was appalled by this philosophy and, in contrast, stood out for absolute standards of justice, compassion and honour. Since it could not be denied that 'for many years past the rich have been growing richer and the poor poorer',[31] or that the poor were being exploited and living in appalling conditions, it was the duty of the government and the ruling classes to do something about it. 'Toryism ought to be the *protective* system . . . It ought to protect the agricultural labourer from the farmer, the factory-child from the mill-tyrant, the Spitalfields weaver from the competition of the men of Lyons.'[32] The Fraserian vision of a just society included a well-established monarchy, Church and landed class, who would protect the working classes from oppression; and a just electoral system in which all householders, including working-class ones, would have a vote.

Fraser's quarrel with Tory politicians was that they had knuckled under to the manufacturers and laissez-faire. They were, in its view, so obsessed with the rights of property that they allowed mill-owners to do what they wanted, and so scared by the idea of revolution that they were unable to distinguish working people with a genuine grievance from demagogues. In 1830–2 *Fraser's* not only bitterly attacked Wellington and Peel, it actually supported the Whigs, even if with reservations. At least the Whigs wanted a fairer electoral system, and professed to be going to legislate to remedy working-class grievances. But the magazine was disappointed with the Reform Act as it was actually passed, and with the ensuing record of the Whig government that passed it. The voting system had merely been changed sufficiently to give the middle classes a stake in Parliament, and to oppress even further the still-unrepresented working class. As a result *Fraser's* gradually went back to supporting the Tories.

The Fraserians clearly had much in common with Digby and *The Broad Stone of Honour*. Not surprisingly, they were sympathetic to chivalry. The most obvious expression of this was the, in its day, famous Fraser's Round Table, around which its contributors ate, drank and wrote their copy. The table had practical advantages, but the Fraserians were also well aware of the Arthurian connotations of what Maginn called *la table ronde*, and welcomed them. The original Knights of the Round Table had been a 'band of brothers', loyal to Church and king, who rode out from Camelot to punish villains, redress wrong and rescue those in distress; and what else were the Fraserians doing?

In 1835 a young Irish artist from Cork, Daniel Maclise, drew the Fraserians seated round their table (Plate 52).[33] It was one of the series of slyly incisive illustrations which he provided for the 'Gallery of Illustrious Literary Characters' published in *Fraser's* between 1830 and 1836. Maclise was full of enthusiasm for chivalry, and the pictures exhibited by him at the Academy between 1835 and 1839 form a kind of symbolic exposition of the *Fraser's* point of view, expressed in chivalric form.

Maclise had been born a Presbyterian, but by the 1830s had become as ardent for Church and king as all the other Fraserians. He lamented the decay of loyalty to both in one of the two poems signed by him in *Fraser's*, 'Our Fathers' Swords'.

> Our fathers' swords are on the wall
> Their blades with rust o'erspread
> And oft these sloth-dimmed brands recall
> The memory of the dead
> For spirits linger round the spot
> And mourn for ages flown
> When brightly flashed those weapons forth
> For the altar and the throne.[34]

In his paintings he portrayed the 'honour, bravery, religion, virtue, high spirit, high feelings' and the happy relationship between people of different classes which Maginn had lamented were being abandoned for a cash relationship.

The Chivalric Vow of the Ladies and the Peacock (Plate VIII) exhibited in 1835 illustrated a custom described by de Sainte-Palaye.[35] Knights about to depart on a quest or a Crusade, or to bind themselves by an especially solemn vow, would swear on a splendidly garnished peacock, which was afterwards cut up and distributed among the company. *An Interview between Charles and Cromwell*, which followed in 1836, moved on several centuries to show one of the later heroes and martyrs of chivalry, surrounded by his loving children and loyal dogs, being asked by a brutal and implacable Cromwell to sign away his royal authority. In *Sir Francis Sykes and his Family* (Plate VII), exhibited in 1837, a

53. Daniel Maclise. *The Chivalric Vow of the Ladies and the Peacock*, 1835

54. Daniel Maclise. *Merry Christmas in the Baron's Hall*, 1838

55. Daniel Maclise. *Robin Hood and his Merry Men entertaining Richard Coeur de Lion in Sherwood Forest*, 1839

contemporary Tory baronet and his family were brilliantly transformed into a mediaeval knight, his demoiselle, dogs and children, caught in a glow of colour and romantic elegance as they walk down a winding newel staircase.[36]

Merry Christmas in the Baron's Hall (1838) was accompanied and explained by a long poem by Maclise in *Fraser's*.[37] The subject was probably inspired by Walter Scott's description of Christmas in *Marmion*, and expressed a similar message, but in an Elizabethan setting. Watched by an indulgent baron and his family in the 'brave old hall', a jovial procession bring in a boar's head, while Father Christmas, St George and the Dragon and their fellows prepare for the Christmas masque, and pages and serving-maids play at hunt-the-slipper.

> An honest mirth flows all around,
> Razing distinction to the ground.
> No stateliness is to be seen,
> Nor dulling distance intervene . . .
>
> Huge was the table; vast the hall
> And free the bounty that gave all . . .
>
> If those were barbarous ages, then
> Let us be barbarous again.

Robin Hood and his Merry Men entertaining Richard Coeur de Lion in Sherwood Forest followed in 1839. It was as large and elaborate as *Merry Christmas* and was also almost certainly inspired by Scott, this time by an episode in *Ivanhoe*. The picture was explained by a pseudo-mediaeval ballad published anonymously in *Fraser's*.[38] Ballad and picture put across two themes, both in full accord with Fraserian philosophy: the ability of the King to mix with his subjects and become the life and soul of a jovial banquet; and the contrast between the open-air and in its way chivalrous life of the outlaws, and the luxury and self-seeking of the barons and priests whom they had stripped of their treasures (seen in the foreground of the picture) in order to give them to the poor. The picture shows Robin drinking Richard's health, in ignorance of his identity. In a moment Richard will reveal himself, and the loyal outlaws kneel to swear fealty to him; like the Fraserians, they are loyal to king and country, in spite of their swashbuckling ways.

★   ★   ★

There were, of course, noticeable differences between the Fraserian Tories and the upper-class Radicals discussed earlier in this chapter. The Fraserians felt much more strongly about the importance of the Crown and the Church; the upper-class Radicals flirted from time to time with republicanism and the doctrines of philosophic Radicalism, both of which the Fraserians abhorred. But none the less they shared a good deal of common ground. Both groups were unable to feel at home with either the Whigs or the Tory Establishment. Both believed in the value of an upper class based on land, one of whose principal duties would be to protect the working classes from oppression. Both admired the kind of relationship symbolised by life in a mediaeval great hall. Both wanted a wider franchise, and were prepared to accept household suffrage, even if not votes for all.

In the early 1830s the differences between the more romantic Tories and the more nostalgic Radicals were small enough for candidates in some elections to try for both the Radical and the Tory vote.[39] The best-known case is that of Disraeli.[40] As a young man his political creed was near enough to that of the Fraserians. 'Toryism is worn out', he declared, 'and I cannot condescend to be a Whig.' By Toryism he meant the Tory politicians of his day, not Toryism as a political creed. Accordingly, in the three elections which he contested unsuccessfully at High Wycombe in 1832–5, he called himself a Radical but asked for the support of the Tories. His political platform throughout was reasonably consistent. He declared himself 'a Conservative to preserve all that is good in our constitution, a Radical to remove all that is bad'. He supported Parliamentary reform, triennial parliaments, repeal of the newspaper tax, abolition of sinecures, legislation to improve the condition of the poor, and any change in the Corn Laws which would 'relieve the customer without impairing the farmer'. In 1833 he wrote a pamphlet, *What is He?*, in which he argued for a National Party, based on a combination of Radicals and Tories. In his election campaign he had the support of the local Tory magnates, Lord Chandos and his father the Duke of Buckingham. He also tried for, but never quite gained the backing of Lord Durham; he had been introduced to him by Lady Blessington in London, had got on very well, and wrote to him as 'a nobleman whose talents I respect, and who, I am confident, has only the same object in view with myself'.[41] But Disraeli's position, although not as illogical or opportunist as has sometimes been made out, fell too much between stools to succeed. In the end, not entirely happily, he committed himself to the Tories, and was elected member for Maidstone in 1837.

Maclise drew Disraeli for his *Fraser's* series in 1833, and Maginn wrote a teasing but not unfriendly text to go with it: 'Benjamin's politics are rather preposterous; but he is young, and may improve.'[42] It is not surprising to find that both the Fraserian Maclise and the Radical Lytton were his friends. He had known Maclise since the later 1820s, and was almost certainly responsible for getting him the commission to paint the Sykes family in 1837. Disraeli was Henrietta Sykes's lover from about 1834 to 1836; when the affair ended Maclise took over from him, until the Sykes marriage broke up in disaster when Sir Francis Sykes found Henrietta and Maclise in bed together in the summer of 1838.[43]

Disraeli first met Lytton in 1830. By 1832 they were going everywhere together; in 1833 he wrote that 'Bulwer is one of the few with whom my intellect comes into collision with benefit'.[44] Through Lytton he met other upper-class Radicals, including Lord Durham and Charles Tennyson d'Eyncourt; in 1837 he noted among the guests at a dinner given by Lytton, 'D'Eyncourt, always friendly to me'.[45] It was probably Disraeli who introduced Lytton to Maclise. The two became friends; Maclise illustrated books by Lytton in 1834 and 1838, drew him for *Fraser's* in 1832, was often at Knebworth in the 1840s and painted his

56. Edward Bulwer-Lytton as Lord Rivers. Detail from *Caxton's Printing Office* by Daniel Maclise, *c.* 1849–50

portrait in 1850.[46] It may have been partly his influence which made Lytton increasingly interested in chivalrous themes. The latter's novel *Rienzi* (1835) dealt with a mediaeval republican; but the most striking character in his play *Duchesse de la Vallière*, which followed in the next year, was Bragelone, to whom, as he put it, 'belonged the essential of chivalric poetry, honour, love and religion, the sword, the favour and the cross'.[47] In about 1840 he bought Maclise's dashing picture *Combat of Two Knights* (Plate 74); in 1849 he posed in full armour for the figure of Lord Rivers in Maclise's *Caxton's Printing Office*.[48]

In his first years in Parliament Disraeli was unhappy with the Tories. Many of them regarded him with suspicion, others did not take him seriously. In 1839 he was frequently voting against his party with the by now diminishing group of upper-class Radicals. The situation changed in 1841. In that year three young Tory aristocrats, all under the age of twenty-three, came into Parliament. They were Lord John Manners, George Smythe and Henry Baillie-Cochrane.

John Manners and his friends had just emerged from a Cambridge undergraduate world not dissimilar to the one in which Digby had moved fifteen to twenty years earlier, a world in which ardent and idealistic young men argued, got excited, pursued campaigns, resolved to change the world, and fell in love with each other. But there was a difference. Their campaigns were now to rescue monarchies, not to promote rebellions; Charles I was their hero, not Cromwell. The enthusiasms which had made Digby seem an amiable oddity to many of his contemporaries had found disciples. John Manners was everything Digby could have hoped for, a Walter-Scott hero come to life and given an extra shot of religious enthusiasm.[49] He was young, ardent, aristocratic, good-looking and entirely without malice or meanness. He was romantic about the Stuarts, loyal to Church and king, distressed by the condition of the working classes and convinced that it was the duty of the upper classes to do something about it. Here, if anywhere, was a modern young knight. 'We have now virtually pledged ourselves', he wrote in his diary on 4 August 1838, 'to restore what? I hardly know—but still, it is a glorious attempt.'[50] Chivalrous metaphors came naturally from the pens of his friends. In 1844 George Smythe, who had loved him since Eton days, dedicated his book *Historic Fancies* to him as 'the Philip Sydney of our generation'. Seven years earlier he had written a sonnet to him at Cambridge:

> Thou should's't have lived, dear friend, in those old days
> When deeds of high and chivalrous enterprise
> Were gendered by the sympathy of eyes
> That smiled on Valour—or by roundelays
> Sung by the palmer minstrel to their praise.
> Then, surely, some Provençal tale of old
> That spoke of Zion and Crusade, had told
> Thy knightly name, and thousand gentle ways.[51]

In 1838 the Reverend Frederick Faber, a High Church clergyman who had become the devoted friend and admirer of both young men, sent him the works of Newman, 'a gift as well suited to your chivalrous propensities as to the clerical character of the donor'.[52] The worst that his friends could say about him was that he was too good for this world. 'You are a miracle of purity in an age of impurity', George Smythe wrote to him in 1848. Those less enthusiastic put it slightly differently: 'There is an impotent purity about John Manners', said Monckton Milnes, 'that is almost pathetic.'[53]

His mind was ardent rather than either creative or complex; he saw everything in black and white. He read and was enthused by *The Broad Stone of Honour* and (probably) the political articles in *Fraser's*; he read Tory political theorists such as Wyndham, Bolingbroke and Filmer;[54] through Faber he became an enthusiastic follower of the Oxford Movement, and a more ardent advocate of the authority of the Church even than the Fraserians. His point of view is expressed clearly enough in *England's Trust*, a volume of verse dedicated to Smythe and published in 1841. In smooth heroic couplets he regrets the diminishing power of Church and king, calls for a return to feudalism and sadly compares the situation of the 'modern slave' to the days when

57. Lord John Manners as Kenneth of Scotland at the Bal Costumé, Buckingham Palace, 1842

> Each knew his place—king, peasant, peer or priest,
> The greatest owed connexion with the least

He describes a traditional Christmas, yearns to have lived in the days of 'King Charles the Martyr', mourns for 'Want of faith and cold disloyalty' at the tombs of the exiled Stuarts and celebrates the chivalrous struggles of the Spanish Carlists—to whom he had paid an impetuous visit in 1839.[55] He pushes one of Digby's sentiments beyond the limits of absurdity, and exclaims,

> Let wealth and commerce, laws and learning die
> But leave us still our old Nobility!

He was never allowed to forget these unfortunate lines. Alas, they are the only memorable ones in the book, with the possible exception of another couplet, descriptive of happy feudal villages 'uncursed by trade':

> O'er them no lurid light has Knowledge shed
> And Faith stands them in Education's stead.[56]

But John Manners and his friends, unlike Digby or the Fraserians, belonged by birth to the upper circle of the Tory hierarchy. None of them had any difficulty in getting into the House of Commons before he was twenty-three. There they met Disraeli, and found him virtually the only Tory M.P. who could talk their language. Disraeli was always attracted to lively good-looking young men of aristocratic birth; they, in their turn, found him glamorous, experienced and fascinating. He may have taken John Manners's more extreme views with a pinch of salt; but on the whole they agreed with each other. Smythe was more cynical and dissolute than his friend; but he loved John Manners, and he loved political intrigue. Baillie-Cochrane came in with the others. After several months of discussion the group that came to be known as Young England formally came into existence in the autumn of 1842.

They spent the next two and a half years in a continuous state of excitement, planning, travelling, making speeches and constantly meeting each other. Disraeli had the gift of turning politics into a highly enjoyable mixture of game and conspiracy. But apart from establishing the beginnings of his own reputation, the political achievements of Young England were minimal. The group manfully spoke up for Lord Ashley's ten-hour Factory Bill, and supported W. B. Ferrand, a Yorkshire landowner who was a pugnacious and remorseless harrier of the iniquities of mill-owners.[57] They did their unsuccessful best to help Don Carlos of Spain, who had fled to France and been imprisoned by Louis Philippe. They supported the idea of land allotments, and voted against their own party in favour of a less tough policy in Ireland. By means of *A Plea for National Holy Days* (1843) John Manners suggested a way of simultaneously supporting the Church and improving the lot of the workers. It was a part of his rather naïve plans for a new feudalism, along with the permanent opening of churches and cathedrals, public games, parks and bath-houses for the working classes, and a 'more personal and therefore more kind' intercourse between 'men of power' and those below them.

But Young England's liveliest achievements in those years were Disraeli's two novels *Coningsby* (1844) and *Sybil* (1845). One dealt with contemporary politics, the other with their social background. Most of the characters, especially in *Coningsby*, are distilled from actual people: Coningsby himself is probably a mixture of Smythe and John Manners. All the latter's pet theories, as expressed in *England's Trust*, reappear transformed with a dash and wit of which Manners was not capable. Almost inevitably, there is a description of a merry Christmas in the tradition of Scott and Maclise, complete with boar's head and Lord of Misrule. But Disraeli's Christmas is made to take place in a Victorian setting. It is a deliberate revival, stage-managed by Coningsby's friend Henry Sydney in the great hall of St Genevieve, the home of their mutual friend Eustace Lyle.[58]

Eustace Lyle is based on Ambrose Lisle Phillipps, a friend of the Young England group through whom it had a direct link with Kenelm Digby. Phillipps had been converted to Catholicism at the age of sixteen, and then gone up to Trinity College, Cambridge, in 1826. Digby, who was still working at Cambridge, although he had graduated in 1819, became his closest friend.[59] Like Charles Tennyson d'Eyncourt he was proud of his descent from a mediaeval family, in this case the de Lisles; the unromantic 'Phillipps' was gradually eroded as he became, first Ambrose de Lisle Phillipps and then (on the death of his father in 1862) Ambrose Phillipps de Lisle.

St Genevieve as described by Disraeli was a 'pile of modern building in the finest style of Christian architecture' complete with a great hall equipped with 'rich roof . . . gallery and screen'. Disraeli's description was almost certainly inspired by the designs which Phillipps's friend Augustus Welby Pugin had prepared in 1841 for rebuilding Garendon, the house of Phillipps's father.[60] The designs were never carried out; but in 1836 and 1837, at exactly the same time as Charles Tennyson d'Eyncourt was building his hall at Bayons, Pugin had

58. Knebworth Hall, Hertfordshire. The staircase, as photographed in 1909

designed two Gothic great halls which actually were built. One was for the Earl of Shrewsbury at Alton Towers, the other for Charles Scarisbrick at Scarisbrick Hall in Lancashire; the designs for the latter (Plate 51) included a splendid fireplace, crowned by knights in armour.[61]

Young England split up over the Repeal of the Corn Laws. Smythe, who had always been an unreliable member of the group, followed Peel; Baillie-Cochrane went with him. Manners remained loyal to Disraeli. Disraeli's own standing among the Tories was dramatically improved, because so many of its leading members had become Peelites; but on the other hand the Tory party was to spend all but five of the next twenty-eight years in opposition.

And what, meanwhile, was happening to the upper-class Radicals? On the whole, they were becoming less radical and moving out of politics. Wildman

59. Knebworth Hall, Hertfordshire, as photographed *c.* 1900

developed into an enthusiastic opponent of Repeal, and busily supported the dukes against whom he had campaigned twelve years earlier.[62] Tennyson d'Eyncourt fell out with his Lambeth electors in 1849, when he refused to support Cobden; he finally lost his seat in 1852. He was still collecting any kind of title he could get hold of; in 1844 he persuaded the Duke of Mantua, 'Successor to the Kingdom of Jerusalem, descendant of Charlemagne and Lothario' (but in exile in London), to creat his wife a Dama Cavaliere and Viscontessa of the Order of Maria Eliza.[63] In 1848 he bought the Château d'Aincourt in France. His friendship with Lytton had become closer than ever. Lytton came frequently to stay with 'the Chatelaine, the Damzelle and the Baron of Bayons'.[64] It was there that he wrote *Harold, the Last of the Saxon Kings* in 1848; he dedicated it to his host.

Lytton was still a force to be reckoned with, but no longer as a Radical. From 1841 until 1852 he was out of Parliament and disillusioned with politics. His mother died in 1844, and he succeeded to Knebworth. Like his friend at Bayons, he immediately set about remodelling it. In 1844–5 he transformed it with remarkable speed (it was all done with stucco) into a Gothic mansion of the time of Henry VIII, bristling with towers and pinnacles.[65] Inside he restored the hall in true feudal style, Gothicised the rooms, and lined hall and staircase with armour. In 1847 he rejected the suggestion that he might stand for Marylebone as a Liberal 'because my prejudices are not with trade, and I fear the constituency is more democratic than I like'. In 1848 he exploded against 'those miserable Cobdens' and the 'wretched money spiders, who would sell England for 1s. 6d.' If there was going to be a republic 'it shall not be, if I and a few like me live, a Republic of millers and cotton spinners, but either a Republic of gentlemen or a Republic of workmen'.[66] In the summer of 1850 Disraeli and his wife made a highly successful visit to Knebworth; in 1852 Lytton returned to Parliament, but as a Conservative.

86

60. (right) The Queen of Beauty processing to the lists at Eglinton, as depicted by E. H. Corbould

CHAPTER 7
The Eglinton Tournament

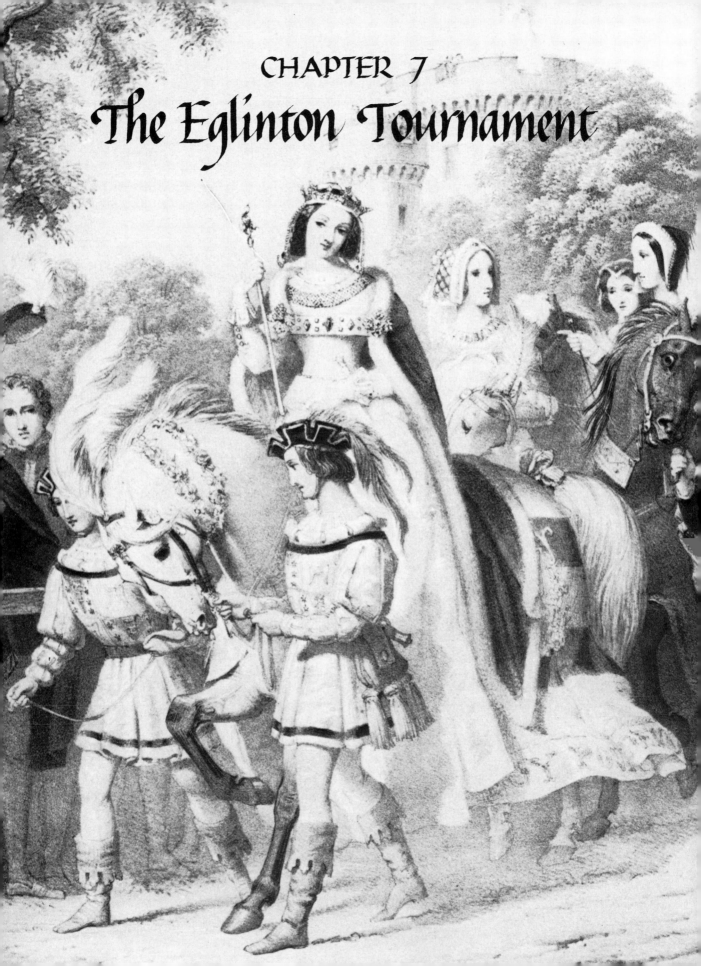

THE EGLINTON TOURNAMENT IS THE MOST OBVIOUSLY FAMOUS PRODUCT OF nineteenth-century chivalry in Great Britain. At the time it aroused almost world-wide interest; even today the fact that there was such a tournament, and that it fizzled out in a cloudburst, is a matter of common knowledge. Two curious stories may help to suggest the background of romanticism which helped to produce it. One concerns a middle-aged nobleman, the other a little boy. Both took place in the years before the tournament; one has only marginal connections with it, the other is directly related.

Charles Stanhope, Viscount Petersham (1780–1850), was a well-known dandy and eccentric in the days of the Regency and George IV. He had a passion for snuff and tea, and lived surrounded by canisters of one and boxes of the other. He never left his house until after six p.m., and when he did his horses, coach and footmen were as brown as his tea and snuff. He wore curiously distinctive hats, and designed a special type of overcoat, known as a Petersham.[1]

Towards the end of the 1820s he met and fell in love with an actress called Maria Foote. Opinions differ as to whether she was a good actress, but it seems agreed that she was both nice and pretty. At the time he took up with her, she was well over thirty and had had a notorious past. She had lived with Colonel Berkeley (later Lord Fitzhardinge) and had several illegitimate children by him; she had been engaged to 'Pea-Green' Haynes, a dandy of the day, and when he had run out on her had sued for breach of promise, and been awarded £3,000 damages.[2]

The Earl of Harrington (as Lord Petersham had become on the death of his father) did not run out on her. He probably lived with her for several years; then, in 1831, he married her. In the 1830s there was no hope of even a countess with such a past being received in society. Lord Harrington took his wife off to Elvaston Castle, his house in Derbyshire. According to one account the Earl, 'animated by romantic jealousy',[3] refused to allow her to go outside the gates; certainly no one else was allowed in. For twenty years Elvaston Castle was sealed to the outside world. Meanwhile, behind the park wall, gardeners worked by the dozen, full-grown trees were carted in and planted, and castle and Countess vanished behind towering walls of clipped yew and spires of exotic conifers.[4]

The house at the centre of this labyrinth had already been partly Gothicised to the design of James Wyatt and Robert Walker. Lord Harrington brought in Lewis Cottingham to add another Gothic wing, and to re-do parts of the interior.[5] Wyatt's Gothic hall was redecorated, and named 'The Hall of the Fair Star' (Plate IX). It became a shrine to the two middle-aged but apparently still ardent lovers, and to Lord Harrington's knight-errantry. Gothic alcoves round the hall were filled with figures in armour and the walls hung with swords and lances. Doors, alcoves and stained-glass windows were decorated with appropriate mottoes: 'Fayre beyond the Fayrest', 'Beauty is a Witch', 'Faithful to Honour and Beauty' (Plate X). Relevant if sometimes mysterious symbols abounded: stars by the dozen, flaming hearts, lovers' knots, quivers of arrows, lyres, pomegranates, peacocks and birds of paradise.[6]

The theme was continued in the gardens. South of the house was the 'Bower Garden' or 'Garden of Mon Plaisir'. A topiary tunnel curved round and enclosed

61. The Garden of Mon Plaisir, Elvaston Castle, from Veitch's *Manual of Conifers*

it. Loopholes were cut in the tunnel, through which it was possible to gaze at the central feature, a 'fair star' laid out in box-edged flower beds. Four figures of kneeling and adoring knights and a ring of topiary sentry-boxes formed an inner circle round the star. From its central point there rose, as the cynosure of the garden—and for what extraordinary reason?—a monkey-puzzle.

Another garden, called the Alhambra Garden, still contains what is known as the Moorish Pavilion. The room inside is encrusted with decoration in the Moorish style, and painted with yet more knightly mottoes and symbols. It is derelict and empty today, and the central feature inserted in it by Lord Harrington has gone. This consisted of 'an image in plaster-of-Paris, of his lady-love, together with one of himself kneeling at her feet and gazing at her, his hands being about to commit his adoration to the strings of a lyre'.[7]

The main lines of the story of Lord Harrington and Maria Foote can be established without doubt, but the personal letters and papers which might have filled it out have all disappeared. The story of Charlie Lamb and his guinea-pigs is amply documented by Charles Lamb himself.[8]

Charles—generally known as Charlie—Lamb, the son of a Sussex baronet, decided shortly after his seventh birthday in 1823 that he was going to write the history of his guinea-pigs, Minnikin, Pin and Toby. *Ivanhoe* had come out four years earlier; Charles Lamb's father had written an epic in twelve cantos, *The Dragon Knight*; Sir Egerton Brydges, genealogist, enthusiast for heraldry and writer of Gothic poems and romances, was a friend of the family. Minnikin, Pin and Toby were gradually transformed into guinea-pig heroes of chivalry. As Charles Lamb grew older, his history grew and multiplied; and so, for that matter, did his guinea-pigs.

He seems to have had the same kind of ardent and lovable nuttiness as Kenelm Digby. Their quests took them in opposite directions; Digby became a Catholic and a monarchist, Lamb ended up an atheist, a socialist and a vegetarian. But from

89

childhood both were mad about chivalry and the Middle Ages. Charles Lamb transformed his guinea-pigs into knights, counts and dukes, constructed elaborate coats of arms for them, and made them the heroes or villains of an epic romance of the kingdom of Winnipeg. In the end *The History of Winnipeg from the foundation to the Present time* BY ROYAL COMMAND extended to eight miniature red-and-green leather volumes. Meanwhile the estate carpenter at Beauport set to work to construct a Camelot of battlemented hutches set in a miniature kingdom of Winnipeg in which swarms of guinea-pigs could roam in safety and content. Here King Geeny and Queen Cavia, Sir Coccus Wallai, the Knight of Kilgynger, the Prince of Rarribu and Turknine de Newton lived, bred and died well into the 1830s. Meanwhile Charles Lamb was growing up, much loved by his family but also a puzzle to them. As his elder half-brother later wrote, 'under the influence of a bad course of reading and an unfortunate choice of friends, he became I fear almost an infidel. He never went into society, and spent his time entirely in the country among his shells, insects, and guinea-pigs, of which latter collection he had several hundred.'[9]

Charles Lamb's half-brother was distressed by his atheism, but amused and intrigued by his enthusiasm for chivalry. He was Archibald Montgomerie, thirteenth Earl of Eglinton, who in 1839 was to give the famous tournament.

★ ★ ★

It was inevitable that someone would give a tournament in the end. Ever since 1819, when Scott had described the tournament at Ashby-de-la-Zouche in *Ivanhoe*, the public had been kept tournament-conscious. Ivanhoe was immediately dramatised, and no fewer than five versions of it were running concurrently in London during 1820. One of these was at Astley's amphitheatre, well known in the 1820s and 1830s both for circuses and for spectacular pageants based on historical events or contemporary best-sellers.[10] The Astley *Ivanhoe* was presented in five set-pieces, culminating in a tournament of twenty knights mounted on horseback. It became a regular feature of the repertoire. Meanwhile, paintings of the Ashby or other tournaments were appearing almost annually at the Royal Academy. In 1827 actual tilting moved modestly from the circus to the country house, in the form of a tilting party given by Viscount Gage at Firle Park in Sussex. Local Sussex gentlemen cantered up and down, poking lances at each other across lines of hurdles, while the ladies amused themselves with archery.[11]

In the summer of 1838 an opera by Lord Burghersh called *The Tournament* was put on at the St James's Theatre. Lord Burghersh (later the eleventh Earl of Westmorland) was an amateur musician who had written the opera when he was Minister at Florence in 1820, but this was its first London presentation.[12] The action centred round a tournament, complete with Queen of Beauty, victorious Unknown Knight, dramas, despair, conflict and ultimate reconciliation.

Two other events helped bring the tournament off the stage into real life. One, to be exact, was a non-event. In April 1838 Lord Melbourne, the Whig Prime Minister, announced that Victoria's coronation would take place without the traditional banquet in Westminster Hall. There would be no Queen's Champion

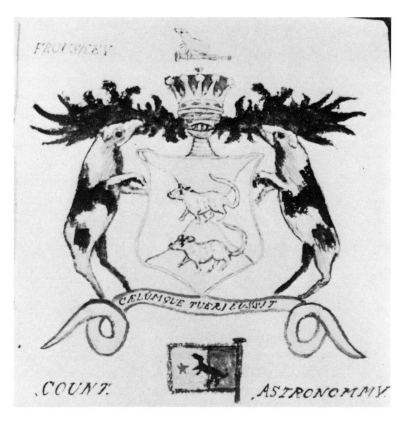

Cabbage Castle.

The ancient residence of the Count of Valence & Cabbage — built by the Emperor Ermineus I. year 10 — 11 — In the year 18. having become ruinous it was taken down & a very splended edifice erected on the same site by Enceladus 1st Count of the house of Waloi —

FROISSEY

CÆLUMQUE TUERI EUSSIT

COUNT. ASTRONOMMY.

Sir Ino FitsRedais of Wittaken. K.W.R.
Sheriff of the border. A.P. 12–13.
From the original picture in the possession of The
Rt Hon. Coccineus Hector.
Earl of Wittaken. &c &c
at
Wittaken Castle.

62, 63, 64. Guinea-pig drawings by Charles Lamb from his *History of Winnipeg*: (top left) 'Cabbage Castle'; (top right) guinea-pig coat of arms; (bottom) Sir Ino FitsRedais of Wittaken casting down his gauntlet, no Earl Marshal, Lord High Steward and Lord High Constable riding into the hall, no presentation to the Queen of two falcons, three cups of maple and a mess of dilligrout. The budget was in deficit, trade was in recession, and thousands of Spitalfield weavers were literally starving. In Lord Melbourne's view it was no time for extravagance; and such ceremonies were anyway becoming ridiculous. His announcement of what became known as the Penny Coronation was greeted with indignation by the Tories, and by all who felt strongly about chivalry or tradition. In the House of Lords Lord Londonderry angrily complained that abandoning 'time-honoured and time-consecrated forms and ceremonies' amounted to an attack on the monarchy.[13] Charlie Lamb's father, Sir Charles, was deprived of the agreeably prominent role he would have played as Knight Marshal, a useful sinecure to which he had succeeded in 1824. Both men were to figure conspicuously in the Eglinton Tournament.

The other event was the opening, in April 1838, of Samuel Pratt's armour showrooms in Lower Grosvenor Street.[14] Pratt had been dealing in armour for some years, but the new shop marked a much publicised expansion of his business. The armour was displayed in a 'truly Gothic apartment' designed by L.N. Cottingham, the architect who a few years earlier had done over Elvaston Castle for Lord and Lady Harrington. Its central feature consisted of 'six grim figures, in full armour, apparently in debate', seated at a table. Pratt also struck out a new line in catalogues, containing illustrations and lavish descriptions of the pieces he offered for sale. 'To gaze on the plumed casque of the Mailed Knight equipped for the Tournament', ran a passage in the first catalogue, 'and to grasp the ponderous mace, yet encrusted with the accumulated rust of centuries, cannot fail to inspire admiration for the chivalrous deeds of our ancestors.'

On 4 August 1838 the *Court Journal* published a rumour that Lord Eglinton was going to hold a tournament. Within a few weeks the rumour had been confirmed. Lord Eglinton was a nice, rich and sporting young Tory earl. Although he later confessed to an early enthusiasm for Malory and Froissart,[15] his main interests at the time seem to have been women and racing. What exactly set him off has never been established. To begin with he envisaged a relatively modest affair, on the lines of the tilting party at Firle. But in the climate of the 1830s, and of 1838 in particular, the suggestion of a tournament acted like sodium dropped into a glass of water. In an instant everything began to fizz. It was not just that Lord Eglinton's stepfather, Sir Charles Lamb, was eager for some compensatory role to make up for his disappointment over the coronation banquet; or that Charles Lamb was driven wild with excitement at the thought of thundering down the lists in real armour; or that Samuel Pratt saw endless potentialities of becoming purveyor of knightly outfits to the British aristocracy. No doubt all three egged Lord Eglinton on. But the reactions reached much wider. Anyone who had ever been inspired by Walter Scott, or filled with chivalrous enthusiasm by Kenelm Digby, or infuriated by the Penny Coronation, or in any way influenced by the now virtually endless gushes of chivalry which had been playing on the public consciousness with increasing vigour for the past twenty years, began to vibrate with expectation. Those who believed in the march of progress, or a rational structure of society, or the greatest good of the greatest number or the rule of the people correspondingly seethed with indignation. Whigs insulted Tories, Utilitarians made fun of romantics. As the excitement grew the tournament grew with it, until it became not only a full-scale re-enaction of a mediaeval event, but even more a symbol of Tory defiance, of aristocratic virility, of hatred of the Reform Bill, of protest against 'the sordid, heartless, sensual doctrines of Utilitarianism'.[16] Lord Eglinton himself was caught up by the tide, and changed by it. He may have started as a young man out for a bit of fun; he ended as a chivalrous gentleman after the best Digby model, possibly better, and certainly poorer, for the experience.

Thirty years later Grantley Berkeley described the reactions of his own friends and contemporaries. 'I know of nothing', he wrote, 'that ever seized on the minds of the young men of fashion with such force as it did, or held out apparently so many romantic attractions. I can safely say that, as far as I was concerned, I was seized with an extraordinary desire to be one of those who would enter the lists, without at first considering the consequences . . . All that I thought of for the moment was a Queen of Beauty, brave deeds, splendid arms, and magnificent horses.'[17] In the autumn he and one hundred and forty-nine other potential knights came to a preliminary meeting in Pratt's showroom. At this and other meetings it was agreed that rehearsals would be held in June and July at the Eyre Arms, St John's Wood; and that the tournament itself would take place on 28 August at Eglinton Castle

Pratt was now in charge of all the arrangements; in addition to armour for the knights he was prepared to sell or hire crests, horse armour and equipment, pavilions, tents, shields, banners, lances, swords, outfits for squires and pages, and mediaeval costumes for the ball which was to be held at the castle after the tournament. In the end he supplied the stands and marquees at the tournament as well, quite possibly to Cottingham's designs. Knight's armour could be bought for one hundred and fifty guineas, or hired for sixty; equipment for a horse bought for fifty guineas or hired for twenty; a tent and pavilions hired for forty guineas. Pratt's bill for Lord Glenlyon, who fought at the tournament as Knight of Gael, survives and comes to £346 9s 6d; it was unlikely that even a more economic knight would get off for less than £200, at least as many thousands at today's values.[18] There were plenty of well-off young men who were not going to balk at that. But, as the rehearsals made clear, tilting needed a bold and skilled horseman, a well-trained horse, and many hours of practice. Of the one hundred and fifty original knights thirty-five came to the rehearsals, nineteen took part in the dress rehearsal, and thirteen finally fought in the tournament.

The dress rehearsal took place at the Eyre Arms on 13 July and could scarcely have gone better. The audience came by invitation only, the indefatigable Pratt was instructed by Lord Eglinton to send out several thousand cards, and 2690 of what the *Court Journal* called 'the very élite of the most élite' attended. The sun shone, the tents and banners were gaily picturesque, the knights looked splendid in their armour, halberdiers in mediaeval dress marshalled the crowds, and the jousting took place with considerable success.

Meanwhile the general public were in a state of some excitement. The tournament, unlike the rehearsal, was to be open to the public. Eglinton Castle was in Ayrshire, about twenty miles from Glasgow; the new railway line from London to Liverpool, the new steamboats running from Liverpool to Glasgow, and the Glasgow and Ayrshire Railway made it relatively easy to get to. Although the tilt-yard could be watched from the surrounding slopes, the best view would be from the open stands which were to be built to either side of the Queen of Beauty's pavilion. Cards of admission to these were free, but had to be applied for.

Applications began to pour in to the estate office at Eglinton. The great majority came from Scotland, but there were others from Calcutta, Copenhagen and Rio de Janeiro, from America and France, as well as from all over the British Isles.[19] Applicants anxiously described what mediaeval or other fancy dress they were planning to wear. Would it be all right to come as Knights Templar, in Highland costume, in hunting coats, as Scottish peasants (early), in sailor's dress with tartan scarves, or (in the case of M. Momsen of Avranches) in 'a large straw hat and Blous of Checked Cotton'? Many stressed their Tory sentiments, for it was known that Whigs or, still worse, Radicals were likely to be refused. The town clerk of Anderston, near Glasgow, claimed that his wife had once nearly killed a Radical with a candlestick; he got a ticket. The notes added to the application from Mr Paxton of Kilmarnock are self-explanatory:

> Granted [scratched out]
> Enquire if a Conservative
> NO
> *Refused*[20]

At the end of August knights and guests began to converge on the castle. There were twelve knights, in addition to Lord Eglinton himself: Viscount Alford, the Earl of Cassillis (later Marquess of Ailsa), the Earl of Craven, J. O. Fairlie, the Hon. H.E.H. Gage, Viscount Glenlyon (later the sixth Duke of Atholl), Sir Francis Hopkins, Bart., the Hon. Edward Jerningham, Charles Lamb, Richard Lechmere, Walter Little Gilmour and the Marquess of Waterford.[21] Their average age was twenty-seven, and, with one possible exception, they were all Tories. At least two came from redoubtable Gothic-revival castles or mansions, Lord Alford from Ashridge in Hertfordshire, Edward Jerningham from be-pinnacled and long-demolished Costessey Hall outside Norwich. H.E.H. Gage's father had been one of the twenty-two peers (known as the 'stalwarts') who had voted against the third reading of the Reform Bill. But on the whole the knights were, as might have been expected, a sporting rather than a political, still less an intellectual, collection. Much the best known to the general public was the Marquess of Waterford, generally thought to be the strongest and wildest young lord in the British Isles. He had stolen the whipping-block from Eton, and gave an annual dinner at which it was the central feature; he had literally painted the town (or at least part of it) red at Melton Mowbray; he had smashed a French ormolu clock to pieces with a blow of his fist; the stories of his escapades and practical

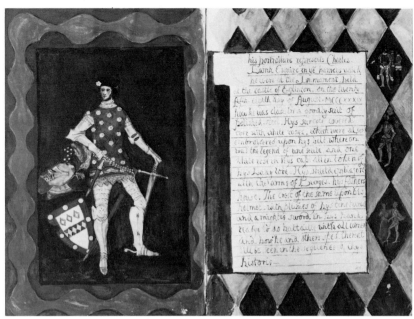

65. Sir Francis Grant. *Charles Lamb*

66. Charles Lamb in armour for the tournament, as drawn by himself

jokes were almost endless. But there was no malice in him; his tearing good spirits were to be one of the most agreeable features of the tournament.

All the knights took suitably mediaeval names, usually derived from their crests or coats of arms. Lord Waterford, for instance, was Knight of the Red Lion; Sir Francis Hopkins, Knight of the Burning Tower; Charles Lamb, Knight of the White Rose. His father, Sir Charles, was Knight Marshal of the Lists. Lord Eglinton was Lord of the Tournament, and a Scottish peer, Lord Fraser of Saltoun, was to help him with the questions of procedure or dispute, as Judge of Peace.

Charles Lamb was in a state of great elation and excitement because, apart from being about to take part in a tournament, he had just rescued a damsel in distress. Earlier that summer he had rented a house outside Bognor for the race-meeting at Goodwood, and one day had come across a fourteen-year-old girl wandering on the Bognor sands. She was in deep distress because her employer was trying to seduce her. He discovered that she was a maid in a nearby house, working for an Indian rajah and his wife. There was no choice for the chivalrous Charles; he rescued her from her Indian and took her off to London. She turned out to be Charlotte Gray, the daughter of a draper in Chichester. Since she was very beautiful, and had coal black hair which fell to her feet when she let it down, Charles soon became her faithful knight. There was a complication, however; he was already engaged to joust for a quite different lady, in whose honour he had agreed to wear one white rose in his cap and display the motto 'une seule' on his belt 'all in token of hys Lady love'.[22]

So he deposited Charlotte in Edinburgh, and joined the other ninety-two people staying in the castle. The Tory aristocracy had come in droves to see the show. Fifty-five peers and peeresses in addition to numerous baronets, knights and younger sons either watched or took part in the tournament. Foreign spectators included Princess Esterhazy from Hungary, Count Persigny from France, Count Lubeski from Poland, and Prince Louis Napoleon—the last already planning the

95

attempted coup that was to land him in a French prison for six years. An interesting and somewhat unexpected spectator (not staying in the castle) was the future Lord Shaftesbury, of the Factory Acts, who was on a Scottish tour with his wife. The ban against Whigs apparently did not extend to the aristocracy; a few grand Whigs were there, notably Lord and Lady Breadalbane and Sir James Graham of Netherby.[23] But on the whole the upper-class spectators were Tory of the most entrenched variety. Living up, perhaps, to *Fraser's* complaint of their 'pusillanimity and desertion of their own principles', top Tory politicians were noticeably absent. The tone was set by the King of the Tournament, the Marquess of Londonderry, general and veteran of Waterloo, ex-Ambassador to Austria, who had been put on the shelf by the last Tory government because he was considered too reactionary. It was believed that Lady Londonderry would have liked to be Queen of Beauty but instead the choice had fallen on the much younger and prettier Lady Seymour (later the Duchess of Somerset), one of the three famously beautiful granddaughters of Richard Brinsley Sheridan.

On the morning of 28 August the sun shone brightly on a picturesque and lively scene. The castle itself had been built by Lord Eglinton's father in and after 1797,[24] to the designs of John Paterson (the architect of Brancepeth Castle); even if its Gothic was already beginning to look a little amateurish, its silhouette and position were sufficiently romantic. Half a mile below it the greensward of the park was gay with the tents and pavilions of the knights and with Pratt's Gothic grandstand, from the middle of which projected the pavilion of the Queen of Beauty. And from every direction, by coach, by carriage, on foot or horse, from local towns crammed to bursting and beyond, pouring off the trains at Irvine or the steamers at Ardrossan, wearing dress of every conceivable variety, filling up the stands and grandstand, crowding the slopes, hanging from the trees, there poured an endless stream of farmers, gentlemen, peasants, thugs, pickpockets, burghers, policemen, shepherds, lords and ladies. It was said that at least one hundred thousand people came to Eglinton that day.

As the opening feature of the tournament a grand procession of all the knights and officers of the tournament were to escort the Queen of Beauty from the castle to the lists. The procession was scheduled to leave at twelve o'clock, but twelve o'clock, one o'clock and two o'clock went by, the sun went in and the waiting crowds grew increasingly restive. In the end it took three hours longer than had been expected to prepare the participants and marshal the procession. All but one or two of the knights had come with a sizeable retinue, and some with a very large one. Lord Glenlyon was escorted by seventy-eight officers and men of his own private regiment, the Atholl Highlanders, in full Highland dress. Lord Waterford's retinue were disguised as monks and friars. The procession included the Ballochmyle Lady Archers, the Irvine Gentlemen Archers, halberdiers, trumpeters, standard-bearers and men at arms innumerable; there was even a real jester, Robert M'Ian, an actor who specialised in comic parts in plays adapted from Walter Scott. Supervising everything, courteous, cheerful, indomitably enterprising and energetic, was Lord Eglinton himself, in a splendid suit of golden armour (Plate XI).

96

IX. (right) Elvaston Castle, Derbyshire. Hall of the Fair Star

X. (following page) Doorway leading to the Hall of the Fair Star, Elvaston

67. Lady Seymour, Queen of Beauty at Eglinton, from a contemporary music sheet

68. The procession forming before Eglinton Castle, from a contemporary music sheet

Just after three, as the procession was at last ready to start, and the Queen of Beauty prepared to mount her snow white palfrey, there was a clap of thunder. Rain began to fall in torrents and continued to fall for the rest of the day. At once, as on the stroke of twelve in the story of Cinderella, the gold and the gaiety vanished, and the whole glittering scene turned to mud. Down at the lists the multi-coloured crowds on the slopes and stands changed in a few seconds to what one onlooker compared to an enormous field of mushrooms, another to the backsides of thousands of elephants,[25] as all who had them put up their umbrellas. Up at the castle the procession began to squelch miserably through the puddles. Lord Londonderry, paladin of 'the chivalric life and gallant bearing',[26] rode in front protecting his coronet and robes under an enormous green umbrella. The Queen of Beauty and her maids of honour were carried ignominiously and invisibly at the back, in closed carriages. The procession was a fiasco, and the tilting even worse. The jester made jokes which nobody laughed at. The knights slithered through the mud and, with a few exceptions, missed each other. In the grandstand expressions of growing horror appeared on the faces of the occupants. Pratt's roofs had failed to keep out the rain; cold water was falling in buckets down the necks of the lords and ladies.[27]

XI. (preceding page) Edward Henry Corbould. *Archibald, Earl of Eglinton and Winton, dressed for the Tournament, c.* 1839

XII. (left) The Eglinton Tournament as depicted by James Henry Nixon for John Richardson's *The Eglinton Tournament,* 1843

69. An illustration from Richard Doyle's *The Tournament*, 1840

When the tournament finally ended, a scene of appalling chaos ensued as tens of thousands of stumbling, slithering people looked in vain for their bogged-down carriages or started to make their way through rain and mud to the nearest available shelter. One participant was reminded of 'the confusion and retreat of a vanquished army'; never had he seen 'the disagreeable and ridiculous so completely mixed together.'[28] Up at the castle one last blow awaited the knights and their associates. The temporary buildings in which the evening's entertainment was to be held had also been constructed by Pratt. Their roofs had proved no better than those of the grandstand; neither the ball nor the banquet could conceivably take place.

That, as far as popular legend is concerned, was the end of the tournament. The humiliations of that terrible day have almost entirely effaced the fact that Lord Eglinton refused to give in. He announced that, if the weather allowed it, jousting would take place again on the next day or the day after. On the next day it continued to rain. Up at the castle maids did their best to salvage the rain-soaked dresses, men-servants scoured the rusting armour, workmen repaired the marquees. The guests amused themselves with a variety of high jinks indoors, culminating in a mêlée between two sides in armour, wearing crests of apples and oranges, and armed with mops and broomsticks. To shrieks of laughter, mops and brooms splintered on helmets, and apples and oranges flew in all directions.[29]

But the weather began to improve, and jousts were announced for Friday. On that day the weather was perfect. Large crowds assembled. The procession took place in brilliant sunshine. The jousting was a reasonable success, and ended with a mêlée, in which, to the delight of the crowd, Lord Waterford and Lord Alford lost their tempers and started laying into each other in earnest; they had to be separated by the Knight Marshal (Plates 70–2).

In the evening the banquet and ball finally took place. Each knight dined with a page holding his banner behind him; conventional nineteenth-century food was interspersed with a real boar's head and numerous mediaeval delicacies. After the banquet two thousand guests danced in Pratt's reconditioned marquee. All wore mediaeval dress, even the band. Louisa Stuart, the beautiful daughter of Lord Stuart de Rothesay, made sketches of it all. 'The ball and banquet one could easily have dispensed with', she wrote, 'but the procession into the Lists, and the tilting, the mêlée, were such beautiful sights as one can never expect to see again.'[30]

102

'Don't you remember', Lycion remarks at the beginning of Edward FitzGerald's *Euphranor*, 'what an absurd thing that Eglinton Tournament was? What a complete failure? There was the Queen of Beauty on her throne—Lady Seymour—who alone of all the whole affair was *not* a sham—and the Heralds, and the Knights in full armour on their horses—they had been practising for months, I believe—but unluckily, the very moment of Onset, the rain began, and the Knights threw down their lances, and put up their umbrellas.'[31]

There were knights at the Eglinton tournament and there were umbrellas, but the two were never combined. It did not matter; a knight under an umbrella became the symbol of the tournament, and to many people seemed sufficiently ludicrous to burst the bubble of modern chivalry for ever. The tournament became the subject of cartoons, satires, squibs, jokes and burlesques innumerable.

The unkindest jokes appeared, not surprisingly, in the Whig or Radical press. The tournament had been a Tory venture, and was bound to be given rough treatment by the other side. In fact, reactions were by no means unanimous. Roughly speaking, commentators fell into three groups: those who derided without mercy; those who pretended that the tournament had been a great success; and those who defended chivalry, but without the mediaeval trimmings.

In *The Broad Stone of Honour* Digby had already attacked the supposition that 'Tournaments and steel panoply, and coat-arms, and aristocratic institutions' were essential to chivalry; rather they were only 'accidental attendants upon it'.[32] The passage was quoted by FitzGerald in *Euphranor*, immediately after Lycion's jokes about the Eglinton Tournament. The tournament, Lycion contended, was absurd because it was a sham; but the real point of chivalry is that it is an attitude to life, not a matter of fancy dress.

FitzGerald and Digby were not alone; the spirit of chivalry was far from dead, as the rest of this book will endeavour to show. However, the feeling that 'shams' must be avoided grew steadily stronger, and was certainly encouraged by the cloudburst at Eglinton. A Victorian tournament, to this way of thinking, was a sham, so was a Victorian gentleman in armour, and so was a Victorian castle. Pugin, although he was a committed enthusiast for the Middle Ages and certainly no enemy to chivalry, made cruel fun of the anomalies of modern castles in his *True Principles of Christian Architecture* (1841): 'Who would hammer against nailed portals when he could kick his way through the greenhouse?'[33] The building of castles was by no means done for, but it had passed its peak.

But even on this view mediaeval-style chivalry was still defensible in book illustrations, pictures, poems or stories of a historical, romantic or symbolic nature; and great halls could still be relevant to modern life, even if battlements or portcullises were not. In fact chivalry even in its most fancy-dress form was still much in evidence all through the 1840s. In architecture the tournament did nothing to discourage the work already described at Bayons and Knebworth; and in 1844 Peckforton Castle, the most complete and archaeologically correct nineteenth-century castle yet to be built in England, began to rise on a hilltop in Cheshire to the design of Anthony Salvin.[34] In 1842 Tennyson set Sir Galahad and King Arthur back in general circulation; in 1845 G. F. Watts painted himself

70, 71, 72. (left) Lords Waterford and Aldford in the mêlée, and scenes at the tilt and the ball, as depicted by Edward Henry Corbould for *The Tournament at Eglinton Castle*, 1840

73. (right) The Eglinton Testimonial. It depicts Lord Eglinton rewarded by the Queen of Beauty

in armour at Florence, where he was being cherished as a young genius by Lord and Lady Holland.[35] The disasters of the tournament may have been a deterrent to some, but the fact that it had taken place, and the mementoes it left behind it, acted as a stimulant to others.

Among the mementoes the Eglinton Testimonial is perhaps the most evocative.[36] Lord Eglinton had been given a banquet at Irvine on 29 September 1839 to congratulate or console him; and in addition two hundred and thirty-nine of his friends (headed by a committee of which Lord Londonderry was chairman, and Lord Burghersh a member) subscribed to present him with a silver trophy. Elkington and Company made it, to designs and models by Cotterill and Sebron. It cost £1775, rises some eight feet high, including its carved wooden base, and is encased in glass, like a wedding cake in a shop window.

The tournament also produced souvenir music-sheets, jig-saws, medals, jugs, plates and scent bottles (with knights' helmets for stoppers).[37] In addition no fewer than eight books on the tournament were published.[38] Of these Richard Doyle's *The Tournament* (1840), was a playful skit; the tone of the rest varied from slight scepticism to adulation. The last to appear, *The Eglinton Tournament* (1843), was the most splendid (Plate XII), and also much the most fulsome; through eighteen superb coloured plates and a very full text rain is never even hinted at, let alone mentioned.

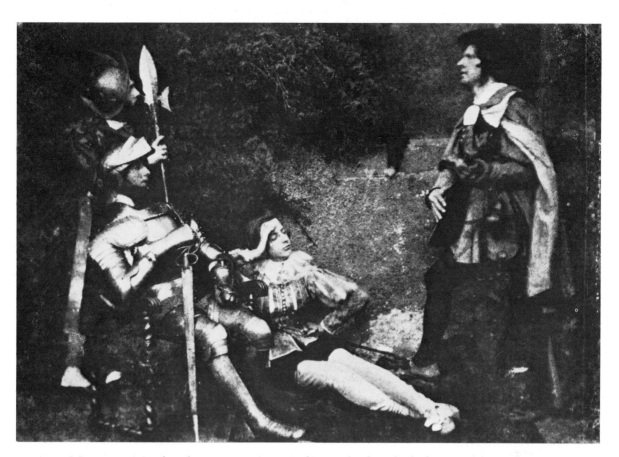

Not surprisingly, the spectators at Eglinton had included a sizeable number of artists, especially those who specialised in mediaeval themes. In addition to Nixon and Corbould it had been watched by Maclise, Landseer, Noel Paton, Bewick, John Franklin, William Allan (a future president of the Royal Scottish Academy) and the pioneer photographer Octavius Hill.[39] Most of these showed the effect of their visit in their work.[40] Maclise's *Two Knights* (which was commissioned by Bulwer-Lytton) may date from the years after the tournament. Corbould produced a spirited portrait of Lord Eglinton on horseback (Plate XI) and in 1842 exhibited a painting at the Royal Academy under the title *At Eglinton. A knight there was and that a weary man*. A photograph by Hill, showing a group in mediaeval dress, is probably directly inspired by the tournament and may even show the outfits which he and his friends wore as spectators.

A group of book illustrators who flourished in the 1840s could almost be called the Eglinton school. Its members dealt largely in chivalrous themes, Corbould and Franklin (and to a lesser extent Nixon) were among its leaders, and the popularity of its style of illustration, and Corbould's own reputation, probably owed a great deal to the two great Eglinton books (even if the style both of these and of the subsequent book illustrations ultimately derived from contemporary work in Germany). Two examples of their style are especially notable, S. C. Hall's *Book of British Ballads* (1842), and the numerous illustrated English editions of the works of La Motte Fouqué.

S. C. Hall's *Book of British Ballads* was a deliberate attempt to show that British book illustrators could equal the best that was being produced in Germany. No

74. (left) Daniel Maclise. *Combat of Two Knights, c.* 1840

75. (above) Costume scene photographed by David Octavius Hill (shown on right) and Robert Adamson

KING ARTHUR'S DEATH.

On Trinity Monday in the morn,
 This sore battayle was doomed to be,
Where many a knight cryed, 'Well-away!
 Alack, it was the more pitie!'

Ere the first crowing of the cock
 When as the king in his bed lay,
He thought Sir Gawaine to him came,
 And there to him these wordes did say:

Chapter XIII.

76, 77. Illustrations by John Franklin for *The Book of British Ballads*, 1842, and E. H. Corbould for La Motte Fouqué's *Wild Love*, 1845

fewer than twenty-seven artists, mostly young, contributed to it, but Hall's 'sheet anchor', as he described him, was John Franklin, another of the Eglinton spectators.[41] He was responsible for nearly a third of the illustrations, and seems also to have acted as general editor. After Franklin, Corbould was one of the biggest contributors; and the book contains some of the earliest work of Joseph Noel Paton, who had walked from Paisley to Eglinton to watch the tournament at the age of seventeen.

La Motte Fouqué was a German romantic writer who had first been translated into English in the 1820s, by, among others, Julius Hare and Thomas Carlyle. But his evocative, slightly dreamy tales of mediaeval life were especially popular in England in the 1840s, twenty or thirty years after they had been written. In that decade there were four English editions of both *Undine* and *Sintram*, his two most popular books, besides editions of several others, including *Wild Love* and *Minstrel Love*. Many of these were lavishly illustrated by Corbould, Franklin and others.[42]

Apart from the artists, what effect, if any, did the Eglinton Tournament have on those who watched or participated in it? Lord Breadalbane, one of the spectators, went home and almost immediately added to and partly redecorated Taymouth Castle, his home in Perthshire. The new work included a full-blown baronial hall, complete with screens and a great deal of armour, and a resplendent drawing-room, on the painted ceiling of which four knights gallop through lushly curling foliage.[43]

At the tournament Lord Waterford fell violently and at first sight hopelessly in love with one of the most beautiful of the guests in the castle: Louisa Stuart, the sensitive and artistic daughter of Lord Stuart de Rothesay. He pursued her with such ardour over the next few years that in the end, to everyone's amazement, she agreed to marry him. But he gave up his wild ways, and settled down in Ireland as a chivalrous husband and model landlord.[44]

For Lord Eglinton, too, the tournament marked a turning point. He ceased to spend most of his time enjoying himself and became the epitome of the Victorian

108

78. (right) The Banner Hall, Taymouth Castle, Perthshire, from an old photograph

79. J. O. Fairlie photographed *c.* 1850 in the armour he wore at the Eglinton Tournament

gentleman, an indefatigable public servant, a faithful husband, unfailingly considerate and courteous to everyone, genuinely loved by all classes, good at everything except money. When he died, *Blackwood's Magazine* wrote, 'Of him it may emphatically be said that honour was his polar star.'[45]

He died of apoplexy at the age of forty-nine. The Eglinton knights, perhaps because they came, on the whole, from a hard-living, hard-riding set, did not enjoy long lives. One died before he was forty, six before they were fifty, two before they were sixty. Lords Cassilis and Waterford died of falls out hunting, aged fifty-three and forty-seven. Charles Lamb married his Charlotte, but the marriage turned out a disaster; he died, at the age of forty, blind and alone.[46]

Almost all the arms and armour were returned to Pratt, who auctioned them in June 1840. A few knights kept theirs. Captain James Fairlie (the Knight of the Golden Lion) kept both his armour and the troubadour dress which he had worn for the ball. About fifteen years later he squeezed into as much of the armour as would still fit him and had himself photographed. His son was painted wearing the troubadour outfit at Rome in the 1860s.[47]

Lady Seymour lived to become Duchess of Somerset and lose her beauty. In 1872, when Disraeli was planning to include an account of the tournament in *Endymion*, he wrote and asked her if she had any souvenirs. 'I do not know what I can find of the Eglinton Tournament', she answered, 'except a coloured print which I will send you—I had all sorts of relics, points of splintered spears with the colours of the Knights, but a stupid old house-maid considered them as "rubbish" as she said and burnt them together with a Blessed Palm that I had caught in mid-air from the Pope's own hands.'[48]

110

80. (right) Details from Landseer's *Queen Victoria and Prince Albert*, 1842

CHAPTER 8
Victoria and Albert

LIKE EVERYONE ELSE QUEEN VICTORIA FOLLOWED BOTH THE PREPARATIONS FOR THE Eglinton Tournament and the tournament itself with fascinated attention; and, like many other nineteen-year-old girls of her time, she put down her news and thoughts every evening in her diary.

June 21, 1839. Talked [to Lord Melbourne] of the Tournament Lord Eglinton is going to have; of the danger of it; of Lady Seymour being chosen 'Queen of the Lists' etc.; of my intending to take a bath . . .

August 11. Talked of my little terrier; of this Tournament being such folly; he understands there is a lady who has paid £1000 for 3 dresses; 'Lady Seymour's is only to cost £40, I was *told* today,' he said, &c.

August 29. Talked of the Tournament, and Lord M. had written to Wilhelmine that she ought to have gone to have attended on the Queen of Beauty, whom they are not very fond of, he says, etc. Of there being no doubt in my opinion about her (Lady Seymour's) beauty; of her saying such odd things, which I thought better for a man than a woman.

September 2. Talked of the horrid weather; of its having poured so at the Tournament, the Queen of Beauty having been obliged to go in a *close carriage*, and that the whole thing had turned out to be the greatest absurdity. Lord M. said he heard from Lord Compton, that is *he* had not seen Lord Compton, but 'a *lady* told me,' (I guess who this *mysterious* lady is from whom he hears so much) that there never was anything like it; the Tent had not been waterproof; all the rain came in, and they were drenched, and Lord Eglinton had to send home the various people who he could not lodge, to their various Inns, etc. etc. I said it served them all right for their folly in having *such* a thing &c.[1]

Less than three years later the Queen gave a fancy-dress ball at Buckingham Palace. The main theme was that of the court of Edward III and Queen Philippa. 'The élite of the nobility', including many who had been at the Eglinton Tournament, danced and paraded in elaborate mediaeval costume; several actually wore armour. 'Her Majesty's fancy dress ball on Thursday night', wrote *The Times*, 'was a scene of such brilliance and magnificence, that since the days of Charles II, with the solitary exception of one fête given in the reign of George IV, there has been nothing at all comparable to it in all the entertainments given at the British Court.'[2] Two thousand people came. The cost was enormous, and was much criticised. What had happened?

What had happened was Albert. In 1839 the Queen was in the full spate of her hero-worship of Lord Melbourne, the Prime Minister. Her ideas were being directed by a sixty-year-old Whig aristocrat, who enjoyed poking fun at the Tories, and whose roots lay in a sophisticated late eighteenth-century society to which the ideals and expressions of chivalry were ridiculous.

But in October Prince Albert came to Windsor; the Queen fell in love with him, and on 10 February they were married. The Prince had been brought up in an atmosphere of German Romanticism; he took chivalry very seriously indeed. Moreover, in the summer of 1841 the Whigs had been disastrously defeated at a General Election, and the Tories had come in. At first

the Queen was distraught; she loved Lord Melbourne and disliked Sir Robert Peel, the new Prime Minister, intensely. But within six months everything had changed. Lord Melbourne's influence waned; Prince Albert got on extremely well with Peel. The Queen moved out of the Whig orbit and into the Tory one.

She was still in touch with Lord Melbourne; but now it was she who was setting the pace. In a letter to him written at the beginning of April she announced that 'on the 6th of May the Queen intends to give a Ball at which all the Ladies are to wear fancy costumes, but this is still a *secret*'.[3] On 13 April she and Albert were thinking of going as Queen Jane of Navarre and Henri Quatre, but by 18 April 'we have settled to go as Edward III and Queen Philippa, and there is such trouble in getting the costumes correct'.[4] In his *History of Chivalry* (1825) James Mill had written that 'the sun of English chivalry reached its meridian in the reign of Edward III';[5] inevitably the final choice of costume suggested the hope that the young Queen and her husband were reviving the great days of chivalry in modern England.

The Bal Costumé (as it was called at the time) finally took place on 11 May. On the next day the Queen wrote in her journal: 'Nothing could have gone better than the whole did, & it was a truly splendid spectacle . . . I danced a Quadrille with George [her uncle, the Duke of Cambridge]—I own with some difficulty, on account of my heels.'

The Queen's and the Prince's costumes are shown in a portrait by Landseer (Plate XIII), and in two sketches made by Queen Victoria herself for her journal. Landseer's painting depicts the two of them standing in front of the throne and canopy from which they surveyed the dancing. The costumes of many of the guests are illustrated in *Dresses worn at Her Majesty's Bal Costumé* (1842) by Charles and Leopold Martin, and the more lavish *Souvenir of the Bal Costumé*, published in 1842, with drawings by Coke Smith and a text by J. R. Planché. Planché was a man of

113

81, 82. Sketches by Queen Victoria show the costumes worn by her and Prince Albert at the Bal Costumé, Buckingham Palace, 1842

83. Lady Elizabeth Villiers, Lord de Grey, Lady Louisa Bruce and Lieutenant Colonel Wylde dressed for the Bal Costumé, 1842

many talents, at once a prolific dramatist, an expert on the history of costume, and a herald in the College of Arms.[6] He was the Pratt of the Bal Costumé, in so far as he advised on the costumes, and in many cases probably designed them. 'Her Majesty', he wrote, 'expressed her desire, in the strongest terms to all parties, that the costumes adopted should be as correct as possible.' He had some difficulty in seeing that her desires were fulfilled; Lord Cardigan, who went, most inappropriately, as the Chevalier Bayard, had to be persuaded out of wearing a costume covered in spangles from neck to ankle.[7]

Not all the costumes at the ball were mediaeval. In addition to the royal couple and their household, representing the court of Edward III, the dancers included eight quadrilles, each dressed to a different theme. Four showed the development of European costume from the fifteenth to the seventeenth century. Four were rather indiscriminately divided into Albanians, knights and ladies of the twelfth century, characters from the Waverley novels, and Merry Muscovites. Lord John Manners was in the Waverley quadrille, dressed as Sir Kenneth of Scotland, from *Ivanhoe*; his feelings veered between disapproval of the 'enormous waste' of the ball, and pleasure at the thought that 'many hundreds of the higher orders have been led to look into the domestic histories of their forefathers'.[8] Those not in the royal entourage or the quadrilles wore a wide variety of dress. Monckton Milnes went as Chaucer; Bulwer-Lytton as one of his own Elizabethan ancestors; Sir Robert Peel was in a magnificent costume after Van Dyck. At least nine of those taking part wore armour, including Prince Albert's two equerries.[9]

Perhaps the sight of the equerries suggested to the Queen how noble her husband himself would look as a knight. At any rate, his birthday presents to her on 24 May 1844 included a minature by Thorburn, in which, as she wrote in her

84. Robert Thorburn. Miniature of
the Prince Consort in armour, 1844

journal, 'my beloved Albert is painted in armour, which I so much wished . . . I cannot say how beautiful it is, nor how it exactly portrays the dear original.' Her Lady of the Bedchamber Lady Lyttelton described it 'as most beautiful indeed. Quite his gravest manliest look, and done when he was rather tanned . . . *in armour* (which is according to an old wish of the Queen's).'[10] The picture marks something of a breakthrough in English iconography. The knights at Eglinton who had chosen to be painted in armour did so in order to commemorate the part they had played in the tournament. When Maclise depicted Sir Francis Sykes in armour in 1837 he was probably commemorating an entertainment of some kind, although the record of it has been lost. But Prince Albert had taken part in no event; he was not assuming a historical character; he had never been near a battlefield. His armour symbolised his chivalrous qualities in civilian life. The application of the code of chivalry to modern gentlemen, as expounded by Kenelm Digby, had been given royal ratification.

The corollary to the Prince in armour was Queen Victoria as Gloriana or mediaeval damozel. The romantic and chivalrous excitement which an innocent, pretty, but determined young queen evoked is nicely expressed in the frontispiece (Plate XIV) to Sir Henry Nicolas's four-volume *Orders of Knighthood*, published in 1842. Here the Queen's Garter robes and dress are not especially mediaeval, but her setting is. She stands ready to dub her loyal knights, holding a sword in what Disraeli's *Sybil* was to describe in 1845 as 'that soft hand which might inspire troubadours and guerdon knights'.[11] In 1842 William Dyce showed Victoria as a mediaeval queen in his design for the so-called 'Gothic' crown, which was not actually minted until 1847.[12] In 1845 Thorburn painted a companion miniature to his one of the Prince Consort. It shows the Queen wearing mediaeval or perhaps Tudor dress—even if looking like an appealingly demure girl of the 1840s.[13] Versions of the miniatures, painted on enamel by Bone,

115

were set into the jewel-cabinet made for Victoria by Elkington and Company in 1851, and exhibited at the Great Exhibition in the same year.[14]

It would be a mistake to make too much of Victoria and Albert's interest in chivalry; there were so many other strands in their lives. But it undoubtedly existed. Further examples of it can be seen in the decoration of the Houses of Parliament; in their patronage of the theatre; and in the work commissioned by them from the painter Edward Henry Corbould.

Of these the first was much the most important. In 1841 Prince Albert became Chairman of the Royal Commission on the Fine Arts, which had been created to advise on and direct the decoration of the Houses of Parliament. It was widely felt that so important a new building offered a great opportunity to British art; here for the first time public patronage might create a school of High Art in Britain, and rival contemporary continental achievements, notably those of Ludwig II in Munich and Bavaria.

The Prince took his appointment very seriously. The membership of the Commission was a large one but, probably because it was so large, it was effectively run by a small inner group. The dominant figures were the Prince Consort himself, and the Secretary of the Commission, Charles Eastlake.[15]

The new Palace of Westminster was divided into three main parts, given over to the Commons, the Lords, and the Crown. Chivalry was to loom large in the decoration of two of them.[16] The Queen's Robing Room, the inner sanctum of the magnificent royal suite, is dominated by scenes from the story of King Arthur

85. (above) The Jewel Casket, made for Queen Victoria in 1851

XIII. (right) Sir Edwin Landseer. *Queen Victoria and Prince Albert as Queen Philippa and Edward III at their Bal Costumé*, 1842

XIV. (following page) Frontispiece to Sir Henry Nicolas's *The Orders of Knighthood*, 1842

86. Daniel Maclise. Detail of cartoon for *The Meeting of Wellington and Blucher*, 1858–9

and the Knights of the Round Table, painted by William Dyce. In the chamber of the House of Lords mailed figures of the signatories of the Magna Carta stand between the windows. Of the four huge paintings that fill the two walls at either end of the chamber, one (by C. W. Cope) shows *Edward III conferring the Order of the Garter on the Black Prince*, the other (by Maclise) depicts the *Spirit of Chivalry*.

'He is in great favour with the Queen', Dickens wrote of Maclise to a friend in 1843, 'and paints secret pictures for her to put upon her husband's table on the morning of his birthday.'[17] The 'secret picture' (there was only one) was a scene from La Motte Fouqué's *Undine* given to the Prince on 26 August. In the same year Maclise had been one of the artists commissioned to decorate a new pavilion in the garden of Buckingham Palace. In 1843–4 he took part in the cartoon competition for the decoration of the Houses of Parliament. Not surprisingly, in view of the chivalric propensities of so many of his earlier paintings, his entry was entitled *The Knight*. On the strength of this, and probably of his work for the Queen and Prince, the Royal Commission asked him to submit proposals for a painted fresco of the *Spirit of Chivalry* in the House of Lords. In the end he painted two subjects for the house, the *Spirit of Chivalry* (1846–7) and the *Spirit of Justice* (1848–9).[18]

The former depicts all aspects of the age of chivalry, not just knights in armour. Representatives of the Church, the laity and the arts are grouped round the Spirit herself, who Maclise admitted was an idealised version of the Queen. The two strongest figures in the composition are a resolute armour-clad king, standing hand on sword next to the spirit, and a young kneeling knight. The latter wears a

XV. (preceding page) Christening cup designed by E. H. Corbould as a gift from Queen Victoria to Prince Albert Victor, 1864

XVI. (left) William Dyce. *Hospitality: The Admission of Sir Tristram to the Fellowship of the Round Table*

88. E. H. Corbould.
Memorial Portrait of the
Prince Consort, 1863

belt with the motto 'à Dieu et aux Dames', holds his sword in the guise of a cross, and gazes up at it while his lady gives him her glove as a favour. In the preliminary studies the young knight was shown bareheaded, in the tradition of West's Black Prince at Windsor; in the final version, perhaps mistakenly, Maclise gave him a helmet.

Dyce's work in the Houses of Parliament came to him by a similar combination of competition and royal favour. His commissions for royalty had included the great fresco of *Neptune resigning the Empire of the Sea to Britannia*, which he painted in 1847 at the head of the stairs at Osborne. The idea of including Arthurian paintings among the Parliament decorations originated in a conversation which he had with Prince Albert while at Osborne in 1847; it was suggested that the Arthurian cycle was the English equivalent of the *Niebelungenlied*. The commission to decorate the Queen's Robing Room followed in July. Dyce did not start on the actual frescoes (Plates XVI, 119) until 1849, and they were still incomplete at the time of his death in 1862.[19]

There is relatively little contrast between these overtly chivalric works and Maclise's last commissions in the Houses of Parliament, his two frescoes in the Royal Gallery—the *Meeting of Wellington and Blucher* (Plate 86) and the *Death of Nelson*.[20] These show scenes from the great contemporary epic of the French wars, the modern equivalent of Agincourt, the Crusades or Arthur's last battle. The *Death of Nelson* was painted after the Prince's death but he took great interest in *Wellington and Blucher* which was painted in 1858–61. The picture

123

87. (left) Daniel Maclise. Oil version of *The Spirit of Chivalry, c.* 1845

culminates in the figure of Wellington himself on horseback, the epitome of the modern chivalrous hero, grave, resolute and noble; his officers are jubilant, but he is not, for he recognises the death and suffering at the cost of which the victory has been won.

The Prince's connection with the decoration of the Houses of Parliament is much better known than his and his wife's theatrical patronage. This was largely confined to one actor–producer, Charles Kean, the son of the famous Edmund. In 1848 the post of Director of the Windsor Theatricals was specially created for him, and over the next eleven years he was responsible for a series of Shakespearian and other productions at Windsor Castle. In 1850 he set up his own company at the Prince's Theatre in London, His Shakespearian productions there were especially notable for the splendour and historical accuracy of their dresss and decor; he made Victorian audiences feel that they had been carried back into the world of mediaeval chivalry. The Royal Family were enthusiastic supporters of his theatre, which owed much of its success to their patronage. Queen Victoria went three times to *King John* (1851), three times to *Richard III* (1854) and four times to *Richard II* (1857) and *Henry V* (1859).[21]

In 1852 Prince Albert's presents to the Queen included a watercolour by E. H. Corbould, showing Act III, Scene I, in Kean's *King John*.[22] Several of Kean's productions were in fact designed by Corbould, and the two were probably brought together by the royal couple.[23] They had been supporters of Corbould since 1842, when the Prince bought his *Woman taken in Adultery*. From 1852 until 1873 he was art teacher to the royal children; they called him 'Cobby' and were very fond of him. He painted numerous pictures for the various members of the Royal Family, almost exclusively showing chivalric subjects; in effect, he became the official depicter of chivalry to royalty.[24]

Corbould was very competent, but no one could pretend that he was more than a minor artist. Much the most curious of his prolific output of royal work was that which came to him as a result of the Prince Consort's death in December 1861. As soon as the Queen began to recover, she set to work to preserve and enshrine the memory of her beloved hero in every possible way. The largest and most elaborate expression of this was the Royal Mausoleum at Frogmore, but it was by no means the only one. The Queen had noticed with wonder that Albert's features on his deathbed bore an extraordinary likeness to Thorburn's portrait of him as a young knight in armour.[25] In 1862 she was deeply touched when Tennyson dedicated a new edition of his *Idylls of the King* to the memory of her husband.

> These to his Memory—since he held them dear,
> Perchance as finding there unconsciously
> Some image of himself—I dedicate,
> I dedicate, I consecrate with tears—
> These Idylls.
>   And indeed he seems to me
> Scarce other than my king's ideal knight,
> 'Who reverenced his conscience as his king;

89. E. H. Corbould. *King John, Act III, Scene I,* 1852

Whose glory was, redressing human wrong;
Who spoke no slander, no, nor listen'd to it;
Who loved one only and who clove to her—'

It was probably the combination of the deathbed resemblance and Tennyson's dedication which led to the idea of Corbould's painting a picture showing the Prince Consort as the true knight who has fought and conquered. It is not certain whether the idea was Corbould's or the Queen's; certainly the latter gave it enthusiastic backing. The picture was completed at Osborne in February 1864; on 12 February the Queen recorded in her journal, 'Saw Mr Corbould about his beautiful allegorical painting of my beloved one. The likeness was not quite good, and needed some alteration which I watched him carry out after luncheon.'

The finished picture is closely based on Thorburn; the face is virtually identical. The armour is more elaborate, however, and the pose has been slightly altered; Prince Albert is sheathing his sword, since his battle is over. An inscription in German under the portrait proclaims, 'I have fought a good fight; I have finished the struggle; therefore a crown of rectitude is awaiting me.' The picture is painted to give the illusion of an open triptych, and the Prince is surrounded by various allegorical scenes, including one showing the crown awaiting him in heaven.[26]

This was by no means the end of this new version of the Thorburn portrait. On 15 February, immediately after the 'beautiful allegorical painting' had been completed, the Queen wrote in her journal, 'Watched Mr Corbould making some drawings for a Christening Cup & Mrs Prothero has written some beautiful lines to have engraved under the plinth.' The cup was to be a christening present for her grandson, Prince Albert Victor, later to be created Duke of Clarence. As the eldest son of the Prince of Wales he was in line to become King of England.

The cup was another version of the picture. As Corbould first designed it was to have consisted of two figures, the second perhaps being of either the baby or his father; but the Queen asked him to change it 'as at my own particular request and

90. Henri de Triqueti. Cenotaph effigy of Prince Albert, Prince Albert Memorial Chapel, Windsor, 1864–73

desire *only* dearest Albert's statuette is to be brought in'.[27] Princess Louise helped him with the final design, and on 20 February the Queen declared it '*most beautiful*'.

In 1864 the design was carried out in silver-gilt and enamel by Elkington and Company, following a model by the sculptor William Theed.[28] It is a most curious combination of Victorian sentiment, piety and chivalry, from which any suggestion of a 'cup' has long since vanished (Plate XV). An inscription records that it was given to Albert Victor 'in memory of Albert his beloved Grandfather', and it was clearly intended to inspire the baby to grow up a true knight, like the Prince Consort. The figure of him which surmounts it is almost identical to that in the memorial picture. On the base of the statue is the inscription 'I have fought a good Fight, I have finished my Course, I have kept the Faith.' Further inscriptions over figures of Faith, Hope and Charity read 'Walk as he Walked', Strive as he Strove' and 'Think as he Thought'. Between Hope and Faith are Mrs Prothero's memorial verses.

In 1864 the Queen began yet another, and much more elaborate, memorial. For nearly a year before its removal to Frogmore the Prince's body lay in the so-called Wolsey Chapel, the free-standing building to the east of St George's Chapel which George III had begun to convert into a chapter house for the Garter. Queen Victoria resolved to make it into a memorial chapel. Sir Gilbert Scott produced elaborate designs. They took nine years to complete, for the chapel is richly embellished with carving, painting, marble, stained glass and mosaics. The central feature is a sepulchral effigy of Prince Albert, which was only placed in position in the summer of 1873. It was sculpted in Berlin by Baron Triqueti, but it is in fact another version of Corbould's picture. The Prince's favourite dog, Eos, lies at his feet. The whole monument was, as a newspaper put it at the time, carved 'in marble as pure and as free from blemish as his own blameless life'. Queen Victoria thought it 'Quite beautiful'.[29]

126

91. Alfred Gilbert. Monument to the Duke of Clarence, Prince Albert Memorial Chapel, Windsor

There is an epilogue to the story of Prince Albert which is worth pursuing, even though it carries the story on into the 1890s. In spite of his grandmother's hopes and the example of his christening present, the Duke of Clarence grew up about as unlike his grandfather as was possible. Although those who knew him well were genuinely fond of him, his combination of a below-average intellect with an above-average sexual appetite made him a continual worry to all those who had to deal with him. His death of pneumonia in 1891, at the age of twenty-eight, was a great grief to his family but somewhat of a relief to those of the Establishment who were in the know.

He was buried in the vault of the Prince Albert Memorial Chapel, and it was decided to erect a monument to him next to that of his grandfather. The commission was given to Alfred Gilbert, probably less on grounds of aesthetic judgement than because Gilbert had been a pupil of Sir Edgar Boehm, who had been one of the Royal Family's favourite sculptors. Fortunately, Gilbert was not only a sculptor of genius, but found such royal commissions exhilarating rather than inhibiting. In January he went to stay at Sandringham, and wrote to his mother about the difficulties and excitements of the commission: 'But I'll do it yet, and you shall go with me to St George's Chapel to see my work and my

92. The figure of St George on the Clarence Monument

children after us. This is the surrounding for an Artist after all. He must be moved, his imagination must be appealed to. He must be moved, attend, even tho' it be called worldly. It is the most worldly things which awaken the deepest suggestions. Think of the beautiful Princess, who one would imagine God himself would not dare to afflict, bowed down like the humblest peasant with the grief for her first born.'[30]

By the 1890s the idea of depicting a contemporary figure in armour was even less acceptable than it was in the 1870s. But the concept of chivalry itself was by no means dead. Gilbert merely put it into contemporary clothing, and showed a chivalrous young officer who had fallen down on the field of battle:

> He lay like a warrior taking his rest
> With his martial cloak around him.[31]

The young men in armour whom Gilbert in fact loved to portray, have been relegated to purely symbolic status, in the person of St George. He is one of the figures incorporated into a grille of sumptuous Art Nouveau foliage which encloses the effigy; he is said to have been modelled from Burne-Jones. At the head of the tomb an angel holds an elaborate crown over the head of the young Prince. It does not matter that the symbolism bears little enough relationship to the poor Duke of Clarence; the effigy is a deeply moving one. The memorial is probably Gilbert's masterpiece; he considered it as such himself.[32]

128

93. (right) Charles Kingsley dressed to go fishing

CHAPTER 9
Muscular Chivalry

IN A SERMON PREACHED BEFORE THE QUEEN AT WINDSOR IN 1865, CHARLES Kingsley expressed a sentiment which Victoria warmly endorsed. 'The age of chivalry is never past', he declared, 'so long as there is a wrong left unredressed on earth, or a man or a woman left to say "I will redress that wrong, or spend my life in the attempt."'[1] Besides being Victoria's favourite preacher, Kingsley was one of the most popular writers, preachers and lecturers in England. He belonged to a small but highly influential group, the members of which were trying to live up to Digby's concept of chivalry as a code for modern gentlemen. But Digby, although not to be discounted as a source of inspiration, was less important to them than Carlyle.

At first sight a craggy, gloomy, dictatorial, puritanical, self-opinionated mason's son from the Scottish lowlands might seem to have little to do with chivalry: a modern Savonarola, surely, rather than a Bayard. But in fact Carlyle played an important part in adapting the concept of chivalry to Victorian life.

Carlyle was one of the most formidable of those who led the counter-attack on Utilitarianism and laissez-faire. He made his reputation with *Sartor Resartus*, first published in instalments in *Frazer's Magazine* in 1831; but it was his *Past and Present* (1843) which captured the imagination of his contemporaries. In an extraordinary mixture of grimaces, growls, prophesy and slapstick he laid into his own times, mercilessly attacking the aristocrats, landlords, manufacturers, politicians and clergymen, the fashions, advertisements, game-preserves and work-houses of an England heading for destruction, full of 'Puffery, Falsity, Mammon-worship' and 'Phantasms riding with huge clatter along the streets'.[2]

Carlyle was a radical in so far as he felt that society was in need of radical reform; but he was very far from being a radical in the sense of believing in the rule of the people. Neither the Utilitarian nor the Radical arguments for universal suffrage convinced him. It was reasonable enough, he felt, for the 'Toiling Millions of Mankind' to try to get free of their 'Mock-Superiors', but what they ought to be doing was looking for 'Real-Superiors'. 'Democracy . . . means despair of finding any heroes to govern you.'[3] He attacked both ruling classes and mill-owners, not because he disapproved of them in principle, but because the former shirked their duty and the latter worried more about their profits than their workpeople.

Carlyle's ideal was a governing hero or heroes, or at least a governing class near enough to heroism to rise above self-interest and dedicate itself to governing justly. He saw the ethic of such a governing class in terms of chivalry. Early chivalry had been a Chivalry of Fighting, a 'glorious chivalry' which could convert the ugly sight of 'men with clenched teeth and hellfire eyes, hacking one another's flesh', into a 'Field of Honour', in which the battle was for ideals, not for self-interest.[4] Such ideals made the difference between 'buccaneers' and 'Chactaw Indians' on the one hand, and 'knights', 'chevaliers' and 'heroes' on the other. 'A Battlefield too is great . . . Here too thou shalt be strong, and not in muscle only, if thou wouldst prevail. Here too thou shalt be strong of heart, noble of soul; thou shalt dread no pain or death, thou shalt not love ease or life; in rage, thou shalt remember mercy, justice;—thou shalt be a Knight, and not a Chactaw, if thou wouldst prevail!'[5]

130

But Carlyle extended the concept of fighting to cover the whole of life. 'Man is created to fight; ... now with Necessity, with Barrenness, Scarcity, with Puddles, Bogs, tangled Forests, unkempt Cotton;—now also with the hallucinations of his poor fellow men.'[6] Such fighting, with tools rather than arms, and covering every aspect of mankind's struggle to make order out of disorder, was glorified by Carlyle under the blanket term of 'work'. Work (or 'godlike Labour') was man's supreme and essential activity. 'The latest Gospel in this world is, Know thy work and do it . . . A man perfects himself by working.'[7] The concept of chivalry needed to be extended to the world of work. 'No Working World, any more than a Fighting World, can be led on without a whole Chivalry of Work, and laws and fixed rules which follow out of that—far nobler than any Chivalry of Fighting was.'[8] Such a chivalry of work could convert idle aristocrats into a real governing class, and hard-working but previously selfish mill-owners into noble 'Captains of Industry'.[9]

Carlyle especially admired two qualities, toughness and idealism. His perfect hero was a tough idealist like Oliver Cromwell. But toughness on its own was better than nothing. He had more than a sneaking sympathy for mill-owners, however selfish; they were the raw material which was capable of conversion into heroes. Toughness, of course, involved more than physical toughness, although it was likely to include it: 'sheer obstinate toughness of muscle; but much more, what we call toughness of heart'.[10]

★   ★   ★

In 1839 well over two million members of the working classes signed a petition—or, as they called it, a Charter—asking for manhood suffrage, annual parliaments, election by ballot, just distribution of electoral districts, payment of M.P.s and abolition of the property qualifications for Parliament. The Charter was presented to Parliament, where a motion that it should be considered was rejected by two hundred and thirty-five votes to forty-six. A rising in Wales was suppressed; Chartists were arrested for sedition, unlawful meetings and unlawful possession of arms; many were tried, and some imprisoned or transported. In his *Chartism*, published in the same year, Carlyle came to the support of the movement. He pointed out that Chartism was the expression of a justified discontent, which could neither be got rid of nor ignored; Parliament, the upper classes and manufacturers were scathingly and brilliantly attacked for evading their responsibilities.

In 1848 rebellions broke out all over Europe. In England, Chartism revived, and its leaders now threatened to use physical force. A new petition was drawn up, and was said to have been signed by five million people and to weigh five tons. A public meeting on Clapham Common was announced for 10 April as a precursor to a mass march to present the petition to Parliament. In London one hundred and fifty thousand special constables were sworn in, the Queen retired to the country, the army stood by and revolution seemed imminent.

But the April meeting proved a working-class Eglinton Tournament. Its enthusiasm evaporated as rain fell in torrents. When the news came through that the Thames bridges had been closed by the military, the march was cancelled. The petition suffered a fate similar to that of the Eglinton Queen of Beauty and her attendants, and was carried to Parliament in three closed cabs; it turned out to be far smaller than had been announced. Organised working-class movements in England were set back by nearly half a century.

At this stage of despondency and disorganisation among the working classes a little group of gentlemen and clerics came to their support. Most of them had read Carlyle, and been inspired by him with enthusiasm to rise above self-interest in the pursuit of an ideal; all had some degree of sympathy for the Chartists, and several had started out to attend the meeting (although none of them had actually got there). They set to work almost immediately to start a periodical, *Politics for the People*, propagating a new doctrine which they called Christian Socialism. The concept behind it was that socialism was a force which could not be ignored or destroyed, and would shake Christianity to its foundations unless it was Christianised. But 'socialism' at that time had connotations not unlike 'communism' today. Many people thought that to combine the two concepts together was little less than blasphemous; gentlemen who could advocate socialism in any form must be traitors to their class.

The behaviour of the Christian Socialists can in fact reasonably be described as chivalrous. Not only did they come to the support of the underdog in causes which brought them no worldly rewards, gave them considerable unpopularity amongst most of their class, and in some cases lost them a great deal of money or actively harmed them in their careers; in addition, most of them were alive to the concept of chivalry, and regularly used its metaphors.

The leaders of the movement were J. M. Ludlow, Frederick Denison Maurice, Charles Kingsley, Thomas Hughes and E. V. Neale.[11] Of these Maurice was the son of a Unitarian minister; he had joined the Church of England and become a clergyman whose character, writings and sermons brought him a large and devoted following. He had been at Trinity College, Cambridge, in the years when Kenelm Digby was living there, and was doubly related to Digby's friend and admirer Julius Hare; each had married the other's sister. Hare was in fact one of the founders of *Politics for the People*.[12]

Charles Kingsley, rector of Eversley in Hampshire, belonged to a once-landed family, 'an ancient house laid low', as he put it.[13] As tended to happen in such cases, he was very conscious of being a gentleman as well as a clergyman. He had been won over to championship of the working classes by a combination of reading Carlyle and seeing the example of his brother-in-law, Sydney Godolphin Osborne. Osborne, who was the vicar of Durweston in Dorset, was a dedicated campaigner for better living standards for agricultural workers, and backed his campaign with statistics which uncomfortably jarred the conscience of the rich. At Eversley, Kingsley worked with crusading zeal for the ignorant and poverty-stricken peasantry in his parish; he wrote to his wife that 'I will never believe that a man has a real love for the good and the beautiful, except he attack the evil and disgusting the moment he sees it.'[14] In 1849, shortly after the Christian Socialist movement had started, he wrote an elegy in which he described himself as a 'joyous knight-errant of God'.[15]

132

E. V. Neale was the richest member of the group's inner circle. He owned a country house in Warwickshire, a house in Mayfair, and a substantial fortune, most of which disappeared in support of the movement. Thomas Hughes was later to describe him as a 'Knight of the Round Table'.[16] Hughes himself was remarkable, as a friend put it, for his combination of 'knightly loyalty, of the most humane geniality, and of the simplest Christian faith'.[17] He was the younger son of a Berkshire squire, and had been brought up on Toryism and Walter Scott; Scott had been a friend of his grandmother and father, and as a child he learnt *The Lady of the Lake* and most of *Marmion* and *The Lay of the Last Minstrel* by heart, and could repeat them for the rest of his life. But Rugby and Oxford changed him from a Tory to a Radical, owing to the combined influence of Dr Arnold and what Hughes called a 'Carlyle fit' at Oxford.[18] To most of those who knew about him in 1848, however, he seemed little more than an indifferent lawyer and a first-rate sportsman. When Maurice first suggested that Hughes might join them there were hilarious cries of 'We're not going to start a Cricket Club.'[19] But Hughes's energy, good temper, enthusiasm and tenacity soon made him a mainspring of the movement.

The blanket of Christian Socialism in fact sheltered a variety of political opinions. Ludlow was an out-and-out democrat. Maurice distrusted democracy and thought that Crown and aristocracy were intended by God 'to rule and guide the land'.[20] Hughes was an impassioned advocate of democracy but an equally impassioned admirer of the paternalistic relationship between a squire and his tenants and dependants; he spent most of his life trying to reconcile his two enthusiasms, but never quite succeeding. Kingsley thought that universal suffrage was a ridiculous idea, and although he intensely enjoyed meeting and championing working men, and was proud of his ability to get on with them, he took the class system for granted: as he put it to his wife, 'the lower orders worship me, and *never* take liberties'.[21]

Such differences did not matter to begin with because they all accepted social and personal regeneration as more important than politics. They accordingly concentrated on bringing the working classes three types of benefit which did not necessarily have political connotations: co-operative associations, better working and living conditions and better education.

The founding of co-operative groups (by means of a Society for Promoting Working Men's Associations) was their principal activity, and the one most closely related to their title. By advocating 'co-operation not competition' they were suggesting an alternative attitude of life to the philosophy of laissez-faire. But to at least some of them the co-operative movement was also attractive because it put them in the position of gentlemen rescuing working men from the trading and manufacturing classes. For, much though the movement was influenced by Carlyle, its members had little of his admiration for mill-owners as potential subjects for conversion into enlightened Captains of Industry. In this quarter they followed Digby. Mill-owners to them were usually the enemy—and also not gentlemen. As Kingsley explained to Tennyson in 1851, brandishing his clay pipe as he paced up and down his study, the only hope for a 'puling, quill-driving, soft-headed, effete and unbelieving age' was an alliance between Church, gentlemen and workmen against shopkeepers and Manchester Radicals.[22] Co-operative associations enabled working men to escape from middle-class exploitation by running their businesses themselves on a profit-sharing basis. The Society for Promoting Working Men's Associations was organised on two levels. A Council of Promoters encouraged the associations to form, and gave them guidance and (in many cases) financial support; the associations themselves consisted of small groups of tailors, shoemakers, printers, bakers, builders, ironworkers and so on, the management of which met from time to time in a Central Board. The Council contained thirty-eight members, thirty-five of whom were classed as gentlemen (distinguished in the printed list as 'Esq.' or 'Rev.' as opposed to 'Mr.').[23] None of them had the slightest commerical experience.

From time to time both *Politics for the People* and its longer-lived successor, the *Christian Socialist,* brought up the subject of improving the conditions in which working people worked and lived. But in this respect the most ardent champion in the movement was Kingsley. His novel *Yeast,* first published in instalments in *Fraser's* in 1848, took up the cause of agricultural workers; in 1849 a cholera outbreak in Jacob's Island in the East End of London spurred him into a furious campaign to give the area a decent water-supply; in 1850 his pamphlet *Cheap Clothes and Nasty* and his novel *Alton Locke* revealed the scandals of the sweating system in the London tailoring industry. By 1851 his reputation as 'the Apostle of Socialism' had made him so controversial a figure that for a time the Bishop of London forbad him to preach in his diocese, and a meeting of working men was held in his support on Kennington Common.[24]

The characters in *Yeast* include the hero, an idealistic young gentleman suitably called Lancelot; a fraudulent banker and a deceitful High Church priest (Kingsley was Broad); Lord Vieuxbois, a Young England–style nobleman of whom gentle fun is made for trying to turn modern agricultural workers into mediaeval peasants; and a gamekeeper, Paul Tregarva. Tregarva is one of nature's gentlemen; Lancelot, having lost all his money, declares that 'I will go with Paul Tregarva, whom I honour and esteem as one of God's own noblemen.'[25] At the end of the novel a mysterious stranger rescues Lancelot from his difficulties, and addresses him in words which drew a response from many idealistic young men of the period: 'Look around you and see what is the characteristic of your country and of your generation at this moment. What a yearning, what an expectation amid infinite falsehoods and confusions of some nobler, more chivalrous, more god-like state.'[26]

The educational side of Christian Socialism began in a very modest way.[27] In 1848 the group started a night school in Great Ormond's Yard, a notoriously rough slum near Maurice's own house. In 1851 a less restricted programme of meetings and classes was mooted, a 'Committee for Teaching and Publication' formed, and the first classes given in 1852, at the movement's Hall of Association in Castle Street.

Projects for expanding these into a full-scale college were brought to a head

when the publication of Maurice's controversial *Theological Essays* in 1853 led to his expulsion from his Chair at King's College, London. In 1854 he took up a new position as Principal of the newly founded Working Men's College in Red Lion Square. By then the Christian Socialist movement was in the process of collapse, partly owing to political and other disagreements among its promoters, partly because of the regular and cumulatively disastrous failure of almost all the co-operative associations. But the College has continued and flourished up till the present day.[28]

Two main principles lay behind it. One was that working men had a right to the kind of education which had previously been considered the preserve of their betters. Universities, Ludlow wrote, should be 'universal in fact as well as in name' and 'cease to be monopolised for the benefit of one or two privileged classes'. The Christian Socialists could not breach the universities but at least they could set up an alternative. The distinctive feature of the Working Men's College was that it offered a liberal education rather than a purely technical one.

But as Maurice honestly admitted, the College was also established for the benefit of the teachers.[29] Educated gentlemen, by coming to the help of those less fortunate than themselves, by getting to know them and even becoming friends with them, would themselves be enriched and improved. This opportunity for service did indeed attract some remarkable people, some of whom were also

135

94. Detail from an engraving of the Metropolitan Rifle Corps, Hyde Park, London, 1860, with members of the Working Men's Corps at the extreme left

actively involved in the Christian Socialist movement, and all of whom approved of it. Those who taught at the College included (in addition to Maurice, Ludlow, Neale and Hughes) F. J. Furnivall, the founder of the Early English Text Society; George Grove, the musician; Lord Goderich, who was to become Marquess of Ripon and Viceroy of India; John Ruskin; and the painters Rossetti, Burne-Jones and Ford Madox Brown.

★   ★   ★

Kingsley had always been a keen sportsman, but soon after the foundation of the Christian Socialist movement he began actively to glory in physical toughness. In 1851, when on a walking tour in Germany, he wrote enthusiastically that 'my limbs are all knots as hard as iron'.[30] In 1852, when staying with his brother-in-law James Anthony Froude in Wales, he described to Ludlow how 'there is a pool at the bottom of the garden into whose liquid ice Froude and I take a header every morning.'[31] In 1854 he wrote his *Ode to the North East Wind*, the theme of which is expressed in the couplet

> Tis the hard grey weather
> Breeds hard English men.

At about this time his reviews and literary essays began to include 'manliness' as one of the necessary qualities of a writer. Shelley and Browning were both tried and found wanting: Shelley was 'girlish', Browning 'effeminate'.[32]

This development was probably inspired by his friendship with Thomas Hughes. Hughes was the epitome of manliness. He had been captain of both football and cricket at Rugby, had played cricket for Oxford and rowed in his college eight, was a skilled and enthusiastic boxer and a tenacious cross-country runner; when Kingsley first met him he was taking young Matthew Arnold for a cold dip at six o'clock every morning.[33] At Rugby he had been scornful of purely clever boys; a distrust of 'cleverness' remained with him all his life. But he had been rescued from a state of unthinking brawniness by Dr Arnold. Arnold, as he later wrote, not only gave him 'faith in and loyalty to Christ', but made him want to join in fight against evil 'which would last all our lives, and try all our powers, physical, intellectual, and moral, to the utmost'.[34]

Hughes took naturally not only to organised games, but to organising others into them. At the Working Men's College he taught comparatively little, modestly believing that there were others better qualified for this than he was. But 'round shoulders, narrow chests, stiff limbs were, I submitted, as bad as defective grammar and arithmetic'. Accordingly he gave lessons in boxing and gymnastics, and sparred with the men himself. It was 'a pretty sight', wrote one of his students, 'to see him, with his lithe well-knit form and cheery smile as, vigorous and alert, he met the onslaught of rougher assailants'.[35]

He went on to organise College cricket and rowing clubs. He believed in games for social reasons as well as a means of developing manliness. They brought the classes together. For the same reasons he became an active supporter of the

136

Volunteer Movement when it swept through England in the early 1860s, set off by fear that Napoleon III was going to be as aggressive as his uncle. Hughes joined with others in seeing volunteer riflemen as the Victorian successors of the bowmen of Agincourt, and dashed into training them as impetuously as any mediaeval knight. He raised and commanded a Working Men's Corps of two companies, largely recruited from the College; at a march-past in 1860 the *Illustrated London News* commented that 'their step was as regular and their front as accurate as if they had been ruled by line'.[36]

As a clergyman Kingsley could not actually join the Volunteers, but he was enthusiastically in favour of the movement. The arrival of the military at Aldershot, a few miles from Eversley, in 1854 had already given him a taste for the army. 'I like to have men of war about me', he said; officers rode over from Aldershot to listen to his sermons, and he rode back to dine in their messes.[37] In 1854 he, like Tennyson, welcomed the Crimean War; it was a chance for the nation to prove its manliness. But the actual conduct of the war drove him to a frenzy. He felt that brave British soldiers were being betrayed by an inept and incompetent government.

He worked off his anger and frustration in *Westward Ho*, which was published in 1855 and proved much more successful than any of his previous books. *Westward Ho* depicted an age of chivalry: but Kingsley chose to write about Elizabethan chivalry because it enabled him to combine his chivalric enthusiasm with an equal enthusiasm for Protestantism and the British Empire.

The young hero of the novel is Amyas Leigh, the son of a Devon squire. He has 'the frame and stature of a Hercules'. His formal education had been limited to reading the Bible, the Prayer Book, the *Morte d'Arthur* and a book on the cruelties of the Spaniards; but he had been taught, like the old Persians, 'to speak the truth and to dread the bad', to endure pain cheerfully, and to believe it 'to be the finest thing in the world to be a gentleman: by which word he had been taught to understand the careful habit of causing needless pain to no human being, poor or rich, and of taking pride in giving up his own pleasure for the sake of those who were weaker than himself.'[38] The book is concerned with his adventures in Devon, in Ireland and on the Spanish Main. In Devon he and his friends form the 'Noble Brotherhood of the Rose', pledged to be true to a local beauty, Rose Salterne, and to roam the world fighting in 'good wars' in her honour. When Rose is abducted to South America by a Spaniard, Amyas and others name a ship after her, and depart to rescue her on 'The most chivalrous adventure of the good ship Rose.' This and other adventures involve a good deal of smashing of bullies and slaughtering of Spaniards; but Amyas never forgets that above all he aims to be a knight of God, a 'Knight-Errant in the everlasting war against the False Prophet and the Beast'.[39]

In 1857 Kingsley's *Two Years Ago* and Hughes's *Tom Brown's Schooldays* brought the virtues of Amyas Leigh into a contemporary context. *Tom Brown's Schooldays* was Hughes's first book; its theme and great influence must be kept for a later chapter. *Two Years Ago* is a forgotten novel, but in its day it was also extremely successful. Its chief characters are Tom Thurnall, a muscular, manly

XIX. (preceding page) George Frederic Watts. *The Eve of Peace*, 1863

XX. (left) Cardiff Castle, Glamorganshire. Chimney-piece in the banqueting hall, designed by William Burges, *c.* 1875

cheerful, self-reliant, boxing, rowing, globe-trotting, grizzly-bear-shooting, extrovert doctor; and Elsley Vavasour, a poet with 'huge beautiful eyes' who unfortunately has none of these qualities, and comes to a bad end. The sub-plot involves a famous actress with a touch of negro blood who reads the *Morte d'Arthur*, enthuses over 'Sir Galahad, the spotless knight', and tries to persuade her American admirer that his Quest of the San Greal should be the liberation of the slaves in the Southern States; he finally comes round to her point of view as a result of a visit to Ehrenbreitstein, Digby's 'Broad Stone of Honour'.[40] Looming in the background of the novel is the Crimean War, and the realisation it brings that war is 'the most necessary human art' after agriculture, and that under its influence 'there are noble elements underneath the crust which will come out all the purer from the fire'.[41] A fight against cholera in a remote Devon fishing village provides a foretaste of the struggles and heroism of the war.

It was probably an anonymous notice of *Two Years Ago* published in the *Saturday Review* of 21 February 1857 which first used the phrase 'Muscular Christianity'. Kingsley had set himself the task, it said, 'of spreading the knowledge and fostering the love of a muscular Christianity. His ideal is a man who fears God and can walk a thousand miles in a thousand hours—who, in the language Mr Kingsley has made popular, breathes God's free air on God's rich earth, and at the same time can hit a woodcock, doctor a horse, and twist a poker round his finger.'

The phrase became so popular as a way of describing Kingsley, Hughes, and all those who imitated them, that in the end both authors had to react publicly to it. In *Tom Brown at Oxford* (1861) Hughes welcomed the nickname, even though it was coined by his critics; but at the same time he distinguished between true muscular Christians and musclemen. 'The muscleman seems to have no belief whatever as to the purpose for which his body has been given him, except some hazy idea that it is to go up and down the world with him, belabouring men and captivating women for his benefit or pleasure . . . Whereas, so far as I know, the least of the muscular Christians has hold of the old chivalrous and Christian belief, that a man's body is given to him to be trained and brought into subjection, and then used for the protection of the weak, the advancement of all righteous causes, and the subduing of the earth which God has given to the children of men . . . For mere power, whether of body or intellect, he has (I hope and believe) no reverence whatever, though, ceteris paribus, he would probably himself, as a matter of taste, prefer the man who can lift a hundredweight round his head with his little finger to the man who can construct a string of perfect sorites, or expand the doctrine of "contradictory inconceivables."'[42]

Kingsley's public reaction came only in 1865, in the first of four sermons on David which he gave at Cambridge during his tenure as Regius Professor of History.[43] A 'thrill of half-expectation half-amusement' ran round the packed congregation of undergraduates when he first used the phrase 'Muscular Christianity'.[44] Having first of all said that it was flippant and meaningless he went on to make a similar distinction to Hughes's one between muscular Christians and musclemen. Muscular Christianity was only acceptable if it meant 'a healthy and manful Christianity, one which does not exalt the feminine virtues to the exclusion of the masculine'.

He linked this concept with mediaeval chivalry. He distinguished two types of mediaeval Christianity, monastic and chivalric. Monks were essentially feminine; they diseased their minds and hearts by trying to unsex themselves. The ideal of chivalry arose in reaction to monasticism; it aimed at producing whole men, and consecrating their masculinity to God in all activities of normal life, including the battlefield. The ideal was to be further developed in the sixteenth century by Protestantism, which believed that 'true religion did not crush, but strengthened and consecrated a valiant and noble manhood'.[45]

Whatever Kingsley might say, the particular form in which he and Thomas Hughes preached 'a valiant and noble manhood' had its own special flavour, which the phrase 'muscular Christianity' caught to perfection. The flavour lay less in the doctrine itself than in the way in which it was presented. The doctrine—that a Christian should dedicate his body, mind and will to the service of God—was unexceptionable, and, as Hughes and Kingsley pointed out, by no means new. But the way in which they wrote and talked made it clear that emotionally they found physical prowess gloriously exciting; that they preferred a strong man to a clever one, and that they regarded a clever man with instinctive suspicion, unless he could prove himself by following hounds, swinging dumb-bells or taking cold baths. Digby had written about the importance of physical fitness; Carlyle had commended 'toughness of muscle; but much more . . . toughness of heart'. Kingsley and Hughes tended to write as though the latter were impossible without the former.

Their heroes are tough, but they are also invariably pure. Wynd in *Two Years Ago*, 'as brave and pure-minded a fellow as ever pulled in the University eight', is a typical example.[46] Purity was a concept of great importance to them. They were far from opposing sex (they left this to unsexed monks), but they believed that it should be confined to marriage. A pure man ardently loved his wife, but outside this one sacred relationship he kept clear of sex, in thought, word and deed. Before marriage he kept clear of it altogether. This was clearly likely to involve a struggle; one of the reasons why they preached manliness was because the hard physical training which it involved helped keep impure thoughts at bay. Cold baths had a special, almost mystical, meaning for them because they were at once a symbol of purity, and a practical means towards preserving it.[47]

Muscular Christianity helped make purity an essential element of nineteenth-century chivalry. The fights in which a modern knight engaged had already been extended by Carlyle to include those against ignorance, disease and the forces of nature; they were now extended again to those with which he gained control over his own passions. Such metaphors of battle against the temptations of the flesh and the Devil had been a commonplace of Christianity since the days of St Paul. They had been given a specifically chivalric twist in the allegories of Spenser's *Faerie Queene*. Bunyan's *Pilgrim's Progress* (of which, not surprisingly, Kingsley was an admirer) had used the images of chivalry for Christian's and Greatheart's fights against Apollyon and the Giants Despair, Grim and Slay-Good. But before the

1850s the concept of self-conquest had played little part in the nineteenth-century revival of chivalry. Digby, for instance, scarcely touched on the subject of purity.

To what extent were Hughes and Kingsley like their own heroes? Hughes was probably much more like them than Kingsley. All the evidence goes to show that besides being a fine athlete he was a thoroughly nice, honourable, generous, open, uncomplicated man of whom the worst that could be said was that he never quite grew up. Kingsley also had good and generous qualities; but under his surface aggressiveness he was neurotic, morbid, and liable to frequent collapses; his heroes were what he would like to have been, not what he was. There is a hysterical edge to his writing that can be very distressing.

It did not, however, distress most of his contemporaries. After the publication of *Westward Ho* Kingsley went from strength to strength. The Prince Consort read *Two Years Ago* with enthusiasm and as a result Kingsley was invited to preach at Windsor; his sermon was so successful that he was immediately appointed the Queen's Chaplain in Ordinary. Royal fvaour won him his appointment as Regius Professor at Cambridge in 1860. Professional historians sneered, but Kingsley was a great success with the undergraduates. Muscular Christianity had become a cult with them.

Kingsley's enthusiasm for working men's causes diminished as he grew older. His being taken up by the Royal Family may have had something to do with this, but he was probably becoming more authoritarian anyway. In 1865, when Governor Eyre's prompt but savage suppression of disaffection in Jamaica divided the English Establishment into two camps, Kingsley supported Eyre, and lost Thomas Hughes's friendship in consequence.[48] He did, however, launch a bitter attack on the mill-owners for abandoning their workers in the cotton slump of 1861; and his revelations about chimney-sweeps in *The Water Babies* led to the immediate passing of the Chimney-Sweepers Regulation Act. Kingsley was now a power in the land. His early death in 1875 was mourned as a national calamity. Dean Stanley, who preached his memorial service in Westminster Abbey, described him as a Crusader struck down in battle. His widow wrote that 'if a love that never failed—pure, patient and passionate, for six-and-thirty years—... could prove that the age of chivalry had not passed away for ever, then Charles Kingsley fulfilled the idea of a "most true and perfect knight" to the one woman blest with that love in time and eternity.'

Thomas Hughes lived on until 1896. For many years he remained a trusted supporter and adviser of co-operative and trades-union movements; but, as tended to be the way with gentlemanly Radicals, he gradually moved away from his working-class affiliations and ended as a Conservative. After 1878 he spent much of his time in an abortive attempt to found an ideal community in Tennessee, to which muscular young gentlemen and honest English yeomen could emigrate and work side by side together. It was called Rugby in memory of his old school, and lost him most of his money. He lived his last years as a County Court judge in Chester, surveyed by the figures of Guenevere, Vivian, Elaine and Enid, the heroines of the first four *Idylls of the King*, whom he had installed in stained glass on his staircase.

95. (right) John Ballantyne. *Sir Joseph Noel Paton in his studio*, 1867 (detail)

CHAPTER 10
A Mid-Century
Miscellany

IN THE 1850S THE IMAGES OF CHIVALRY WERE ABSORBED INTO THE PATTERN of everyday life. Knights in armour jostled each other on the walls of the Royal Academy, and filled the drawers of the print-sellers. Knights in literature were two a penny. Baron Marochetti's Richard Coeur de Lion, first introduced to the public outside the Crystal Palace, proudly championed chivalry in his final station outside the Houses of Parliament. But knights in armour were now as likely to suggest moral struggles as military battles, and to symbolise modern gentlemen as depict mediaeval heroes. Chivalric metaphors came naturally to the lips of any educated man or woman. Chivalry was working loose from the Middle Ages.

THREE NOVELS AND THEIR HEROES

The Broad Stone of Honour was able to fill young men with ardour to, in John Manners's words, 'restore—what?—I scarcely know, but still it is a glorious attempt'. But his barrage of examples and quotations was too diffuse to provide them with a concrete model for imitation. Heroes of literature like Scott's Quentin Durward or even, in their own day, Kingsley's Amyas Leigh suffered from being presented in a period setting. Thackeray's Colonel Newcome was as chivalrous a contemporary figure as any one could wish for (did not Thackeray himself compare him to both Lancelot and Bayard?);[1] but he was too old for young men to imitate, and a little too gullible. Some of the heroes of Scott's eighteenth-century novels came closer to what they were looking for. Better still, a number of best-selling novels of the 1850s had heroes who were young, chivalrous and contemporary. Something has already been said about Tom Thurnall; Tom Brown will be discussed in the next chapter; but it is also worth taking a look at Guy Morville in Charlotte M. Yonge's *Heir of Redclyffe* (1853); Guy Livingstone in the novel of the same name by G. A. Lawrence (1857); and John Halifax in Dinah Mary Mulock's *John Halifax, Gentleman*.

Charlotte M. Yonge was the unmarried daughter of a small Hampshire landowner. She had started her literary career by writing stories for children's magazines. *The Heir of Redclyffe* was her first novel; it was written in 1850–1 but not published until 1853. Its immediate and well-deserved success set her off on her career as a novel-writer.

She was a deeply religious member of the High Church movement (Keble was a close personal friend), a Tory, a believer in discipline and obedience, but also a romantic. Walter Scott was her first literary hero, and she was a warm admirer of the stories of La Motte Fouqué, especially *Sintram*.[2] *Sintram* was written to provide a context for Dürer's mysterious engraving *The Knight, Death and Satan* (a copy of which hung in C. M. Yonge's drawing-room). It tells the story of the high-spirited son of a Norse war-lord, who lies under a curse, owing to his father's crimes. He is plagued with terrible dreams and frequently tempted by the Devil in person; several times he falls, but always recovers and fights on. In his final ordeal he meets with Death and the Devil when riding through a dark and ghastly valley to see his sick father; by resisting the Devil's temptations and emerging

triumphant, he wins his father a peaceful death and frees himself from the curse.

When her brother Julian was given a commission in the Rifle Brigade in 1852, Charlotte compared him 'to a young squire obtaining knighthood, and felt it to be a sort of revival of the romance of an older day'.[3] *The Heir of Redclyffe* was a variant on *Sintram* set in modern times and given a hero who was even more of a modern young knight than Charlotte's brother Julian. This hero, Sir Guy Morville, is seventeen when the story starts and twenty-one when he dies towards the end of it. He is the heir of an ancient, strong-willed and passionate line; his grandfather's pride and temper had been indirectly responsible for his own father's death. He has read *Sintram* and believes that he too is under a curse. Although basically gay, affectionate and full of fun, he is painfully aware that he has a furious temper; as his cousin Philip Morville puts it: 'how thin a crust covers the burning lava'.[4]

The interest of his character lies in the resulting 'extraordinary mixture of gaiety of heart and seriousness', the 'serious ascetic temper combined with very high animal spirits'. He has 'hawk's eyes' and 'the eager head of a listening greyhound'. As a boy he goes 'shouting, whooping, singing, whistling' through the great gloomy house at Redclyffe. The house is on the edge of a cliff, and he loves 'the free feeling as you stand on some high crag, the wind blowing in your face across half the globe, and the waves dashing far below'. He is instinctively sweet and tender to anything small or weak; he is driven to a fury by seeing a dog being ill-treated; he jumps impetuously into a river in flood to rescue a ram who is being carried out to sea. But he is always mortifying himself because

147

96. (left) Baron Carlo Marochetti. *Richard I*

97. (right) Albrecht Dürer's *The Knight, Death and Satan*, as framed in La Motte Fouqué's *Sintram*, 1844

he is terrified of his character getting out of control; he gives up hunting and dancing because they over-excite him; he keeps losing his temper and bitterly repenting. The main thread of the story concerns the frictions between him and his insufferably complacent and disapproving elder cousin Philip Morville. In the end Guy nurses Philip when he is down with fever in Italy, catches the fever himself, and dies.

Guy's character as a modern knight is left in no doubt. His cousin Charlotte calls him 'a true knight'. He is 'a very chivalrous lover'. As a boy he starts writing an epic on King Arthur; Malory is 'his boating-book for at least three summers'. At Oxford a drawing of Sintram is one of the few features of his rooms. In a game in which the participants have to write their favourite plant, quality and character in history and fiction, his contribution is 'Heather—Truth—King Charles—Sir Galahad'.[5] Shortly before he dies he even models for a painting of Sir Galahad; 'Mr Shene, the painter' is struck by an expression on his face which is exactly what he wants for Sir Galahad 'when he kneels to adore the San Greal'.[6]

When William Morris and Edward Burne-Jones were young men at Oxford *The Heir of Redclyffe*, alongside *Sintram* and *The Broad Stone of Honour*, was one of their favourite books.[7] Julian Yonge told Charlotte that most of his fellow-subalterns in the Rifle Brigade had copies.[8] But in 1857 G. A. Lawrence's *Guy Livingstone* produced a rival to compete as a model for young men. He was a serious rival; for although the novel in which he featured was infinitely worse than *The Heir of Redcliffe* it had the image-making quality which the over-simplification of bad novels sometimes produces.

Like Guy Morville, Guy Livingstone is the heir of an ancient line; but there is much more of the beast-of-prey in him. His own ancestors have been 'hunters and soldiers beyond the memory of man'. He is a giant in size and strength, but 'lean in the flanks as a wolf-hound'. His huge hand is 'corded across with a network of tangled sinews'. Behind 'the heavy moustache that . . . fell over his lip in a black cascade' looks out the face of a 'stone Crusader'—not surprisingly, since his ancestors, in addition to Beau Livingstone and Livingstone the Cavalier, included Sir Malise 'Point-de-Fer' Livingstone, who had gone east with Richard Coeur de Lion. Guy moves in a set of lean, tough, hard-drinking and hard-riding friends. At Oxford he fights with 'Burn's Big 'un,' a famous professional boxer, and leaves him 'a heap of blind, senseless, bleeding humanity'. He believes in rough justice for any 'base, brutal hound'; but he would never strike a woman, or be disloyal to a friend.[9]

When not occupied in violent sports, Guy's relaxations are flirting with pretty women and swapping yarns with his friends in his smoking-room 'with its great divans and scattered card-tables'. His affections are divided between the good and beautiful Constance Brandon, and Flora Bellasys, a *femme fatale*; for anyone hearing her voice 'it was very easy to believe the weird stories of Norse sorceresses, and German wood-spirits and pixies, luring men to death with their fatally musical tones'.[10]

Guy becomes engaged to Constance Brandon; but Flora Bellasys over-excites him at a ball, and Constance catches them kissing in the conservatory. Naturally she breaks off the engagement. Guy retires to dissipation in Paris. (He takes a break, however, to save an English girl-artist from being molested—'By G-d . . . I believe it's an Englishwoman they are bullying.') Constance relents, and sends him a letter, but Flora prevents it getting to him. A second letter, telling him that she is dying, reaches its destination. After a harrowing deathbed scene, Guy goes down with brain-fever.

He recovers, a broken, but also a better, man. In Italy he gallantly rescues a boatload of fishermen from drowning. When an Italian *lazzerone* insults him, he merely 'lifted him by the throat and held him suspended against the wall'. On his old form 'a straightforward blow from the shoulder would have settled the business'. Then a hunting accident back in England breaks his spine ('You always told me I went too fast at timber, Jack'). He dies in great agony, 'but the brave heart and iron nerve ruled the body to the last imperially'.

Towards the end of the novel a parallel is drawn between Guy's story and that of Lancelot and Guenevere. Flora is his Guenevere; and his repentance and grief after Constance's death are like those of Lancelot after the death of Arthur. The last chapter, in which Guy dies, is headed by Malory's famous lament for Lancelot: 'Ah, Sir Lancelot, there thou liest, that never wert matched of earthly hands . . .' Guy, too, was a noble knight who sinned and repented.[11]

A clergyman figures briefly in *Guy Livingstone*, and attends his deathbed: 'Guy soon trusted him implicitly when he spoke of the Past and of the Future which was so near.' G. A. Lawrence was the son of a clergyman, and had been at Rugby just after Thomas Hughes.[12] He intensely admired Kingsley, as he made clear in at least one of his novels.[13] To the embarrassment of the two men, *Guy Livingstone* tended to be classed with their writings as an example of 'Muscular Christianity'. They indignantly denied any resemblance in their outlooks, and ponderous articles in public-school magazines and elsewhere came to their support.[14] Nevertheless, the resemblance was there, even if muscularity was much more in evidence in *Guy Livingstone* than Christianity. The novel had a great, if controversial, success. Guy was to breed a line of knightly toughs, always ready to smash a mean hound to jelly; Bulldog Drummond was his most notable descendant.

In spite of their differences, both C. M. Yonge and G. A. Lawrence had upper-class connections and unhesitatingly identified themselves with the landed gentry. The background of Dinah Maria Mulock (or Mrs Craik, as she became) was completely middle-class.[15] Her mother's family had been prosperous tanners; her father had been in business in Liverpool (and, briefly, secretary to Canning) but gave up his job to start his own religion. In *John Halifax, Gentleman* his daughter tackled the problem of 'trade'. Could someone in trade be a gentleman? Kenelm Digby had come down with a firm 'No': 'it did not appear necessary to enter upon a review of those pursuits which are chiefly directed towards the attainment of wealth, because I had no reason to suppose that there was any motive or influence that could induce you to embrace them.' One of the few appearances of trade in *Guy Livingstone* is in the person of 'Buttons'—the son of a Birmingham button-manufacturer who attempts to bully Guy at school; Guy hits him between the eyes with a brass candlestick and marks him for life. In *The Heir of Redclyffe* the subject is not mentioned. But according to Mrs Craik a tanner and a mill-owner could be more of a gentleman than an earl. Such an answer (even if, as will appear, she cheated to get it) combined with Mrs Craik's own skill as a writer to ensure her book's success; by 1900 it had gone into over forty editions.

The hero of the novel first appears as an illiterate and half-starving young boy walking the streets of Norton Bury. A Quaker tanner gives him a job, and his ensuing friendship with his master's sickly son, and his own ability and honourable nature, lead him to success and ultimately affluence. He becomes a partner in the tannery, takes it over, starts a cloth-mill and makes a fortune. His career keeps crossing the path of the Earl of Luxmore, a corrupt and haughty local aristocrat; after he has made his money the Earl's son wants to marry his daughter, but John Halifax sends him away, because Lord Luxmore's debauchery and extravagance, and his daughter's immorality, have made 'the so-called "honour" of Luxmore' unworthy of 'the unsulled dignity of the tradesman's life'.

In spite of his trade, John Halifax—strong, tender, courteous, honourable—is essentially chivalrous, and moreover he looks it. His friend Phineas Fletcher once says to him, 'John, when you're on horseback you look like a young knight of the middle ages.' He himself admits, 'If there was one point I was anxious over in my youth, it was to keep up through life a name like the Chevalier Bayard—how folk would smile to hear of a tradesman emulating Bayard—"sans peur et sans reproche!"'[16]

Towards the end of the novel John's son Guy, embarrassed when his father refers to his origins, remonstrates: 'Father, we may as well pass over that fact. We are gentlefolk now.' His father rebukes him: 'We always were, my son.'[17] John's gentlemanliness is underlined all the way through the book. A review in the *Scotsman* described him as 'one of nature's own nobility'.[18] But this is where Mrs Craik cheats; she has to have it both ways. As a penniless boy, John Halifax's only possession is a Greek Bible inscribed with the name of his father: 'Guy Halifax, Gentleman.' He knows nothing more about his father, and nothing emerges about him; but John not only takes it for granted that he is a gentleman born, it is made obvious by his looks, his manners and his cleanliness: 'He loved and delighted in what poor folk generally abominate—water.' Readers are left uncertain. Clearly a gentleman can be a tradesman; but can a tradesman, without the advantage of John Halifax's mysterious Bible, be a gentleman? Many were unwilling to take the risk; it is remarkable how many Victorian middle-class families cherished the belief that they were in fact descended from landed gentry who at some period had lost their estates in a suitably gentlemanly way, such as fighting on the right side in the Civil War.[19]

THREE PAINTERS: WATTS, NOEL PATON AND MILLAIS

Sir Galahad (Plate XXV) is probably Watts's best-know painting, but it is only one of a sizeable group of chivalric pictures painted by him. Three of them—*Sir Galahad*, *Aspirations* and *Una and the Red Cross Knight*—stem from the same

98. (right) George Frederic Watts. *Una and the Red Cross Knight*, 1869

99. (below left) George Frederic Watts. *Aspirations*, c. 1866–87

100. (below right) Arthur Prinsep as a young officer in the Indian Army

model, the fifteen-year-old Arthur Prinsep, whose mother had welcomed Watts as a friend and lodger into Little Holland House in Kensington in 1852. In the winter of 1855–6 Watts took Arthur Prinsep over to Paris, where he had been lent a studio.[20] He made a number of sketches of him, persuading him with the greatest difficulty not to have his hair cut before they were finished. Over the ensuing years he gradually worked them up into pictures; it is not certain that he envisaged the ultimate chivalric themes at the time of the sketches. *Sir Galahad* was exhibited at the Royal Academy in 1862, the *Red Cross Knight* in 1869; *Aspirations* was begun about 1866, but not completed or exhibited until 1887. In the 1860s he had also painted, or started to paint, the *Standard Bearer* (1862); a grave and beautiful self-portrait in armour called the *Eve of Peace* (1863, Plate XIX); and *Watchman, What of the Night* (1864–5). The last was modelled for by Ellen Terry during her disastrous fifteen-month marriage to Watts; the *Standard Bearer* (Plate 132) is the only completed portion of a portrait which was to have shown Reginald Talbot as standard-bearer, by the side of his father the Earl of Shrewsbury as a knight on horseback. Later armour pictures include *Joan of Arc*, which was painted in 1878–9, and the *Condottiere* and *Happy Warrior*, which may date from as late as the 1880s.[21]

All through the 1860s and the first half of the 1870s Watts was living and working in Little Holland House, protected from the outside world by the loving admiration of Mrs Prinsep and her sisters Lady Somers, Lady Dalrymple, Mrs

152

101. George Frederic Watts. *The Happy Warrior*, 1884(?)

Jackson and Julia Margaret Cameron. But, however protected, he was by no means isolated from the chivalric currents of the 1850s. Tennyson, Rossetti, Burne-Jones and Thomas Hughes were all involved in the Little Holland House circle. Watts became friends with Tennyson in the summer of 1857, if not earlier, and from then on saw him constantly. These were the years in which Tennyson was working on the *Idylls of the King*. (When Watts took Ellen Terry to stay with the Tennysons at Freshwater in 1864, she used to escape from the grown-ups to play Indians and Knights of the Round Table with the Tennyson children.)[22] Watts had known Rossetti since the early 1850s; he first met Burne-Jones in 1857, and became a close friend. He encouraged Val Prinsep, the younger brother of his model of Sir Galahad, to become a painter, and in 1857 further encouraged him to join with Rossetti and others in decorating the Oxford Union with Arthurian scenes;[23] so he knew exactly what was going on there.

Thomas Hughes's sister, Mrs Nassau Senior, was one of Watts's closest friends and the confidante of numerous letters from him. Thomas Hughes came to Little Holland House through her; Watts painted his portrait in 1868 or 1869.[24] The Kingsley–Hughes brand of muscularity was probably a bit too breezy for him, but in essence he was sympathetic to it. For although his own bad health kept him from obtaining any distinction in what the Victorians liked to call manly sports, he loved watching them; moreover he was at least a competent horseman, and went hunting whenever he could.[25] He was also an enthusiast for the Volunteer Movement when it started in 1859, joined the Artists' Rifles, and in 1860 designed a shield for the National Rifle Association, one of its side products.[26] 'I wish I were strong enough', he wrote to Mrs Nassau Senior, 'to go where deeds of heroism and daring are done, and privations are suffered. The aspirations, even with the violence, of an heroic age would have suited me better.'[27] Watts in fact joins with FitzGerald and Johnson Cory (and later with Henley, Barrie and Kipling) as one of a line of Victorians who admired manliness from the sidelines; the Prinsep brothers were perhaps to him for a time what Kenworthy Browne was to FitzGerald, or the Llewellyn Davieses to Barrie.

In 1879 Watts regretted that chivalry had been allowed to decay: 'Had it been encouraged to penetrate all ranks in the army of life, many of our greatest difficulties might never have arisen.'[28] By pervasion of all ranks he seems to have meant no more than appreciation and help for the working classes from an upper class alive to its duties and aware that its possessions were only there in trust, to do good with. Although he wrote little to expand the message of his chivalric pictures, one can interpret them with reasonable confidence. They are types of upper-class manliness enlisted in the fight for good: *Aspirations* shows a young man just entering on life's battles; in the *Red Cross Knight* he is in action, protecting a woman; in *Sir Galahad* he is briefly resting from the fight;[29] in the *Happy Warrior* he has died in the fight and is being rewarded by the ideal for which he has struggled. The *Standard Bearer* is the completed part of a picture which would have shown modern chivalry personified in a great nobleman and his son. In the *Eve of Peace* Watts shows himself as one of those engaged in the struggle (and endows himself with a considerably more impressive physique than

in fact he possessed). Finally, his memorial effigy of Reginald Cholmondeley (Plate 165), in the church at Condover in Shropshire, clearly shows a modern knight at prayer, even though the only traditional chivalric symbol retained is the sword.

'A great work of high art', Watts wrote, 'is a noble theme treated in a noble manner, awakening our best and most reverential feelings, touching our generosity, our tenderness, or disposing us generally to seriousness.'[30] The chivalric pictures form only a comparatively small section of the much larger corpus of pictures in which he endeavoured to depict noble themes. Towards the end of the century large numbers of them (including almost all the chivalric pictures) reached a wide audience by way of reproduction. In the 1860s and 1870s they were known only to a small but influential circle, the members of which reverenced Watts as the greatest living artist. One of them later wrote that 'he seemed to sanctify Holland House'.[31] When Mary Seton Tytler, who was to become his second wife, first visited his studio in 1870 as an enthusiastic young girl, he 'so distinctly suggested to me the days of chivalry that I believe I should not have been surprised if, on another visit, I had found him all clad in shining armour'.[32]

At much the same time as Watts was using knights to symbolise moral and spiritual values his slightly younger contemporary Sir Joseph Noel Paton (1821–1902) was working on the same lines in Scotland.[33] Paton's father was a successful fabric designer, a Jacobite and an antiquarian; his mother was an

154

102. The Hall of Sir Joseph Noel Paton's house in George Square, Edinburgh, c. 1895

enthusiast for Highland legends and stories; his sister married David Octavius Hill, the photographer. In 1838 he walked forty miles there and back from Paisley to attend the Eglinton Tournament; his experiences on the terrible first day were bad enough to make him do his best (with success) to discourage a projected tournament at Taymouth Castle in 1880.[34] In 1843 he studied for a time at the Royal Academy schools, and entered on 'an unclouded friendship of fifty years' with Millais.

Back in Edinburgh he rapidly became one of the leading painters in Scotland. As soon as he could afford it he began to collect arms and armour, on the basis of a few pieces left him by his father. He bought lavishly at the sale of the Meyrick collection in about 1871, and in the end his house in George Square was crammed with the collection which is now in the National Museum in Edinburgh.[35]

Paton's life was increasingly dominated by two passions, armour and religion. He combined the two by painting moral allegories featuring knights in armour. He started by way of Arthurian subjects; but even these increasingly assumed religious rather than purely literary or romantic significance. Besides making charming illustrations for Aytoun's *Lays of the Scottish Cavaliers*, he painted *Sir Lancelot of the Lake* in 1860, and the *Death Barge of King Arthur* in 1865. In 1866 he exhibited two armour pictures, one whimsical and the other religious. *I wonder who lived in there* featured his little son Diarmid. *Mors Janua Vitae* showed a mail-clad Christian warrior, wounded and weary from the conflict, being rewarded with the crown of life as he passes through the gates of death.[36] In 1879 he started

155

104. Sir Joseph Noel Paton. *Sir Galahad and his Angel*, 1884

on the first of three different paintings of Sir Galahad.[37] They were completed at intervals, and in a number of different versions, over the next ten years; one was titled from the Beatitudes *Beati Mundo Corde* (Blessed are the pure in heart) and all were variants on the same theme. In 1881 *In Die Malo* showed Faith among the Christian warriors. *The Choice*, which occupied him on and off from 1883 to 1886, is best described in the words of the *Art Journal* in 1895: 'A Knight completely armed in mail stands upon the verge of a precipice, grasping with his right hand the hand of an angel, while with his left he rejects the advances of a Circean temptress—a luridly beautiful, bold and attractive woman, arranged in luxurious deshabille.'[38]

Although his pictures ran on into the 1880s, stylistically the later ones belong to the 1860s, when the series started. Watts had left spirits and angels out of his chivalric pictures, with the exception of the *Happy Warrior*; artistically Paton would have been well advised to do the same, for the saccharine quality of his angels oversweetens even so striking and romantic a picture as *Sir Galahad's Vision* (Plate XVIII).

The excursions into chivalry made by Paton's friend Sir John Millais provide a curious story of failure in both life and art. Superficially he was an ideal knight. His slightly superior background, dashing gentlemanly bearing and amazing good looks set him a little apart from all his fellow-artists. To William Blake Richmond, when a boy, he seemed wonderfully glamorous: 'how he roused my admiration for his manly beauty, his splendid physique, and his glorious head of curly hair. He was like some knight of old who only needed to be clad in golden

156

105. (right) Sir Joseph Noel Paton. *The Choice*, 1883–6, after an engraving

armour to appear a perfect Sir Galahad.'[39] This was in 1852 or 1853; Richmond was then ten or eleven years old and he and his friend Thomas More Palmer (Samuel Palmer's son) were in a state of continual romantic excitement; they had made suits of armour out of pasteboard and glue, and thought of themselves as 'knight-errants, whose duty it was to guard the Castle of Independence from evil comers and influences'.[40]

At exactly the same time Millais was in fact achieving the classic exploit of chivalry, and rescuing a damsel in distress. For John Ruskin's wife Effie, married to a sexually mixed-up and possibly impotent husband, was certainly in distress; and Millais came to her rescue by falling in love with her, persuading her to leave her husband and ask for an annulment, and finally marrying her. They should have lived happily ever after, but unfortunately they did not. Both were essentially conventional people; and for a wife to leave her husband in the 1850s was a highly unconventional, and in the eyes of many a reprehensible, act. It imposed too many strains for the happiness of their subsequent marriage.

In 1844–5 Millais had put together a manuscript book, *Sketches of Armour*, elaborately illustrated with drawings made in the Tower of London armoury.[41] He was then still a boy; and in the first years of the Pre-Raphaelite Brotherhood he kept off chivalric subjects, perhaps because he instinctively realised that they were not his forte. However, by 1856 chivalry had become so much the fashion among artists that he succumbed, and painted *Sir Isumbras at the Ford*. This shows a kindly knight who has taken two peasant children on his horse to give them a lift across a river. It was exhibited at the Academy in 1857, accompanied by some verses from a pseudo-mediaeval ballad by Thomas Taylor. The critics slaughtered it, largely because the horse was grotesquely too large for the knight. Frederick Sandys drew a caricature, in which the horse was changed to a donkey, and its

158

106. Sir John Everett Millais. *Sir Isumbras at the Ford*, 1857

three riders to Millais, Rossetti and Holman Hunt. The horse had to be repainted before the picture could find a buyer.[42]

In 1858 Millais started work on a picture to be called the *Crusader's Return* but never completed it. His *Joan of Arc*, exhibited at the Royal Academy in 1865, attracted little attention.[43] The *Knight-Errant* (Plate XIX), which followed in 1870, was as much a disaster as *Sir Isumbras*.[44] It aroused howls of protest, on the reasonable grounds that it was pornographic. Millais could not sell it, and had to hang it in his own house. As originally painted the woman was looking at the spectator; but Millais decided, as his son later put it, that 'the beautiful creature would look more modest if her head were turned away', and repainted it accordingly. In its new state he finally managed to sell it in 1874 to a dealer who resold it to Sir Henry Tate, the sugar magnate; it is now in the Tate Gallery. Millais painted no more chivalric subjects. His unfortunate essays in the genre suggest that basically he was not a chivalrous character: Holman Hunt said that he was the kind of man who always got other people to carry his parcels for him.[45]

A CLUTCH OF CASTLES

Chivalry in Victorian architecture was a different matter from chivalry in novels or pictures. Chivalry in novels did not necessarily imply mediaevalism; pictures of knights need not affect the life-style of their owners. But chivalry in architecture was hard to express except by building castles, and the temper of the times was increasingly against building castles for modern gentlemen. The bias of Victorian chivalry was towards absorbing the ideals of mediaeval chivalry into contemporary life, rather than trying to re-create it in something approaching the

159

108. East Horsley Towers, Surrey. Detail of the courtyard

mediaeval form. Nevertheless, castles continued to be built; but since their builders were pushing against the current their appearances were sporadic and largely unrelated.

The castle architecture of the mid and later nineteenth century includes the Duke of Northumberland's formidable remodelling of Alnwick Castle in 1854–65; the fortifications, gatehouses and moat added by the Earl of Lovelace to what then became Horsley Towers in 1855–60; Lord Beaumont's only partially completed transformation of Carlton Hall into Carlton Towers in 1873–7; Lord Bute's virtually total remodelling of Cardiff Castle in 1868–85 and rebuilding on the ruins of Castell Coch in 1872–9; and the Duke of Norfolk's visually sensational but perhaps not sensitive rebuilding at Arundel Castle in 1879–90.[40] Of these the work at Cardiff Castle and Castell Coch is much the most fascinating owing to the combination of Lord Bute's discrimination and immense wealth with the extraordinary talents of his architect, William Burges. But although themes and motifs drawn from mediaeval chivalry abound in the two buildings (Plate XX), they stand apart from the mainstream of Victorian chivalry, just as Burges as an architect and designer developed away from the mainstream of Victorian architecture.

An alternative to their overpowering mediaevalism was to keep the castle

109. (left) Killyleagh Castle, County Down, Ireland, as remodelled by Lanyon and Lynn, 1849–51

110. (below) Gilt spurs and roses paid as rent for the gatehouse

111. (bottom) The gatehouse, Killyleagh, by Benjamin Ferrey, c. 1858–60

elements to the silhouette, thus allowing a client with romantic tastes to both have his castle and live in it in contemporary comfort. Pugin had in effect done this in 1847–51 for the Earl of Shrewsbury, when he created the dramatic skyline of Alton Castle on the brow of a gorge in Staffordshire.[47] A rather similar efflorescence at the skyline has a similarly romantic effect at Killyleagh Castle, County Down, remodelled for Archibald Rowan Hamilton in 1849–51 by the Belfast architect Charles Lanyon. It is in fact an Ulster version of Scottish Baronial, a style which owed much of its popularity to its potential combination of comfort and romance. But to anyone concerned with the revival of chivalry the interest of Killyleagh lies less in the main building (splendid though that is) than in the curious story of the gatehouse.[48]

Owing to the freakish results of a will made in the seventeenth century the original castle and fortified bawn at Killyleagh had been split into two: the castle and half the bawn went to the Hamiltons, the other half and the gatehouse to the Blackwoods. In the early nineteenth century the Blackwoods built a sizeable house on the site of the gatehouse, and by doing so completely blocked the Hamilton's best view across the town to Strangford Lough. In 1841 the Blackwood portion was inherited by the fifth Lord Dufferin, the future Governor-General of Canada and Viceroy of India.

Lord Dufferin (whose aunt the Duchess of Somerset had been Queen of Beauty at the Eglinton Tournament) was addicted to romantic building projects, most of which, owing to his limited fortune, remained on paper. Two, however, came to fruition, Helen's Tower in the demesne of his own house at Clandeboye, and the new gatehouse at Killyleagh. Helen's Tower was designed in 1848, but begun much later and only completed in 1862. It was built as a symbol of the love between him and his mother. A room near the top of the tower was inscribed with poems expressive of this, written especially for the tower. That by Tennyson started:

> Helen's Tower here I stand
> Dominant over sea and land.
> Son's love built me, and I hold
> Mother's love in lettered gold.

At Killyleagh Lord Dufferin made the romantic gesture of demolishing the Blackwood house, building a Gothic gatehouse, towers and crenellated wall to replace it, and presenting the result to the Rowan Hamiltons. Although the gatehouse was built in about 1858–60, the formal deed of gift was not drawn up until 1869, by when Archibald Rowan Hamilton had died, and Lord Dufferin had married his daughter. In return for a lease of 999 years the Rowan Hamiltons were to present the Blackwoods with a yearly rent of 'one pair of silver spurs of the ordinary size, and of the value of £10 at the least, and a golden rose of like value, alternatively, the spurs one year and the rose the other'. The rent was to be paid on Christmas Eve, and be 'a memorial of the friendship' between the two families. It was paid in this form until 1914, and the resulting spurs and roses continue to be displayed on the Clandeboye dinner table on special occasions.[49]

162

112. (right) The Boer War Memorial, Clifton College, Bristol

CHAPTER 11

The
Public
Schools

IN 1829 THOMAS ARNOLD, THE HEADMASTER OF RUGBY, WROTE TO JULIUS Hare: 'If I were called upon to name what spirit of evil predominantly deserved the name of Antichrist, I should name the spirit of chivalry—the more detestable for the very guise of the "Archangel ruined" which has made it so seductive to the most generous spirits.'[1] In 1917 Sir Henry Newbolt described with approval (and complete lack of accuracy) how the public school 'has derived the housemaster from the knight, to whose castle boys were sent as pages; . . . prefects, from the senior squires; . . . and the love of games, the "sporting" or "amateur" view of them, from tournaments and the chivalric rules of war'.[2] By then chivalry was everywhere in public schools, and this kind of view was taken for granted. What had happened in the interval makes an instructive story.

The common belief that the public-school ethic emerged, like Minerva from the head of Jupiter, ready-made from the brain of Dr Arnold is exaggerated rather than absurd. Arnold did indeed exert a formidable influence, partly through his own example as headmaster of Rugby from 1827 to 1842, partly through the masters who served under him, and moved on to headmasterships at other public schools. In the eighteenth century schoolmasters had confined themselves to teaching and beating boys; Arnold tried to make them good as well. Not only did he carefully collect together a staff in sympathy with his aims; he selected sixth-formers with equal care, inspired them with his ideals, and aimed to form their characters by giving them the responsibility of running the school out of class.

But two elements which were to loom large in later Victorian public schools were entirely lacking in Arnold's Rugby. In the first place, though he was not against organised games, he took little interest in them, and would never have conceived of making them compulsory. Secondly, he showed active hostility to the idea of chivalry, because he thought that it set personal allegiances before God, and the concept of honour before that of justice.

Arnold died in 1842. Within forty years games were dominant and chivalry rampant in most public schools. The way things were going is shown in Edward FitzGerald's *Euphranor*, a dialogue on education published in 1851. *Euphranor* owed a good deal to Kenelm Digby and to FitzGerald's friend Carlyle, but as much or more to William Kenworthy Browne, with whom FitzGerald had first picked up acquaintance on a steam-packet to Tenby, when he was twenty-four and Browne sixteen. He became Browne's devoted friend and admirer. FitzGerald was short-sighted and physically clumsy, but Browne grew up an enthusiastic hunter and angler, an active squire, a captain in the Militia, 'quick to love and quick to fight—full of confidence, generosity and the glorious spirit of Youth'.[3] *Euphranor* was concerned with devising a system of education which would produce more Brownes.

It takes the form of a dialogue between the narrator ('the Doctor') and four undergraduates: Euphranor, Lexilogus, Lycion and Phidippus. Euphranor is reading *Godefridus*, the first volume of *The Broad Stone of Honour*. Digby's definition of chivalry, and his contention that it is permanently valid as 'the state of mind which disposes men to heroic and generous actions', is read and approved; so is his association of chivalry with youth. It is agreed that, if possible, men ought to be so imbued with ardour when young that age and experience 'should serve not to freeze, but to direct, the genial current of the Soul'. The talk then moves on to education, and the Doctor argues for the importance of training the body, so as to provide the soul with 'a spacious, airy, and wholesome tenement becoming so Divine a Tenant'. He suggests compulsory gymnastics, military drill and manoeuvres, working the land or grooming a horse as ways of strengthening the will and acquiring a 'sense of Order, Self-restraint, and Mutual Dependence'. In addition, cricket, boxing and similar sports instil presence of mind, a 'habitual Instinct of Courage, Resolution, and Decision', and 'the Good Humour which good animal Condition goes so far to ensure'. Eton is praised for teaching its boys 'to sublime their Beefsteak into Chivalry in that famous Cricket-field of theirs by the side of old Father Thames murmuring of so many Generations of chivalric Ancestors'. Although Euphranor makes fun of the idea of 'turning out the young Knight from Cricket on the World', the Doctor contends that there is no reason why such a young man should not prove worthy of the Round Table and quotes Tennyson's 'Morte d'Arthur' about Arthur returning as a 'modern gentleman'. The dialogue finally ends as the party watch the college boat races: 'and suddenly the head of the first boat turn'd the corner; and then another close upon it; and then a third; the crews pulling with all their might compacted with perfect rhythm'—visual demonstration of what the Doctor had been getting at.[4]

In 1852, the year after *Euphranor* was published, G. E. L. Cotton went from Rugby to become the second headmaster of Marlborough. Marlborough, which had been founded in 1843, had got off to a bad start. A feeble headmaster, a brutal staff and appalling living conditions had led to a mass rebellion in 1851; the whole school ran berserk for a week. Cotton transformed it. He used two tried Arnoldian methods: he established a responsible sixth form and recruited a 'devoted band of young men' as masters. But, in addition, as the school historian puts it, 'the organization of games which was due to his initiation was in some ways a still more potent factor . . . a civilized out-of-door life in the form of cricket, football, and wholesome sports, took the place of poaching, rat-hunting and poultry-stealing'.[5] Cotton was totally unathletic himself, but he took care that his young men (one of whom was the future Dean Farrar, of *Eric or Little by Little*) were athletes as well as scholars.

Previously, public-school games had just been one of the ways in which boys occupied their time out of school. Matches between schools had been organised by the boys, and headmasters had often tried to prevent them, as an unsettling influence. For a headmaster actively to encourage games as a means of improving the character of his boys was something new. It was the result of a changing climate, to which *The Broad Stone of Honour*, Carlyle, *Euphranor* and a growing cult of games at the universities had all contributed. But perhaps the most important influence was that of Hughes's and Kingsley's muscular Christianity.

The two men's involvement with Christian Socialism helped bring their influence to the public schools. The movement's Council of Promoters had included William Johnson, who taught at Eton, and G. G. Bradley, who taught at Rugby and was an intimate friend of Cotton, the new headmaster at Marlborough;[6] moreover, Cotton had been Thomas Hughes's tutor at Rugby. What Kenworth Browne was to *Euphranor* and to Edward FitzGerald, Hughes was to the whole Christian Socialist movement. He was much the youngest of its leaders—only twenty-five when the movement started in 1848—and he seemed to the others the epitome of what a young, ardent, Christian gentleman should be. In 1857 he produced his own view of the point of a public school in *Tom Brown's Schooldays*. *Euphranor* had gone into two editions, enough to exert an influence upon a small group of thinking men of the time; but *Tom Brown's Schooldays* went into at least fifty different editions and reprints by the end of the century, and was read by grown-ups and schoolboys all over the world.

Hughes overlaid his vivid memories of his own experiences at Rugby with the philosophy of life which he had evolved in the fifteen years since he had left it. It was a philosophy that owed much to Carlyle: life was a constant fight between good and evil; strength of intellect was useless and even dangerous without strength of character. But *Tom Brown's Schooldays*, like other writings of Hughes and Kingsley, went far beyond Carlyle in suggesting that the best way to moral prowess was physical prowess, in actual fighting or in sport.

Hughes lumped moral and physical fighting together in one of the frequent asides which pepper the book. 'From the cradle to the grave, fighting, rightly understood, is the business, the real highest, honestest business of every son of man. Everyone who is worth his salt has his enemies, who must be beaten, be they evil thoughts and habits in himself or spiritual wickednesses in high places, or Russians, or Border-ruffians.'[7] The theme of the book is how Tom Brown, a strong, brave boy with an inherited instinct to stick up for the underdog, is saved by Dr Arnold from becoming just a young tough and enrolled in the 'band of brothers'[8] who use their toughness to fight for God. As his character develops he proves himself, not just by prowess at football and cricket, by bravely enduring bullying and finally doing down the bully, and by sticking up for a smaller boy in a knock-down fight with 'Slogger' Williams (although these and similar episodes occupy the greater part of the book); he also kneels down to say his prayers in a hostile dormitory, looks after and encourages clever but sickly little George Arthur, and finally (hardest of all) gives up the use of cribs in class.

But he gives up cribs so as not to deceive Dr Arnold, not because he wants to learn Greek and Latin properly. Although George Arthur is allowed to be clever (but Tom Brown teaches him to be good at games too) and Martin, who makes stinks in his study and knows all about birds and lizards, is depicted as an engaging if eccentric character, the space given to any form of intellectual activity is minimal. Squire Brown, when sending Tom to Rugby, ruminates 'I don't care a straw for Greek particles and the digamma . . . If he'll only turn out a brave, helpful, truth-telling Englishman, and a gentleman, and a Christian, that's all I want.'[9] Brooke, the head of School House, is enthusiastically cheered when he declares, 'I know I'd sooner win two School-house matches running, than get the Balliol scholarship any way.'[10] Tom, in mid-career at school, announces his ambitions: 'I want to be A1 at cricket and football, and all the other games, and to

CHAPTER VII

HARRY EAST'S DILEMMAS AND DELIVERANCES

"The Holy Supper is kept indeed,
In whatso we share with another's need—
Not that which we give, but what we share
For the gift without the giver is bare :
Who bestows himself with his alms feeds three,
Himself, his hungering neighbour, and Me."
LOWELL, *The Vision of Sir Launfal*, p. 11.

THE next morning, after breakfast, Tom, East, and Gower met as usual to learn their second lesson together. Tom had been considering how to break his proposal of giving up the crib to the others, and having found no better way (as indeed none better can ever be found by man or boy), told them simply what had happened; how he had been to see Arthur, who had talked to him upon the subject, and what he had said, and for his part he had made up his mind, and wasn't going to use cribs any more : and not being quite sure of his ground, took the high and pathetic tone, and was proceeding to say, "how that having learnt his lessons with them for so many years, it would grieve him much to put an end to the arrangement, and he hoped at any

TOM'S VISIT TO THE TOMB OF DR. ARNOLD.

113, 114. Two illustrations made by Arthur Hughes for the 1869 edition of *Tom Brown's Schooldays*

make my hands keep my head against any fellow, lout or gentleman. I want to get into the sixth before I leave, and to please the Doctor; and I want to carry away just as much Latin and Greek as will take me through Oxford respectably . . . I want to leave behind me the name of a fellow who never bullied a little boy, or turned his back on a big one.'[11] Nowhere is it suggested that these points of view are possibly limited.

In another passage Brooke explains why 'the dear old School-house—the best house of the best school in England'—has won its match : 'It's because we've more reliance on one another, more of a house feeling, more fellowship.'[12] Games are valuable, it is made clear, not just because they encourage individual bravery and determination, but because they teach leadership and fellowship. A sympathetic 'Young master' (who in fact was based on Cotton of Marlborough) expands on this when watching a cricket match : 'The discipline and reliance on one another which it teaches is so valuable, I think . . . It ought to be such an unselfish game. It merges the individual in the eleven; he doesn't play that he may win, but that his side may . . . And then the Captain of the eleven! what a post is his in our School-world! almost as hard as the Doctor's; requiring skill and gentleness and firmness, and I know not what other rare qualities.'[13]

The young master surmises that, under the doctor, 'perhaps ours is the only little corner of the British Empire which is thoroughly wisely and strongly ruled just now'. Young Rugbeians, one feels, will learn from the doctor and the cricket field how to be wise and strong, and go out to rule the Empire properly. Tom's friend East does in fact join the Indian Army and is likely to make a capital officer: 'no fellow could handle boys better, and I suppose soldiers are very like boys'. Other Rugbeians are heading for jobs in 'country curacies, London chambers, under the Indian sun, and in Australian towns and clearings'.[14] Tom himself is the son of a Tory squire; Browns have been soldiers, lawyers and clergymen. Trade and industry are never mentioned in connection with either the Browns or Rugby boys.

Although passages in *Tom Brown's Schooldays* are reminiscent of Digby's views as to the qualities and occupations suitable for a gentleman, and FitzGerald's as to how he should be educated, the language of chivalry never obtrudes into the cheerful mixture of slang and breeziness in which the book is written; only occasionally, in terms such as 'fellowship' and 'band of brothers', does one sense it. But in the illustrated edition which first appeared in 1869, the chivalric implications of the book are allowed to surface in two illustrations by Arthur Hughes. The initial letter at the beginning of the chapter in which Tom fights against cribbing depicts him as a young knight kneeling in prayer. In the final illustration, *Tom's visit to the Tomb of Dr Arnold*, Tom, now a young undergraduate, has hurried back from a holiday in Scotland on hearing of Arnold's death, and is standing by his tomb in Rugby chapel. He is of course in ordinary dress. But the rug over his shoulder suggests a military cloak; and his attitude—pensive, bareheaded, one leg forward—is in the tradition of West's Black Prince and Watts's recent Sir Galahad. He is a young knight in mufti, keeping vigil before entering on the battles of life.

From the 1850s onwards Cotton's example at Marlborough and the attitude expressed in *Tom Brown's Schooldays* began to spread to other public schools; and many new schools were founded in the same image. Rugby, not surprisingly, was one of the first to change; moreover Rugby was still exporting headmasters, who now tended to be as much disciples of muscular Christianity as of Arnold. Bradley succeeded Perceval at Marlborough in 1858, Perceval went to Clifton in 1862, Potts to Fettes in 1870, Hart to Sedbergh in 1880.[15] Wellington was founded in 1859, and from the start Kingsley exerted a great influence there. His son was one of the first pupils, his rectory was only a few miles away and the headmaster, E. F. Benson (another Rugby export), was a close personal friend.

Games were now enthusiastically furthered by headmasters and their staff, as a means towards training character. The inevitable end was that they became compulsory. By the end of the 1870s compulsory games were the rule rather than

the exception. By the 1880s it could be said of Hart at Sedbergh that 'character more than scholarship was the aim of his teaching':[15] in effect games were more important than work.

In 1876 an article in the *Marlburian* stated that 'a truly chivalrous football player . . . was never yet guilty of lying, or deceit, or meanness, whether of word or action.'[17] Chivalry was much in the air in the public schools of those days. Actual knights in armour appear as school trophies, and abound in the form of statues (Plate XXVI) or stained-glass figures, especially as memorials to the Crimean, Boer or Great Wars. Although the figures are usually ostensibly St Georges or St Michaels, the faces that look out from under the helmets tend to be those of Victorian public-school boys. Gareth, the young man who had earned his knighthood by uncomplaining service and had been the hero of one of Tennyson's *Idylls of the King*, was installed in stained glass on the main staircase of Glenalmond.[18] In school magazines, the articles interspersed among the ever-increasing accounts of school games include ones on muscular Christianity, Kingsley, King Arthur, Tennyson's *Idylls*, chivalry, and the *Niebelungenlied*.

115. (left and right) Great War memorial windows showing King Arthur and Sir Galahad in Clifton College chapel

116. (centre) The Bell Trophy, Marlborough College, Wiltshire

An alternative to the knight almost inevitably appeared as well: the Greek god or hero. In the school magazines poems on Theseus or Thermopylae rub shoulders with those on Agincourt or Camelot. *The Broad Stone of Honour* had long since pointed out the chivalric elements in Greek life and literature. In one of his most popular books, *The Heroes* (1856), Kingsley retold the stories of Perseus, Theseus and Jason: two Greek heroes who rescued maidens in distress, and one who went on a quest. Public schools, now that their time was largely divided between the study of the classics and the cult of athletics, were bound to be attracted to Greece.

The catch to the Greeks of course, apart from their paganism, was their attitude to sex. But most Victorians of the period accepted and even admired Greek ideas of male friendship, as long as they did not go too far. Love between men or boys, and men and boys, was beautiful and praiseworthy; sex was disgusting. In a school context many schoolmasters were extraordinarily naïve about the dangers of love crossing over into sex, until experience disillusioned them. The contrast between the ideal and reality imposed considerable strains, especially on those who were either consciously or unconsciously homosexual. As public-school life was now anyway conducted on a plane of constant moral struggle, most Victorian schoolmasters found it hard to relax. Life was a continuous fight with sin, and one of the ways to keep the body under control was by hardship and physical exercise. Cold dips at dawn (and breaking of the ice if necessary) combined with endless games to keep them and the boys busy out of school. In the holidays they climbed mountains (preferably the Alps) or went on bicycle tours or thirty-mile tramps from church to church, or battlefield to battlefield.

Typically, they also read Carlyle, did social work in the slums, and were rather more radical than their pupils, as Arnold had been before them. Many of them were very able. It is easy to make fun of Victorian public schools, especially if one looks at them in the years around 1900. In the years around 1870 they were often exciting places. Clever, energetic and idealistic young men were attracted to teach in them in large numbers. Muscularity was only part of their creed, and, to begin with especially, it was kept under control. To train the body and will as well as the mind, to inspire boys to think of something more than themselves was not, after all, an entirely ignoble ideal.

By the 1890s J. H. Skrine, the Warden of Trinity College, Glenalmond, could write about public-school systems with an edge of criticism, but still with enthusiasm. 'Yes, it is the knightly life once more, with its virtues and its perversions . . . with the narrowness, the pride of caste, the soldier scorn of books and of industry which is not of the open air, as war, the chase, the game . . . But, with all its glory and its faults, chivalry it is again, and that is the reason why the life of the school has romance.'[19] Glenalmond was full of chivalry, but so, for that matter, were almost all British public schools in the second half of the nineteenth century. The material is so over-abundant that it is perhaps best to concentrate on two examples, one old and one new: Eton College, founded by Henry VI in 1440, and Clifton College, founded on the outskirts of Bristol in 1862.

117. Detail from the memorial window, Trinity College, Glenalmond, showing scenes from Tennyson's *Gareth and Lynette*, c. 1890

Public-school chivalry is still much in evidence at Clifton. The court between its cricket fields and high range of formidably Gothic buildings is dominated by the figure of a knight in armour, erected as a Boer War Memorial in 1904. Inside the chapel, knightly figures in stained glass abound as mementoes of the Boer and later wars: Joan of Arc, the Black Prince, various St Michaels and St Georges and even King Arthur and Sir Galahad (Plate 115). In his poem on Clifton Chapel Sir Henry Newbolt urged Clifton boys

> To set the cause above renown,
> To love the game beyond the prize,
> To honour, while you strike him down,
> The foe that comes with fearless eyes.

Newbolt was at Clifton from 1867 to 1881 and already as a schoolboy was writing poems on Camelot and Tintagel for the school magazine.[20] Although the visible symbols of chivalry at Clifton date from after 1900, chivalry played an important part in its code from the days when John Perceval came from Rugby to be its first headmaster in 1862.

Perceval was a formidable but also a curiously lovable man: formidable because of his huge size, craggy features, vibrant Westmorland accent and the intensity with which he drove masters and boys harder than most of them could stand; lovable because he was so patently a good man, who loved his school and cared passionately about the welfare of everyone in it.

He was inspired by a vision of creative conformity. Whenever people worked together in a unified body, he believed that 'a certain infection of nature which goes from man to man as if by some chemical process' would make the whole greater than the parts.[21] A public school and its house system could produce the same kind of intense loyalty and patriotism which had flourished in the old city-states, but which the size and complexity of England and its empire tended to discourage.[22] Such loyalty was admirable, as long as it was infused with Christian ideals of worship and service. Sustained by pride, loyalty, and high purpose, the school was to march forward shoulder to shoulder, a united army of the Lord.

An army needs leaders, and Perceval had a gift for picking an able and dedicated staff. Among its members were T. E. Brown, whose poems in Manx dialect are among the lesser classics of Victorian literature; Graham Dakyns, who had been the much-loved tutor of Tennyson's children, and of whom Emily Tennyson wrote that 'he is still to us what no one else is, almost';[23] W. W. Asquith, the elder brother of the Prime Minister;[24] and John Addington Symonds, who taught on and off at Clifton as a young man, before he made his name with his seven-volume *History of the Renaissance in Italy*. Many of the masters had, like Perceval himself, radical and reforming views inspired by Arnold, Carlyle and Christian Socialism. Perceval started one of the first public-school missions, to a poor area of Bristol, and did his best (without conspicuous success) to encourage Cliftonians to become involved in it and similar organisations.[25] Typical old Cliftonians were more likely (with Perceval's entire approval) to be in the army or the colonial service, working loyally for little financial return in remote parts of the Empire. Some inevitably went into business, for, apart from anything else, Clifton drew heavily on the sons of Bristol businessmen. But 'trade and business and money-making generally were looked at rather askance by Perceval, and by very high-minded Cliftonians who accepted his ideals'.[26]

Compulsory uniform and compulsory games came to the school at about the same time, in the early 1870s. For Clifton, uniform was 'the outward and visible sign of that uniformity of spirit of which it was so proud'.[27] As for games, Perceval believed in them not only because they developed manliness (about which he felt as fervently as any Victorian headmaster), but because they encouraged school pride and loyalty. The cult of games at Clifton was carried to extreme limits. According to Henry Newbolt, 'there were very few members of the school who would not have bartered away all chance of intellectual distinction for a place in the Cricket Eleven or Football Fifteen'. Newbolt recognised the dangers of this, but thought it was worth it. 'The consciousness of belonging to a militant fellowship was exhilarating and sustaining, and a great part of our happiness came from it. The days of our youth are the days of our glory.'[28] In his semi-autobiographical novel *Twymans* he describes the effect the cricket field at Clifton had on him when he first came there as a new boy and saw 'a multitude of white figures, standing, running walking, bowling, throwing, batting . . . Something broke over his spirit like a wave: he took it for the tide of joyful anticipation, but I think it was more than that . . . a glimpse, behind the mere beauty of the white young figures shining so coolly in the slant evening sunlight, of the finely planned order and long-descended discipline it symbolized.'[29]

Perceval managed to instil similar feelings of romanticism and excitement into a high proportion of his masters and boys. They could move easily enough from cricket to chivalry. According to Newbolt's contemporary Herbert Warren, 'it seemed to us no less than the dawn of a new age, the creation of something which, while like, was yet unlike any school that had gone before. Outside the school the age was one of optimism, of eager chivalries and idealisms. It was the time when Tennyson was completing the "Idylls of the King" . . . Whatever may be felt about them now, these "Idylls" had an immense influence upon us as boys at the time. The contrasted knightly types, Galahad, Percivale, Lancelot, Bors, the sage Merlin, above all King Arthur himself, were very much to us. Side by side with Homer and Greek history, they gave us our standards. We saw them in our Head, in our Masters, and in our comrades.'[30]

Warren was reminiscing in middle age, but contemporary sources bear him out. Early numbers of the *Cliftonian* are full of chivalry. Perceval himself named two of his sons Arthur and Lancelot, and in one of his sermons urged 'the new chivalry of personal purity and the suppression of the baser animal appetites'.[31] Among the masters, Charles Hope Cay, who died at the age of twenty-eight, was described by Perceval as 'the singularly pure and chivalrous master whose life burnt out so quickly in the service of our young society'. Of F. M. Bartholomew, who was thought to be the closest in character to Perceval among the masters, it was said that 'in appearance and character he was like a knight of the age of chivalry'. Of J. G. Grenfell, T. E. Brown wrote, 'Did you ever meet a Paladin like Grenfell? Gentle and faithful, unselfish, and of the purest chalybean, stainless and pure.' W. O. Moberley was compared by Canon Glazebrook (who became headmaster in 1891) to Sir Bors of the Round Table.[32]

And then, among the boys, there was Cecil Boyle: Boyle of the aristocratic connections (a rarity at Clifton) and splendid good looks, Boyle who was a superb cricketer, whom his house and the school adored (and Symonds and Dakyns loved rather too well), 'strenuous in work as in games, patient of reasonable discipline, kind to the least conspicuous of his school fellows, courteous to all'.[33] In 1871 Symonds found him 'as resplendent as a young paladin on the Crusades'. 'Good Knight!' he wrote to him when he left Clifton in 1872, 'to whom God has given strength, and with it gentleness and anger. Use these rightly and be always the nobleman you ought to be!'[34]

Boyle over-excited Clifton, which seems to have seen him as its answer to Eton heroes such as the Lytteltons; in fact his surviving letters suggest that his character was much less splendid than his physique.[35] In later life he disappointed his admirers by becoming a stockbroker. However, on the outbreak of the Boer War he rushed to join the Imperial Yeomanry, and was the first of his regiment to be killed.[36] He had vindicated himself. Herbert Warren wrote a memorial poem in the *Spectator*:

> Life's business came, you passed into the stress
> Of gainful rivalry, and 'Lost' we cried . . .
>
> Not so. Through lulling ease alert and trained
> You kept your manhood's force and your desire;
> Still quick, though slumbering, in your breast remained
> The seed of sacred fire.[37]

Patriotism was one of the qualities which Clifton was proud to instil in its members; three hundred of its old boys served in the Boer War, and forty-four were killed or died as a result of it. Inevitably there was a war memorial, and much discussion as to what form this should take. Two rival groups formed, one wanting an officer in khaki, the other a knight in armour.[38] The knight won, and was duly produced by the sculptor Alfred Drury (Plate 112). The choice was surely the right one, for the resulting young man (ostensibly St George) standing high on his pedestal and looking towards South Africa over the cricket fields epitomizes everything that Clifton of those years stood for.

Did the spirit of mid and late Victorian Eton differ substantially from that of Clifton? Inevitably its age and great social prestige set it a little apart from other public schools. It was a training-ground for stars: a proportion of its boys were certain to end up as cabinet ministers, viceroys, ambassadors or field marshals. Accordingly, it perhaps tended a little more to develop boys as individuals, rather than as members of a team. The master who established warm (sometimes too warm) personal relationships with individual boys was a distinctive new feature of most Victorian public schools. But at schools like Clifton he appeared in spite of, rather than because of, the system; at Eton there was more place for him.

The most famous Eton example of the type was William Johnson (better known today as Johnson Cory), who was a master there from 1845 until 1872. When reading his journals and letters, or his pupils' memories of him, it is hard not to become attached to this short-sighted, intelligent and affectionate man.[39] He joked and laughed with his boys, shouted abuse at them, lent them his books, took them riding or boating and taught them everything which interested him, whether it was in the curriculum or not. With loving myopia he blinked at the blurred images of his especial friends, on the river or cricket field. For although he had a genius for teaching boys of all kinds, there was a particular type—'the bold, gay, confident, alert and beautiful', as a former pupil put it—with whom he regularly fell in love.[40] His favourites included a number who were later famous: Dalmeny, who was to become Lord Rosebery and Prime Minister; Reginald Brett, who as Lord Esher was the *eminence grise* of Edwardian politics; the future Lord Halifax, Chancellor of the Exchequer and Secretary of State for India; and the Lyttelton brothers, who were not only superb sportsmen but included a future Colonial Secretary, Eton headmaster, bishop and Commander-in-chief.

Like many Victorian schoolmasters Johnson was more radical than the majority of his pupils and their parents. He ended up an agnostic and republican; as a young man he was an enthusiastic supporter of the Christian Socialists, sat for a time on their Committee of Promoters, wrote for their periodicals and lectured at the Working Men's College.[41] Among his fellow Christian Socialists he found Thomas Hughes especially sympathetic; he seems to have had reservations about Kingsley.[42]

Almost inevitably he was attracted to the concept of chivalry, and even gave a series of lectures on it.[43] But he was an individualist: he worked out his own views on the subject. In the 1840s he had read *The Broad Stone of Honour* and for a time was set on fire by it;[44] but he came to think that Digby had been much too starry-eyed about the Middle Ages, that the chivalry of mediaeval tournaments and romances bore little relationship to the behaviour of mediaeval knights, and that 'the courteous treatment of (1) women, (2) captives, (3) enemies is hardly to be found in mediaeval history'. Chivalry, in his view, derived from the Greeks and

174

Romans, was essentially a literary concept in the Middle Ages, and only really started to affect practical conduct in the sixteenth century: 'Bayard was the first rather than the last of true knights.'[45] He found chivalry in Shakespeare, in Sidney, in the Civil War, and in the code of the professional officer as it solidified in the eighteenth century and survived to his own day. Like his boyhood hero Walter Scott he loved soldiers, glory and the Empire. 'Brats, the British Army', he would shout if a detachment marched by; immediately the whole class would clatter into the street, and Johnson would stand on the pavement with eyes closed and hands folded until the soldiers had passed.[46]

He was as enthusiastic over sport as soldiering, probably for the same mixture of reasons: he was attracted to brave, active and ardent men and boys, and because of his sight could never join their number. He was one of the first Eton masters actively to encourage school games. In 1860 he helped revive Eton cricket by presenting an inter-house cricket cup; he wrote a poem in praise of the school Volunteers; more memorably, in 1863 he wrote the 'Eton Boating Song'.[47] There was an edge of melancholy to Johnson's sentiment, and both were expressed in his poems. His beloved boys were Greek heroes or young knights, preparing for an active life in which he could take no part.

> I shall not tread thy battlefield,
> Nor see the blazon on thy shield;
> Take thou the sword I could not wield
> And leave me, and forget,

he wrote in 'A New Year's Day'; and in 'Academus',

> I cheer the games I cannot play;
> As stands a crippled squire
> To watch his master through the fray,
> Uplifted by desire.[48]

There is no evidence that desire carried him across the acceptable Victorian boundaries until 1872. In that year something happened; a parent made a fuss; Johnson left Eton, resigned his King's College fellowship, and changed his name from Johnson to Cory. His last years were devoted, with considerable success, to tutoring clever young girls in Hampstead.

To some extent his position at Eton was taken by his younger friend H. E. Luxmoore.[49] Luxmoore was a less emotional character, or at least kept his emotions under control: but he exerted a strong influence on a certain type of intelligent and sensitive boy. He was more interested in the arts than Johnson; as a young man he became an enthusiastic admirer of William Morris and the Pre-Raphaelites, and later he was to present Eton with the Burne-Jones tapestry that now hangs at the east end of the chapel. He was equally enthusiastic about Watts. After Watts's first public exhibition in 1882 he wrote to ask if the *Sir Galahad* exhibited there was available for Eton; but it was not. He wrote again after the Watts exhibition of 1897. Watts found an unfinished study, worked it up, and presented it to the school, where it was hung in the chapel.

'I think', he wrote to Luxmoore, 'it may be of use as a peg whereon to hang an occasional little discourse . . . upon the dignity and beauty of purity and chivalry, which things should be the characteristic of the gentleman, probably with more effect and brought more home to the minds of the youth hereafter to have so much to do with the Government and character of the Nation than by cut and dried lectures.'[50] Luxmoore used to give prints of *Sir Galahad* to selected boys when they left Eton (Plate XXV). In January 1900 he described to Watts how 'I have this very morning a letter from a heartbroken mother whose boy (only child) was shot last week in Ladysmith. She says "His favourite picture was the one you gave him . . . he also was an innocent knight."'[51]

But masters like Johnson and Luxmoore were in a minority, even at Eton. Masters in the mould of Edmond Warre who, as one of his successors put it, 'cared more for the whole than the individual'[52] were much more typical. Warre was a housemaster at Eton from 1861, headmaster from 1884 to 1905, and Provost from 1909 to 1918. He was a big man, and the energy and strength of character which he exuded made him seem bigger; when he sailed into a room, gown flowing behind him, 'he seemed hardly mortal in his bigness'.[53] He had been a rowing-blue at Oxford; at Eton he virtually created rowing as an organised sport. He was equally enthusiastic in establishing the Eton Volunteer Corps, and in promoting what later became the Officer Training Corps in public schools all over England. One of the boys in his house compared him to a mixture of Kingsley's Amyas Leigh, Scott's Front-de Boeuf and Bunyan's Mr Greatheart. In visual matters he was completely Philistine. In literature he distrusted Browning and was a fervent admirer of Tennyson, whom he once persuaded to read the manuscript of 'The Holy Grail' in an Eton garden.

In spite of their different styles (which prevented any kind of friendship between them) Warre had a good deal in common with Johnson and Luxmoore. All three admired and supported the British Empire, the military virtues and the cult of games. All three sympathised with ideals of service of the kind advocated by Christian Socialism; Warre and Luxmoore were among the main founders and supporters of the Eton Mission to the East End of London at Hackney Wick. Between them they helped to establish the Eton of the years around 1900 in which the Lyttelton mixture of sport and public service seemed to epitomize the ideal of the English gentleman; patriotism was virtually exalted into a religion; and to die for one's country was the supreme sacrifice.

Clifton subscribed to the same ideals; the proportions of its mixture may have been different but the elements were much the same. Eton chapel had Sir Galahad in oil, Clifton chapel had him in stained glass. Eton produced Field Marshal Earl Roberts, Clifton produced Field Marshal Earl Haig. Johnson swooned over Rosebery at Eton a few years before Dakyns swooned over Boyle at Clifton. Eton boys swung together in Johnson's 'Boating Song'; Clifton boys thundered towards the twilight goal in Newbolt's 'The Best School of All'. Indeed, if one looks beyond Eton and Clifton to the whole formidable corpus of late Victorian public schools, however considerable the differences between them in style or background, the resemblances seem even greater.

176

118. (right) Arthur Hughes. *Sir Galahad* (detail)

CHAPTER 12

The
Return
of
Arthur

Interest in Arthur and his knights rose and fell, not surprisingly, with interest in chivalry. Malory's *Morte d'Arthur* went out of print a few years after the last tournament and a few years before Milton finally rejected the possibility of writing an Arthurian epic in favour of *Paradise Lost*.[1] For over a hundred years Arthur made no more than occasional, and not very significant, appearances.[2] His rehabilitation only really got under way with Walter Scott. As early as 1792 Scott was making notes on the *Morte d'Arthur*.[3] He introduced references to Sir Lancelot and the Holy Grail into the first canto of *Marmion* (1808), and supported them in the footnotes with long extracts from Malory; 'many of the wild adventures which it contains', he remarked, 'are told with simplicity bordering upon the sublime.' The best part of *The Bridal of Triermain* (1813) is 'Lyulph's Tale' about King Arthur; in it Sir Galahad makes probably the first of his innumerable nineteenth-century appearances.

> There Galahad sate with manly grace
> Yet maiden meekness in his face.[4]

When Washington Irving visited Abbotsford in 1817, one evening passed in Scott's reading 'from the old Romance of Arthur, with a fine deep sonorous voice'.[5] By then there were three new editions of Malory in print, two pocket-sized reprints published in 1816, and the extremely handsome edition produced with an introduction and copious notes by Robert Southey in 1817. In 1805 Scott's friend George Ellis had already published modern versions of the romances of *Merlin* and the *Morte d'Arthur* in his *Specimens of Early English Metrical Romance*; the latter (quite distinct from Malory's) was edited for the Roxburghe Club in 1819. Original Arthurian material was now easily available. One of the 1816 editions of Malory was in the rectory library at Somersby, and Tennyson almost certainly read it there as a boy in the 1820s.[6] Meanwhile, from 1822 onwards, Digby was freely quoting and drawing examples from Malory in the various editions of his *Broad Stone of Honour*.

In 1832–4 Tennyson produced his first crop of Arthurian poems: 'The Lady of Shalott', 'Sir Launcelot and Queen Guinevere', of which only fragments survive, the 'Morte d'Arthur' and 'Sir Galahad'. Of these only 'The Lady of Shalott' was ready in time for his 1832 volume of poems. Then in 1837 Lady Charlotte Guest, the wife of Sir John Guest, the self-made maestro of the Dowlais Ironworks in South Wales, was encouraged by a hint in Southey's edition of Malory and by her own residence in Wales to translate *The Mabinogion*, the main Welsh collection of Arthurian legends. This remarkable young lady of twenty-five taught herself Welsh and, in the intervals of London social life, childbearing and keeping the accounts of her husband's ironworks, produced a translation in seven volumes. The first came out in 1838, the seventh in 1849; little Arthur Guest, born in 1841, arrived between the third and fourth volumes, and Enid, born in 1843, coincided with the fifth one.[7]

In 1842 Tennyson's 'Sir Launcelot and Queen Guinevere', 'Morte d'Arthur' and 'Sir Galahad' first appeared in print. In the same year S. C. Hall's *Book of British Ballads* included two Arthurian ballads, illustrated by John Franklin. But many

people still considered King Arthur a somewhat bizarre subject. Mediaeval history was by now completely acceptable, but mediaeval romance was not. In an endeavour to make the 'Morte d'Arthur' palatable for his 1842 volume, Tennyson inserted it into a new setting, 'The Epic' (probably written in 1837–8). It now became a story told in a Victorian house on Christmas Eve; Edward FitzGerald thought that this was done 'to give reason for telling an old-world Fairy-tale'.[8] None the less John Sterling, reviewing it in the *Quarterly*, dampingly remarked, 'the miraculous legend of "Excalibur" does not come very near to us, and as reproduced by any modern writer must be a mere ingenious exercise of fancy'.[9] Tennyson took this so much to heart (Sterling was a personal friend) that he abandoned his plan to write the Arthurian epic for which he had already drafted out a structure. The first Victorian epic on Arthur to be published was, as a result, Lytton's *King Arthur* (1848). But Lytton's epic bore little relation to Malory, or any other mediaeval source; he took over some of the traditional Arthurian characters and gave them new adventures, mainly in Switzerland and among polar bears and Eskimos in the Arctic. The result, much to Lytton's chagrin, was a complete flop.[10]

The first Arthurian cycle actually based on the legends to come to fruition took the form of painting rather than poetry. Dyce's frecoes for the Queen's Robing Room in the Palace of Westminster were decided on in 1847 and painted between 1849 and 1862; owing to Dyce's death in the latter year, only five of the seven projected paintings were completed. None the less the official adoption of the Arthurian cycle as a worthy subject for a major room in the most important new building in the kingdom, and the Prince Consort's enthusiastic backing of the project, made it clear that Arthur had well and truly returned at last.

179

119. William Dyce. *Religion: The Vision of Sir Galahad and his Company*, 1849–51

The 1850s were, indeed, studded with Arthurian projects. Matthew Arnold's 'Tristram and Iseult' (which Arnold probably started in 1849) was published in 1852 and republished in 1853. Charlotte M. Yonge's *Heir of Redclyffe*, with its many Arthurian allusions and hero modelling for Sir Galahad, came out in 1853. Tennyson began his first four *Idylls of the King* in 1855 and published them in 1859. Watts probably started studies for *Sir Galahad* in 1855 or soon afterwards. Almost all Rossetti's Arthurian paintings date from between 1855 and 1859. Moxon's illustrated Tennyson, containing Arthurian engravings by Holman Hunt, Rossetti and Maclise came out in 1857. The Oxford Union was decorated in 1857–8 with Arthurian paintings by Rossetti, Burne-Jones, Morris, Val Prinsep, Spencer Stanhope and Hungerford Pollen (with a sculptured entrance tympanum by Alexander Munro). Morris was painting a small group of Arthurian paintings in the same years and published *The Defence of Guenevere* in 1858. In that year Thomas Wright produced a new edition of Malory's *Morte d'Arthur*. The extent to which Arthurianism was in the air is shown by the fact that in 1857 a tough middle-brow novelist like G. A. Lawrence could quote at length from Malory in *Guy Livingstone*, and suggest that his hero was a modern Sir Lancelot.

Roughly speaking, attitudes to the Arthurian story in the mid-nineteenth century divide into two groups, one moral and the other romantic. The romantics read Malory and were deeply moved and excited by the vividness of his stories of love, quests, fighting and marvels. The moralists saw Arthur and his knights as epitomizing (at their best) virtues which were still valid as a source of moral lessons for contemporary life. The moral school might be described as Tennysonian, and the romantic as Pre-Raphaelite, except that Tennyson's approach in his four early Arthurian poems of 1832–4 was largely a romantic one.

Although there are moral elements in both 'Sir Galahad' and the 'Morte d'Arthur' they are chiefly memorable as a series of vivid images. Purity, and indeed virginity, were popular subjects of discussion in the 1830s; it was at this time, for instance, that Richard Hurrell Froude was urging 'the severe idea of virginity' on his friends in the Oxford Movement.[11] But Tennyson gives the impression of being attracted to Sir Galahad's purity less for its moral implications than as one extreme of knight-errantry, the other being represented by Lancelot's passion for Guenevere. The passion is as exciting to him as the purity. Tennyson's poem about Lancelot and Guenevere came much nearer completion than the fragment which was published in 1842 suggests. According to his friend J. M. Kemble, a substantial part of it was written in June 1833, when Tennyson read or showed it to him. Kemble was excited by its description of how 'in the Spring, Queen Guinevere and Sir Lancelot rode through the forest green, fayre and amorous: and such a queen! such a knight!' He copied out the song which Lancelot sang—to quote one verse:

> Bathe with me in the fiery flood
> And mingle kisses, tears and sighs
> Life of the Life within my blood,
> Light of the Light within mine eyes.

He sent the song to his friend W. B. Donne with the warning, 'for the sake of my future clerical views and Alfred's and Sir L's character, I must request that it be kept as quiet as possible'. It was, he confessed, 'but a loose song', sung, apparently, as Lancelot took Guenevere to live with him at Joyous Gard, having rescued her from being burnt as an adulteress.[12]

Kemble's comments make clear how stringent the moral climate had already grown by the 1830s; to appear to condone, or even describe, an adulterous relationship was likely to cause a fuss. It was perhaps for this reason that Tennyson only published a portion of the poem in his 1842 volume, and that this did not include the song.

The problem of how to treat the Arthurian story surfaced again with Dyce's commission for the Queen's Robing Room in 1847. On 20 July 1848 he wrote to the Fine Art Commissioners suggesting two possible approaches. One was a chronological series of pictures telling the main story of the *Morte d'Arthur*, from Guenevere's infidelity to Arthur's final disappearance in the barge, Guenevere's remorse and Lancelot's conversion. The other was to 'consider the Companions of the Round Table as personifications of certain moral qualities, and select for representation such adventures of Arthur and his Knights as best exemplified the courage, magnanimity, courtesy, temperance, fidelity, devoutness and other qualities which make up the ancient idea of chivalric greatness'.[13]

It is not surprising that the Commission opted for the moral qualities; Guenevere presented problems for proper Victorians, even if she did repent in the end—and was perhaps considered especially unsuitable for a room to be used by a woman. The subjects finally decided on were mercy, hospitality, generosity, religion, courtesy, fidelity and courage. Dyce started on the frescoes in 1849, but *Hospitality* was not quite finished at the time of his death in 1864, and *Fidelity* and *Courage* were never started.[14] Eight small compartments under the big ones were filled in 1867–70 with wood sculptures by H. H. Armstead showing other episodes in the Arthurian story.

In spite of their mediaeval trimmings, the Arthurian 'moral qualities' which the pictures express are clearly being presented for admiration and imitation by the monarch and aristocracy of Britain. All are entirely appropriate for a Victorian gentleman. *Hospitality* (Plate XVI), for instance, in fact depicts 'The Admission of Sir Tristram to the Fellowship of the Round Table', that is to say to the Arthurian equivalent of an officers' mess; the word 'fellowship', frequently used in Malory, was to become powerfully emotive in Victorian England. *Mercy* and *Courtesy* stress the obligation on gentlemen to be courteous to women and to come to their protection. In *Generosity* Sir Lancelot spares his opponent King Arthur when he is unhorsed and at his mercy; all Victorian gentlemen knew that one did not hit a man when he was down.

In 1855, when Tennyson finally took up the Arthurian story again, his approach was much closer to Dyce's than to that of his poems of the 1830s. In the twenty or so intervening years he had married and become a national figure. He had never been in the least sexually promiscuous, and after marriage became increasingly disapproving of sexual adventures; moreover his wife Emily, in spite of her deliberately self-effacing image, was a powerful personality completely wedded to conventional Victorian morality. In the *Idylls of the King* not only has adultery become shameful rather than glamorous; but the main theme is how Arthur's achievements as king are brought to nothing as a result of Guenevere's guilty love for Lancelot, and everything that flows from it. Arthur himself hammers this home in the celebrated scene in 'Guinevere' where, like a grim but sorrowful god, he speaks to the Queen as she grovels at his feet:

> Then came thy shameful sin with Lancelot;
> Then came the sin of Tristram and Isolt;
> Then others, till the loathsome opposite
> That all my heart had destined did obtain,
> And all thro' thee.[15]

'Guinevere' was one of the first four *Idylls*, all published in 1859. The title which it was first intended to publish them under, 'The False and the True', sums up their theme; false as against true womanhood. Enid unquestioningly follows and serves her husband, even though he humiliates her owing to his groundless belief that she has been unfaithful to him. Elaine, 'delicately pure and marvellously fair',[16] dies of grief owing to her innocent but overwhelming love for Lancelot, who would have done much better to marry her than to carry on with Guenevere. In contrast the lissom and snake-like Vivien, who is incapable of believing that anyone is not, under the surface, as rotten as herself, successfully seduces Merlin, whose wisdom is not proof against his lust; and Guenevere betrays her husband, and repents too late.

Between 1859 and 1873 Tennyson wrote six more *Idylls*, and adapted his 'Morte d'Arthur' to make a final one, so as to produce something resembling a logical and chronological sequence, carefully designed to underline and expand on the moral of the original four. In the process he worked out symbolisms which he may not have fully envisaged in the 1850s: Arthur, for instance, represents 'the Ideal Soul of Man coming into contact with the warring elements of the flesh'.[17] The whole sequence forms a powerful and extremely depressing account of the decay and defeat of an ideal; the only consolation lies in the possibility of the ultimate return of Arthur, carried away wounded but still alive on the barge of the three queens.

The ideal for which Arthur stands is expressed in the oath sworn to him by his knights (and later applied by Tennyson to the Prince Consort, in shortened and slightly altered form):

> I made them lay their hands on mine and swear
> To reverence the King, as if he were
> Their conscience, and their conscience as their King,
> To break the heathen and uphold the Christ,
> To ride abroad redressing human wrongs,
> To speak no slander, no, nor listen to it,
> To honour his own word as if his God's,

> To lead sweet lives in purest chastity,
> To love one only, cleave to her
> And worship her by years of noble deeds,
> Until they won her; for indeed I knew
> Of no more subtle master under heaven
> Than is the maiden passion for a maid,
> Not only to keep down the base in man,
> But teach high thoughts and aimiable words,
> And courtliness, the desire of fame,
> And love of truth, and all that makes a man.[18]

Literary historians disagree as to Malory's own views. Did he or did he not fashion his *Morte d'Arthur* out of earlier romances in order to point a moral not dissimilar to Tennyson's? Tennyson himself seems to have thought not. His own Arthur, he wrote in 1872, was 'ideal manhood closed in real man', in contrast to

> . . . him of Malleor's, one
> Touched by the adulterous finger of a time
> That hovered between war and wantonness.[19]

In his presentation of the Arthurian story he consciously and deliberately bowdlerised Malory in many particulars. Malory can say of Guenevere 'that while she lived she was a true lover, and therefore she had a good end'. His Arthur,

183

120. (left) *Elaine*, as photographed by Julia Margaret Cameron for her edition of *Idylls of the King*, 1874–5

121. (right) Johnston Forbes Robertson as *Sir Lancelot* in J. C. Carr's *King Arthur*, 1895, for which Burne-Jones designed the sets and costumes

far from being a loving but deceived husband, shows little interest in Guenevere and is much more concerned about the quarrel with Lancelot and his followers than the loss of his wife: 'for queens I might have enow, but such a fellowship of good knights shall never be together in no company.'[20] Tennyson's Arthur tells Guenevere that 'I was ever virgin save for thee', but in Malory the false Sir Mordred who finally betrays Arthur is in fact his illegitimate son. Malory's Nimue (from whom Tennyson's Vivien derives) is a benevolent rather than baneful sorceress, and her enchantment of Merlin is considered a feather in her cap rather than a foul deed.[21]

Tennyson was, as a result, criticised both at the time and later for turning Malory's king and knights into pattern Victorian gentlemen.[22] But he did so out of intention rather than ineptness; his Arthur was deliberately designed to be an inspiration to modern members of the ruling class, just as Gareth in 'Gareth and Lynette' ('the young knight who can endure and conquer', as Edward FitzGerald described him)[23] was taken as model for modern public-school boys; hence his appearance in stained glass on the main stairs at Glenalmond (Plate 117).

To many thousands of Tennyson's readers Arthur, 'selfless man and stainless gentleman', was 'the great pillar of the moral order, and the resplendent top of human excellence', as Gladstone described him.[24] To others he seemed a cold cuckold, whose forgiveness of Guenevere

> Lo, I forgive thee, as Eternal God
> Forgives . . .

was self-satisfied rather than moving. George Meredith thought that he sounded like a 'crowned curate'.[25] To them Lancelot, like Milton's Satan, stole the show in spite of the author.

> The great and guilty love he bare the Queen,
> In battle with the love he bare his lord,
> Had marr'd his face, and mark'd it ere his time . . .
>
> His mood was often like a fiend, and rose
> And drove him into wastes and solitudes
> For agony, who was yet a living soul.
> Marr'd as he was, he seemed the goodliest man
> That ever among ladies ate in hall.[26]

The *Idylls of the King* were designed as a warning. Their pessimism reflected Tennyson's own belief that the age was getting worse, and would continue to do so until the English were to live up to the moral standards necessary for members of an imperial nation. His worries were, by his own standards, justified, at any rate as far as concerned sexual morals. A different attitude to that of the *Idylls* had already begun to make its appearance before the first *Idylls* were published, and grew steadily more prevalent during the 1860s and 1870s.

In 1852 Matthew Arnold published a volume of poems which included 'Tristram and Iseult', a poem mainly written in 1849–50 under the influence of a frustrated love affair in Switzerland and his subsequent marriage to Frances Lucy Wightman. In Tennyson's 'Guinevere' Arthur condemned the adulterous 'sin of Tristram and Isolt', but there is no hint of condemnation in Arnold's poem. It depicts an emotional triangle—Iseult of Cornwall in love with Tristram but married to Mark, Tristram in love with Iseult of Cornwall but married to Iseult of Britanny, Iseult of Britanny in love with Tristram—without praise or blame, just as something tragic which happened. The poem centres round Tristram on his deathbed in Britanny, yearning for Iseult of Cornwall, and the tragedy is summed up in the couplet:

> TRISTRAM   Soft—who is that, stands by the dying fire?
> PAGE   Iseult.
> TRISTRAM   Ah! not the Iseult I desire.[27]

The action takes place many years after Tristram's love affair with his lost Iseult, and this time-gap throws a veil of wistful melancholy over the whole poem. The poems in Morris's *Defence of Guenevere*, published in 1858, treat a similar situation with much more immediacy.

Morris was the son of a City merchant who had done well out of Devon copper mines and acquired a country property on the edge of Epping Forest. Morris himself had read all of Scott by the age of seven, and as a child was given a little suit of armour in which to ride through the Forest.[28] In 1853 he went to Exeter College, Oxford, and formed a deep and life-long friendship with Edward Jones (not yet Burne-Jones), the son of a Birmingham picture-framer. Both young men were planning to become clergymen. Jones introduced him to a group of his undergraduate friends from Birmingham whose experience of slum conditions in that city had given them Radical or at least Christian Socialist leanings.

The group came under all the influences likely to affect chivalrous and ardent undergraduates of that date. Their enthusiasms included *The Broad Stone of Honour*, Tennyson, Kingsley's novels, the Pre-Raphaelites, the Christian Socialists (they 'must be glorious fellows', wrote Burne-Jones in 1853), *The Heir of Redclyffe*, La Motte Fouqué's novels, and Dürer's *Knight, Death and Satan*, which they came to by way of Fouqué's *Sintram*.[29] Finally, in the summer of 1855, they discovered Malory, and were completely knocked over by him.

Inspired, apparently, both by Christian Socialism and by reading Hurrell Froude (with his 'high severe idea of virginity'), Burne-Jones involved his friends in a project for a religious order intended to work among the poor in the cities. 'Remember', he wrote to his friend Cormell Price in 1853, 'I have set my heart on our founding a Brotherhood. Learn Sir Galahad by heart. He is to be the patron of our order.'[30] Sir Galahad was, of course, Tennyson's Sir Galahad. But then the group discovered not only Malory but what they called 'stunners', in particular Jane Burden, the beautiful daughter of a groom in an Oxford livery stable. At the beginning of 1856 Morris and Burne-Jones got to know Rossetti, the Pre-Raphaelite whom they had always especially admired. Virginity, the Brotherhood and plans for clerical careers vanished; Sir Galahad had to share the stage, and was soon largely superseded by Lancelot, Guenevere, Tristram and Iseult.

185

The poems in *The Defence of Guenevere* are essays in bringing Malory to life for modern readers by using the techniques of direct broken verse evolved by Browning. Such an analysis can give no idea of the power and originality of these remarkable poems. With the exception of two poems on Galahad their themes are sex and violence. The sex seldom leads to happiness; it is either frustrated or interrupted by violence. Sudden openings and awkward hesitating rhythms give the reader an extraordinary feeling of being present in person, of actually feeling physical surfaces and sensing physical contacts. There is no moralising. Guenevere is not shown as a guilty wife lying at the feet of her husband, but as a splendid and sensuous woman, defying her accusers, celebrating her love (though denying that it went as far as adultery), and minimising her marriage:

> '. . . for a little word
> Scarce ever meant at all, must I now prove
> Stone cold for ever?' . . .

> 'I scarce dare talk of the remembered bliss
> When both our mouths went wandering one way
> And aching sorely, met among the leaves.'

The few products of Morris's brief career as a painter were nearly all produced or at least started in 1857, and were all of lovers or people in love. He painted or drew Guenevere, Tristram, Iseult, Palomides, and St George tenderly lifting up Princess Sabra. His painting of Guenevere (Plate XXI) is as direct as his poem on her. A beautiful and desirable Guenevere is shown fastening her belt by the side of a rumpled bed; a knight plays a harp in the background. Guenevere is in fact Jane Burden, and Morris is said to have written on the picture: 'I cannot paint you, but I love you.'

At this period the work of Morris, Rossetti and Burne-Jones was all of a piece. Rossetti and Burne-Jones also painted or wrote about love and lovers, without adopting any moral stance about the background of the love; intensity of emotion, not morality, was what concerned them. Before he met Morris and Burne-Jones, Rossetti had already been moving in that direction, away from the moral and religious themes which he had painted under the influence of Holman Hunt. His *Paolo and Francesca* derives from Dante's description of how Francesca and her brother-in-law were encouraged by reading about Lancelot and Guenevere to become lovers; Francesca's husband murdered them, and they continued to be lovers in hell. Rossetti started in 1849 with drawings of a decorously courting couple, but in the finished version of 1855 the lovers are embracing very passionately; Ruskin told Ellen Heaton, who was thinking of buying it, that 'Prudish people might perhaps think it not quite a young lady's drawing', even though the figures were draped. If she bought it (she didn't) he advised her to keep it locked up.[31]

Rossetti's Arthurian pictures of the 1850s veered, like Morris's poems, between the two extremes of the Holy Grail on the one hand and Lancelot and Guenevere, or Tristram and Iseult, on the other. His other mediaeval pictures include knights

122. Dante Gabriel Rossetti. *Sir Galahad at the Ruined Chapel*, as engraved in Moxon's *Tennyson*, 1859

123. Dante Gabriel Rossetti. *Paolo and Francesca da Rimini* (detail)

124. Dante Gabriel Rossetti. *Sir Launcelot in the Queen's Chamber*

125. Edward Burne-Jones. *Going to Battle*, 1858

embracing or kneeling at the feet of their ladies (Plate XXIII), and many celebrations of the love of Dante and Beatrice. In his illustration of *St Cecilia and the Angel* for Moxon's *Tennyson* the angel is about to give (or in one version giving) St Cecilia an extremely unspiritual kiss; Tennyson did not like it at all.[32] Similarly Burne-Jones's subjects include (in addition to the inevitable Sir Galahad) knights being seen off to battle by their loves, the Blessed Damozel of Rossetti's poem looking down from heaven for her lover, and May Margaret about to admit Clerk Sanders to her house and bed; the last comes from the ballad of Clerk Sanders in Scott's *Border Minstrelsy*, which ends with Clerk Sanders being murdered by Margaret's brothers when in bed with her, and returning as a ghost.

In the 1860s and 1870s Rossetti, Burne-Jones, Morris and their new friend Swinburne continued to celebrate Love—now very much spelt with a capital *L*: *Love is Enough, Love's Greeting, Love at Sea, The Boat of Love, Love among the Ruins, Love and Sleep, The Triumph of Love, Laus Veneris, The Hill of Venus, Dantis Amor.* These later works lack the peculiar vividness of the work of the 1850s. They move in a world of dreams which seems to have little to do with real people, even real mediaeval people. It has been said that in Morris's *Earthly Paradise*, 'to prevent offence to Victorian sensibility, sexual events are bowdlerised';[33] Burne-Jones's women of the period are often described as 'sexless'. Sexless to whom, though? It is a mistake to judge them by the standards of twentieth-century viewers or readers conditioned to be stimulated only by very obvious symbols.

The Defence of Guenevere was too direct for most Victorians. One achievement of Morris's later poems, and the later pictures of Burne-Jones and Rossetti, was to

XXI. (right) William Morris. *Queen Guenevere*, 1857

XXII. (following pages) Walter Crane. *The White Knight*, 1870 (detail)

126. Edward Burne-Jones. *Sir Galahad*, 1858

make sex acceptable in Victorian drawing-rooms. They achieved this by calling it Love, and all Victorians knew that Love was superior to sex. Sex could come in under its skirts, however; many Victorians found the dreamy rhythms of Morris's poems, or the far-away beauty of Burne-Jones's women extremely suggestive. They helped inaugurate a new form of love affair, conducted on a high plane, excitingly spiced with guilt or frustration, involving much talk of the 'passion of the soul' and a total absence of erotic language or even mention of sex, but always moving towards the final act and sometimes getting there.

In the 1850s and early 1860s the later Pre-Raphaelites had little success, and were scarcely known outside a small circle. Their new manner brought them fame, to the extent that the sales of their poems seriously affected those of Tennyson's. But they did not escape criticism, especially for being 'morbid' or sensual. In 1871 Buchanan attacked Rossetti in a celebrated article 'The Fleshly School of Poetry'; the Fleshly School consisted, in his view, of Morris, Rossetti and Swinburne, all of whom were criticised for their 'spasmodic ramifications in the erotic direction'.[34] In 1872 the heroines of the *Earthly Paradise* were called 'as forward as the heroes are languid . . . Mr Morris, in fact, seems to think that shame and reserve are qualities incompatible with simplicity.'[35] Swinburne was the most obviously outrageous of the group, and was always being attacked from the time of his *Poems and Ballads* (1861), which was dedicated to Burne-Jones.

In 1870 Burne-Jones was asked to remove his *Phyllis and Demophoon* from the Royal Water-Colour Society's exhibition. The reasons seem to have been partly that Demophoon was naked and had visible private parts, partly because Phyllis had the features of the granddaughter of the leader of the Greek community in London, Mary Zambaco, with whom Burne-Jones was having an affair at the

193

XXIII. (left) Dante Gabriel Rossetti. *Before the Battle*, 1858

time.[36] The art critic Harry Quilter later commented that his work 'all has some trace in it of that purely physical side of love, which he depicts in such strange conjunction with its most immaterial aspect'.[37] Why 'strange'? Perhaps because many Victorians believed that love and sex were separate and unrelated; it was one of the achievements of the later Pre-Raphaelites to make the conjunction seem less strange.

The group provided models for imitation in their own lives as well as their works. The way in which Morris, Rossetti and Jane Morris relived the story of Arthur, Lancelot and Guenevere has often been described. In the 1850s both Rossetti and Morris were painting Jane as Guenevere. This was before the situation had really developed, although there is a possibility that it already existed in embryo and that Jane had preferred Rossetti, but been unable to marry him because of his commitment to Elizabeth Siddal. Once Rossetti's infatuation with Jane became obvious and public in the mid-1860s, for him to paint her as Guenevere would have been too near the knuckle; the closest that he came was in a drawing in which she is holding a copy of *The Defence of Guenevere*.[38] But he painted or drew her over and over again in other roles, or just as herself. As Harry Quilter wrote in the year of Rossetti's death, 'there is probably no record of a painter whose personality grew to be so submerged in the form and face of one woman as did that of him of whom we are writing'. He was 'possessed by the strange beauty of the face he made so familiar to us'.[39] The paintings made his infatuation with his friend's wife clear enough, but there must have been much surmise then, as there has been since, as to the lengths to which it was carried. It seems most likely that it stopped just short of the final act, and went exactly as far as the relationship between Lancelot and Guenevere as portrayed by Morris rather than Tennyson.

Burne-Jones never had a relationship as long-lasting or publicised as that between Rossetti and Jane Morris, but he was always getting emotionally involved with women and had at least one really passionate affair, that with Mary Zambaco, which nearly broke up his marriage. His loves tended to appear in his painting; during the two or three years of his affair with Mary Zambaco he painted her several times, most notably as Phyllis in *Phyllis and Demophoon* and as the sorceress or enchantress Nimue in *The Beguiling of Merlin*.[40]

Burne-Jones was attracted to sorceresses and sirens all through his career, and he painted a whole sequence of them.[41] But they clearly had a different significance for him from that which, for instance, Vivien had for Tennyson. For both men, sorceresses were possibly symbols of sex unadorned by love; but whereas Vivien was clearly intended to inspire abhorrence, Burne-Jones gives the impression of reacting to his sorceresses with delicious fascination.

All this has carried the story a long way from Tennyson's 'love one only, cleave to her', with marriage as the end, or indeed from his own long and unruffled marriage to Emily Selwood; but perhaps it has brought it a little closer to mediaeval courtly love. Courtly love *à la* Pre-Raphaelite did indeed provide an alternate model of chivalry to Tennyson. The innumerable Arthurian

127. (top left) Royal Windsor Tapestry Manufactory. *Arthur forgives Guinevere*, from the *Idylls of the King* series designed by Herbert Bone, 1879

128. (bottom left) John Melhuish Strudwick. *The Enchantress: Acrasia lures Sir Guyon, c.* 1888

129. (top right) Edward Burne-Jones. *The Beguiling of Merlin*, 1873–7

130. (bottom right) Dante Gabriel Rossetti. *Mrs William Morris*, 1868

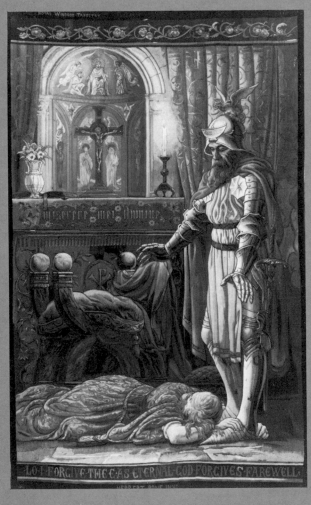

paintings of the period tend to divide themselves between the two, with one school (to which, for instance, Arthur Hughes, Noel Paton and the artists of the Royal Tapestry Works at Windsor belong)[42] favouring Arthur, Galahad, Enid, Elaine, and purity vanquishing the Wicked Woman, the other (of which Aubrey Beardsley is an extreme example) preferring Lancelot, Tristram, Guenevere, Iseult, and sorceresses deliciously triumphant (Plates 118, 127–9).

It was Tennyson's version of chivalry, 'Live pure, speak true, right wrong, follow the King', which provided what might be called the establishment ethic of chivalry, approved of by the public schools and, not surprisingly, by the Queen. One result of Tennyson's great prestige and popularity was a spate of books retelling Malory for children: the first of them, J. T. Knowles's *Story of King Arthur* (1862) was actually dedicated to Tennyson. The versions were all written in pseudo-mediaeval language, but they inevitably involved a good deal of cutting and also careful editing. The object (as U. W. Cutler put it in 1905, in his *Stories of King Arthur and his Knights*) was to remove whatever was 'so crude in taste and morals as to seem unworthy of the really high-minded author of five hundred years ago'.[43]

Lancelot and Guenevere clearly presented problems. Lancelot, in particular, was so powerful and attractive a character that even if given the moral treatment of the *Idylls* there was a danger that he might set boys off on the wrong path. The solution was to bowdlerise him, on lines in fact suggested by Tennyson. According to a 'minstrel of Caerleon' in the *Idylls*, it was 'out of naked knightlike purity' that

> Sir Lancelot worshipped no unmarried girl
> But the great Queen herself.[44]

As treated by Tennyson this was, indeed, the way in which the relationship started, but it soon went much further. In Cutler's *Stories of King Arthur*, it stays at its starting point; Mordred's accusations are baseless; Guenevere's supposed adultery is a put-up job; Lancelot remains a pure and honourable gentleman throughout. Not surprisingly, this was the version recommended by Baden-Powell to his Boy Scouts. Sidney Lanier's *Tales from King Arthur* (1880) went even further. Adultery is never even hinted at; in the final drama Lancelot and Guenevere are accused of a mysterious 'treason', the nature of which is never explained.

Of course Victorians were not attracted to the Arthurian story solely by its morals or lack of them. To many its chief claim was simply that it provided an escape into a magical world—or rather a series of magical worlds, varying from Malory's own to Burne-Jones's. Walter Crane described the effect of paintings by Burne-Jones on young men coming across them for the first time. 'The curtain had been lifted and we had a glimpse into . . . a twilight world of dark mysterious woodland, haunted streams, meads of dark green starred with burning flowers, veiled in a dim and mystic light, and stained with low-toned crimson and gold.'[45] He himself painted his own version of such a world (which did not necessarily have to be inhabited only by Arthurian figures) in his *White Knight* (Plate XXII) of the early 1870s.

131. (right) Wilfred Scawen Blunt photographed in fancy dress in the 1860s

CHAPTER 13

Modern Courtly Love

MANY MEN OF TENNYSON'S TIME FOLLOWED, OR DID THEIR BEST TO FOLLOW, his ideals of love; Tennyson almost certainly did so himself. They remained pure until marriage and faithful after it: 'For I was ever virgin save for thee', as Tennyson made King Arthur say to Guenevere.[1] They married for love, and once they had found the woman they loved were prepared, if there were obstacles, to wait faithfully and patiently until they were removed. In their attitude to all women, but above all to their wives, they aimed to be courteous, tender and protective. They never, under any conceivable circumstances, struck a woman, or let her hear, see or read anything which could be considered impure.

Much of this was an adjustment of mediaeval courtly love to fit it to Victorian standards. Courtly love was not of course a hard and fast set of rules; the literature of chivalry is full of variations. But on the whole it had little to do with marriage, which it was assumed would be arranged on dynastic or financial grounds. Nor did ideals of purity figure nearly so prominently in it, and when they did it was for different reasons. To the Victorians purity was a permanently desirable virtue, but in the literature of mediaeval chivalry it was more a means of refining individual love affairs; the lover was to be purged, exalted and enriched by refraining from physical love in the long period during which he served and courted his mistress. Some poets suggested that this period was the most worthwhile one, and that the final consummation was always an anti-climax; some exalted love without sex as the purest form of it; but more often the ultimate aim was a consummated love with a mistress who was not necessarily, or even usually, a wife. Sir Galahad played a much smaller role in the Middle Ages than in the nineteenth century; as heroes Tristram and Lancelot were far more representative.

Purity as an element of modern chivalry only began to loom large in the 1850s. Kenelm Digby has remarkably little to say on the subject of women and nothing about purity, except by implication when he attacks 'habits of licentious enjoyment' as coarsening the character and blunting the finer feelings.[2] Hints in his biographical poems suggest that as a young man he enjoyed the kind of sexual adventures that were then taken for granted as a way of getting experience.[3] The theme of purity derived from Dr Arnold and other serious-minded clergymen who reformed the public schools in the 1830s (and, in Arnold's case, at any rate, disapproved of chivalry). It was Tennyson and the muscular Christians who grafted it onto modern chivalry. Thomas Hughes showed it in action in *Tom Brown at Oxford* (1861): Tom, about to start an affair with a bar-maid, is dissuaded by his friend Hardy, who believes (as Tom does too, basically) that 'the crown of all real manliness, of all Christian manliness, is purity'.[4]

Purity was, of course, distinct from virginity. Virginity was an ideal almost entirely confined to Catholics and High Churchmen, and even with them only concerned those who devoted their lives to religion. Purity was for all men and women, and entailed accepting sex only as an accompaniment to love and marriage. But virginity and purity were sufficiently related for it to be easy enough to change Sir Galahad from a mediaeval symbol of virginity to a Victorian symbol of purity. Hanging Watts's *Sir Galahad* in Eton College chapel was not intended to put Eton boys off marriage.

If Victorian emphasis on purity was a graft onto earlier concepts of chivalrous love, devotion, tenderness, courtesy and protection were essential parts of the original code which the Victorians could take over without qualms. Even here, however, there were adaptations to be made, once the code was extended to cover the relationship between husband and wife. The accepted symbol of mediaeval courtly love was the knight kneeling at the feet of his mistress, as a superior and adored being. According to early Victorian practice the image was acceptable in courtship but not after marriage; the husband was expected to be tender, reverent and protective, but he was also undoubtedly superior. The position of women as presented in *The Broad Stone of Honour* suggests nineteenth-century wives rather than mediaeval mistresses: 'they sacrificed with pleasure their own feelings for the sake of his duty; they became his adviser, his support, his consolation in trouble, and the source of his purest terrestrial joy'.[5] The only women on pedestals in the *Idylls of the King* are there as warnings, not for admiration, and they do not stay on them. Guenevere ends on the ground at Arthur's feet; Ettare ends up wasting and pining for Pelleas, whose adoration she had started by despising. Tennyson's ideal is represented by Enid and Elaine, rather than by the queenly and imperious Guenevere. Enid loyally obeys an unreasonable husband; and it is Elaine, the shrinking but true and pure 'lily maid of Astolat', who dies for love of Lancelot, not the other way round.

None the less chivalry brought queenly women back into fashion in the end—and even in some cases at the beginning. Queenly heroines feature in some numbers in Walter Scott: in an obviously chivalric context there is Rowena in *Ivanhoe*, tall dignified, with a 'noble cast' of head and features, and a 'clear blue eye . . . capable to kindle as well as melt, to command as well as to beseech'.[6] The four statuary knights kneeling in worship of the Fair Star at Elvaston, and the kneeling troubadour in the Moorish Temple there, show Lord Harrington prepared to introduce the convention of worship into marriage in the 1830s.

In 1865 Ruskin, addressing women in *Sesame and Lilies*, wrote that 'queens you must always be; queens to your lovers; queens to your husbands and your sons; queens of higher mystery to the world beyond, which bows itself, and will for ever bow, before the myrtle crown and the stainless sceptre of womanhood'. 'The first and necessary impulse of every true knight and knightly heart', he laid down, 'is this of blind service to its lady; . . . in this rapturous obedience to the single love of his youth, in the sanctification of all man's strength, and the continuance of all his purposes.' Ruskin went on to condemn the common belief that this situation was 'right in the lover and mistress, not in the husband and wife'. Rather, marriage should only be 'the seal which marks the bowed transition of temporary into untiring service, and of fitful into eternal love'.[7]

Sesame and Lilies was dedicated to Lady Mount Temple. She epitomized Ruskin's argument, for she belonged to a notable feature of the 1850s and 1860s, a group of queenly ladies, noble by nature and usually noble by name as well, chatelaines of great houses, as good as they were beautiful and as artistic as they were good, sailing serene and splendid through Victorian drawing-rooms in a distinctive atmosphere of love, worship and deference. They included Lady

Waterford (wife, and after 1859 widow, of the Knight of the Red Lion at the Eglinton Tournament) and her sister Lady Canning, of whom Augustus Hare wrote his joint biography *Story of Two Noble Lives*; Lady Marion Alford (wife, and after 1851 widow, of the Eglinton Knight of the Black Lion) and her niece Lady Cowper; Lady Waterford's three nieces Lady Pembroke, Lady Brownlow and Lady Lothian; Ruskin's confidante Lady Mount Temple, famous for the missionary meetings which she and her husband held at Broadlands in Hampshire; and Mrs Russell Gurney, who could reasonably be described as a poor man's Lady Mount Temple.

Augustus Hare tended to refer to Lady Waterford as 'the Lady of Ford' or 'our dear Lady'. The painter Frederick Shields, whom Mrs Russell Gurney commissioned to fill an entire church with frescoes in memory of her husband, usually addressed her as 'dear Mistress'.[8] Ladies of this type tended to inspire this kind of language. They all had one thing in common, that they were at least equal, and often superior, members of their marriage partnership. (In 1889 Wilfred Scawen Blunt, talking of Lady Brownlow, described 'her husband as always in devoted attendance'.)[9] Of the list given above, only Lady Marion Alford had children. No doubt there were a variety of explanations for this; but one cannot help wondering whether in at least some cases the wives elevated love so far above sex that their marriages were never consummated.

★   ★   ★

A feature of the mid-century which related very closely to mediaeval courtly love was the chivalrous relationship between a man and a married woman. On the continent such relationships had lasted on far beyond the Middle Ages in the form of *cavalieri serventi*. But in England there had been no such tradition, and its appearance in Victorian England was a direct result of the revival of chivalry. In its purest form the relationship was entirely Platonic; a man, having suffered the misfortune of falling in love with a married woman, or a woman who refused him and married someone else, became her faithful servant, met and corresponded with her, but never contemplated having an affair with her.

A celebrated but by no means typical variant was the relationship between Queen Victoria and Disraeli. Its distinctive note was struck from the moment Disraeli kissed hands as Prime Minister in 1868. On 4 March Victoria wrote to her daughter: 'he is full of poetry, romance and chivalry. When he knelt down to kiss my hand wh. he took in both his—he said: "In loving loyalty & faith." '[10] By the 1870s he had started calling her 'the Faery', as his variant on the Faerie Queene—Spenser's symbolic representation of Queen Elizabeth. He was in fact playing a dual role of chivalrous lover and loyal subject, based on the prototype of Elizabethan courtiers, and his own experiences in Young England days. As is so often the case with Disraeli, it is not clear where play-acting ended and reality began—probably Disraeli did not know himself. But both he and the Queen enjoyed themselves enormously.

Royal ladies have always tended to attract cavaliers, and, at much the same time as Disraeli was, in semi-earnest, prostrating himself before Victoria, Oliver

132. George Frederic Watts. Reginald Talbot as *The Standard Bearer* (detail)

Montagu was metaphorically kneeling in more serious adoration before the Princess of Wales. He was the younger son of the Earl of Sandwich, and became Colonel of the Blues. He never married. His 'chivalrous devotion to a beautiful woman', in the person of Alexandra, was well known in upper-class society.[11] Lady Antrim describes in her memoirs how 'Oliver Montagu was looked upon with awe by the young as he sauntered into a ball-room, regardless of anything but his beautiful Princess, who as a matter of course always danced the first after-supper waltz with him.' The fast set in which she and her husband tended to move was full of scandal, but none ever touched her. 'He shielded her in every way, not least from his own great love, and managed to defeat gossip.'[12] When he died in 1893, aged only thirty-nine, Alexandra wrote to his father calling him 'the best and truest of men, one to be relied on in every relation of life, faithful, discreet and trustworthy, gentle, kind, just and brave, and noble, both in his life and death'.[13]

Another devoted cavalier, Reginald Talbot, had an unimpeachably chivalric background. The Eglinton Marquess of Waterford was his uncle; the queenly Ladies Brownlow, Lothian, and Pembroke were his sisters; his elder brother Lord Ingestre was a champion of working-class causes who flirted with Christian Socialism.[14] In 1862 Watts painted Reginald as the *Standard Bearer*, the only completed portion of a picture which was to have included his father, Lord Shrewsbury, as a knight on horseback. He became the devoted servant of Georgiana Sumner, the wife of another of the Prince of Wales's friends. In 1871 Wilfred Scawen Blunt described him as 'one who had been content to worship for years, not asking more'.[15]

Blunt did ask for more, and made 'Georgie' Sumner his mistress in the same year. The other kind of relationship did not appeal to him. In his diaries he describes another example in more scathing terms: 'Lady Kenmare did not pretend to love her husband and had a certain Sir Charles Douglas generally in attendance on her, who she made run on errands for her, and called her "paramour."'[16]

A more sympathetic variant on the faithful-cavalier theme, and an example of Victorian chivalry carried to what some may consider absurd limits, is exemplified in the story of the four friends of Baddesley Clinton.[17]

In 1859 Edward Heneage Dering, a rich young officer in the Coldstream Guards, fell in love with Rebecca Dulcibella Orpen. He went to her aunt and guardian Lady Chatterton, the widow of an Irish baronet, to ask permission to pay his addresses to her ward. Lady Chatterton misunderstood him (whether deliberately or not remains unestablished), took the proposal as addressed to herself, and accepted it. Heneage Dering was far too chivalrous a gentleman to cause her the pain and embarrassment of disillusioning her. He married her, even though she was old enough to be his mother.

In 1865 Dering, his wife and Rebecca Orpen were all received into the Catholic Church. Two years later Miss Orpen, his real love, married his close friend Marmion Edward Ferrers. Ferrers was also a Catholic and lived, as many generations of his family had before him, at Baddesley Clinton, a romantic moated house in Warwickshire. He invited his friend and Lady Chatterton (as she still called herself) to come and share it with him.

The friends settled down together, and all four lived at Baddesley Clinton for the rest of their lives. Ferrers had very little money, and Dering had plenty. He paid off the mortgage on Baddesley Clinton, restored the parish church, and established a Catholic church, convent, school and chaplain on the property. He settled his own property on Marmion Ferrers's great-nephew and heir; Marmion and Rebecca Ferrers never had children. The friends devoted their lives to good works, piety and the study of Catholic theology and philosophy; they read

133. The four friends of Baddesley Clinton, painted in the library by Rebecca Orpen

134–7. (right) Rebecca Orpen's paintings of herself, Marmion Ferrers (top left and right), Edward Heneage Dering and Georgiana Lady Chatterton

Tennyson together in the evenings. Dering wrote novels (not very good ones). Ferrers liked to think that he resembled Charles I, and dressed and cut his beard to the part. Rebecca, who was a watercolourist of considerable ability, drew portraits of all four of them, separately and together. On her own she wrote: 'Heneage called her his Pearl.'

Lady Chatterton died in 1876, but Heneage Dering continued to live with his friends. Marmion Ferrers died in 1884. Dering was at last free to reapproach Rebecca. She married him in 1885, twenty-six years after his first abortive proposal. He died in 1892; she lived on at Baddesley Clinton until her death in 1923. All four were buried next to each other in the Catholic churchyard 'within sound of the Sanctus bell'[18] as they had always planned.

★   ★   ★

Mediaeval courtly love could vary from the worship of an untouchable mistress by her adoring swain to passionately physical love affairs only differentiated from other affairs by the style of high literary romance with which they were conducted. It is not, perhaps, surprising that courtly love in nineteenth-century England was similarly varied; once an attraction was started, and physical desire stimulated, it was always tempting for the man to push things further or alternatively for the woman to become bored of Platonic worship and fall for a more down-to-earth lover. To do so, however, she usually had to break through very strong scruples imposed as a result of her background and education; so, in many cases, had the man. If an affair could be embellished with talk of Art and Love, seen in terms of mediaeval romance or Pre-Raphaelite art, and sublimated as a 'passion of the soul', in which sex played only a subordinate part, scruples became that much easier to overcome.

Almost every variety of romantic relationship, as played out by the English upper classes from the 1860s to the early 1900s, is described in the diaries, letters and 'secret autobiography' of Wilfred Scawen Blunt, anti-imperialist, Home Ruler, Arabist, country gentleman, poet and insatiable womaniser. Even though what he wrote needs to be treated with a little caution,[19] it provides a unique and valuable window on an aspect of English society which, by its nature, was not publicly written about at the time.

Blunt is full of information about the relationships between other people, but the bulk of his diaries is concerned with his own. The world in which he chose to move was heavy with chivalrous language and images, which no one was more ready to use than himself. To say that he was a seducer who employed a particular technique because it brought in good results is not altogether fair to him. He believed (or persuaded himself that he believed) in what he called the 'passion of the soul', in which a spiritual relationship was what really mattered, but a physical one was a necessary part of it. Sexual intrigue was only worthwhile to him if conducted with high drama, and on an elevated literary and artistic plane. Chivalric romance spiced with Morris, Rossetti and Burne-Jones provided him with what he needed. He 'never could stomach' Tennyson's *Idylls*,[20] but loved the stories of Malory's *Morte d'Arthur*, for much the same reason as the Pre-Raphaelites. They were:

> Tales touching still, and still thro' time renowned
> Though less, methinks, for their high deeds who wear
> Their crests so proudly, than for the lost sound
> Of Lancelot's steps at the Queen's chamber door.[21]

In 1891, when he was re-reading Malory, he actually compared himself to Sir Lancelot[22]—not only because his own step had been heard at many chamber doors but because, like Lancelot (who ended up in a monastery), he saw himself as torn between the life of love and the life of the spirit. This kind of tension was in fact half the fun of the game; although prepared to contend that the union of two kindred souls (with its necessary sexual element) should be above guilt, he also enjoyed feeling guilty on occasions. He wrote about his affair with Minny Pollen: 'how happy I could be serving God with Minny and sinning sin with her, for which we should both sit in sackcloth'.[23]

In 1865, when he was a young diplomat in Portugal, Edward Bulwer-Lytton's son Robert became, and remained, his closest friend. Together they spent many hours imbibing the atmosphere of German Romanticism in the 'fantastic castle in the Clouds' which Don Fernando, German widower of Queen Maria of Portugal, had built for himself and his mistress at Pena, concealing 'a wild garden of many acres, a delectable pleasaunce', behind it walls, towers, drawbridge and portcullis.[24]

The most irresponsible of his sexual escapades took place in 1875, to the accompaniment of chivalric themes derived from the 1830s and 1840s. The scene was Parham in Sussex, an Elizabethan house which Lord Zouche, the traveller and collector of manuscripts, had filled to bursting in the 1840s and later with one of the biggest collections of armour in England. The heroine was 'Doll' Fraser, newly married to the current Lord Zouche, and the niece of that Lord Fraser of Saltoun who had been the Judge of Peace at the Eglinton Tournament. Lord Zouche's armour, memories of the Eglinton Tournament, and perhaps recollections of the Order of the Rose in Kingsley's *Westward Ho* combined to produce an outburst of semi-serious and, as it turned out, disastrous chivalry during what Blunt described as 'a week of extravagant amusement, one of sublime unreason in an Earthly Paradise, for Parham is . . . the perfectest and best, the most ideal framework of romance'.

It all centred on a tournament, given in honour of Doll Zouche. Two of the guests, Alec Fraser and Lord Mayo, 'had got up what they called an order of chivalry connected with our proposed journey [to Abyssinia] the next winter. She was to be Queen of Abyssinia and they her knights, and we were all to have medals and ribbons and wear them at the tournament for her sake.' The tournament took place on 15 October 1875; all the neighbouring gentry came. The culminating feature was a sham fight in which Doll Zouche and others, representing Christian ladies, were attacked by Moorish marauders and rescued

138. Armour in the Hall at Parham, Sussex

by two knights on horseback. Blunt was one of the marauders: Lords Zouche and Mayo, wearing two of the Zouche suits of armour, were the knights.

'Jealous as we were of each other', according to Blunt, 'the fight begun in play became one soon almost in earnest.' The background to these chivalric high-jinks was that Doll Zouche had been pushed into marriage by her mother, and very much disliked her husband. Blunt saw her 'as the sleeping beauty to be called to life by her prince of fairyland'. He had spent a previous visit creeping every night 'through the uncurtained hall watched by the moon and by the effigies in armour' in order to get from his end of the house to hers (he had been married for six years, and his wife was at Parham with him). Fraser and Mayo were also in love (and had probably slept) with their hostess, and Mayo wanted to elope with her—as he ultimately did. On the day after the tournament she quarrelled with her husband, and galloped romantically away on her favourite pony. Blunt was nearly cited as a co-respondent in the ensuing divorce case.[25]

But perhaps the most interesting revelation of Blunt's papers is the number of much more reputable upper-class women, not, on the surface, in the least fast but good, beautiful and artistic (for that was Blunt's favourite type), with whom he succeeded, or nearly succeeded, in having affairs. Blunt's explanation was that their reading and education had made them hungry for romance, which their husbands could not supply; they were 'in a phase of poetic romance of the neo-pagan kind then beginning to be popular with our fine London ladies, whose Bible was Morris's Earthly Paradise and book of hours the pre-Raphaelite art revival as preached by Rossetti'.[26] Indeed, almost all the women with whom Blunt was involved had some kind of Pre-Raphaelite connection—or, failing that, a link with some other aspect of the chivalric revival, which disposed them for romance, or made them romantic to Blunt, or both.

Georgiana Sumner, whom Blunt made pregnant in Madeira in 1871, had Pre-Raphaelite bronze-red hair and looks, and was later to be painted by Rossetti.

Minny Pollen had become friends with Morris, Rossetti and Burne-Jones through her husband, who had collaborated with them on the Arthurian decorations of the Oxford Union in 1857. Rosalind Howard lived in a house on Palace Green, Kensington, which Burne-Jones had decorated with frescoes of Cupid and Psyche for her and her husband (the latter 'of too mild a temper to inspire her with all the romance she asked of life'); Blunt's courtship of her in 1872 was one of his few failures, but he was convinced she intended an affair, and that things only went wrong through his clumsiness. Madeline Wyndham (wife of Blunt's cousin Percy) was one of the queens of the artistic world, painted by Watts (Plate 139), friend of Burne-Jones, owner of many Pre-Raphaelite pictures, including a version of Rossetti's *Beata Beatrix*. Violet Singleton was the daughter of Charles Lamb, the inspirer of the Eglinton Tournament; she had had Clare Vyner as a cavalier, 'content with an ideal love', but got bored of this, started a long liaison with Philip Currie, but broke it off briefly to have a passionate affair with Blunt in 1880.[28]

Ella Baird, whom Blunt liked to address as 'Juliet', lived in Switzerland and had no Pre-Raphaelite or chivalric connections. Even so, Blunt linked her to the Pre-Raphaelite world on the strength of her looks. In 1875, fresh from seeing her in Monaco, he visited Burne-Jones's studio in London. Among the pictures which he saw there was *Laus Veneris*, the theme of which derives from an episode in the story of Tannhäuser, as related in Morris's *Earthly Paradise*. Venus, reclining among her attendants, is gazed at through an open window by wondering knights; Tannhäuser is among them, and will later become her lover. Blunt was fascinated to find that Venus, as depicted by Burne-Jones, 'with her deep set melancholy eyes, her classic forehead, her fair hair and full red lips, was no other than Juliet. She was there, reclining on a couch, in the very posture and with the very same hard sad face which I had seen the day she read my letter and I kissed her hand and said good-bye.'[29]

By the 1880s it was with the excitement of a collector (although Blunt would never have put it like that) that he had an affair with no less a person than Jane Morris, the modern Guenevere. To succeed where Rossetti (so Jane herself told him) had failed was indeed a triumph, and he began to identify himself with Rossetti 'as his admirer and successor'. In 1889–90 he tried, but this time failed, to hit another Pre-Raphaelite bull's-eye in the glorious person of Maria Stillman, whom Graham Robertson once described as 'Jane Morris for beginners' and Rossetti and Burne-Jones had both loved to paint. Blunt had to content himself with covering her hand with kisses: 'so we sat together for half an hour with the life pulsing through our fingers. I shall never forget it while I live.'[30] Unconsummated love of this kind made in fact a stimulating change, especially when it could be alternated with a consummated affair with Margaret Talbot, whose forehead was 'pure with a strange nobility as of a soul immaculate of earthly sin, and yet she is the most passionate woman in the world'.[31]

In 1895 Blunt had an especially fervent affair in the Egyptian desert with Lady Elcho, the daughter of his earlier mistress Madeline Wyndham. But by now he was approaching sixty, and beginning to move from married women to young girls. Among them was seventeen-year-old Lady Margaret Sackville, whom he first met in August 1899 and found 'as pretty in her muslin frock as a child'. She showed him a sonnet which she had written beginning 'Arthur still lives for those who love him well', and Blunt wrote in return 'Why wait for Arthur, he too long has slept.'[32] He gave up after two months of romantic but unsuccessful love-making. In 1900 he had more success with Dorothy Carleton, who liked to address him as Merlin. In 1906 she came to live with him; the relationship finally broke up his marriage. She spent much of the rest of her life industriously copying out records of his earlier conquests from his diaries. She could do this without too much embarrassment because in all Blunt's voluminous accounts of his affairs the physical details of love-making are never described; there is nothing in them which could be considered even remotely pornographic.[33]

Blunt represents one extreme in the spectrum of nineteenth-century courtly love, just as Oliver Montagu represents the other. In between there are numerous variations. All had in common, however, the assumption that spiritual love was more important than sexual; Blunt believed that the two were incomplete without each other but many were prepared to contend that the purity of the first was spoilt by the physical crudity of the second. In extreme examples of hopeless passion, the lover was in constant attendance, but never even expressed his love. More often the apparatus of courtship—meetings carefully and discreetly arranged, endless letters, presents, retreat on one side and pursuit on the other, quarrels and reconciliations—was important and enjoyable, more so to many than the final consummation, if indeed that was ever arrived at.

It was a kind of relationship that needed time, money, the right sort of education, and if possible a variety of available country houses to provide an appropriate background for the more romantic episodes. Those who engaged in it took it very seriously, but, with few exceptions, they never allowed it to upset the structure of their lives, least of all to become public; in spite of ritual protests of despair, grief or ecstasy it was often little more than an enjoyable game, designed to pass time for rich bored people.

The relationship flourished among the Souls, the small but influential upper-class coterie presided over by Arthur Balfour. 'Souls' was a term applied by others, often in no friendly spirit, to a group which had no formal existence, but was none the less a social and political fact because the people of whom it consisted were all close personal friends, went round everywhere together, had certain beliefs and attitudes in common, and looked down on the rest of the world. The rest of the world tended to resent it, not without reason, for the Souls were not quite as good as they thought themselves to be. Their cleverness tended to be superficial, their vision was limited and their wit curiously streaked with sentimentality. None the less their ability, resources and self-confidence made them a force to be reckoned with.

In addition to Arthur Balfour, their members included George Wyndham, his wife Lady Grosvenor, his sister Lady Elcho and her husband, Lord Elcho's brother Evan Charteris, Lady Granby (later the Duchess of Rutland), Lady Windsor (later Lady Plymouth), Lady Horner, Lord and Lady Pembroke, Mr and Mrs Grenfell (later Lord and Lady Desborough), Henry Cust, St John Brodrick, Lord Curzon, Alfred Lyttelton and the Tennant sisters.[34] The group came together in the 1880s, and flourished all through the 1890s. Nearly all its members were young, all were intelligent, most were rich and well-born. Politically, although a few were Liberals, the great majority were Conservatives, and almost all were imperialists. They believed in an empire, and in themselves as providing an inner élite to run the empire. Curzon became Viceroy of India, Lyttelton Colonial Secretary, Broderick Secretary of State for India, Wyndham Secretary for Ireland, and Balfour Prime Minister.

Among the enthusiasms of the Souls were Burne-Jones, the *Morte d'Arthur*, games of all kinds, including intellectual games after dinner, Wagner, Rodin, bicycling and the cultivation of personal relationships. None of the women Souls had any intention of becoming self-effacing wives on the Tennysonian model. At least three of them—Lady Granby, Lady Horner and Mrs Grenfell—were much more powerful characters than their husbands. They took for granted their right to lead independent lives, and to have at least one admirer and often a string of them. When Blunt first got to know them they believed, according to him, in 'unlimited license in love save only the one connubial act . . . Poetry was the basis of their ambition, poetry put in practice, a reality in their lives . . . They read the Bible and they read the Morte d'Arthur in the same spirit & with the same reverence, & they had founded on both a code of superior morals suited, as they considered it, to women of their own superior kind. It allowed them almost every latitude of feeling, including passion as between the sexes, for they held that without passion life would be colourless & the higher emotions could not be enjoyed. Only . . . there was a line drawn short of complete indulgence.'[35]

This type of relationship was exemplified in Balfour's long, profound but almost certainly Platonic relationship with Lady Elcho, or Lady Horner's equally long friendship with Burne-Jones, which, although rather more emotionally charged, was unlikely ever to have become a consummated love affair. It was not an aspect of the Souls with which Blunt sympathised, and he claimed to have helped 'break down their restrictions' by a one-night affair in Margot Tennant's 'little virginal bed' in 1892, and by his passionate affair with Mary Elcho in Egypt in 1895.[36] Whether or not his claim was justified, by the end of the 1890s Lady Granby and Lady Windsor had certainly had affairs with Harry Cust and George Wyndham—so, probably, had Mrs Grenfell with Lord Revelstoke.

However, in the endlessly ramifying love-life of Ettie Grenfell (as her friends called her) the chase was clearly more important than the kill, and this probably remained true with most of the Souls, whether they consummated their loves or not. Ettie Grenfell[37] managed with conspicuous success to play the dual role of siren and *grande dame*; all through her life she expected and received love and adoration. She had strings of lovers, some permanent, others passing, and with each of them she played a complex game of acceptance and rejection; it seems unlikely (although certainty is virtually never possible) that more than one or two of her affairs went the full way. Those with Lord Revelstoke and Evan Charteris lasted many years, and ran concurrently; both remained bachelors for her sake. Her

other less permanent conquests included Lord Revelstoke's novelist brother Maurice Baring (whose novels encapsulated the atmosphere of the group and period) and Blunt's cousin and close friend George Wyndham.

Like Blunt, the latter was always romantically in love with somebody, but because he was less promiscuous (perhaps four *grandes passions* rather than forty) his contemporaries tended to describe him as chivalrous, an epithet they never applied to Blunt. The last and longest of his relationships was with Lady Windsor (who was to become Lady Plymouth in 1905). He died of a blood clot in 1913, when she was visiting him in Paris. Blunt was convinced 'that love was the true cause', and wrote a valedictory poem, 'To a Happy Warrior', in which he compared him to Lancelot.[38]

In 1895 George Wyndham wrote enthusiastically to Blunt about St Fagan's Castle, Lady Windsor's home in Wales. It was 'an enchanted land of Arthurian romance'. The castle was not in fact a castle but 'Elizabethan with gables, built within the enceinte of a Norman fortress . . . There is a pleasaunce and terraces and fishponds, and mazes of cut yews.'[39] Blunt went to stay there for a week in 1897 and found it 'a paradise'.[40] He arrived in white, drawn by four white Arab horses, and was greeted by Lady Windsor, also in white. They walked round the gardens discussing love and friendship; they drove over to St Donat's Castle, and talked about Lancelot and Guenevere. On the next day Lady Windsor (by now wearing black, to reject him) told Blunt that she could only be his friend. On the day after she was wearing white again, and agreed to go with him to Jerusalem and Damascus. Blunt wrote her a poem:

Ghost of the beautiful past, of the days long gone, of a queen, of a fair sweet woman Ghost with the passionate eyes . . .[41]

Nothing happened, however, because Lady Windsor fell for George Wyndham instead; Blunt acted like a loyal friend, invited them to stay, and sent them out into the woods to read Swinburne together.[42]

Women like Lady Windsor needed a setting, to go with the *Morte d'Arthur* or the *Earthly Paradise* or whatever else they fancied. To build a new castle was by now considered hopelessly inept; yet something was needed, with a special quality to take it out of the ordinary into the world of romance.

In the 'Morte d'Arthur' Tennyson described the island of Avalon or Avilion, to which Arthur is taken by the three queens:

> the island valley of Avilion
> Where falls not hail, or rain, or any snow
> Nor ever wind blows loudly; but it lies
> Deep-meadow'd, happy, fair with orchard lawns
> And bowery hollows crowned with summer sea.
> There will I heal me of my grievous wound.[43]

The picture which this suggests, of peaceful English countryside intensified to the point of enchantment, was taken up by the later Pre-Raphaelites. For them the enchantment took place when countryside of this kind became the setting for a

139. (top left) George Frederic Watts. *Madeline Wyndham*

140. (top right) Edward Burne-Jones. *Lady Windsor*, 1893

141. (left) Edward Burne-Jones. *Laus Veneris*, 1873–8

142. St Fagan's Castle, Glamorganshire, in 1902

mellow gabled house set behind walls and clipped hedges. Morris and Rossetti felt it at Kelmscott—'a heaven on earth! an old stone Elizabethan house . . . and such a garden! close down by the river.'[44] Rossetti retired to Kelmscott, literally to heal himself of a grievous wound, the psychological wound caused by Buchanan's criticism of his poetry. But it also became a setting for his romance with Jane Morris. It was an Avalon with a touch of Joyous Gard, the castle setting of the loves of Lancelot and Guenevere, and Tristram and Iseult.

The image was transmitted to those rich, romantic and cultivated people who admired the later Pre-Raphaelites—the Souls among them. They flourished in settings of this kind, and if they did not have the good fortune to inherit them did their best to buy or create them. To some, just the creation or intensification of the setting was enough; but the setting, once it existed, also provided the ideal background to foster or create romance, whether an actual *grande passion*, or some more delicate relationship. Hence the 'Arthurian romance' of St Fagan's for Blunt and Wyndham. It was a house that had all they could desire: gables, cut yew, water, the romantic connotations of 'a pleasaunce' and the hint of a castle.

Such mellow old houses lovingly and gently done over in the years around 1900 have a highly individual character, made up of the interaction between their original character, often sufficiently strong in itself, and the sensibility that has been poured into them. Blunt's own Earthly Paradise was Newbuildings, a brick house of the early seventeenth century which he embellished with a formal garden, Burne-Jones tapestries, and a miscellany of old and new furniture, which included a table that had belonged to William Morris. He lived there on and off throughout his life as an alternative to his main house, Crabbet. Crabbet represented his aspect as squire, landowner and head of an old county family—one which he took very seriously. Newbuildings stood for his romantic side—it 'was to be for me a palace of supreme romance through many generous years, and is so still'.[45]

Another example was Stanway, a Cotswold house the beauty of which still takes the breath away, where Lady Elcho held court with Arthur Balfour. Or, on a grander scale but with the same kind of magic, Montacute, which Lord Curzon leased as the setting of his *grande passion* for Elinor Glyn. Or Sutton Courtenay, 'the place of all others for romance and gathering rosebuds, and making hay and jumping over the moon',[46] where Lady Granby's brother and sister-in-law, Henry and Norah Lindsay, lived. Or—a somewhat different mix, but clearly related—Garsington, where Lady Ottoline Morrell unleashed her extraordinary looks on her numerous lovers.

The influence of the image can be seen in the occasional new house, built by people in the circle of the Souls, or one of the circles that overlapped with it. There are signs of it at Percy and Madeline Wyndham's Clouds, and at Avon Tyrrell, where Lord and Lady Manners lived, but it is strongest at Lambay, built by Edwin Lutyens for Cecil and Maude Baring. Lambay was built in consequence of a *grande passion*, but one of a somewhat different nature from those described earlier in this chapter. Cecil Baring was the brother of Ettie Grenfell's Lord Revelstoke (whose title he ultimately inherited), and of Maurice Baring, the novelist. He had been working in New York as one of the partners in the American branch of Baring's Bank, and fell in love with the wife of his American partner. She was the daughter of Pierre Lorillard, a tobacco millionaire who, among much else, created Tuxedo Park as a chic commuting community in New York State. Maude Lorillard was married very young to a glamorous but unfaithful husband, and found herself increasingly unhappy in the circle of smart, rich New York young-marrieds in which she moved. Cecil Baring rescued her, ran off with her, and married her in 1902.[47]

In doing so he was breaking the conventions; in Edwardian society *grandes passions* were expected to be an alternative to divorce, not a cause of it. Inevitably the Cecil Barings left New York, but to begin with they did not return to London. Instead, in 1904, they bought a retreat from the world, in the form of the little island of Lambay, three miles from the mainland of County Dublin. The only buildings on it were a few cottages and a derelict house, originally built as a 'fine little castle of freestone' in 1555. In 1905 they called in Lutyens, and in 1907 he began to remodel and enlarge the castle for them.[48] He became one of their closest friends.

Three-quarters of a century earlier Lord Harrington had reacted to a not dissimilar situation with castellations and figures of kneeling knights. Lutyens and the Barings were more subtle but equally romantic. Lambay became a magic island, a refuge from the world, a Tennysonian Avalon of 'bowery hollows crowned with summer sea', an Earthly Paradise in miniature. It has something of Burne-Jones's mixture of Greek and Gothic romance. Cecil Baring loved Homer, and when his second daughter was born on the island in 1905 christened her Calypso, after the nymph who lived on the island of Ogygie, on which Odysseus was shipwrecked; she fell in love with him, kept him there eight years, and wanted to make him immortal. One of Lambay's most memorable features is the great wall, with a battlement walk along the top of it, which encloses the house in

a magic circle, filled with a grove of trees. The island itself, by virtue of being an island, is a little world on its own; the wall forms a smaller secret world, at once a sacred grove and a hidden bower or pleasaunce enclosed within the bigger one.

Lutyens added onto the original fort with artful simplicity; there are no battlements or fortifications, but romantically winding stone steps, vaulted rooms, or ceilings of massive timbers. For the Barings' own bedroom (the room in which Calypso was born) he designed a four-poster bed reminiscent of a bed in a mediaeval manuscript, and a massive stone fireplace which rises up, like the bed, into a barrel-vaulted ceiling. He continued to do work on the island for the Barings for the rest of their lives; when they died they were buried on the battlement wall in sight of the house, and Lutyens designed their tombs.

In Lutyens's own courtship Victorian chivalry at its most highminded had combined with whimsicality, house-parties and bicycle outings typical of the late nineteenth century. The objective was Lady Emily Lytton, the daughter of Lord Lytton, ex-Viceroy of India and Ambassador to Paris, who had been Scawen Blunt's best friend. When Emily Lytton first met Lutyens in 1896 her father was dead, and she was recovering from Blunt's attempts to seduce her.[49] In contrast to the sixty-year-old amorist, Lutyens was twenty-seven, a rising young architect, penniless except for what he earned, sexually innocent, but full of idealistic enthusiasm to conquer the world for his love. He epitomized in fact Tennyson's arguments for the ennobling effect of a 'maiden passion for a maid'; the history of their marriage was to show that maiden passions could have their drawbacks.

He first met Emily at a musical evening in Kensington in the early summer of 1896. Almost immediately he started to court her, not with sonnets, but with a casket, made to symbolise his love for her and the life which he hoped that they would live together. The casket still exists. It is $9\frac{5}{8}$ inches high, including the stand, and contained, among other things, a ring, a crucifix, a heart, an anchor (symbol of hope), a minute Bible, plans of a dream house, and a poem inscribed in writing so tiny that it cannot be read with the naked eye.[50]

As the casket began to take shape, he reinforced it with letters. On 17 October he wrote to her that 'one word from you would turn my world to one great sphere of happiness and I would become a man—give me some chance to prove it'. On 23 October Emily wrote back that 'It is hopeless of you to think of me any more.' They did not have enough money between them to satisfy her family. However, she urged him to 'go forth like a knight of old (as you said) and conquer a name and fortune for yourself.' He answered on 25 October: 'If only like that knight of old I could have some hope—some Grail—how I would fight.' On 27 October she felt able to give him 'a gleam of hope . . . Come to me when you feel that you are man sufficient, and that like that knight of old you have proved your knighthood.' His reply came the same evening: 'I have seen the *Holiest* grail and I can now go forth with great comfort.'[51]

A few ritual months then elapsed during which Emily's mother, backed up by her relations, played the part of the dragon, and stopped all communications between them. But in December Lutyens proved his knighthood to the satisfaction of the Lytton family, by showing them his bank statement. He was

143. (top) Lambay Island, County Dublin. The house inside its enclosing wall

144, 145. (bottom) The staircase and a bedroom at Lambay

now earning enough to support a wife in reasonable comfort and to pay the premiums on a life-insurance policy for £10,000. Lady Lytton gave in at the end of January; they became engaged, and were married in August.

During their engagement the tone of their letters changed gear from Charlotte M. Yonge to James Barrie. Lutyens was in fact about to make friends with Barrie, and designed the sets for the first production of *Peter Pan* in 1904. Although he was over six feet tall, he became Emily's 'sweetest little boy-man', 'my own little boy husband to be', 'my own beloved little darling Ned'. But he still drew and described himself on occasion as her knight.[52] On their honeymoon they found that he hated the sea as much as she loved it; they sat in deck-chairs, facing opposite directions, but holding hands. The position symbolised their marriage; the collision between ideal and reality which chivalry tended to produce was in their case an especially violent one. They had almost no tastes in common; moreover Lutyens's purity made him so clumsy a lover that Emily was put permanently off sex, to their great subsequent unhappiness. Emily took up Theosophy and fell spiritually in love with Krishnamurti; she also acquired a *cavaliere servente*, Arthur Chapman, who followed her round faithfully until his death in 1925.[53] Lutyens had a less spiritual love affair with Lady Sackville. Yet in some ways they continued holding hands until Lutyens died in 1944.

*   *   *

Chivalry could encourage close relationships between men as well as between men and women. Romantic friendships had always been an inevitable feature of the male life at public schools and universities. They tended to be more in fashion, however, at some periods than others. In the 1820s and 1830s they were very much the vogue at Cambridge; they were called 'arm-in-arms'. Monckton Milnes reports on them in his letters as an undergraduate around 1830: 'Garden and Monteith have not cooled at all'; 'Cavendish's brother is a charming creature

216

146. (left) Edwin Lutyens's casket, designed and made for Emily Lytton, 1896

147. (right) Lutyens as knight, drawn by himself in a letter to Emily Lytton

and so well fitted for Fitzroy.'[54] The especial fervour of such relationships at this period was a product of the Romantic movement, and scarcely connected with the revival of chivalry; there was little in the chivalric tradition to encourage close male friendships. Later on Tennyson may to some extent have identified Arthur Hallam with King Arthur, but there is no evidence that he did so while Hallam was alive.

However, as people began to think more and more in terms of chivalry, it was inevitable that its language should be applied to love and friendships between males, as well as between the sexes. In particular, friendships between older and younger boys, or boys and dons or masters, could be seen in terms of knights and squires, or alternatively of young knights being advised by wise mentors.

In the 1860s William Johnson Cory reversed the metaphor and thought of himself as the 'crippled squire' of a young Etonian knight. In the early 1870s J. A. Symonds at Clifton was busy advising his 'young Paladin', Cecil Boyle. It was almost certainly as a side product of his love for Boyle that he commissioned a painting of a young knight from Edward Clifford in 1871; it was titled *Moriturus*.[55] A few years earlier his friend Graham Dakyns, a master at Clifton, had fallen in love with Arthur Carré, one of the Clifton boys. Symonds advised Dakyns to encourage him by holding up 'the life of Arthur or of Lancelot'.

Such romantic friendships need not necessarily, or even usually, lead to sexual relationships. But the dangers were obvious, and as Victorian schoolmasters grew more and more concerned with purity, they tended to become obsessional about them. They are discussed in F. W. Farrar's *Eric or Little by Little* (1858) by Eric's two friends Montagu ('such a little gentleman') and Russell:

'You mean you don't like the "taking up" system?'
'No, Montagu; I used once to have fine theories about it. I used to fancy that a big fellow would do no end of good to one lower in the school, and that the two would stand to each other in the relation of knight to squire. You know what the young knights were taught, Monty—to keep their bodies under, and bring them into subjection; to love God, and speak the truth always. That sounds very grand and noble to me. But when a big fellow takes up a little one *you* know pretty well that *those* are not the kind of lesson he teaches.'[57]

During the second half of the nineteenth century opinion about love between males among schoolmasters and adults tended to harden into three groups: those who regarded it with suspicion or disquiet, once it went beyond the 'best pal' stage; those who believed in love without sex; and those who believed in the two together.

The last two groups can conveniently be described as homoerotics and homosexuals. The former not infrequently developed into the latter, as J. A. Symonds did while he was teaching at Clifton. Both groups, not surprisingly, tended to be more drawn to Greece than to chivalry; apart from anything else the Greek tradition naturally expressed itself in naked bodies rather than bodies covered in armour.

Nevertheless, chivalry continued as a minor theme, especially in the curious concept of the 'New Chivalry'. The idea behind this was that the exaltation of women in mediaeval chivalry was essentially bound up with the need to procreate; now that the world was sufficiently well populated, women should be replaced by young men. Another feature of the new chivalry was that it was to be democratic: beauty and spiritual quality, not birth, were to be the passports to entry.

Such a democratic male-oriented chivalry was hinted at in J. A. Symonds's *Song of Love and Death*, privately printed in about 1875:

> O nobler peerage than that ancient vaunt
> Of Arthur or of Roland! Chivalry
> Long sought, last found! Knight of the Holy Ghost!
> Phalanx Immortal! True Freemasonry![58]

But it was spelt out in detail in an article by Charles Kains-Jackson, entitled the 'New Chivalry' and published in April 1894 in a homoerotic magazine, the *Artist and Journal of Home Culture*.[59]

Kains-Jackson was its editor, and Symonds had already written to him appreciatively in 1892: 'I see you continue to be very indulgent to the claims of "lovely knights" upon public attention.'[60] 'Just as the flower of the early and imperfect civilisation', Kains-Jackson argued in the 'New Chivalry', 'was in what we may call the Old Chivalry, or the exaltation of the youthful feminine ideal, so the flower of the adult and perfect civilisation will be found in the New Chivalry, or the exaltation of the youthful masculine ideal . . . A beautiful girl will be desired before a plain lad, but a plain girl will not be considered in the presence of a handsome boy. Where boy and girl are of equal outward grace the spiritual ideal will prevail over the animal and the desire of influencing the higher mind, the boy's, will prevail over the old decree to add to the population.' The article (which led to Kains-Jackson losing his job) went on to extol the 'tenderness of elder for younger' and the pleasures of 'the evening tent-pitching of campers-out, and the exhilaration of the early morning swim'. It suggested that there was more companionship in such relationships than in ordinary marriage.

Similar ideas were put into verse in a volume of poems by Edwin Emmanuel Bradford, *The New Chivalry* (1918):

> Nay, boys need love, but not the love of women:
> Romantic friendship, passionate but pure,
> Should be their first love . . .
>
> And linked in love the knight and squire shall run
> To seek adventures . . .
>
> But earth is earth—not heaven: well I know
> Full many a squire will fail to win his spurs
> Woman will call him, and the lad will go.

'Dr Bradford's poems are vigorous and refreshing', commented the *Oxford Review*. 'The book should be read by all earnest schoolmasters.'

218

148. (right) An Indian Army polo team, *c.* 1890

CHAPTER 14

Knights of The Empire

ON 3 DECEMBER 1857 J. A. FROUDE WROTE TO HIS FRIEND WILLIAM LONG: 'We had been doubting, too, whether heroism was not a thing of the past: and what knight of the Round Table beat Havelock and Sir John Lawrence?'[1] The Indian Mutiny had been a traumatic experience for the British, but its suppression by, relatively speaking, a handful of British isolated in a country of millions, was greeted with ecstatic relief and produced a new circle of heroes to be added to the existing Pantheon. Lord Curzon recited the list in a speech given in 1907; among them 'John Lawrence, that rugged tower of strength; Nicholson, the heroic Paladin of the frontier; Outram, that generous and gallant spirit, the mirror of chivalry; Hugh Rose, that prince among fighting men'.[2] Outram, who died in 1863, lies in Westminster Abbey under a tombstone on which is proudly inscribed 'the Bayard of India'. The term had first been applied to him in the 1840s by Sir Charles Napier.[3] Napier was one of the most chivalrous of those who had fought in the Peninsular War; but in Peninsular days chivalric epithets were not yet being used for modern heroes. By the mid-century the language of chivalry was sufficiently current to come naturally to hand for their celebration.

In the letter quoted at the beginning of the chapter Froude also wrote, 'When smooth times have made one doubt whether there is such a place as Hell, and such a being as the Devil, it breaks out right in the middle of us in forms as fiendish as ever Dante imagined.' The hell of the Mutiny was especially terrible because it was unexpected. India was generally believed, both in England and by the English in India, to be one of England's triumphs. Its peoples were being exposed to English law and education, English Protestantism and English trade. Indian ignorance and superstition were, it was believed, beginning to crumble, slowly but inevitably because the English represented a superior civilisation, and the good must automatically drive out the bad. The process would take some time, but as soon as it had got far enough, the Indians would be ready for constitutional self-government, on the English model. England would welcome the relief from responsibility. As Palmerston put it, 'all we want is trade, and land is not necessary for trade'. The ideal situation was one in which England spread its way of life to other nations by trading with them, and owned no more than naval bases, spread round the world, from which it could police the seas, and punish any offence against British nationals in foreign parts.

Although they sometimes found his expression of it too aggressive, this was also the view of the Utilitarians and the Manchester school—that is to say of the two groups which those who supported the revival of chivalry most disliked. For several decades in the mid-century it was the prevailing view. But when two hundred British women and children were killed in cold blood at Cawnpore, their hair and limbs hacked off and the mangled pieces thrown into a well, it was clear that something had gone wrong. The ground was ripe for an alternative approach. This was worked out or supported in the ensuing decades by individuals and groups who have already featured in these pages. Carlyle was its founding father, Kingsley and his brother-in-law Froude his disciples; it was increasingly supported by the public schools, given a boost by Ruskin, put into verse by Tennyson, and transmuted into cloudy visual allegories by Watts.

The view ran on these lines. Good would not spread of its own accord. Evil and the devil were real and powerful facts. Most people were not able to govern themselves and needed wise and strong rulers. The English, of all races, were the most capable of justly ruling those not able to rule themselves. It was their duty to take the leading role in the world. For this two separate approaches were necessary. England should send her own people to settle on as much as they could of all land still uncultivated, whether by means of emigration to existing English colonies or by the acquisition of new ones, and should unite these English-settled colonies in a federation with herself; in this way a Greater England would be created which would carry far more weight than one little island, and ensure world leadership. At the same time England should continue to provide just and strong rule to the non-English people already under her sway, and be prepared to extend it over others; and she should accept it as a fact that, even if her subject peoples might one day develop to the state when they were capable of self-government, this would not be for many generations to come.

The fully fledged doctrine of what came to be known (but scarcely until the 1880s) as Imperialism took some time to evolve, and even more time to win wide acceptance. Before the 1880s Froude and Kingsley (and, sporadically, Ruskin) were more concerned with encouraging the development and federation of colonies based on Anglo-Saxon settlers than with England's role as a ruler of 'inferior' races. This role had long been taken for granted in India, and there is no doubt that what might be called the school of Carlyle heartily endorsed it; but it seems not to have been explicitly stated by Froude until 1888. He then expressed it succinctly: 'We have another function such as the Romans had. The sections of men on this globe are unequally gifted. Some are strong and can govern themselves; some are weak and are the prey of foreign invaders and internal anarchy; and freedom, which all desire, is only obtainable by weak nations when they are subject to the rule of others who are at once powerful and just. This was the duty which fell to the Latin race two thousand years ago. In these modern times it has fallen to ours, and in the discharge of it the highest features in the English character have displayed themselves.'[4]

In fact the two types of colonies, those initiated by English settlers and those in which the English governed native peoples, shaded into each other. There were virtually no cultivable lands which were totally uninhabited; settling them involved some kind of relationship with an indigenous population. The relationship could take two forms: either English settlers provided the work force as well as the managers, and the indigenous natives were pushed into reserves; or English settlers took over the land but used a native work force. The argument most commonly used to justify appropriating the land of 'inferior' races was based on Carlyle's doctrine of work: people had a duty to work the lands they occupied to the utmost, and if they did not they had no exclusive right to them.

Kingsley expressed this doctrine in an essay published in 1859: 'the human species have a right to demand . . . that each people should either develop the capabilities of their own country, or make room for those who will develop them.'[5] In the same year he was telling an audience of London ladies that 'the English race is the very noblest race the world contains'.[6] In remarks like these one can see the imperialism of the 1880s developing. One can see too how it related to the worlds of Christian Socialism and muscular Christianity. The Empire provided an alternative and wider field in which Christian English gentlemen, instead of pleading laissez-faire as an excuse for inaction, could actively come to the aid of those less well off than themselves. As the Warden of Glenalmond put it, they could play the part of 'a knight-errantry fit to keep the marches of an empire, and to purge the land nearer home of wrong, violence, lust'.[7] In England they could rescue English working men from poverty, ignorance, drink and exploitation by greedy employers; overseas they could fight against the forces of nature to produce abundance from forest and scrub, or redeem inferior peoples from slavery, superstition or unjust rulers, and give them peace and wise but firm government. In doing so they themselves would find worthy fulfilment; indeed, the preachers of imperialism often give the impression that they think of the Empire less in terms of the benefits its confers on the ruled than as a training ground for the character of the rulers.

Imperialism had a period of formulation, during which it was evolved and preached by writers, theorists and teachers, and a period of practice, during which it began to influence politicians and administrators. In the 1860s and 1870s the Liberals, who were in power for much of the two decades, were still dominated by Free Trade doctrines, and the Conservatives, with a few exceptions, were not especially interested in the Empire; even Disraeli never expressed a fully worked-out imperialist doctrine, although he gave hints of it from time to time. Laissez-faire was still working to England's advantage; it was only when other European countries reached the stage when they began to threaten England's markets and English supremacy, that imperialism began to win wide acceptance. The threat only became apparent in the 1870s, and serious in the 1880s.

The 1870s were in fact the key decade during which future members of the ruling class were bitten by the imperialist bug. It was in 1870 that Froude first began to work out his views in detail, in an article on 'England and her Colonies' in *Fraser's Magazine*, to be followed by many articles and books plugging the same theme. Oxford in the 1870s was electric with the twin ideals of service to the poor at home and the Empire abroad. In a famous lecture given there in 1870 Ruskin called on the youth of England to 'make your country again a royal throne of kings; a sceptred isle, for all the world a source of light, a centre of peace; . . . amidst the cruel and clamorous jealousies of the nations, worshipped in her strange valour, of goodwill towards men'. To achieve this England 'must found colonies as fast and as far as she is able, formed of her most energetic and worthiest men; seizing every piece of fruitful waste ground she can set her foot on, and there teaching her colonists that their chief virtue is to be fidelity to their country, and that their first aim is to be to advance the power of England by land and sea.'[8]

In 1874 Ruskin invited the youth of Oxford to work with their own hands in a more limited form of service, the improvement of a lane running past Ferry

Hinksey, on the outskirts of Oxford, which had become a quagmire. 'My chief object', he wrote, 'is to let my pupils feel the pleasure of *useful* muscular work, and especially of the various and amusing work involved in getting a Human Pathway rightly made through a lovely country, and rightly adorned.'[9] But the significance of the road which Ruskin and his undergraduates toiled away to make was less the result (which was virtually useless) than the ideals behind it, and the undergraduates who took part in making it. These included Alfred Milner, future Governor of South Africa and arch-imperialist; Arnold Toynbee, future apostle of service to the working classes, in whose honour Toynbee Hall was founded; George Parkin, a schoolmaster from Canada who was to devote the rest of his life to preaching Imperial Federation and the importance of the Empire; and Oscar Wilde, whose appearance in this company seems less odd if one reads his imperialist poem 'Ave Imperatrix'.[10]

George Parkin had come to Balliol and Oxford as what would now be known as a mature student. He was a schoolmaster from Fredericton in Canada, and his enthusiasms included the *Idylls of the King*, Rossetti, Dr Arnold, Swinburne, the English public schools (he was very conscious of being a gentleman) and the British Empire.[11] He had already met Edward Thring, the headmaster of Uppingham, and been inspired with a hero-worship which later led to his writing Thring's biography. In Canada he had already tried, without success, to remodel the collegiate school at Fredericton on public-school lines, and later became headmaster of Upper Canada College, the nearest that Canada had to offer to an English public school. At Balliol he became one of the moving spirits of a group of Liberal imperialists which included Milner and Asquith. Milner imbibed imperialist ideas from Parkin and sympathy for the working classes from Toynbee; he was later to be an enthusiastic supporter of Toynbee Hall. Indeed Balliol, presided over and inspired by Jowett, was seething with ideas of service, and the conviction that Balliol would provide the élite to carry them out. The next generation of undergraduates, of which George Nathaniel Curzon was perhaps the most notable, was to be equally enthusiastic.

Cecil Rhodes was studying as an undergraduate at Oriel at intervals from 1873 until 1881.[12] Like Parkin he was a mature student, not so much in point of age (he was only twenty when he first came up) as in experience; by 1873 he had already made a modest fortune in the Kimberley diamond mines, and he considerably increased it during his Oxford period. He neither knew the Balliol group, nor worked on the Hinksey road; but he read Ruskin's famous lecture, and it inspired him with the idea of making a yet greater fortune and using it for the furtherance of the Empire, on the lines laid down by Ruskin. In 1877, when he was still at Oxford, he wrote down his intentions in two documents, a will and a declaration of belief. 'I contend', he wrote, 'that we are the first race in the world, and that the more of the world we inhabit, the better it is for the human race . . . Added to which the absorbtion of the world under our rule simply means the end of all wars.' Accordingly he left his money for the creation of a secret society, dedicated to promoting England's settlement and subsequent absorbtion of the whole of Africa and South America, the Holy Land, the Euphrates valley, the islands of the

Pacific, the Malay Archipelago, the seaboard of China and Japan, and the United States.[13] He went on to become Prime Minister of the Cape Colony and founder of the British South Africa Company, which developed into the colony of Rhodesia.

Between 1874 and 1902 the British Empire was in fact increased by 4,750,000 square miles. But Rhodes in particular and the imperialist creed in general can only claim a portion of the responsibility for this. As with earlier additions to the Empire it was mostly the result of decisions made for a variety of different reasons and often *ad hoc*, rather than of any deliberate policy—fear of potential threats to the routes to India and elsewhere, fear that another European power would step in if England did not, desire to open up areas to trade, or to secure existing traders from molestation by aggressive local rulers. What imperialism did was to provide a super-charge, in the form both of men on the spot and of opinion at home, which was positively in favour of expansion. Even more it provided a moral justification for England's rule both of newly acquired territory and of the existing Empire.

The sources of imperialism and the sources of the Victorian code of the gentleman are so intertwined that it is not surprising to find this code affecting the way in which the Empire was run. Most obviously, the great majority of the officials who ran it came from public schools. But there are a number of particular attitudes which it is worth looking into.

The philosophy of imperialism was essentially élitist. It was not only that it saw the British people as a ruling race; within the British people it saw British gentlemen as leading, loyally supported by what it liked to think of as British yeomen; and within the ranks of British gentlemen it tended to create little individual 'bands of brothers', conscious of their traditions or believing in their superiority. In addition to the innumerable army messes and naval gun rooms, which developed their inherited codes to new heights of rigour and

149. Edward VII as Prince of Wales being welcomed by the Princes at Agra, 1876

demandingness, a number of one-off groups gave dedicated and devoted support to individual heroes. Wolseley had his 'ring' in India; Kitchener had his 'cubs' in Egypt and the Sudan; Milner had his 'kindergarten' to help him with the reorganisation of the Transvaal after the Boer War; back in England the kindergarten developed into a closely knit group of imperialists known as the Round Table, from the magazine which they founded in 1911.[14] A couple of decades earlier the Souls were solidly imperialist, conscious of being clever and abler than other people, and united in respect and affection for their leading member, Balfour, whom they liked to refer to as 'King Arthur'.[15]

Being élitist, imperialists tended to distrust democracy. Not all imperialists were anti-democrat, but a great many were, including, over the decades, figures as important as Carlyle, Kingsley, Froude, Milner and Curzon. Imperialism found support not only from members of both parties but from people who belonged to neither party and hankered for the arrival of what Milner called 'a head for the show' under whose leadership the whole Empire could unite. One of the attractions of the colonial and Indian services for many people was that it put them in positions in which they could exert much greater authority than was possible in England; they were at least free from control by local democracies, even if they were occasionally, often to their great indignation, interfered with by the democracy at home. The society which they dreamed of creating was paternalistic, hierarchic and rural, such as in England only survived on great landed estates, and even there was being eroded. Sir Hugh Clifford, who was to become one of the ablest colonial governors of the twentieth century, never forgot his memories of being taken as a child in the late 1870s round the farms and cottages of his cousin, Lord Clifford, at Chudleigh in Devon: 'It seemed to me . . . as though I had suddenly become part of a great family and congregation of the essence of which I had up to that time been ignorant. It imbued me even at that early age with a tremendous sense of responsibility.'[16]

225

150. George V as King-Emperor receiving the homage of the Princes, Delhi Durbar, 1911

Sir Hugh Clifford spent his life governing native races; but even in the British-settled colonies imperialists tended to look rather wistfully for the development of a ruling class, plan for the creation of a colonial House of Lords, and be encouraged by anything which might be described as neo-feudalism. In Australia in 1885, for instance, Froude was delighted to find a full-blown country house in the Scottish Baronial style set in its own park near Melbourne, with a couple of real English lords staying in it, and a son of the house who was 'tall, spare-loined, agile as a deer, and with a face which might have belonged to Sir Lancelot'.[17]

Distrust of democracy encouraged a tendency to deal with and support surviving feudal rulers in the 'native' colonies and in India, rather than with the emerging middle classes in the towns. This was a reversal of the usual policy in the first half of Victoria's reign. It meant, for instance, that no more of the maharajahs' territories were taken over by the Indian government, and that in Africa Lugard and others developed 'indirect rule', in which local chiefs and sultans were allowed to continue administering their territories, under English supervision.[18] In general imperialists tended to disapprove of cities and city-life; one of the functions of the Empire, as they saw it, was to draw away the English working classes from the unhealthy atmosphere of the cities and, as Froude wrote in Australia, 'to empty our towns of half the squalid creatures that draggle about the gutters, and pour them out here to grow fat and rosy again'.[19]

One of the dominant notes sounded by imperialists was that of duty. Since, as W. T. Stead put it in the opening number of his *Review of Reviews* in 1891, 'the English-speaking race is one of the chief of God's chosen agents for executing coming improvements in the lot of mankind',[20] it was its duty to take up what Kipling later called the White Man's Burden. Curzon celebrated this 'call to duty ... more inspiring than has ever before sounded in the ears of a dominant people'.[21] In 1901 Haig wrote about it to his nephew: 'It has been your *good fortune* not only to become a soldier, but to have served and risked your life for the Empire—you must continue to do so, and consider that it is a privilege, and not that by so doing you are losing time and money! ... Aim at being worthy of the British Empire ... It is not ambition. This is *duty*.'[22]

As Haig made clear, serving the Empire had nothing to do with making money. Many years previously Digby, in *The Broad Stone of Honour*, had discussed the careers open to gentlemen and ruled out any that were 'chiefly directed towards the attainment of wealth'. His proud insistence that gentlemen should not be interested in making money was endorsed to the hilt by the Colonial Service and the Indian Civil Service as they developed in the second half of the nineteenth century. Their members could look forward to no more than retirement on a comfortable pension and whatever they might have been able to save from their adequate but certainly not princely salaries. The vast fortunes made by Indian nabobs were a thing of the past; the Empire as it developed under Victoria was the most incorruptible that has ever existed.

The corollary to contempt for money-making was that those who actually were in the Empire to make money were looked down on. Businessmen were 'box-wallahs'. The attitude survived far into this century and is epitomized in the

answer given to an eminent travelling businessman, who asked what his wife should wear for dinner at Government House: 'Oh, Sir Christopher, we have a very simple rule in this colony. Commercial wear short, government wear long.' Many colonial officials saw the protection of native races from businessmen as one of their principal roles. The British Empire has been criticised for failing to develop local industries; if the charge is justified it was probably due as much to the desire of colonial servants to save the natives from what they saw as corruption as to business interests at home lobbying to prevent competition.

★   ★   ★

Such desires related to the ideals of chivalry and the enthusiasm of Victorian gentlemen to protect those less well off than themselves; the Empire had become one of the obvious fields in which to serve. Empire and chivalry were linked together in 1872 when Tennyson finally completed his *Idylls of the King*. He prefaced them with an ode to Victoria, which (among other themes) urged that the Empire should not be dismembered, and praised Lord Dufferin for speaking up in favour of keeping Canada within it. Three years later Lord Dufferin invited the Northern Irish architect W. H. Lynn out to Quebec, and commissioned designs from him which, had they been carried out, would have transformed the city into a modern Camelot or Carcassonne, encircled with cliff-top wall and towers.

But whereas the most superficial research into, for instance, the public schools and the Boy Scouts, brings up chivalry in bucketfuls, its images and metaphors occur less frequently in the context of the Empire. Imperialists, however much the ideals of chivalry lay at the back of their thinking, were not often compared to knights, or even described as chivalrous. One reason for this was the size, complexity and power of the Empire; the language of chivalry is easiest applied to simple situations, and the Empire was not simple. A complex mixture of motives and causes lay behind it; chivalry rubbed shoulders with religion, pride of race, and self-interest. Moreover, colonial officials were so obviously elevated in a position of power and prestige that it was easier to see them as rulers ruling, than knights protecting, the peoples of the countries in which they served. Indeed, chivalrous metaphors could more naturally be used for those who tilted against

227

151. A. Chevalier Tayler. *Gentlemen, The Queen, c.* 1893

THE STAIN OF CENSURE.

Britannia to Lord Milner. "LEAVE YOUR SHIELD IN MY KEEPING. I SHALL MAKE IT BRIGHT AGAIN."

"OUT OF THE WOOD!"

the Empire rather than for it. When Scawen Blunt went against his own class to the support of the Land League in Ireland, he not unreasonably described his motives in a sonnet: 'I thought to do a deed of chivalry.'[24] The politician most often depicted by cartoonists as a knight was Gladstone, whom imperialists detested.

In contrast, imperialists tended to see themselves as modern Romans. The analogies between the Roman and British empires were obvious enough, and were often drawn. At New Delhi, Pretoria and elsewhere, classical architecture became the accepted vehicle for expressing imperial authority. Governors and viceroys were referred to as 'great proconsuls'. At a humbler level it was easier for colonial officials bogged down in administrative routine to think of themselves in terms of Kipling's centurion, patiently watching on the Roman wall, than as Knights of the Round Table, performing gallant exploits.

Even so, chivalry continued to provide an alternative source of images, especially for moments of exhilaration or emotion. In particular the Queen, as the head of the Empire, became the object of a loyalty such as had no parallel in England since at least the days of Charles I, and probably came closer to the ideals of mediaeval chivalry than the mediaeval actuality ever did. It was an emotion at once mystical and personal; the Queen symbolised the Empire, but she was also an individual whom her subjects longed to serve, and for whom they were prepared to die. Such feelings reached their crescendo in the Diamond Jubilee ceremonies in 1897; 'it would be impossible', wrote Henry Newbolt, 'to express in words the exaltation of the day . . . we dreamed an impossible but not ignoble dream of world leadership, and rededicated ourselves to the service of a twice-crowned queen.'[25]

The Queen had her knights, both living knights and knights of legend. One of the most obvious effects of the revival of chivalry was the great expansion of the Orders of knighthood. At the beginning of her reign Victoria presided over some three hundred and fifty knights; by the end they were approaching two thousand. The Order of the Bath had been enormously expanded; the Order of St Michael

228

152, 153. W. E. Gladstone and Lord Milner as knights, from *Punch* cartoons, 17 August 1881 (showing Gladstone rescuing Ireland) and 29 March 1906

and St George, which when it was founded in 1818 had been confined to Malta and the Ionian Isles, was remodelled, greatly enlarged, and extended to all the colonies in 1869; the Order of the Star of India was founded in 1861 and that of the Indian Empire in 1878; the Victorian Order followed on in 1896; the Order of the British Empire was inaugurated in 1917.[26]

The knights of legend were the heroes who had made Britain's greatness and were in all the story-books. They extended from mediaeval to modern times. The most notable additions in Victoria's reign were the heroes of the Mutiny and General Gordon. They were treated as heroes of chivalry although, in many cases, the Bible meant a great deal more to them than the *Morte d'Arthur*—if, indeed, they had ever heard of the latter.

Gordon was a key figure, in that his death was a catalyst which did as much as anything to create imperialism as a mass emotion. In some ways he was an odd figure to become a legendary knight of the Empire. He had gained his reputation fighting for foreign masters—the Emperor in China and the Khedive in the Sudan and Equatoria. Far from being a supporter of the Empire, he delivered, on occasions, sentiments that could only be described as anti-imperial. There is no evidence that he was in the slightest degree influenced by the ideals of chivalry. But he died in the service of the Empire; Gladstone, whom all good imperialists hated, was held responsible for his death; and his purity, bravery and freedom from self-interest could be described as chivalrous, even if he did not see them as such himself. In fact, the intensity of the cult which he stimulated was due to the fact that he could be hero-worshipped both by Bible Christians and chivalrous gentlemen. Biographies poured from the press in his praise. He united 'all that is noble and chivalrous in man'.[27] He combined 'the attributes of Sir Lancelot, of Bayard, of Cromwell, of John Nicholson, of Arthur Connolly, of Havelock of Burley, of Livingstone, of Hedley Vicars'.[28] He was 'as unselfish as Sidney, of courage dauntless as Wolfe, of honour stainless as Outram, of sympathy wide-ranging as Drummond, of honesty straightforward as Napier, of faith as steadfast as More. Doubtful indeed it is if anywhere in the past we shall find figure of knight or soldier to equal him, for sometimes it is the sword of death that gives life its real knighthood, and too often the soldier's end is unworthy of his knightly life; but with Gordon the harmony of life and death were complete . . .'[29] The fact that he was also a very odd character indeed vanished beneath such eulogies.

The chivalry of the Empire was presided over by the figure of St George slaying his dragon. In the early nineteenth century he was most often shown as a classical figure wearing a Roman helmet, but by the mid-century he normally appeared transformed into a knight in armour. The fact that he was England's traditional patron saint, that he was also accepted as the patron saint of chivalry and that slaying dragons, and rescuing those in distress by doing so, beautifully symbolised what imperialists believed the Empire was all about, ensured his popularity. When the fourth Earl Grey was Governor-General of Canada in 1904–11 he asked his friends in England to send him banners of St George and the Dragon to hang 'like silent sermons on the walls of colleges', proclaiming the mission of the British Empire.[30]

Lord Grey had been a director of Cecil Rhodes's British South Africa Company, and Administrator of Rhodesia from 1894 to 1897. The biographical study of him by Harold Begbie, and his own short life of Hubert Hervey (an employee of the British South Africa Company) make curious reading today.[31] Grey himself is said to have had a 'spiritual and almost religious enthusiasm for the British Empire', and is portrayed as mixture of saint, great gentleman and knight. He starts as 'the beau-ideal of English manly youth', and develops into 'the deliberate knight of the chivalry of Christ', and 'a Paladin of Empire'.[32] His own account of Hubert Hervey is written in similar language. It starts with a plea for chivalry. 'There is a tendency, in the present day, . . . to assume that those finer feelings which were once regarded as the heritage of our race are becoming extinct, or, at most, are kept alive by sordid motives. Chivalry is dubbed Quixotism; honour is sneered at as sentimentality; and patriotism is too often attributed to a mere desire for personal aggrandisement.' Grey protested against this tendency, and seems to have written about Hervey in order to show his ideal of a young Englishman. Hervey was 'one of the most chivalrous and high-minded men it has been my privilege to meet'.[33]

Grey hero-worshipped Rhodes, as did George Wyndham, another aristocratic Englishman who was often described as chivalrous. Rhodes himself could scarcely be called chivalrous, but he was attracted to men of this type, and had the gift of attracting them. The Rhodes scholarships, which he left as his principal legacy, were designed to produce more Greys and Wyndhams, not more Rhodeses. In the qualities which he laid down as necessary for his scholars the qualities of the chivalrous gentleman as taught in public schools loomed large. They were to show 'fondness of, and success in manly outdoor sports, such as cricket, football, and the like' and 'qualities of manhood, truth, courage, devotion to duty, sympathy for the protection of the weak, kindliness, unselfishness and fellowship'. He considered the combination of these qualities more important than 'literary and scholastic attainments'. He hoped that his scholars, drawn from both the colonies and the United States, would form an élite, and spread over the world to bring about the permanent supremacy of the Anglo-Saxon race.[34]

Rhodes made millions out of the Kimberley diamond mines, and employed his wealth in bribery on a lavish scale. This was scarcely in accordance with the code of chivalry; his admirers had to turn a blind eye to the bribes, and assure themselves that he only made money in order to serve the Empire. It was hard, however, to believe that the gold-millionaires of the Rand were similarly dedicated. The doctrine that Britain was in the Empire for duty not for gain looked especially odd in South Africa. Milner, the great South African pro-consul, may have been above money himself, but he worked closely with men who thought of little else. When he brought in cheap Chinese labour to work the mines, and allowed corporal punishment to be administered to the labourers, there was an outcry at home, but imperialists rallied to his support; no mud could be thrown at the most dedicated of the champions of Empire (Plate 153). One of the advantages (or dangers) of chivalry was that it could lift people to so lofty an emotional level that inconvenient facts could be disregarded.

154. (right) Healthy boy and loafer, as illustrated in Baden-Powell's *Scouting for Boys*, 1908

CHAPTER 15

Playing
The
Game

IN 1977 THE LONG-ESTABLISHED AUSTRALIAN CRICKET BOARD DECIDED TO choose a symbol with which to launch their campaign to defeat England in that year's Test Matches, and bring back the Ashes to Australia. They chose a logo of two knights fighting. Many Australians considered it ludicrously inapposite; moreover, England won the matches. The Australian financier Kerry Packer moved into Australian cricket, complete with bunnygirls, theme songs, flood-lighting, coloured cricket flannels, and a commitment to 'get bums on seats'. The Cricket Board crumbled, and the knights with it.[1]

The knights may have been out of date, but there was a point to them. Chivalry helped to create the Victorian gentleman; and the Victorian gentleman created, or rather re-created, cricket. Indeed, the whole vast fabric of contemporary sport derives, not just from Victorian England, but from the small percentage of Victorian Englishmen who went to the public schools. The games which public-school men took up or invented, the rules which they laid down for them, the clothes which they wore, the settings and equipment which they devised, the language which they used and the seriousness with which they took the whole business gradually spread down the social scale and out to the rest of the world. As they spread they changed; but even though there is much about sport today that would horrify Victorian gentlemen, it still shows its origins.

The operative term is 'public-school men' rather than 'public schools'. Victorian sport was created as much by those who had left public schools as those who were still at them. University and amateur clubs, country-house, county and college teams all played their part. As pioneers, the universities were especially important. Team games first became a noticeable feature at Oxford and Cambridge in the 1820s, inter-college matches appeared in the same decade, and regular inter-university matches started in the late 1830s. The first inter-university boat race and cricket match were in 1829 and 1827, and from 1839 and 1838 they became annual events.

The reasons for this development have never really been examined, and can only be guessed at. It perhaps started through the combination of a growing craze for physical fitness with a new class of undergraduate. Physical prowess had become an upper-class fetish in the late eighteenth century, but to begin with it expressed itself mainly in hunting, racing and boxing, and was closely tied up with betting. In the 1820s, as upper-class patronage declined and middle-class independence increased, Oxford and Cambridge were increasingly filled with the lively and often idealistic sons of clergymen and professional men, most of whom lacked the money to keep a stable or move in smart sporting circles, and many of whom were morally averse to the betting and womanising that sporting young lords and their hangers-on went in for. Team games were an acceptable alternative, in which they, as initiators, could set the style. No doubt most of them played games simply because they enjoyed them. But Digby and Carlyle provided a moral basis for those who wanted it. Digby, pioneer of rowing and the cold dip at Cambridge, preached the knightly values of fellowship, discipline, exercise and physical prowess; Carlyle praised toughness of muscle as an accompaniment to toughness of heart.

It was young men who had played and enjoyed games at public school, and continued to play and enjoy them at university, who went back to teach at public schools in the 1850s, and revolutionised the prestige of sport by using school games to improve their boys' characters, rather than just to amuse them. Kingsley and Hughes encouraged them; games became not just an acceptable, but a praiseworthy, activity for grown men as well as for schoolboys. To play them was both morally creditable and the mark of a gentleman. Throughout the British Isles public-school men founded clubs in which they could continue to play games into middle age, and even beyond it.

The moral value of games was given official recognition in 1864, when the Royal Commission on the Public Schools reported that 'the cricket and football fields . . . are not merely places of exercise and amusement: they help to form some of the most valuable social qualities and manly virtues.' In 1884 Edward Bowen, Harrow schoolmaster and author of *Forty Years On*, was of the opinion that 'I had rather regenerate England with the football elevens than with average members of Parliament.'[2] In the same year Bowen's friend the Hon. Robert Grimston died. He was an Old Harrovian who had given much of his time to coaching Harrow boys in cricket. His biography, which came out in 1885, quoted the remark of a friend: 'It was not cricket *only* that the boys learnt from poor old Bob Grimston, but they acquired the true principles of chivalrous honour.'[3] When his fellow-coach the Earl of Bessborough died a few years later they were commemorated by a joint memorial at Harrow. 'While teaching skill in cricket,' the inscription ran, 'they taught manliness and honour.'[4]

It is still widely believed that the Duke of Wellington said 'The Battle of Waterloo was won on the playing fields of Eton.' He never said anything of the sort, but the legend that he had, which had been taking shape since the 1850s, was given its final form by Sir William Fraser in 1889.[5] In 1893 Andrew Lang wrote that 'there is more teaching in the playground than in schoolrooms'.[6] In 1908 Baden-Powell told his Scouts that football was 'a grand game for developing a lad physically and also morally, for he learns to play with good temper and unselfishness, to play in his place and "play the game," and these are the best of training for any game of life'.[7]

Once the moral value of games was recognised they inevitably began to supply this kind of metaphor. It became a commonplace, in an everyday rather than sporting context, to condemn an action as 'not cricket', or to commend someone for being a sportsman or for playing the game. The popularity of the last phrase derives largely from Henry Newbolt's 'Vitai Lampada', first published in 1897. To quote so hackneyed a poem in full may seem unnecessary; but perhaps it becomes forgivable if presented, as the National Anthem sometimes is, in an unfamiliar arrangement, in this case as adapted by Baden-Powell in 1908 for public performance by Boy Scouts.

Scene I: Tableau of boys playing cricket

RECITATION

There's a breathless hush in the close tonight

Ten to make and the match to win—
A bumping pitch and a blinding light,
An hour to play and the last man in.
And it's not for the sake of a ribboned coat
Or the selfish hope of a season's fame,
But his captain's hand on his shoulder smote.

[*Action: The captain steps up to the batsman, puts his hand on his shoulder, and says to him urgently—*]

'Play up! Play up! And play the game!'

Scene II: Tableau. Soldiers in a hard-fought fight retreating—a young officer among them

RECITATION

The sand of the desert is sodden red—
Red with the wreck of the square that broke;
The gatling's jammed and the colonel dead,
And the regiment blind with dust and smoke.
The river of death has brimmed its banks,
And England's far and Honour a name,
But the voice of a schoolboy rallies the ranks.

[*Action: The young officer stands forward pointing his sword to the enemy, and the retreating soldiers turn ready to charge with him as he cries—*]

'Play up! Play up! And play the game!'

Scene III: A procession of all kinds of men, old ones at the head, middle-aged in centre, young ones behind—soldiers, sailors, lawyers, workmen, footballers, etc., etc.—Scotch, Irish, English, Colonial—all linked hand in hand

RECITATION

This is the word that year by year
While in her place the school is set
Every one of her sons must hear,
And none that hears it dare forget.
This they all with joyful mind
Bear through life like a torch in flame,
And falling fling to the host behind.

[*Action: The leader flings out a Union Jack, and calls to the rest—*]

'Play up! Play up! And play the game!'

[*One in the centre then calls back to the juniors: 'Play up! Play up! And play the game!' The smallest of the juniors steps forward and cries to the audience—*]

'PLAY UP! PLAY UP! AND PLAY THE GAME!'[8]

The phrase 'playing the game', or something close to it, had in fact been used as early as 1849 in Charles Kingsley's couplet:

Up, Up, Up and Up
Face your game and play it.[9]

Twenty years or so after 'Vitai Lampada' it was adapted to celebrate the dead of the 1914–18 war:

234

And though there is no need to tell
Their answer to the call
Thank God we know they batted well
In the last great game of all.[10]

A verse in 'Alumnus Football' written in the 1920s by the American poet Grantland Rice was so rapidly acclimatised into England that it tended to be misattributed to Newbolt:

For when the One Great Scorer comes
To write against your name
He marks—not that you won or lost—
But how you played the game.[11]

In the 1890s *Punch* defined the qualities of a sportsman as follows: 'He is one who has not merely braced his muscles and developed his endurance by the exercise of some great sport, but has, in the pursuit of that exercise, learnt to control his anger, to be considerate to his fellow men, to take no mean advantage, to resent as a dishonour the very suspicion of trickery, to bear aloft a cheerful countenance under disappointment, and never own himself defeated until the last breath is out of his body.'[12] Self-control, courtesy, consideration of one's opponent, honour, rejection of deceit, cheerfulness under difficulty and refusal to surrender were in fact knightly qualities selected by Digby as worthy of imitation by modern gentlemen. So were other qualities associated with sportsmanship but not mentioned by *Punch*: modesty, fellowship, capacity to lead or loyalty to a leader.

At much the same time the poet laureate Alfred Austen described cricket as chivalry in modern form:

Why mourn ye the age of bright chivalry fled
While each knight of the bat has a fair one to win?
Why deem we that courage and honour are dead
While cricket enobles the young heart within?[13]

In 1915 Newbolt stated the public-school 'love of games, the "sporting" or "amateur" view of them', derived 'from tournaments and the chivalric rules of war'.[14] If taken to mean that a continuous tradition joined mediaeval chivalry to Victorian games, this was nonsense; but in the sense that Victorians selected the qualities which they admired in chivalry and remodelled games in the light of them, he was saying no more than the truth.

For playing the game had not always had its Victorian connotations. Eighteenth-century football was an affair of undisciplined mobs of boys or yokels kicking and hacking each other in disregard of what few rules existed. Eighteenth and early nineteenth-century cricket was closely tied up with betting for high stakes; winning was all-important, matches were fixed by bribery or cunning, opposing sides not infrequently came to blows over a disputed decision, and the

235

losing side tended to be beaten up by its infuriated supporters. Many early cricketing heroes were far from sporting in the Victorian sense. The famous Squire Osbaldeston resigned from the M.C.C. in a fury because he was unexpectedly bowled out. Lord Frederick Beauclerk, one of the most gifted cricketers of his day, was famous for his bad temper and unscrupulous tricks. Football had to be codified and civilised, and cricket to pass through what the great late-Victorian amateur Lord Harris called 'a cleansing fire',[15] before they became acceptable. As late as 1874 the *Cliftonian* had to issue a warning: 'There are people in the school who need to be reminded not to forget themselves so far as to applaud when a stroke falls short, or when a catch is missed by strangers playing against us.'[16]

By the end of the century the code and prestige of sportsmanship were triumphantly established. The lords who presided over cricket were now unimpeachably chivalrous gentlemen like Lord Harris in Kent or Lord Hawke in Yorkshire ('my job has been to play the game both on and off the field in a spirit of sportsmanship', the latter declared in his autobiography).[17] New or newly popular games like golf and tennis had enriched the repertoire of games and been imbued with an acceptably sporting spirit. Even boxing had been cleaned up by the Queensberry Rules and the National Sporting Club. Racing admittedly, even though under the gentlemanly direction of the Jockey Club, was still dominated by betting and professional jockeys; and the newly professionalised football teams of the North were a worrying new feature. But from the school almost to the grave the range of sports, teams and clubs available to and dominated by amateur gentlemen was virtually endless.

None was more typical than country-house cricket (and its extension, the country-house cricket week). Owners of country houses who were also cricketing enthusiasts formed their own teams out of their families, their relatives, their friends, and sometimes their servants, employees and tenants. They played matches with other country-house teams, with teams from neighbouring towns and villages, and with teams formed by travelling amateur clubs, of which I Zingari, founded in 1845, was the first and most famous. Country-house cricket got under way in the 1850s, but its elaboration into actual cricket weeks was a development of the end of the century. Since a cricket week involved having one or more visiting teams to stay, country houses were sometimes enlarged to accommodate them. The elaborate half-timbered extensions made to Wightwick Manor, near Wolverhampton, in the 1890s, were said to be largely for the annual cricket week.[18] The cricketing wing added at about the same time to Ballywalter Park in Ulster was suitably equipped with twenty-two bedrooms.[19]

The make-up of teams varied considerably. At Gorhambury rival teams of Harrow schoolboys were got together by Frederick Ponsonby and Robert Grimston, and played cricket against each other from 1868 into the 1870s. Often teams were formed largely, and sometimes entirely, from one family. Arnos Grove, just outside London at Southgate, was the home of the seven Walker brothers, none of whom ever married and all of whom devoted their lives to

cricket. The most famous cricketing family of all, the Graces, produced an entire eleven on occasions, as did the Lytteltons of Hagley.[20]

At Lorbottle in Northumberland Frank Coltman, an Old Etonian judge who 'had kept from his days in the Eton XI a perfect faith in cricket, not merely as a pastime, but as a strategical and even a moral exercise', held an annual cricket week. His team included Henry Newbolt, the novelist J. Meade Falkner, and Lancelot Perceval, the Arthurian-named son of the headmaster of Clifton.[21] The team collected together by the American painter Edwin Austen Abbey for cricket weeks at his house outside Fairford in Gloucestershire consisted entirely of artists. In the intervals of cricket, convivial meals took place in Abbey's studio-barn, under the shadow of the vast pictures of the *Quest for the San Greal*, which Abbey was gradually painting for the Boston Public Library.[22]

Abbey's gatherings, like almost all cricket weeks, involved a good deal of jokiness during the matches, and charades and high jinks in the evenings. But their juxtaposition with Abbey's intensely serious pictures was not inapposite, for the surface frivolities of cricket weeks tended to have a serious base, which came to the surface at times of stress. During the 1914–18 war, for instance, I Zingari, which was perhaps the most facetious of all the cricket clubs, presented the freedom of the club to Kitchener, French and Beatty. The accompanying letter quoted the couplet about those who 'batted well/In the last great game of all'. Beatty replied appreciatively that 'The precepts of I Zingari are very familiar to the Navy, and indeed might be said to form the basis of the unwritten laws which we try to instil into the minds of all Naval Officers in our endeavours to teach them to "play the game."'[23]

For a gentleman with sufficient private means to devote the greater part of his life to playing or promoting games was now entirely acceptable. But another typical product of the late nineteenth century was the prominent public servant who was passionately addicted to games. The Lyttelton brothers were perhaps the

237

155. Edwin Austen Abbey's cricket eleven at Morgan Hall, Fairford, in 1903

156, 157. Surcoats of mediaeval knights, as illustrated in S. R. Meyrick's *Critical Inquiry into Antient Armour*, 1824

best-known example. Alfred Lyttelton (1857–1913), the most gifted of the brothers, was the finest football player of his day at Eton, captained Eton and Cambridge at cricket, played cricket for Middlesex until 1884 (and was considered the best wicket-keeper in England) and was amateur champion at tennis from 1882 to 1896. He was also a busy and successful lawyer, an M.P. from 1895, and Secretary of State for the Colonies from 1903 to 1905. In middle age he took up golf; he built Grey Walls, Gullane (designed for him by Lutyens), in 1900–1, in order to be next to the Muirfield golf course at North Berwick.[24]

Lyttelton, according to his admirers, was equally generous to an opponent whom he was beating at tennis, and to a political opponent in the House of Commons; 'he had an ingrained sense of "the rules of the game" and, whatever the provocation, he was no more capable of taking what he thought an unfair advantage of his opponent than of disputing the umpire's decision at Lords.'[25] He died, sadly but perhaps suitably, as the result of being hit in the stomach by a cricket ball. Asquith compared him to Wordsworth's Happy Warrior; his widow believed that 'he had stood for all that was pure, chivalrous and high-minded in England of his time'.[26]

Being a sportsman, being a gentleman and being chivalrous were such overlapping concepts that it is scarcely surprising to find sport using terms and practices derived from chivalry. Mediaeval knights went out to joust from their pavilions and so did Victorian 'knights of the willow'; indeed, the tent which preceded the provision of permanent buildings at the edge of cricket fields had a curious, though perhaps fortuitous, resemblance to the mediaeval pavilions that

238

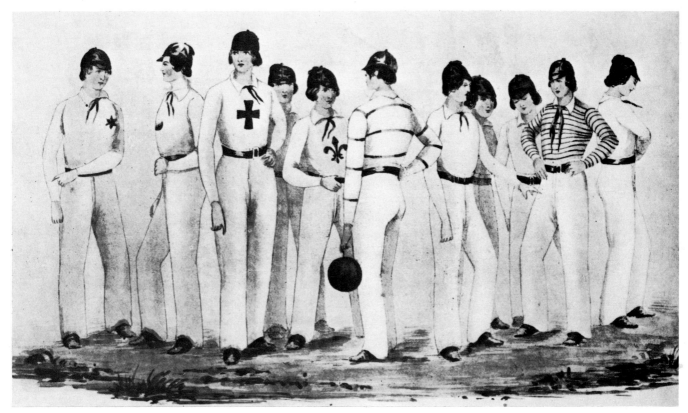

158. Early football costume at Rugby School, drawn by T. L. Johnson, *c.* 1850

were to be imitated at the Eglinton Tournament in 1839.[27] Victorians competed for shields and took part in golf or tennis tournaments. Opposing teams were described as 'entering the lists' or 'throwing down the gauntlet'. A winning competitor or captain of the team went up to the stand to receive his shield, cup or trophy from a gracious lady of title, just as a knight received his reward from the Queen of Beauty.

Even football jerseys may have had chivalric origins. In the football matches at Rugby described in *Tom Brown's Schooldays*, which are set in the years around 1840, no particular dress is worn. Distinctive clothes seem to have appeared in the early or mid–1840s. According to the account of 'An Old Rugbeian', published in 1848,[28] 'considerable improvement has taken place within the last few years, in the appearance of a match, not only from the great increase in the number of boys, but also in the use of a peculiar dress, consisting of velvet caps and jerseys. The latter are of various colours and patterns, and wrought with many curious devices, which on their first introduction were accompanied by mottoes . . . as, for instance, *Cave Adsum* [Look out, here I am].'

This new gimmick at Rugby seems to have been directly inspired by the dress and devices of mediaeval knights, by way of Scott's account of the tournament in *Ivanhoe*. When he first touches on the competing knights Scott disclaims any intention of describing 'their devices, their colours, and the embroidery of their horse trappings', but in fact he later deals with their devices in some detail. For instance 'the gigantic Front-de-Boeuf, armed in sable armour, was the first who took the field. He wore on a white shield a black bull's head, half defaced by the

239

numerous encounters which he had undergone, and bearing the arrogant motto, *Cave Adsum.*'[29]

The appearance of the same motto at Rugby as in *Ivanhoe* seems to be beyond coincidence. Moreover the resemblance between a modern football jersey and the surcoat of a knight, as exhibited in many plates of Meyrick's *Critical Inquiry into Antient Armour* (1824), is striking; *Ivanhoe* and Meyrick combine to suggest that chivalry, rather than racing colours, provided the inspiration of football dress. By 1848, according to the Old Rugbeian, mottoes had gone out of fashion, and the modern jersey was well on the way: 'these vanities have, as far as we could judge from a match at which we were present a few months ago, now gone out, leaving, however, the many coloured caps and Jerseys to contrast with the white trowsers and give a very lively and pleasing appearance to the game.'[30]

By the 1860s gay heraldic stripes and chequers had spread to cricket. The Oxford Harlequins were especially colourful; Lord Harris explained how 'you might see eleven young gentlemen in caps and shirts, quartered brown, blue, and red, with a broad stripe of the same colour down their trousers'.[31] But on the whole cricketers confined their colours to caps, blazers, or ribbons on straw hats.

Racing trophies were another aspect of sport in which chivalry figured prominently. Because of the social prestige of racing and the amount of money involved in it, its so-called cups and trophies were far more elaborate than those in any other sport. Winners of famous races found themselves the owners of massive allegories in silver, designed to load their sideboards or provide centrepieces for their dinner parties. Goodwood, Doncaster and Ascot (where the Queen annually commissioned and presented the Gold Cup) were especially prolific in examples; but even obscure Hunt steeplechases could on occasion produce trophies of amazing elaboration. All sorts of themes were expressed in these pieces, but chivalry was among the most popular. An early example is the cavorting knight who forms part of the Goodwood Prize Plate of 1849. Later examples include St George, the Black Prince, the Red Cross Knight and William the Conqueror.[32]

★　　★　　★

In sport, as in everything else which felt the influence of chivalry, the relationship between the classes played an important role; and in sport, as in so much else, the ideal situation which chivalrous gentlemen dreamed of did not always work out quite like that in practice.

The ideal had already been suggested by eighteenth-century cricket—as long as certain features in it were ignored. A number of eighteenth-century teams were funded and captained by aristocrats and country gentlemen; and it was a common practice for them to have tenants or employees in their teams, or alternatively to employ professional cricketers in their households, in order to give them an occupation and livelihood out of season. The model of benevolent feudalism which this suggested appealed to all those who approved of benevolent feudalism; and although feudalism and chivalry are not synonymous, approval of one tended to go with approval of the other. The situation seemed to epitomize

240

XXIV. (right) Cover of Baden-Powell's *Young Knights of the Empire*

XXV. (following page) George Frederic Watts. *Sir Galahad*, from a late nineteenth-century colour reproduction by Emery Walker

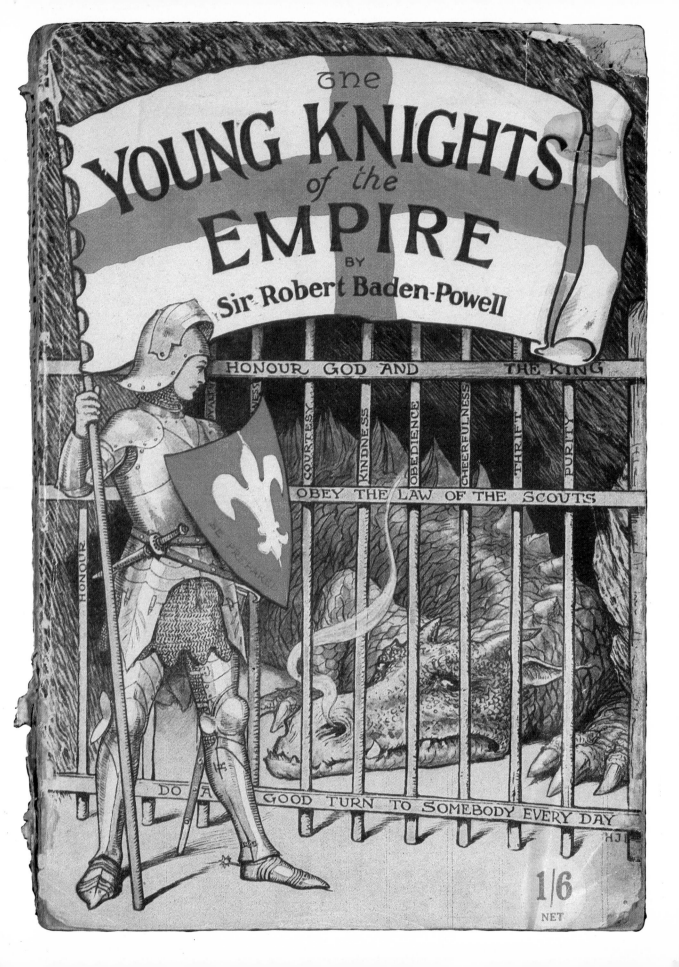

THE
YOUNG KNIGHTS
of the
EMPIRE

BY
Sir Robert Baden-Powell

HONOUR GOD AND THE KING

OBEY THE LAW OF THE SCOUTS

DO A GOOD TURN TO SOMEBODY EVERY DAY

1/6
NET

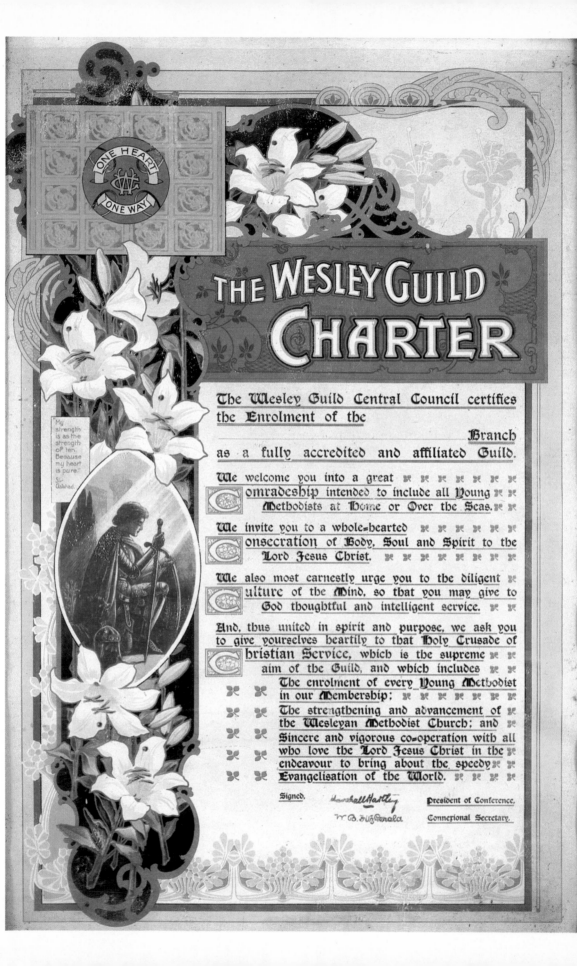

ONE HEART
ONE WAY

THE WESLEY GUILD CHARTER

"My strength is as the strength of ten. Because my heart is pure."
Sir Galahad.

The Wesley Guild Central Council certifies the Enrolment of the

.... Branch

as a fully accredited and affiliated Guild.

We welcome you into a great ✖ ✖ ✖ ✖ ✖
Comradeship intended to include all Young ✖ ✖
Methodists at Home or Over the Seas. ✖ ✖

We invite you to a whole=hearted ✖ ✖ ✖ ✖ ✖
Consecration of Body, Soul and Spirit to the
Lord Jesus Christ. ✖ ✖ ✖ ✖ ✖ ✖

We also most earnestly urge you to the diligent
Culture of the Mind, so that you may give to
God thoughtful and intelligent service. ✖ ✖

And, thus united in spirit and purpose, we ask you
to give yourselves heartily to that Holy Crusade of
Christian Service, which is the supreme ✖ ✖
aim of the Guild, and which includes ✖ ✖
The enrolment of every Young Methodist
in our Membership; ✖ ✖ ✖ ✖ ✖ ✖
The strengthening and advancement of
the Wesleyan Methodist Church; and ✖
Sincere and vigorous co-operation with all
who love the Lord Jesus Christ in the ✖
endeavour to bring about the speedy ✖ ✖
Evangelisation of the World. ✖ ✖ ✖

Signed,

Marshall Hartley   President of Conference,

W. B. Fitzgerald   Connexional Secretary.

159. The Black Prince and King John of France: Doncaster Race Cup, 1853

160. The Red Cross Knight and Una: Queen's Cup, Ascot, 1852

that 'sympathy of feeling and affection' between gentlemen and 'the lower classes of society' which was believed in by Kenelm Digby.

Not surprisingly, this kind of attitude won the support of Young England. It can be seen in operation in connection with the much-publicised festivities with which William Busfield Ferrand celebrated the opening of the Cottingley allotment gardens in Yorkshire in 1844. Ferrand was a Radical Tory M.P. whose attacks on mill-owners for exploiting their work-force had won him the friendship and support of Young England. The provision of allotments formed part of his campaign to give working people a fair deal. Having failed to get a 'Bill for the Allotment of Waste Lands' through Parliament as 'an act of justice to the poor', he persuaded his aunt, Mrs Walker Ferrand, to present fifteen acres near Bingley for allotments. These were inaugurated on 11 October 1844 with a parade, a dinner and a series of cricket matches; the Bingley Cricket Club was another of Ferrand's ventures.

Disraeli and Lord John Manners attended the celebrations, and both took part in the cricket. Manners is said to have captained one of the teams, and Disraeli to have gone in to bat with a local shoemaker. At the ensuing dinner, Ferrand sat between Disraeli and Manners, and declared to a mixed company of two hundred people that 'if there be one position more than another in which an English country gentleman may stand proud and happy in his own parish, it is when he is surrounded by every grade of society within it, cheering him when his health is proposed at a vast meeting like the present'.[33]

There were many other examples of local landowners or their families taking part in village or small-town cricket; Thomas Hughes, for instance, was an active member of local teams near his father's house in Berkshire.[34] A nostalgic picture of a similar situation with regard to football is depicted in the standard early twentieth-century history of Association Football: 'A younger son, with his school career behind him, was dumped down in a distant country, and as winter

245

XXVI. (preceding page) Detail of the reredos, Marlborough College chapel

XXVII. (left) Wesley Guild Certificate of c. 1900

came along and he pined for the thrill of the beloved game, he would gather round him the village tenantry, the squire's boy, the blacksmith's prentice, and the schoolmaster, and in one of the Manor fields, there would be transplanted the old game under new conditions.'[35] In fact football entered the country-house scene much less than cricket—perhaps because hunting and shooting kept the upper classes busy in the winter, whereas in the summer they had time to fill. But there were occasional examples. James Kay, for instance, the son of a Lancashire landowner, founded the Turton Football Club in 1872 jointly with the village schoolmaster; games were played on a ground in front of the village inn.[36]

But sporting contact between the classes did not necessarily have to take place in so obviously neo-feudal a context. It could result from the formation of a city or town club which did not confine its membership to one class; or from a clergyman with a public-school background in charge of a poor parish encouraging his parishioners to start a club; or from the owner or partners of a family business with a similar background getting involved with a football or cricket club at the works; or from public-school men bringing the gospel of sport to a settlement, mission or related organisation.

Such spreading of the message had been pioneered by Thomas Hughes at the Working Men's College in the 1850s, and became the almost inevitable accompaniment of any attempt by public-school men to improve the quality of life in working-class districts. A high proportion of football, cricket and other sporting clubs emerged from this kind of background. Some of the clubs later became well known. The Bolton Wanderers were originally the Christ Church Wanderers, founded in the 1870s by 'some of the scholars and teachers connected with Christ Church Schools, Bolton'. West Ham United emerged from the Thames Ironworks Football Club, set up in 1895 by A. F. Hills, the owner of the largest shipyard on the Thames.[37]

As the later history of clubs like these makes clear, selling football to the working classes was not a difficult matter. Football had originated with them, and they took it back with enthusiasm. Sheffield was the pioneer. Its first club, the Sheffield Football Club, was formed in 1857, and was limited to the social élite of Sheffield. By 1865 twelve more clubs had started up, at least eleven of which were working-class or lower-middle-class in character.[38] By the end of the 1870s football clubs by the hundred had appeared all over the north of England: town clubs, street clubs, pub clubs, works clubs, clerks' clubs, chapel clubs, most of them started up independently of public-school or Church of England patronage. Even the church clubs were beginning to have rows with the vicar, and go off on their own.

By the 1880s the mainly public-school committee of the Football Association had to face the problem of professionals. Public-school men could get enough free time to train up to a high standard; working men could not. Was this fair to working men? Should the Association allow clubs to pay working men, either on a full-time or part-time basis? In 1885, after protracted debate, professionalism was allowed. It had, after all, been an acceptable feature of cricket since the eighteenth century.

161. Amateur and Professional: Lord Desborough (right), perhaps the best-known all-round amateur sportsman of the late nineteenth century, out punting with his water-bailiff

The analogy was not a good one. Amateur cricketers were on the average both richer and grander than amateur footballers. A proportion of them were in effect professionals, in the sense that they could afford to be full-time cricketers; their resulting prowess at the game, combined with the prestige of titled cricketers and cricketing country houses, kept cricket, including county and national cricket, firmly under gentlemanly control. Professionals had entered cricket on an upstairs–downstairs basis, and remained there.

But amateur footballers were on the whole doctors, lawyers, journalists or businessmen. They owned no country houses, and could not afford full-time training. Within twenty years they had been virtually pushed out of all the more

247

important club teams—or at least those which competed for the F.A. Cup. The professionals played, on the average, better football. The old pattern of amateur-dominated football was replaced by one of teams of working-class professionals organised and financed by local businessmen who thought in terms of money at the gate and were less interested in playing the game than winning it.

Rugby football, for a variety of rather complex reasons, took longer to spread and catch on than Association. It was approximately ten years behind, and accordingly it had its crisis over professionalism in the mid-1890s, rather than the mid-1880s. Warned by what was happening in Association football the Rugby Football Union banned professionalism. In 1895 a large group of Northern clubs split away. The world of Rugby was divided into two, amateur Rugby Union and professional Rugby League.

The amateur–professional debate was carried on with great heat and bitterness, especially in the 1890s. The effect of professionalism, it was averred, would be to make players play to win rather than for the enjoyment of the game; to cause money to loom much too large; to encourage bribery; to separate the classes instead of bringing them together; and to reduce most working men to the status of a Roman mob watching a gladiatorial contest. Courtesy to opponents, sympathy for the loser, unquestioning obedience to the decision of the referee, would all vanish. 'Twenty thousand people', wrote Edward Ensor in an article, 'The Football Madness', published in 1898, 'torn by emotions of rage and pleasure, roaring condemnation and applause, make an alarming spectacle . . . As regards morality, the old English feeling for "sport" or "fair play" has receded to thinly-populated or remote districts.'[39] H. H. Almond, the headmaster of Loretto, expressed similar reactions in 1893, writing on 'Football as a Moral Agent'. Football ought to be 'an education in that spirit of chivalry, fairness, and good temper'. Instead, owing to professionalism, there was a danger that 'ultimately the game, instead of promoting sentiments of chivalry and honour, would become a byword for everything that is most opposed to old English notions of fair play and genuine sport'. There was an imminent threat 'of the grand old Rugby game becoming one in which no gentleman, after he leaves school, will take part'.[40] In fact Rugby, or the greater part of it, was saved for the amateur. As a result, within a few decades gentlemen, on the whole, played Rugger and working men played Soccer.

Amateurism in the latter went down with glory, however. From 1882 to 1907 the Corinthian Football Club battled with professional sides like an outpost of Crusaders fighting to the last against the infidel. The Corinthians were recruited from the cream of public-school footballers; not only did they have a brilliantly successful record playing against professional clubs, but for many years most (and in some years all) the English team was drawn from their members. Their play, according to their historian, B. O. Corbett, exemplified the natural superiority of the gentleman: 'the excellence of professional play generally gives the impression that the many tricks and intricacies of the game are mastered by mechanical activity and laborious training. But the passes of the amateur, though made as often and accurately, appear to be the result rather of natural instinct.'[41]

248

162. (right) Heading to 'Chivalry of the Knights', Chapter VII of Baden-Powell's *Scouting for Boys*, 1908

CHAPTER 16

Chivalry
for
The
People

ALTHOUGH CHRISTIAN SOCIALISM AS AN ORGANISED MOVEMENT, WITH ITS OWN headquarters, structure of committees, and periodical, only lasted a few years, as a point of view it continued to exert a great influence for the rest of the century. It left behind it one flourishing institution, in the form of the Working Men's College. Its ideas were carried to Oxford and Cambridge (in somewhat different forms) by two of its apostles who were professors there, Kingsley at Cambridge and Ruskin at Oxford; Ruskin, admittedly, had not been involved in founding the Christian Socialist movement, but he taught at the Working Men's College and his economic and social theories were greatly influenced by those of Carlyle and of Christian Socialism. At the public schools Christian Socialism was much the most important force among the masters, whether it worked through those who had been actively involved in the movement, like Bradley at Rugby and Marlborough and Johnson Cory at Eton, or those who absorbed elements of its teaching, like Warre at Eton and Perceval at Clifton.

Two concepts stressed by Christian Socialists are especially relevant from the point of view of chivalry. One is the need for the better off to go to the help of the worse off. The other is the value of sport as an aid to strengthening the character. The latter had nothing to do with the intellectual basis of Christian Socialism, but through the influence of Hughes, Kingsley and others it became inextricably mixed up with it.

The most obviously picturesque, if slightly ridiculous, expression of the concept of service is John Ruskin at Oxford and his band of idealistic undergraduates constructing an unusable road from Hinksey to Oxford with their own hands, for the benefit of the community. Service for Ruskin was closely bound up with the ideals of chivalry; he adjured the upper classes of his own day to retain 'the ancient and eternal purpose of knighthood, to subdue the wicked and aid the weak'.[1] Like Maurice and Carlyle, although he was passionately concerned about the condition of the working classes, he was very far from being a democrat; he believed in a ruling class, but wanted it to be so altruistic, noble, and free from self-interest that people would freely accept its rule. His ideals were expressed in his Guild of St George (St George, he believed, was essentially the 'type of Christian gentlemen'),[2] which absorbed most of his energies from 1870 onwards. He hoped that the Guild would develop into an ideal society, working its own lands away from the corruption of the cities, and divided into a carefully graded hierarchy of Marshal, landlords, Companions, tenants and retainers. Landlords would have to be able to work 'as much better than their labourers at all rural labour as a good knight was wont to be a better workman than his soldiers in war'.[3] The Guild was a considerable failure, and embittered Ruskin's last years.

A more typical product of chivalrous ideals of service was the almost endless stream of missions, clubs, institutes, halls and societies which upper and middle-class money and personnel brought into existence in the East End of London and other working-class areas between 1860 and 1914. What were the motives of those who answered what one writer called 'the call to the East'?[4] It is often hard to separate fear and guilt on the one hand from genuine compassion and desire to serve or help on the other. Fear of the political results of a disaffected and neglected working class, and guilt of the rich comparing their easy lives to those of the poor, certainly produced much of the money which was so liberally subscribed; so did fears that city dwellers were physically deteriorating, brought to a head by the poor physique of most of the volunteers in the Boer War.

A different and perhaps more sympathetic type of guilt, as an element leading to an active desire to serve, was expressed by Arnold Toynbee in 1883: 'we—the middle classes, I mean, not merely the very rich—we have neglected you; instead of justice we have offered you charity and instead of sympathy we have offered you hard and unreal advice; but I think we are changing. If you would only believe in us and trust us, I think that many of us would spend our lives in your service. You have—I say it clearly and advisedly—you have to forgive us, for we have wronged you; we have sinned against you grievously—not knowingly always, but still we have sinned, and let us confess it; but if you will forgive us— nay, whether you will forgive us or not—we will serve you, we will devote our lives to your service, and we cannot do more . . . We are willing to give up something much dearer than fame and social position. We are willing to give up the life we came from, the life with books and with those we love.'[5] When Toynbee died in 1883, aged only thirty, Toynbee Hall in Whitechapel was founded in his memory, and became the base for Residents, dedicated to work in the East End. Francis Fletcher Vane, one of the first of them, saw its work as 'not only an anti-slum campaign—but directly a revival of Chivalry'.[6]

The desire to serve was by no means confined to those of the upper or middle classes influenced by Christian Socialism, with its strong Church of England connections: it was felt by Quakers, nonconformists and agnostics as well as by High Church Anglicans, whose relationship with Christian Socialism had always been an uneasy one. Nor has serving the poor necessarily anything to do with chivalry; it is, after all, part of the basic message of Christianity. The connection depended on whether those who served saw themselves as Christians helping their fellow men, or gentlemen coming to the rescue of the oppressed.

They were probably often not at all clear in their own minds as to the answer. But their behaviour could be, and at the time often was, described as chivalrous, especially when it involved giving up the comforts of a rich man's life and the rewards of a conventionally distinguished career. The concept of chivalry undoubtedly helped release or inspire a great deal of genuine idealism among ardent young men of the upper and middle classes at the time; but it had the danger that, by elevating them on, as it were, spiritual chargers, it could create awkward barriers between helpers and helped.

How should they be helping anyway? With rare exceptions they were concerned with making the existing social system work more equably, rather than with radically changing it. Common to many of them, especially those influenced by Christian Socialism, was the desire to bring to the poor some of the advantages enjoyed by the rich. The Working Men's College had been started in order to give working men something of the education in the humanities which the rich took for granted at Oxford and Cambridge. Canon Barnett's East End art exhibitions, and the Whitechapel Art Gallery which developed out of them, had a similar aim as regards works of art; Emma Cons's Old Vic Theatre extended the concept to the plays of Shakespeare.

But what more precious gift could gentlemen bring to those whom they were helping than their own code? Being a gentleman, most gentlemen devoutly believed, had nothing to do with money; nor, many of them would insist, did it necessarily have anything to do with birth (though of course birth helped). Why should not the best type of working-class boy, given the training and opportunity, be just as loyal to queen and country, tender and respectful to women, manly in sport and war, pure in thought and true to his word as the best type of public-school boy?

Since manliness was the necessary first step to gentlemanliness, boxing, cricket and football were considered essential elements of the boys' clubs which were the inevitable appendages to missions and settlements. Sir John Gorst, an early friend and backer of Toynbee Hall, described how the University Settlements had succeeded in changing the boys of their local slums, and remarked, 'it is said that when a boy of this class begins to learn to box, his reformation has commenced'.[7] It continued when he learnt leadership and team spirit (and of course improved his physique) in a cricket or football team.

He could also learn them in one of the numerous organisations of a military or para-military nature founded for boys in the same period as the clubs. These did not necessarily have a gentlemanly element. There seems, for instance, to have been little emphasis on gentlemanliness in the Boys' Brigade, founded in 1883 by a Glasgow businessman, William (later Sir William) Alexander Smith. On the other hand the boys who joined its rather less successful rival, the Church Lads' Brigade (founded in 1891) were told to 'Remember that the C.L.B. aims at all its boys being gentlemen.'[8] The point was expanded on in its Fifth Annual Report in 1896–7: 'these lads have had a sound elementary education, but the Brigade aims at giving them something hitherto denied them—something of the free discipline, the manly games, the opportunities of wholesome society which a Public School gives.'

The Jewish Lads' Brigade, founded in Spitalfields in 1891, was designed to help the boys of the desperately poor Jewish immigrants who had come flooding into the East End as the result of the Russian pogroms. These Jews were somewhat of an embarrassment to the prosperous, Anglicised and in many cases gentrified Jews of the existing Jewish community—of which the Brigade's founder, Colonel Albert Edward Goldsmid, was a member. The Brigade, it was hoped, would help to make little immigrant Jews, if not more gentlemanly at least more acceptably English. One of the boys who joined it described the puzzled reaction of his father, when its officers came to visit him about his son's membership: 'They were English gentlemen, of course, and when they had gone my father asked "They're Jewish?"'[9]

Most of the various elements which coalesced in 1891 to form the London Cadets also had gentlemanly origins and aims. The First London Cadet Battalion, for instance, was made up of the Eton College Mission Cadet Company, the East

London Cadet Corps and the Southwark Cadet Corps. The East London Cadet Corps was an offshoot of Toynbee Hall, and had been founded in 1886–7 by a Toynbee Hall Resident, and ex-Guards officer, Sir Francis Fletcher Vane. The Southwark Cadet Corps acquired close links with Sherborne through one of its officers, Lancelot Bennet, who had been to school at Sherborne, and through the fact that Sherborne had a mission in Southwark.[10]

Its treasurer was the redoubtable Octavia Hill, Maurice's former secretary and friend and disciple of Ruskin. One of her other spheres of influence was Notting Hill, where she was also associated with a Cadet Company. In 1910 she described the virtues which it instilled; as in the case of the Church Lads' Brigade these were essentially public-school ones. 'The cadets learn the duty and dignity of obedience; they get a sense of corporate life and of civic duty; they learn to honour the power of endurance and effort . . . and they come in contact with manly and devoted officers . . . These ideals are in marked contrast with the listless self-indulgence, the pert self-assertion, the selfishness and want of reverence, which are so characteristic of life in a low district.'[11]

But among the various boys' organisations which came into existence in the years around 1900, the Boy Scouts were far and away the most successful. They owed their success to the remarkable character of their founder, Sir Robert (later Lord) Baden-Powell, and to the skill with which he worked out a formula which was as attractive to the boys who joined the movement as to the grown-ups who promoted it. The formula was a complex one, but chivalry formed a sizeable part of it. Whenever Boy Scouts make the Scout Promise, learn the Scout Law, or do their daily good deed, they are carrying on the traditions of the knights—at least as Baden-Powell saw them.

Baden-Powell was tremendously jolly, tough to the verge of ruthlessness, not in the least conventional, and a convinced believer in the need and duty of the white races (the British in particular) to lead the rest of the world. Jollity, toughness, unconventionality and belief carried him triumphantly through the siege of Mafeking and made him a national hero when it was relieved in 1900.

As a soldier he had always been somewhat scornful of conventional military discipline; what interested him were the tactics of reconnaissance and guerilla warfare, and the effect which these had in developing resourceful and independent soldiers. He had written two books on the subject, *Reconnaissance and Scouting* in 1884, and *Aids to Scouting* in 1899. In the early 1900s people involved in various boys' organisations who had found his ideas applicable to their work began to write to him for advice. He started to work out his own system of training for boys; at first he envisaged it as a system which could be used by existing organisations, but the interest it aroused was so great that it soon escalated into an independent movement.

Although he was far from being an intellectual, he had an academic background. His father, the Reverend H. G. Baden-Powell, had been Savilian Professor of Geometry at Oxford, and one of the contributors to *Essays and Reviews* (1860), the controversial Broad Church publication which nearly lost Jowett his job as Regius Professor of Greek. The elder Baden-Powell (whom

163. Two examples of chivalry in Boy Scout literature

Ruskin had known and admired)[12] had died in the year of its publication. But his library remained, at 32 Prince's Gate in London, where his widow kept a home going for her tribe of bachelor sons, the hero of Mafeking among them. The library formed the basis of Robert Baden-Powell's reading when he was working out the shape of his new movement; some of the books he had already read and been influenced by as a young man. He worked through Epictetus, Livy, Fraser's *Golden Bough*, and any other book that he could find, in order to discover about methods of training boys and initiating them into manhood in Sparta, Rome, Japan, Ancient Britain, Ireland and other early or primitive societies. He read Kenelm Digby's *Broad Stone of Honour*. He studied a wide range of contemporary organisations and themes, including all the relevant boys' organisations in England, the German gymnasiums and the writings of Pestalozzi.[13]

But he was probably more influenced by two American organisations for boys, the Woodcraft Indians and the Knights of King Arthur. The former had been founded by the novelist Ernest Thompson Seton as a means of encouraging boys in an enterprising out-of-door life by training them in Red Indian methods of woodcraft.[14] The Knights of King Arthur had been founded in 1893 by a Congregational minister from Vermont called William Byron Forbush. Its members (led by adult Merlins) met round a Round Table, took the names of knights or contemporary heroes, and transformed their games and outings into Arthurian quests and battles. Their object was to revive 'the spirit of chivalry, courtesy, deference to womanhood, recognition of the *noblesse oblige*, and Christian daring'.[15]

If Forbush and Ernest Thompson Seton are mixed together, something not unlike the Boy Scout movement emerges. Scouting and chivalry were its two dominant elements. Scouting derived from Baden-Powell's own experiences in Africa, and from what he had read about the Woodcraft Indians. It involved what now makes up most people's image of the Boy Scouts: tents, camp-fires, billycans, slouch hats, staffs, knots, signs, patrols with animal names, little boys rubbing two sticks together. But chivalry was equally important.

254

This is made clear in Baden-Powell's best-selling *Scouting for Boys*, which first came out in fortnightly parts in 1908, and thereafter went into innumerable editions.[17] Chapter VII is devoted to 'The Chivalry of the Knights', and consists of two 'Camp-Fire Yarns', one on 'Chivalry to Others', and the other on 'Self-Discipline'. What was to become one of the most familiar elements of the Scout code appears early on. 'In peace time, when there was no fighting to be done, the knight would daily ride about looking for a chance of doing a good turn to any wanting help, especially a woman or child who might be in distress. While engaged in thus doing good turns he was called a "Knight Errant." ' The origins of the code of chivalry are pushed back, with cheerful disregard of history, to the days of King Arthur, who is assumed to have been a real person living in A.D. 500. 'The Knight's Code' is given, in nine rules, ostensibly as laid down by King Arthur but in fact apparently distilled by Baden-Powell from Malory and Digby.[15]

The various rules are enlarged on in sections on Honour, Courtesy, Loyalty, Fair Play, Obedience, Discipline, Humility ('Don't Swagger') and so on. Examples are cited, drawn from chivalry ancient and modern and increased in number from edition to edition: King Arthur, Captain Oates, General Gordon, Sir Nigel Loring in *The White Company*, the soldier who died at his post at Pompeii, F. C. Selous (the African explorer), various cases of 'women and children first' and captains refusing to leave sinking ships. St George is introduced as the patron saint of chivalry, and therefore of Scouts. The word 'gentleman' is explained, in similar terms to those used in *The Broad Stone of Honour*: 'A knight (or Scout) is at all times a gentleman. So many people seem to think that a gentleman must have lots of money. That does not make a gentleman. A gentleman is anyone who carries out the rules of chivalry of the knights.' A London policeman, for instance, is a gentleman, because he is 'well disciplined, loyal, polite, brave, good-tempered, and helpful to women and children'. A final section, besides describing the game of 'Knight-Errantry' in which Scouts, like little knights, were to look for women or children in want of help, gave a reading list: books on chivalry and King Arthur, Scott's *Ivanhoe*, Conan Doyle's *White Company*, Kipling's *Puck of Pook's Hill* and Digby's *Broad Stone of Honour*.

The Boy Scouts were to achieve a great and rapid success in the public schools, but Baden-Powell was thinking mainly of working-class boys in the cities when he evolved his ideas. Like the Cadet Forces and the Church Lads' Brigade, his movement aimed not only to improve the physique of its boys by physical exercise in the open air, but to improve their character by inoculating them with the code of the Victorian gentleman. By the early twentieth century the chivalric elements of this code had been so thoroughly absorbed into it that they tended to be forgotten or taken for granted. Baden-Powell presumably brought them up to the surface again to make them more romantically attractive to boys.

Rules in the Scout law such as 'A Scout's Honour is to be trusted', 'A Scout is loyal to the King . . .', and 'A Scout is courteous' derive from Baden-Powell's Knight's Code. Even Law 8, 'A Scout smiles and whistles under difficulties', derives from the *Broad Stone*: 'Chivalry requireth that youth should be trained to perform the most laborious and humblest offices with cheerfulness and grace.'[18] Rule 6, 'A Scout is a friend to animals', was purely nineteenth century in origin. Rule 9, 'A Scout is thrifty', was tailored to the situation of working-class boys; encouraging the working classes to be thrifty had formed a major element in nineteenth-century philanthropy. Even here, however, Baden-Powell states (on very doubtful ground) that 'the knights of old were ordered by their rulers to be thrifty'. Rule 10, 'A Scout is clean in thought, word and deed', first appeared in the 1909 edition of *Scouting for Boys*. It relates to nothing in the Knight's Code, except, possibly, Rule 8, 'Rather die honest than live shamelessly.' But its connection with the Sir Galahad of Tennyson and Watts is obvious; Watts did in fact paint Baden-Powell's portrait, and although he did not live to see the Boy Scout movement, his widow was convinced that had he done so 'he would have welcomed it with enthusiasm, as probably the most hopeful movement of the century'.[19]

In 1907 Baden-Powell had held a first experimental camp on Brownsea Island, off Poole. Twenty boys came to it, some from public schools, some from the East End. The publication of *Scouting for Boys* and the formal inauguration of the movement followed in the next year. The first 'official' camp was held in 1908, at the end of August and beginning of September. The venue was Humshaugh, near Hexham and the Roman Wall. Baden-Powell described the camp as 'in a wild country teeming with romance—in fact our theme for two days and nights is "The Quest of King Arthur" who lies asleep in some hidden cave in the neighbourhood. This will I hope make his story and chivalry very real to the boys.'[20] As he wrote at the time to *The Scout*, 'even if we fail to find King Arthur, and to awaken him to revive chivalry we may still awaken his memory and revive chivalry among ourselves.'[21]

An engraving of St George and the dragon in which St George is transformed into a Boy Scout appears in the later editions of *Scouting for Boys*. Chivalry also makes occasional other appearances in Boy Scout iconography.[22] The most elaborate and curious is on the cover of the paperback edition of Baden-Powell's *Young Knights of the Empire*, of 1916 (Plate XXIV). This is an account of Scouting and its ideals, based on the concept of 'thousands of boys all over the British Empire carrying out the same idea' as mediaeval knights. On the cover, St George, displaying the Boy Scout fleur-de-lis on his shield, is gazing at a dragon whom he has caged in with bars made up of Scout virtues and mottoes.

Baden-Powell's formula proved triumphantly successful. It had the supreme advantage of appealing to both boys and adults. Boys enjoyed learning the novel but manageable skills of woodcraft, and getting involved in an organisation which had some of the qualities of a gang or secret society. Moreover, unlike most other boys' organisations of the period, the Scout Movement (on the surface, at any rate) was not authoritarian. Scout masters wore the same clothes as the boys and were deliberately encouraged to be like jolly elder brothers.

It is debateable how much the idea of being little knights appealed to working-class boys. But it was calculated to appeal to all the gentlemanly adults who supported and helped with the movement. Many of these had links with Christian Socialism, and were especially sympathetic to both chivalric language and the idea of a movement which would bring the classes together—whether by putting

Under the Searchlight.

THE ALLIANCE HAS NOW ENTERED UPON ITS 21st YEAR.
    Following upon a period of eighteen months of quiet endeavour and surveying of the ground, an unobtrusive, semi-private Conference was held at Islington, on *January 29th, 1903*, which was destined to cause an impact upon millions of lives—many at that time yet unborn. The years have sped quickly, filled with glad service for God and man—and the best is yet to be!

    The **JUNIOR SECTION** is steadily making its mark, but we lack funds to broadcast its existence. Our representative at Silcoates writes that it is greatly strengthening the power of Purity in the School and says that almost all possible boys are now enrolled as "Young Knights."

    THE MEETINGS continue in force in many parts of the country. During one period of 11 days no less a number than *15,280 persons* (men and women) received an appeal for Purity of life, both through eye-gate and ear-gate, as at each of the 12 gatherings held during that period (February 20th to March 2nd) "The Gift of Life" has been shown in addition to powerful speeches delivered. Many have joined in Membership—thus signifying their intention to take an active share in helping on the cause.

    In a number of instances the audience has risen *en masse* in signification of its avowal to stand boldly for the principles of the Alliance of Honour.

    Such work is counting in the Nation's life and its fruit will be seen in the days to come, for Purity and Nobility of life are essential factors in a Nation's greatness.

    ABROAD. Promising developments are transpiring in Bombay, Johannesburg and Sierra Leone (Freetown) where we are in correspondence with earnest workers.

    A MOTHER writes to notify us of the death of her son and send a subscription in his name—"He was a good noble son, and was proud of being a Member of the Alliance of Honour." Happily the Alliance is helping to produce many noble sons.

    "The work you are doing is a splendid one"—writes a subscriber—"and must do a tremendous amount of good, I hope you will get all the support you need to carry on the good work."

    We do need greatly enhanced support. No amount is too large and no amount too small to help.

    EVELYN E. BAGNALL } Joint Acting
    ALFRED B. KENT } Directors.

CHIVALRY

The Quarterly MESSENGER for ASSOCIATES of the ALLIANCE of HONOUR.

CONTENTS

Vol. VII.   No. 24.

MAY, 1923.

EDITED by the JOINT ACTING DIRECTORS
LONDON: MORGAN & SCOTT Limited

COPYRIGHT.
PRICE 1d. from International Hqrs. 112 City Rd., London, E.C.

164. Front and back cover of *Chivalry*, May 1923

gentlemanly Scout masters in charge of working-class Scouts, or getting working-class and public-school Scouts together around the same camp-fire. It was not surprising that the movement was enthusiastically supported from the start by Toynbee Hall.[23]

In his Camp-Fire Yarn on 'Health-Giving Habits' in *Scouting for Boys*, Baden-Powell gave a few slightly embarrassed and embarrassing words on 'beastliness';

257

'bathing at once in cold water' was suggested as a help. The section on 'Books to Read' at the end recommended 'publications by the Alliance of Honour, 118, City Road, London, who can give the best advice and help'. The Scout movement placed a strong emphasis on purity; so, for that matter, did almost all religious organisations of the period (Plate XXVII). But the Alliance of Honour was perhaps the only organisation exclusively concerned with purity.

The Alliance had been founded in 1903 as an inter-denominational movement 'to impress upon men and youths the necessity of living pure lives'. It grew rapidly, and soon acquired a formidable array of bishops, clergymen, ministers and minor celebrities as sponsors. In 1911 it started its own magazine, the *Alliance of Honour Record*; in 1915 this was renamed *Honour*. Its cover incorporated a reproduction of Watts's *Sir Galahad* as the 'type of perfect manly courage and purity'. From 1916 it also published a separate quarterly pamphlet called *Chivalry*. Membership was open to males of eighteen and over; boys under eighteen and over fifteen could become associates. It was possible to enrol separately as a Young Knight of the Alliance of Honour.[24]

The first issue of the *Alliance of Honour Record* reported a 'Monster Demonstration' in the Great Assembly Hall, Mile End Road. The speakers included Sir Robert Anderson, K.C.B. He told 'a harrowing story of an Eton boy, son of a colonel in the army, a brilliant lad "always head of his class, popular and successful both in his work and in the playing fields," who had been reduced to drivelling imbecility as the result of a secret sin, induced by the sight of an obscene photograph exhibited by a scoundrel whom he met in the railway train. "I had the satisfaction," adds Sir Robert, "of hunting the villain down and of procuring him a long stretch of penal servitude." '

Masturbation and fornication were the two dragons against which the Young Knights of the Alliance were urged to fight. Doctors told them how sexual abstinence was compatible with perfect health. Explorers wrote about Scott of the Antarctic and how 'we may safely assert that among the heroes of that dreadful journey from the South Pole there were no victims of the vice which the Alliance seeks to combat'. The Bishop of Durham distinguished between 'admirers of women' who were 'frankly animal' and 'reverencers of woman who look upon her as God's masterpiece of truth and virtue, made to be man's guiding star, his better self, that for which he shall feel it is a joy to live pure, to serve her with a loyal life, to find in her a perpetual inspiration for all that is noblest in himself'. Chivalry for the Alliance meant especially chivalry towards women. Members were told to think of 'the sacredness of your sister's body' and to remember that every woman, however low she had fallen, was likely to be someone's sister.[25]

By the 1930s the Alliance claimed branches in sixty-seven countries. In England it does not seem to have survived the last war, but there is said still to be a branch in South Africa.

258

165. (right) George Frederic Watts. Monument to Reginald Cholmondeley (d. 1864), Condover, Shropshire

CHAPTER 17

The Chivalrous Gentleman

BY THE END OF THE NINETEENTH CENTURY A GENTLEMAN HAD TO BE CHIVALROUS, OR at least if he were not he was not fully a gentleman. At the beginning of the century no one had talked about chivalrous gentlemen and the term would have been virtually meaningless to most people. The change was not simply one of a fashion in words; the concept of what a gentleman ought to be had changed.

The change was the most conspicuous result of the revival of chivalry. It was not, of course, the only one. When Rossetti and his fellow Pre-Raphaelites fell in love with Malory and tried to re-create his spirit in their poems and paintings, or young Wesleyans thought of Sir Galahad and tried to lead pure lives, neither group were particularly concerned with being gentlemen. Even here, however, gentlemanliness had a way of creeping in. Once a man started thinking in terms of being, or at least trying to be, a knight of God, the implications and associations of the metaphor were likely to start working. The concept of a Christian soldier was an ancient one, but being a Christian knight was not quite the same thing; it was more like being a Christian officer. And officers were of course gentlemen.

A chivalrous gentleman was brave, straightforward and honourable, loyal to his monarch, country and friends, unfailingly true to his word, ready to take issue with anyone he saw ill-treating a woman, a child or an animal. He was a natural leader of men, and others unhesitatingly followed his lead. He was fearless in war and on the hunting field, and excelled at all manly sports; but, however tough with the tough, he was invariably gentle to the weak; above all he was always tender, respectful and courteous to women, regardless of their rank. He put the needs of others before his own; as an officer, he always saw that his men were looked after and made comfortable before thinking of himself, as a landlord he took good care of his dependants. He was always ready to give up his own time to come to help of others, especially those less fortunate than himself. He was an honourable opponent and a good loser; he played games for the pleasure of playing, not to win. He never boasted. He was not interested in money. He was an ardent and faithful lover, but hated coarse talk, especially about women.

Certain beliefs were accepted by most (though by no means all) chivalrous gentlemen. Politics was a dirty business and most politicians not to be trusted; if only all decent men could get together, they could run the nation without party strife and bitterness. The countryside was better than the town. A natural affinity joined working men to gentlemen. Women who competed with men were betraying the essential role of womanhood.

The chivalrous gentleman was not an accident; he had been deliberately created. The aim of Digby, Carlyle, FitzGerald, Kingsley and others had been to produce a new model for the ruling classes, to train, in fact, an élite. They had undertaken this aim in conscious reaction to certain features of their own age which they disliked, especially the increase of democracy, and what they saw as the worship of money, and the placing of expediency before principle. Although they accepted many existing features of the tradition of the gentleman, they radically altered its balance. The eighteenth century had believed in a ruling class which ruled by right of ownership of property; it was hoped that this property-owning class would acquire sufficient of the right moral qualities to make them

good rulers, but property, not moral qualities, was the basis of their rule. The aim of the revival of the chivalric tradition was to produce a ruling class which deserved to rule because it possessed the moral qualities necessary to rulers. Gentlemen were to run the country because they were morally superior.

To those trying to create a new image for a ruling class, the code of mediaeval chivalry had a number of advantages. In the first place it *was* a code, and moreover one devised for an upper-class élite and designed to make those who adopted it think of more than their own self-interest. Secondly, it was made glamorous and therefore attractive by its romantic associations, which clothed gentlemen in metaphorical armour and mounted them on metaphorical chargers. Thirdly, it proved remarkably adaptable to the nineteenth-century situation. Although it had been specifically devised for a warrior caste, the use of fighting as a metaphor to cover self-conquest or the conquest of evil enabled it to be extended without difficulty to every aspect of life. Self-conquest included purity, a virtue on which nineteenth-century chivalry laid much more stress than mediaeval; none the less mediaeval chivalry could produce Sir Galahad as purity's ideal symbol.

The gentleman as he emerged at the end of the nineteenth century was not of course entirely a product of the revival of chivalry. Chivalry was superimposed

166, 167. Chivalrous gentlemen in and out of armour: the Scottish novelist William Black, by John Pettie, 1877, and A. N. Hornby, Captain of Lancashire Cricket XI, by John Collier, *c.* 1893

on earlier traditions, or used to give extra force to qualities already considered desirable for a gentleman. The model of the squire, for instance, kindly, honest, sturdy, down to earth and a good master, retained its popularity into the nineteenth century and helped to leaven the more quixotic aspects of knight-errantry. The concept that being a gentleman involved living up to standards as well as enjoying privileges had always existed; what the concept of chivalry achieved was to give it a new intensity. Sporting pursuits had always been considered a suitable recreation for gentlemen; chivalry, Victorian style, made them morally prestigious as well as enjoyable. On the other hand certain previously accepted aspects of the gentleman were much weakened through its influence; the concept of the gentleman as a man of taste, for instance, which had become strong in the eighteenth century, had almost disappeared by the end of the nineteenth.

The changing image of the gentleman had obvious attractions to those born into the ruling class; it meant that, at a time when inherited privilege was increasingly under attack, they were presented with a powerful weapon with which to overcome criticism and keep their position. But it also had attractions to those born outside the ruling class; it enabled them to enter it without having to acquire property, at any rate to anything near the extent that had been necessary in the eighteenth century. But if property was not necessary, the right sort of training was; hence the enormous prestige of the public schools as a means of creating new gentlemen as well as training existing ones.

The new image of the gentleman provided a magical means of dissolving much of the antagonism between middle and upper classes which had been a conspicuous feature of the early nineteenth century. By the end of the century thousands of middle-class Victorians, if asked their social rank, would have unhesitatingly answered not that they belonged to the middle class, but that they were gentlemen. As gentlemen, they identified with the upper classes and joined with them in running the country. And owing to England's great expansion in power and population, there were jobs for all—or if there were not, each expansion of the Empire created new ones. A wide range of careers was in fact (though almost never in theory) only open to gentlemen. Gentlemen dominated diplomacy, the colonial service, the Treasury, the Church of England, the army and navy, Oxford and Cambridge, the public schools, large sections of medicine and the law, and many of the most reputable firms in the City.

Being a gentleman was also a necessary key to society with a capital S, and to select preserves of male or male-dominated fellowship, from White's Club to the MCC. But it would be a great mistake to suppose that people only wanted to be gentlemen because it helped them to get on in the world. It was the additional moral aura and the glamour derived from chivalry that gave Victorian gentlemanliness its special quality and led many people to pursue it with the ardour of those looking for the Holy Grail. The business of being a gentleman had assumed a mystical quality. Gentlemen carried the seal of the elect, were conscious of doing so, and were recognised by others as carrying it. As Rider Haggard put it they were 'sealed with the indescribable stamp of the English gentleman'.[1]

How was this seal acquired? The easiest way was by a combination of birth and education. However much those who preached the gentlemanly code said that birth was not essential, or even important, and however genuinely many of them believed it, birth was historically so tied up with the concept of being a gentleman that it was virtually impossible to get rid of it. A gentleman by birth remained a cut above other gentlemen. Middle-class gentlemen clung tenaciously to any hint, myth or shred of gentlemanliness in their origins. Arthur Conan Doyle thought of himself not as the great-grandson of a Dublin silk mercer, but as descended from Norman Doyles who came to Ireland in the twelfth century, and linked with the Percies, the Plantagenets and the Conans, Dukes of Britanny.[2] Oscar Wilde ignored the Durham master-builder from whom he was actually descended in favour of a mythical Colonel de Wilde of Cromwellian days; he refused to leave England before his trial, because an Irish gentleman must stay to face the music.[3] Even W. H. Smith, the tycoon of the bookstalls, whom most people thought of as the epitome of solid self-made middle-class virtues, liked to believe that his grandfather was an Old Harrovian who came of Somerset gentry stock, but had been disinherited for marrying beneath him—a family legend for which there seems to have been absolutely no foundation.[4]

Education at a good public school was enough to make someone a gentleman, as long as he subsequently behaved like one; even so both he and his fellow gentlemen were likely to be conscious of his origins, so that he lacked the complete self-confidence of a gentleman born. The less prestigious the school, the less secure he was likely to feel. Education at Oxford or Cambridge might make a gentleman even out of someone who had not been at a public school, or at least it set him on the road; it depended on his friends at university and his subsequent career. John Buchan (Hutcheson's Grammar School, Glasgow, and Brasenose) and H. H. Asquith (City of London School and Balliol) were successful examples, even thought for a good many years Asquith was described as 'not quite a gentleman' by those who met him.[5] It is unlikely that this sort of reaction bothered Asquith; but it did bother those less formidably equipped than he was to get to the top.

In theory, as advocated for instance by both Digby at the beginning of the period and Baden-Powell at the end of it, neither birth nor education was absolutely essential to being a gentleman; anyone who lived up to the standards of a gentleman automatically became one. In fact it never worked out like that; such 'natural gentlemen' were at best gentlemen of the second class, whom few real gentlemen would for instance contemplate asking to dinner. To be a gentleman, for all practical purposes, involved not only adhering to the moral code of a gentleman, but looking and talking like one.

Both the code and the manners were normally acquired by a combination of home influence with public-school education. Formal training was supplemented by the informal education which came from reading the right sort of books, becoming familiar with the right sort of pictures, and going to the right sort of plays. The right sort of books need not necessarily include what might be called the textbooks of chivalry, such as Digby's *Broad Stone of Honour*, Carlyle's *Past and*

Le bon Chevalier sans peur et sans reproche

HERBERT COLE - 1911

BAYARD

168. Herbert Cole's frontispiece to Christopher Hare's *The Story of Bayard*, 1911

Present, FitzGerald's *Euphranor*, Kingsley's sermons, or even Baden-Powell's *Scouting for Boys*. Many, and perhaps most, Victorian gentlemen got through life without reading them. But by the end of the century most Victorian schoolrooms had accumulated several strata of books which inculcated the principles of chivalrous behaviour by means of memorable poetry or gripping stories.

Among them was likely to be Malory's *Morte d'Arthur* in the original or, more probably, in one of numerous modernised versions; Lanier's *Froissart for Boys* (1880); Christopher Hare's *The Story of Bayard* (1911); and the story of chivalry through the ages as told in Newbolt's *Happy Warrior* (1917). Successive waves of novels about the Middle Ages included Scott's *Talisman*, *Ivanhoe* and *Quentin Durward*, Charlotte M. Yonge's *Little Duke* and *Dove in the Eagle's Nest*, and Conan Doyle's *White Company* and *Sir Nigel*. Tennyson's *Idylls of the King* were probably too slow-moving for most schoolboys, even if enlivened by the romantic illustrations of Gustave Doré. But his 'Morte d'Arthur' on its own was memorable enough; or the exotic place-names and clashing armies of Matthew Arnold's *Sohrab and Rustum*, and the ringing couplets of Macaulay's *Lays of Ancient Rome*, both, in their different ways, pursuing chivalry into other civilisations. Henley's anthology *Lyra Heroica* was a good source for rousing shorter poems; and there were always the gripping ballads of Henry Newbolt.

Such poems were not of course confined to the Middle Ages; for chivalrous themes could be pursued all the way up to the present day. Among actual history books there were Charlotte M. Yonge's *Book of Golden Deeds*, W. H. Fitchett's *Deeds that Won the Empire*, and endless more specialised books, from W. H. D. Adams's *Famous Shipwrecks* to Butler's *General Gordon*. The relevant novels came once again in waves, starting with Scott and moving on to *Westward Ho* and *The Heir of Redclyffe*, by way of Captain Marryat's *Children in the New Forest*. In about 1880 G. A. Henty began his series of stories, and sent public-school boys thinly disguised in period dress on adventures of every date and in every climate—from *Beric the Briton* to *With Kitchener at the Soudan*.

Then there were the new brand of thrillers and romances, appearing sleek and dashing among the old heavyweights with their leisurely pace and pages crowded with small type. The idea that a story should be written in instant clear prose and move as fast as possible, gripping the reader so that he could not put it down until he had finished it, caused a revolution in English fiction, and its first results were heavily spiced with chivalry. Robert Louis Stevenson's short novel *The Pavilion on the Links*, first published in 1878, was followed by further adventure stories by Stevenson himself, by Anthony Hope, Stanley F. Weyman, Conan Doyle, Rider Haggard, Baroness Orczy and others; in 1910 Buchan's *Prester John* showed that a new master in this vein had arrived, although his great days were not to come until the Great War and afterwards.

In spite of their superficial variations the books of these various authors had much in common. To keep the pace going they needed simple characters and situations that were simple too, even if spiced with mystery. Nothing was better than a contest between easily identifiable enemies, be they Cavaliers and Roundheads, Citizens and Aristos, cowboys and Indians, or honest Englishmen and mysterious foreign secret societies. Anthony Hope's inspired invention of Ruritania allowed him to move his English hero straight from modern clubland into a world of castles, kings, beautiful women, and feudal loyalties.

A good villain made all the difference and a good hero was of course essential. The latter might be misanthropic, effervescent, eccentric, dashing, sleepy or humorous, but he had to be brave, clean-minded, true to his friends and his word, chivalrous to women, always ready to help someone in distress, and a gentleman. If he ever fell below the standards of his code, he was likely to spend the rest of the novel making up for it. Even Raffles, the gentlemanly cracksman whom E. V. Hornung daringly set in circulation in 1899, expiated his transgressions in the end by dying for his country.

In *The Scarlet Pimpernel* Baroness Orczy's Sir Percy Blakeney, noble and resourceful behind the camouflage of his billows of exquisite lace, was followed by Sir Andrew Ffoulkes, Lord Anthony Dewhurst and the rest with all the devotion that contemporary young Englishmen were bestowing on Wolseley, Kitchener and Milner. In fiction such bands of brothers were to be given a great future by Buchan, 'Sapper' and others; but before the Great War their main appearance outside Baroness Orczy was in school stories, in the off-beat and anti-establishment gang of Kipling's *Stalky & Co.* and the enormously popular 'Famous Five' of St Dominic's as endlessly retailed in the *Magnet*.

The *Magnet* was first published in 1908, the *Boy's Own Paper* in 1879. In the interval boys' magazines had started up by the dozen. They mixed stories of school-life and adventure with practical articles on how to blow eggs or stuff birds, and exhortatory articles on the armed forces or the Empire. Some, like the *Boy's Own Paper*, catered mainly for public-school boys, others, like the *Gem* and *Magnet*, aimed for boys of all kinds; but their heroes, schoolboys or otherwise, were almost universally gentlemen, up to pranks but never to mean tricks, and always ready to do down a bully or a dago, face a cobra or walk into an opium den.

Bound volumes of *Chums* or the *Boy's Own Paper* were soon appearing in Edwardian schoolrooms, along with full-length school stories. Tom Brown continued to keep his end up, but *Eric or Little by Little* was already becoming a bit of a joke. Horace Annesley Vachell's *The Hill* brought Tom Brown up to date, in a Harrow rather than a Rugby context, to the accompaniment of generous dollops of honour, sentiment and snobbery. Other school stories were coming out by the hundred, endlessly varying on the old mixtures of playing or not

266

169. (left) W. F. Yeames. *And when did you last see your father?* 1878 (detail)

170. (right) Little Lord Fauntleroy with his grandfather, the Earl

playing the game, good sportsmen, excitable foreign masters, Cock House, and the discomfiture of school bullies or bounders.

Somewhere in all this mass of literature there were likely to be characters with whom most boys could identify. It is to be hoped that few put themselves into the buckled shoes of Little Lord Fauntleroy, whom Frances Hodgson Burnett introduced to the world in 1885. But their mothers were likely to identify for them, and even to invest in Fauntleroy suits. For Fauntleroy was as gallant and chivalrous a little fellow as any mother could have wished for, all fearless, winning and loving as he was, facing the gouty old earl so bravely, and galloping along on his pony, with his cavalier locks flaring out over his little cavalier suit.

The pictorial equivalent of Lord Fauntleroy was the little boy in W. F. Yeames's *And when did you last see your father?*, painted in 1878. The picture was enormously popular, and reproductions of the gallant lad in his blue silk suit won hearts all over the country. Other reproductions likely to be found in nurseries or schoolrooms included Watts's *Sir Galahad* or *Happy Warrior*, Noel Paton's *The Choice*, Pettie's *The Vigil* and a wide variety of depictions of scenes of heroism or battle, including such old favourites by Lady Butler as *Balaclava* and *Steady the Drums and Fifes*. They supplemented the lessons of the books, as did visits to suitable plays, from *Henry V* to *Where the Rainbow Ends*.

The English gentlemen who emerged at the end of this conditioning were a remarkable phenomenon; moreover they were a successful one, in so far as they did to a large extent run England and its empire for the best part of a century. But they had their disadvantages.

They tended to take it for granted that they were better than non-gentlemen. This could work both ways of course. It could produce that total self-confidence which, for instance, enabled H. J. Huddlestone in 1924 to put down a mutiny of native troops in the Soudan by walking single-handed and unarmed into their camp; when asked what made him think they would surrender, he answered, 'It never occurred to me that they would do otherwise.'[6] But it could also mean that those who had no more than the social qualifications of a gentleman assumed that they were morally superior as well; similarly, many gentlemen found it hard to trust people who dropped their *H*s. It meant moreover that most people who considered themselves gentlemen were so conscious of the fact that they found it almost impossible to talk naturally or on equal terms with those who were not gentlemen, however hard they tried (and most of them did not try). In theory this should not have been so: Clement Attlee, when he worked at the Haileybury College mission in Limehouse, was delighted as a young man by the definition of one of the boys at the club: 'a gentleman is a bloke wot's the same to everybody'.[7] But in effect a deep and virtually uncrossable ditch prevented not just a small caste but a sizeable proportion of the population of England from doing more than shout across to those on the other side of it.

The division is all too visible in *A Little Military Knight*, an appalling children's story by E. M. Green published in about 1911 by the S.P.C.K. (which should have known better). It tells the story of Adrian Cunningham, son of a famous general, a little boy who lives in an apartment in Windsor Castle, and is inspired

"CAN I SEE THE PRIME MINISTER, PLEASE?"

by the banners and stalls in St George's Chapel to try to become a true knight himself. He models himself on Charlotte M. Yonge's *Little Duke*, is taken to see Watts's *Sir Galahad* in Eton College chapel, and is read the *Idylls of the King* by his tutor. He wins his spurs in the end when he overhears a plot to assassinate the King, and goes up to London to warn the Prime Minister.

Earlier in the book he lets a rough town boy ride his pony and the boy goes off without saying anything. The following conversation with his nurse ensues:

'I thought he would just have said "Thank You," ' . . .
'He isn't a gentleman, my dear,' said his nurse . . .
'Yet we have got to be kind to every one whether they are gentlemen or not.'
'Still,' she answered wisely, 'you can always see the difference.'

The gulf between ungentlemanly boys and this 'gallant little figure' in 'his little black suit with silk stockings and buckled shoes' is made overpoweringly obvious. When he goes up to see the Prime Minister 'it never occurred to him, although his

268

funds were small, to travel anything but first class'. He tells the Cabinet that 'there are some things that a person does not tell to servants'. At one stage a group of 'ragged boys' kidnap him, and even go as far as to throw mud at him; but his gallant and gentlemanly little ways so impress them that they end by cheering him to the echo.

Such infiltrations of chivalry by snobbery were rather too common. And there were other chivalrous attributes of the gentleman which had disadvantages. One was the concept that gentlemen should not be interested in money; another, the related concept that gentlemen should not engage in trade (in the widest sense, of trade, commerce and industry). The latter dated back to the eighteenth century, if not earlier, but chivalry gave it a new moral stamp; gentlemen should keep away from trade not only to show that they had no need to make money, but because making money was a morally inferior and spirit-soiling occupation. It was assumed, for no very obvious reasons, that no one could conceivably want to engage in trade except to make money.

For such sentiments to become powerful in a nation the greatness of which was based on trade was of course absurd, so absurd that the doctrine in its full purity was never accepted by more than a small proportion of those who called themselves gentlemen. It could only have been effective if there had been a rigid separation in background and education between those in the professions and those in trade but in fact there was not; both went to the same public schools, and married each other's sisters. What it did mean, however, was that gentlemen (whether by birth or education) who engaged in trade tended to be apologetic about it; and, in order to show that their hearts were in the right place, spent as much time as they could in more acceptable occupations, such as farming, fox-hunting, fly-fishing and county cricket. It also meant that large numbers of those in trade got out of it as soon as they could afford to, and that the cream of the country's talent tended to go into the professions.

The underlying attitude is nicely expressed by the remark made by the novelist P. C. Wren about his publishers, that they had 'somehow strayed into the muddy paths of commerce, but somehow contrive to remain sportsmen and gentlemen and jolly good businessmen'.[8] Successful English novelists tended to be afflicted by the same kind of inferiority complex and get out of it in the same way; there were few more dedicated cricketers than J. M. Barrie or Conan Doyle, or country gentlemen than Rider Haggard and John Buchan. How good this was for their writing is debatable; it certainly seems unlikely that the energies which businessmen and manufacturers diverted into disguising themselves as country gentlemen helped England to hold its own against foreign competition.

The doctrine that character was more important than intellect was an equally debatable feature of the chivalrous gentleman. If carried to extremes, as it too often was, it could result in the belief that grit and pluck could deal with every problem and that it was not necessary nor even desirable for a gentleman to learn his job too well; that was for the professionals. More generally, it led to a distrust of 'cleverness'; many chivalrous gentlemen were not only not very bright, but proud of it. But it is dangerous for a ruling class to be suspicious of intelligence. In practice, the people who actually got to the very top were seldom conspicuously chivalrous; they tended to be both too complex and too ambitious, and chivalry does not go well with either quality. None the less there were large numbers of loyal, honourable but limited men in positions of responsibility; and although this was all very well when things were going well, it was less good in times of crisis.

Purity, too, and the reverence for women that went with it, had their disadvantages. The massed ranks of gentlemanly Victorian and Edwardian bachelors were partly the result of social conventions which made it difficult for those of modest income to find wives of their own class; but they were also the result of gentlemen so conditioned by their upbringing that they were as incapable of making contact with a woman as with a working man. Even if they did win through to marriage, the collision with a woman in the flesh rather than on a pedestal could have its problems, as the case of Lutyens and Emily Lytton made clear.

Back in the 1820s, when Dr Arnold let off a blast against chivalry, he had said that 'it sets up the personal allegiance to the chief above allegiance to God and law'.[9] By the end of the century chivalry had helped make loyalty one of the most admired virtues. Even though the political powers of the Queen were on the decrease, she had acquired a formidable, if less measurable, new power as the principal focus of this loyalty. In the shadow of loyalty to queen and country numerous other loyalties flourished; loyalty to a regiment or a school, loyalty of gentlemen to each other and to their code. The emotional charge behind all this was enormous, but, as Dr Arnold had seen, it had its dangers. Religion, which had loomed large as a constituent of chivalry earlier in the century, was playing a much smaller part by the end of it. The code of the gentleman, and the loyalties which it encouraged, tended to become an alternative to religion; and in moments of crisis the loyalties, especially when unaccompanied by critical intelligence, could overpower both sense and justice.

Indeed one of the great dangers of chivalry was that it could make people totally out of touch with reality. Revering women who did not want to be revered, serving others, who would have preferred to serve themselves, gallantly charging in the wrong direction, chivalrous Galahads and Lancelots were always in danger of turning into White Knights.

But no human system is perfect; and almost all the qualities discussed in previous paragraphs had advantages as well as disadvantages. What the ideals of chivalry, as adopted and adapted by English gentlemen, achieved was sufficiently remarkable. They inspired very large numbers of men of the upper and middle classes with the resolve to think of something other than themselves. They kept them to rigorously high standards of conduct, and gave them extraordinary confidence and powers of leadership. They provided an almost inexhaustible reservoir of people prepared to work long hours for nothing in support of what they judged to be a good cause. They helped keep England free from political rancour and war between the classes. They were inextricably bound up with the concept of a ruling class; but the ruling class which they produced was, on the whole, brave, honest, honourable and self-controlled. For the best part of a century it brought peace, security and a degree of justice to a large portion of the world.

Much though they shared in common, chivalrous gentlemen were not of course all exactly the same. There was a good deal of variety; by no means all corresponded exactly to what might be called the Tennysonian ideal. Many gentlemen lived up to high standards in personal relationships without feeling any obligation to serve others. Many, however high their standards in other fields, were by no means pure; even so, they were likely to respect purity in others, rather than to consider it a sign of aberration or lack of virility.

Among the varieties of chivalrous gentlemen two conspicuously different types can be distinguished as fellowship knights and knights-errant. Knights-errant liked working on their own. They were always pursuing some quest or other, regardless of how odd or hopeless it appeared to other people; they tended, as a result, to be called quixotic. Although they were invariably proud of being gentlemen, loyalty to groups or even to the monarch did not loom large in their lives. Wilfred Scawen Blunt, for instance, spent much of his life tilting ferociously against the Empire, in Egypt and Ireland. His motives, even if mixed with an element of exhibitionism, could genuinely be described as chivalrous,[10] and form a much more sympathetic aspect of his career than his exploits as a lover.

A visit to the Bedouins in Algeria in 1874 provoked him to draw a scornful contrast 'between their noble pastoral life on the one hand with their camel herds and horses, a life of high tradition filled with the memory of heroic deeds, and on the other hand the ignoble squalor of the Frank settlers with their wine shops and their swine'.[11] Knights-errant tended to be drawn to Arab countries, or to countries relatively untouched by Western civilisation, partly because they could get away on their own there, partly because they found such traditional ways of life preferable (in short spells, at any rate) to modern civilisation.

There were elements of the knight-errant in both Aubrey Herbert, the younger son of the fourth Earl of Carnarvon (1879–1923) and his friend and contemporary Sir Mark Sykes (1880–1919). Neither man was against the Empire in quite the way Blunt was, but both were great travellers in remote places. Aubrey Herbert was described in his *Times* obituary as 'a devoted champion of certain smaller nationalities, possessed perhaps of more enthusiasm than judgement, and enjoying to the utmost the amusement of insisting on the unpopular view.'[11] Like a good many other people he is said to have been invited to become King of Albania. He once kept a pet shark.[12] He inspired John Buchan to draw the character of Sandy Arbuthnot: 'He's blood brother to every kind of Albanian bandit . . . In shepherds' huts in the Caucasus you will find bits of his cast-off clothing, for he has a knack of shedding garments as he goes. In the caravanserais of Bokhara and Samarkand he is known, and there are shikaris in the Pamirs who still speak of him round their fires . . . In old days he would have led a crusade or discovered a new road to the Indies. Today he merely roamed as the spirit moved him . . .'[13]

Aubrey Herbert was pro-Turk, his friend Mark Sykes was pro-Arab. Like other knights-errant he enjoyed shocking people, and despised city life and the bourgeoisie. He had his doubts about imperialism, heartily disliked Anglo-Indians, and thought that 'the White Man's burden is a bag of gold'. He became increasingly concerned to prevent 'the smearing of the east' with the 'slime of the west'.[14] Not unlike Blunt, he reached out from his private kingdom of twenty thousand acres at Sledmere in Yorkshire to greet sheikhs and Kurdish chiefs as fellow aristocrats. He is best known for the Sykes–Picot agreement, which he negotiated on behalf of the Foreign Office in 1915, and which laid down British and French spheres of influence in the near East. But his enthusiasms all lay in creating genuinely independent Arab kingdoms within these spheres. On his memorial brass, inset into the modern Eleanor Cross which stands at the gates of Sledmere, he is shown in full armour, as a modern Crusader. He had already filled other panels on it with brasses to friends, tenants and employees killed in the Great War, including one to Edward Bagshawe, his friend since schooldays, 'chevalier sans peur et sans reproche'.[15]

It was easier to be a knight-errant if one had a private income; it was not coincidence that Scawen Blunt, Herbert and Sykes were all upper-class landowners. Fellowship knights were more likely to be working in the professions or the Empire. Chivalry for them involved, above all, loyalty to a group or a leader. Sir Henry Newbolt was their laureate.

Newbolt's poems may give the impression of being written by a jolly table-thumping extrovert, but in fact he was a spare scholarly man, very much at home at common-room tables. Two kinds of romanticism dominated his life: he felt strongly about what he liked to call 'fellowship' and, as he put it himself, he was 'a man to whom heroism, and even more courage and the primitive passion for the fight, appeal strongly'.[16]

Both feelings owed much to Clifton, where he was educated. The school, the house, the cricket team, the school shooting eight (which he captained), his college rowing eight, a boys' club in Notting Hill, his fellow authors, the establishment, England, the Empire, all in turn inspired him with ardent loyalties. A visit to his old school and house in 1898 elicited the enthusiastic comment: 'It's a pure marvel, a School, and the intangible invisible thing we call "House feeling" is about the most wonderful thing in it.' The boys roared out his poems at the House Supper. An artillery captain back from Omdurman made 'the most ripping speech . . . speaking in a quiet dry voice, soldier fashion'; before the battle, he told them, the school had sent a letter to all Old Cliftonians saying, 'God bless you', and that night 'they lay rolled in their blankets in the desert, and thought of the great fellowship that was thinking of them'.[17]

Newbolt himself was never more than moderately good at cricket or football, and was never in a battle, or anywhere near one. But his most successful poems celebrated the heroic acts of men like the 'ripping' captain, and the fellowships to which they belonged; in doing so they made public-school boys the world over feel that, however modest their role, they belonged to a glorious company:

> Today and here the fight's begun
> Of the great fellowship you're free.[18]

It was scarcely surprising that by his schooldays he was already an enthusiast for chivalry and the Round Table, and that he continued throughout his life to feel that it 'still gives the answer'.[19] In his poem 'Craven' he rolls out the list through the centuries:

> Sidney thirsting a humbler need to slake
> Nelson waiting his turn for the surgeon's hand
> Lucas crushed with chains for a comrade's sake
> Outram coveting right before command.
> These were paladins, these were Craven's peers
> These with him shall be crowned in story and song
> Crowned with the glitter of steel and the glimmer of tears,
> Princes of courtesy, merciful, proud and strong.

There were a good few people in the early 1900s who might have been, and sometimes were, called paladins. There was Arthur Conan Doyle, once described by a journalist as 'that paladin of lost causes', who had been brought up by his mother on poverty, chivalry and tales of his ancestors, who slapped his son's face for calling a woman ugly ('just remember that no woman is ugly'), and wanted to be remembered for *Sir Nigel* and *The White Company* rather than Sherlock Holmes. The code of chivalry took the place of religion for him until, in the last years of his life, he set off on a long and elusive quest after Spiritualism.[20] There was Francis Younghusband, marching with his little escort of troops up into the remoteness of the Himalayas in order to talk face to face with the Chief Lama, and writing to Newbolt of 'our race and its high destiny' and England's 'genius for leading Asiatics'.[21] There was C. E. Tyndale-Biscoe, who spent his life teaching Hindu boys in Kashmir to respect women, live purely, train their bodies, serve others, take cold dips and play the game.[22] There was General Lord Methuen, who, when his opponent, the gallant and chivalrous Comte de Villebois-Mareuil, leader of the International Brigade in the Boer Army, fell fighting against him at Boshof, buried him with the full honours of war: fifteen hundred men came out on parade to do him honour in the little moonlit cemetery at Boshof; the Last Post was sounded over his grave; his comrades, now prisoners of the British, filed past it to pay their last respects; a fellow officer gave the funeral address and then turned to Lord Methuen and said, 'Mon General, we are here your prisoners and we thank you for your courtesy. We recognise that we are prisoners of an army which is the bravest of the brave.'[23]

And then there were the knights of the future, brave handsome boys fearlessly riding their ponies and looking life in the face with clear blue eyes. The image of a little boy on a horse had acquired a special poignancy as a symbol of chivalry in embryo, especially in upper-class families of the time. When the sculptor Alfred Gilbert came to Avon Tyrrell in 1901, to stay with Lord and Lady Manners and model a bust of their son John, he never forgot the sight of him returning from a paperchase, riding up a valley towards the house, sparkling with excitement: 'he was a gallant boy with all the makings of a hero, which he looked; a true type of what England alone can produce to the highest point of excellence.'[24] George Wyndham wrote a poem about his own little son Percy on horseback:

172. 'Heart's Delight'. Percy Wyndham in 1892

173. John Manners on horseback

Heart's Delight is five years old
And rides an old white pony
With the easy seat of a rider bold
By grassy ways and stony . . .

Heart's Delight is five years old
His face is fresh and sunny
His English hair just touched with gold
Amidst a browner honey
And English eyes of deepest blue
Whose courage looks you through and through.[25]

'Heart's Delight' and John Manners were both killed in the Great War in September 1914. Their friends Julian and Billy Grenfell, Edward Horner, Charles Lister and Patrick Shaw-Stewart, with whom they had spent their boyhood in what Billy Grenfell called a 'band of brothers'[26] were all killed too.

274

174. (right) Frontispiece to Henry Newbolt's *Book of the Happy Warrior*, 1917

CHAPTER 18

The Great War

OPINIONS WILL ALWAYS DIFFER AS TO WHETHER THE GREAT WAR COULD OR SHOULD have been prevented. But one conclusion is undeniable: the ideals of chivalry worked with one accord in favour of war.

During the nineteenth century the upper and much of the middle classes had been increasingly encouraged to believe that a fight in a just cause was one of the most desirable and honourable activities open to man, and that there was no more glorious fate than to die fighting for one's country. The purging or ennobling effect of contemporary war had been written about by numerous poets, Scott, Tennyson and Newbolt among them.

> And as months ran on and rumour of battle grew,
> 'It is time, it is time, O passionate heart,' said I
> (For I cleaved to a cause that I felt to be pure and true)
> 'It is time, O passionate heart and morbid eye,
> That old hysterical mock-disease should die.'
> And I stood on a giant deck and mix'd my breath
> With a loyal people shouting a battle cry,
> Till I saw the dreary phantoms arise and fly
> Far into the North, and battle, and seas of death.
>
> Let it go or stay, so I wake to the higher aims
> Of a land that has lost for a little her lust of gold,
> And love of a peace that was full of wrongs and shames,
> Horrible, hateful, monstrous, not to be told;
> And hail once more to the banner of battle unroll'd![1]

Tennyson wrote these lines about the Crimean War in *Maud*, a poem that was in almost every literate Victorian household. In 1892 a poem published in W. E. Henley's *National Observer* exhorted the Almighty:

> Give us war, O Lord,
>   For England's sake,
> War righteous and true
>   Our hearts to shake.[2]

Henley himself wrote his *Song of the Sword*:

> Ho then the music
> Of battles and onset
> And ruining armours . . .
>
> I am the Sword
>
> Sifting the nations,
> The slag from the metal,
> The waste and the weak
> From the fit and the strong.

And here is Newbolt in his *Vigil* of 1898 (what could be more chivalrous than a vigil?) writing on the eve of Omdurman:

276

XXVIII. (right) *Britain Needs You At Once*. A poster issued by the Parliamentary Recruiting Committee
XXIX–XXX. (following pages) Postcards of the 1914–18 War

BRITAIN · NEEDS

YOU · AT · ONCE

ENLISTED UNDER THE CROSS! AM I?

From the painting by W. H. Margetson

"THE ANGELS OF MONS."

OLD ENGLAND FOR EVER!
(I KNOW THAT I SHALL DIE AT SEA)
JE SAIS QUE C'EST SUR MER QUE JE MOURRAI
Pressentiment de LORD KITCHENER

JUSTICE   SACRIFICE

THERE SHALL DAWN A RADIANT PEACE

The Angel of Justice watches the Peace Star
breaking through the Clouds of War while the
Angel of Sacrifice mourns the tragedy of her loss

Copyright printed in England

Let the bugles sound the truce of God
To the whole world for ever. — Sumner

16ᵀᴴ (THE QUEENS) LANCERS
CHARGE !!!

THE REAL ANGEL OF MONS.
L'ange de nos blessés.

GREATER
THAT A MAN

LOVE HATH NO MAN
LAY DOWN HIS LIFE FOR

THAN THIS
HIS FRIENDS

So shall thou when morning comes
Rise to conquer or to fall
Joyful hear the rolling drums
Joyful hear the trumpets call.
Then let Memory tell thy heart;
'England! What thou wert, thou art!'
Gird thee with thy ancient might
Faith! And God defend the Right!

In thousands of nurseries and schoolrooms children had been brought up on the exploits in battle of heroes new and old: Hector and Achilles, Horatius holding the bridge, Arthur and his knights, Roland blowing his horn, Richard Coeur de Lion charging the Saracens, the Black Prince at Crecy, Henry V at Agincourt, Sir Philip Sidney at Zutphen, Richard Grenville on the *Revenge*, Prince Rupert charging with his cavaliers, Sir John Moore at Corunna, Nelson at Trafalgar, Wellington at Waterloo, the charge of the Light Brigade, Nicholson falling at the gates of Delhi, Gordon proudly facing the screaming Dervishes, the heroes of Rorke's Drift dying to the last man, the gallant little garrison at Mafeking playing cricket in the jaws of the enemy.

'Fighting' was one of the most honourable words in the vocabulary, 'the real, highest, honestest business of every son of man', as Thomas Hughes put it.[3] The language of battle and of chivalry had been used to provide metaphors for every aspect of life; life was a battlefield on which a gentleman had to fight impure thoughts in himself, injustice or ignorance in others, 'whatever was mean and unmanly and unrighteous in our little world'.[4] The approval attached to the metaphors almost inevitably attached itself to the basic meaning. Of course, the fight had to be for a good cause. But one of the effects of imperialism had been to imbue very large numbers of people with a religious belief in Britain as the great force for good in the world. Like Francis Younghusband, they 'had the greatest possible faith in our race and its high destiny'.[5] That England could be in the wrong was almost inconceivable. Moreover, once war was declared, or likely to be declared, all those who had been at public schools knew exactly what was expected of them. But so, outside the public schools, did all Boy Scouts, past and present, all Cadets, all members of boys' clubs and boys' brigades, all readers of the right adventure stories in the right magazines. Giant forces of loyalty to king and country were ready to be triggered off, submerging all doubts in the process.

Many people had long accepted that a war with Germany was inevitable. Here is Henley in 1898: 'It is written, or so it seems, that the world is for one of two races, and of them the English is one. Let us English, then, consolidate—consolidate—and still consolidate . . . accordingly as we are found prepared for the inevitable Pharsalia, so shall the question, which of the twain shall come forth Caesar, be answered.'[6]

There was, perhaps, a touch of hysteria in Henley. But Henry Newbolt, besides being the friend and admirer of Edward Grey, the Foreign Secretary, was (superficially, at any rate) an urbane and sensible man. In 1916 he described how

XXXI. (left) Stained-glass window depicting *War* made by Morris and Company for St Bartholomew's, Wilmslow, Cheshire, 1920

he had 'spent most of the years of my life under the certainty of war, the conviction that my country must pass through the trial of a great war: the necessary effort of training for it the force and the thoughts and the character'.[7]

For many years public schools all over the country received regular visits from Field Marshal Lord Roberts. He came to urge the necessity of preparing for war: 'However little we may wish it, we may some day find ourselves involved in a serious war with a great nation trained in arms, and, if we do not take the trouble to be prepared, we shall not only deserve defeat, but most certainly suffer it.'[8] He was invariably greeted with tumultuous applause, for it was an age in which public-school boys hero-worshipped famous British soldiers, and 'Bobs'—a 'Happy Warrior', a 'real little saint'—was one of their favourite heroes.[9]

Baden-Powell was another one. He believed in preparation for war too; it was partly with this in mind that he chose 'Be Prepared' as the Scout motto. He saw moral benefit in such preparation, as well as practical necessity. 'The Damoclesian sword of war', he wrote, 'ever hanging over a country has its value in keeping up the manliness of a people, in developing self-sacrificing heroism in its soldiers, in uniting classes, creeds and parties, and in showing the pettiness of party politics in its true proportion.'[10] Both Roberts and Baden-Powell were talking about preparation in order to prevent war; but such talk has a way of making people expect it, and indeed manliness, self-sacrifice, heroism and the disappearance of party-government seemed more likely to be encouraged by war itself than by preparation for it.

When the moment of crisis finally arrived, most people saw it in terms that were familiar to them from school days, and that gave a chivalrous people no option. They were, in the first place, as Baden-Powell put it, going 'to give the big bully a knock-out blow, so that other nations can live afterwards in peace and freedom'.[11] Everyone knew that that was what one did to bullies. Even more important, going to war was a matter of honour. For, although the big bully had been throwing his weight about all over the place, the particular nation which he was bullying at the moment was 'little Belgium'; and England was bound by treaty to come to Belgium's help. The Boer War had called for a certain amount of soul-searching before honourable men could accept it; the possibility that big England was knocking down little Transvaal in order to take her bag had to be considered and dismissed; some people were unable to dismiss it. But in 1914 there was no need for this kind of hesitation; Germany was an equal opponent.

People could approach the war in a black-and-white yes-or-no spirit because they lacked the faintest prevision of what it was going to be like. The most recent war, the Boer War, had, admittedly, been the biggest and bloodiest since the time of Napoleon. It had lasted two and a half years and had involved nearly 450,000 British or colonial soldiers, some 22,000 of whom had died. But twelve years later its unhappier episodes were beginning to gloss over in people's minds: it was becoming the war of the glorious reliefs of Kimberley and Mafeking, 'a gentleman's war', 'a very pleasant time for a young fellow'.[12] Its main military lesson, that the combination of trench warfare with modern rifles and machine-guns was likely to result in a long and cruel stalemate, had escaped almost everyone. If the military experts believed that war with Germany would be a brief affair of a few knock-out and decisive battles, ordinary people could scarcely be blamed for thinking the same. And as the great majority of them had no experience of war at all, there was nothing to stop them thinking of it in terms of their education—a war of glory, honour and cavalry charges.

'War declared by England', Patrick Gray, a schoolboy still at Rugby, wrote in his diary on 5 August (he was to go to the front in 1917, and be killed almost at once). 'Intense relief, as there was an awful feeling that we might dishonour ourselves.'[13] On the same day Kitchener made his first call for volunteers. They came in hundreds of thousands, filling the streets outside the recruiting offices with queues of patient, cheerful, innocent faces. Between August 1914 and January 1916, 2,467,000 men volunteered to fight for their country, and went on volunteering even when it became clear how many of them were going to die. The first few months were ones of excitement. As George Wyndham's sister Pamela Glenconner put it: 'Those were the days of the Singing Armies; Armies that went singing through the streets, with crowds running beside them, and the air rang with cheers.'[14] On 24 August Henry Newbolt described how his son Francis 'writes in a glorious state of suppressed exaltation—it simply escapes him, like a halo from under his hat'.[15] A few months later Newbolt himself 'can't help wishing this war could have come when I was young. I envy F. and his friends their happiness.'[16] Two days before the war was declared an entry had appeared in the personal column of *The Times*: 'PAULINE—Alas, it cannot be. But I will dash into the great venture with all that pride and spirit an ancient race has given me.'[17] John Manners, the same John Manners whom Alfred Gilbert had seen as a little boy on horseback and thought 'a gallant boy, with all the makings of a hero', volunteered in the first month. Before he left he gave his mother a piece of paper on which he had written

> Mon ame a Dieu
> Mon vie au Roi
> Mon coeur aux Dames
> Et honneur pour moi[18]

He was killed at the beginning of September, less than a month later.

The Great War probably produced more poetry than any other in the history of the world. There were poets at home and even more poets on the front. Their poems were published in *The Times* and other dailies, in the weeklies, in anthologies by the dozen and in literally hundreds of individual volumes. Chivalry featured in them either directly in terms of knights, vigils, Galahads and Holy Grails, or indirectly in terms of sportsmen and playing the game. Newbolt's 'The Vigil' was published in *The Times* on the first day of the war; it sold so many copies, and was thought to have had such a great effect on national morale, that he was given a knighthood. Herbert Asquith's 'The Volunteer', first published in 1915, attracted much admiration, both in its own right and because it was written by the son of the Prime Minister:

> Here lies a clerk who half his life had spent
> Toiling at ledgers in a city grey,
> Thinking that so his days would drift away
> With no lance broken in life's tournament.

All was well, however:

> His lance is broken; but he lies content
> With that high hour, in which he lived and died . . .

> Nor needs he any hearse to bear him hence
> Who goes to join the men of Agincourt.

J. S. Arkwright's 'The Supreme Sacrifice' was translated into both Latin and Welsh, set to music, and sung as a hymn at innumerable memorial services.

> Oh valiant hearts, who to your glory came
> Through dust of conflict, and through battle flame.
> Tranquil you lie, your knightly virtues proved
> Your memory hallowed in the land you loved.[19]

Mildred Huxley's 'A Song of Oxford', published in the *Spectator* on 23 September 1916, was later to be recommended as suitable for war memorials:

> They who had all, gave all. Their half-writ story
> Lies in the empty halls they know so well,
> But they, the Knights of God, shall see His glory
> And find the Grail ev'n in the fire of hell.[20]

Chivalry appeared in prose in the stories written by Arthur Machen for the *Evening News*, especially in 'The Bowman', which came out on 29 September 1914. 'The Bowmen' succeeded beyond most authors' dreams—much to Machen's embarrassment. It tells how a British soldier, while fighting a forlorn hope, remembers and repeats a motto which he had seen under figures of St George on the plates of a restaurant: 'Adsit Anglis Sanctus Georgius.' Immediately he hears 'a great voice' and 'thousand shouting . . . Array, array, array . . . St George! St George! . . . St George for merry England . . . a long bow and a strong bow . . . Heaven's Knight, aid us . . . High Chevalier, defend us!' In front of the trench in which he is standing he sees 'a long line of shapes, with a shining about them'. The day is saved; 'the grey men were falling by thousands'; he realises that St George has brought in Agincourt bowmen to help the English.

Almost immediately Machen began to get requests from parish magazines to print, and reprint, the story. Their congregations, it turned out, believed that it was a true one. Soon reports began to come in of officers who had seen St George, of arrow wounds having been found in dead Germans, of how clouds had come down to conceal British soldiers and shining shapes appeared from them. A wounded Lancashire Fusilier had asked his hospital nurse for a picture or medal of St George 'because he had seen him on a white horse, leading the British at Vitry-le-François, when the Allies turned'. French troops had seen St Michael or Joan of

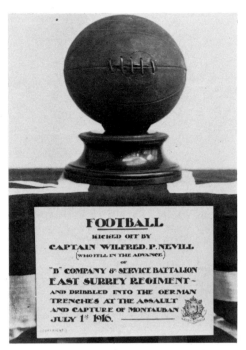

Arc playing the same role. In many versions the 'shapes with a shining about them' of Machen's story had become actual angels. The story was discussed or reported in magazines from *John Bull* to the *New Church Weekly*; sermons were preached on it; it was the subject of numerous pictures and postcards. In the popular form of the legend St George and the bowmen disappear and only the angels remain.[21]

Another prose best-seller of the war was *The Love of an Unknown Soldier*. It had gone into eight editions by 1919. Ostensibly it was based on letters from a tin box found in an empty dug-out on the front line; but it is hard (though perhaps not quite impossible) to believe that they are genuine. The letters are highly romantic ones, purporting to have been written to an American Red Cross nurse by an English officer who was too shy ever to send them. He compares her to a modern Joan of Arc, whose 'charger is a Ford car'. He writes to her about the 'mediaeval romance' of their meeting, about how as an unhappy schoolboy he used to dream of being 'a King Arthur kind of person, who rode to the rescue of great ladies', of how Gaston de Foix used to lead storming parties to success with his lady's kerchief tied to his arm: 'I have no kerchief, but your letter lies near my heart, and goes with me everywhere as a talisman.' His last letter is written as the enemy close in, and is unfinished.[22]

Henry Newbolt's *Book of the Happy Warrior* came out in 1917; it told the story of chivalry and was clearly intended to inspire boys in wartime England with chivalrous enthusiasms. The chapter about Agincourt was titled 'France v. Gentlemen of England'. 'The Germans, and even our Allies', wrote E. B. Osborn in an anthology of war poems called *The Muse in Arms* (1917), 'cannot understand why this stout old nation persists in thinking of war as sport; they do not know that sportsmanship is our new homely name, derived from a racial predilection for comparing great things with small, for the *chevaleries* of the Middle Ages.'[23] A section of the anthology is headed 'Chivalry of Sport', and its highlight is 'Rugby

175. (left) *Angels of Mons*. A music cover of 1915

176. (right) Postcard of Captain Nevill's football

Football—Written on receiving [in the front line] the football-match list from Ilkley Grammar School':

> There's a roar from the 'touch' like an angry sea
> As the struggle moves from goal to goal
> But the fight is as clean as a fight should be
> And they're friends when the ball has ceased to roll.

The influence of Newbolt's 'Vitai Lampada' is obvious, and sure enough the analogy with the battlefield is soon drawn:

> Can you hear the call? Can you hear the call
> That drowns the roar of Krupp
> But hark! can you hear it? Over all—
> Now, School! Now, School! Play up'.

Such metaphors of sport were carried over into action: on at least two occasions troops going over the top dribbled a football as they advanced. The most famous of these was on 1 July 1916, when the football was produced by Captain W. P. Nevill and dribbled by his company of the East Surrey Regiment, in the disastrous Battle of the Somme. Captain Nevill was killed, along with most of the company.

> On through the heat of slaughter
> Where gallant comrades fall
> Where blood is poured like water
> They drive the trickling ball
> The fear of death before them
> Is but an empty name
> True to the land that bore them
> The Surreys play the game.[24]

Memorial volumes to commemorate individuals who had been killed were published in large numbers. They took the almost invariable form of a biographical account, memorial inscriptions, and extracts of letters of condolence from commanding officer, friends, N.C.O.s and soldier-servant. References to the dead man could move through all levels of chivalric allusion. He could be called 'a gallant gentleman', 'a sweet and gallant English gentleman who died that the England he loved might live', 'a chivalrous soldier', an officer who 'played the great game manfully'.[25] Brigadier Frank Maxwell, V.C., who as a young man had been Kitchener's favourite among his 'cubs' was described on his memorial as 'the bravest of the brave—a true gentleman—a sportsman—and a great companion'.[26]

Poets were liable to be described in a more specifically knightly way. Shortly after Rupert Brooke's death Sir Iain Hamilton gave a memorial address on him at Rugby. He told the boys how 'I went into his tent, where he was lying stretched out on the desert sand, looking extraordinarily handsome, a very knightly presence.'[27] A. St. J. Adcock's *For Remembrance: Soldier Poets who have fallen in the*

War (1918) is studded with chivalric epithets. Robert Sterling 'went about life in the same manner as did the knight-errant of old'. Edward Thomas showed the 'chivalry . . . we always knew that he had'. Colwyn Philipps was 'a very perfect gentle knight'. The last was one of a group of poets who were the sons of peers: Colwyn Philipps, Robert Palmer, Edward Tennant and Julian Grenfell, 'the fearless and perfect gentle knights that they were . . . such dear and heroic souls'.[28]

Although Adcock was emphatic that equally heroic souls had emerged from the ranks, knightly epithets were more likely to be attached to upper-class soldiers. In particular they burgeoned in the circle of the Souls—among whom the metaphors of chivalry had been flourishing since the 1880s.

Edward ('Bim') Tennant, the beloved eldest son of Pamela Glenconner, had been an avid reader of poetry, Malory and stories of adventure since childhood; a picture of Sir Perceval sent by him aged eight to his uncle George Wyndham had drawn a whimsical letter from the latter ('I would have been very happy if I had lived in those days riding through forests in quest of adventure'),[29] and their common love for romance and chivalry became a strong bond between them. Besides writing poetry himself—including a 'Ballad of Sir Bedivere'—'Bim' Tennant knew all the speeches in *Henry V* by heart, and was kept going in his year at the front by a mixture of *Henry V*, Keats, and Scott's *Border Ballads*. 'Today is a great day for me. That line of Harry's rings through my mind', he wrote home on 20 September, two days before he was killed. One of his friends described him as 'intensely chivalrous . . . it was enough to see him speak to an old, or unlucky, or poor or sorrowful person'.[30]

His cousin Ego Charteris, who was killed on 23 April 1916, was described by his sister-in-law Diana Cooper as 'of all men the nearest to a knight of chivalry'.[31] Maurice Baring applied similar epithets in his 'In Memoriam' poem to Auberon Herbert, Lord Lucas, who was in the Royal Flying Corps, went out on a flight on 3 November 1916, and never returned.

> Surely you found companions meet for you
> In that high place
> You met them face to face
> Those you had never known, but whom you knew
> Knights of the Table Round
> And all the very brave, the very true
> With chivalry crowned.

The death of Auberon Herbert's cousins, Julian and Billy Grenfell, on 26 May and 30 July 1915, released a flood of chivalrous epithets. Norah Lindsay saw Billy 'in one flash riding into Valhalla amongst the heroes and saviours of England'. To Angela Manners 'the world is all black now. When Billy was here there was still one perfect gallant knight left; and now he too has joined the noble company.' Lady Barrington recalled, 'I never forget seeing Billy once at Westminster Abbey after the King's Funeral. He was standing against the Dryden Monument, and a shaft of sunlight came down on his head; and I thought what a beautiful picture of manly youth . . . He looked like a young Knight who would ride into battle with joy.'[32]

177. Julian and Billy Grenfell, from
Lady Desborough's *Pages from a
Family Journal*, 1916

Diana Wyndham 'could never forget Julian's lovely face of sunshine, and his beautiful strong figure; and now he is a shining radiant knight, and he can never grow old, or be tarnished by the sorrows of this world'. Sibell Grosvenor could 'always see the vision of Julian's St Michael face shining into this house'. Evan Charteris wrote, 'The name of Julian has come to be linked in my mind with all that is swift and chivalrous, lovely and courageous . . . of all men he the Happy Warrior, for gathered around him seems to be all that has been said or thought of the glory and romance of War.'[33]

'Others are left to whom he may leave his sword', Charles Lister wrote about Julian. '. . . Surely the Lady he sought with tireless faith, the Lady for whom he did and dared so much on lonely paths, will now reward him.'[34] Who was this Lady? Could he have been referring to Watts's *Happy Warrior*, in which the warrior is rewarded by an undeniably female angel who represents the ideals for which he has been striving? The aura which rapidly grew round the Grenfell brothers certainly had a strong flavour of Watts; the frontispiece of the memorial volume written about them by their mother consists of a double photograph in which Billy Grenfell stands in the exact position of Watts's Sir Galahad.[35]

Within a few days of Julian Grenfell's death Newbolt was off again: 'However we suffer, we have seen the England of our dreams—the Black Prince and James

288

Audley and Philip Sidney and Christopher Cradock, and all the Company of the High Order of Knighthood. I am sorry Lord Bobs died so soon—he didn't see half of it.'[36] At much the same time Alan Lascelles, writing a little desperately from the front about the death of Billy Grenfell and all his friends, still felt able to say, 'Some days one is glad and thankful that one is not too old to take part and to see for oneself the bigness and wonder of this war.'[37] But it was becoming harder for those at the front to find war wonderful. Siegfried Sassoon's 'They', first published in 1916, struck another note:

> The Bishop tells us: 'When the boys come back
> They will not be the same; for they'll have fought
> In a just cause: they lead the last attack
> On Anti-Christ; their comrades' blood has bought
> New right to breed an honourable race.
> They have challenged Death and dared him face to face.'

> 'We're none of us the same!' the boys reply,
> For George lost both his legs; and Bill's stone blind;
> Poor Jim's shot through the lungs and like to die.
> And Bert's gone syphilitic: you'll not find
> A chap who's served that hasn't found *some* change.'
> And the Bishop said: 'The ways of God are strange.'

There are times when the Great War can seem like a nightmare parody of the Eglinton Tournament. The chivalry of England, young, brave, dashing and handsome, line up to process to the tournament. They are filled with ardour for the fight, escorted by loyal yeomanry, and longing to do great deeds and win honour for themselves and their lady-loves. Trumpets blow, attendant bards recite heroic poetry, and all is ready for the glorious combat. Then the rain starts falling. The shining knights cannot charge, for their horses are bogged down and they themselves are wallowing in mud up to the groin. Mud totally obscures their glorious armour. They fall over, their armour splits open and their blood and entrails spill out into the mud. But the audience, watching the ludicrous but ghastly scene, appear impervious to what is going on. The trumpets continue to blow. The ladies cry out, 'Well fought, my noble heroes.' Watching artists paint canvases in which heroic combats are waged under a cloudless sky. Poets enthuse about Roland and Lancelot. Journalists survey the squalid carnage and intone: 'Even as he lies on the field he looks more quietly faithful, more simply steadfast than others.'[38]

The first and last British cavalry charge on the western front took place at Audreques on 24 August 1914. John Buchan found the charge 'as futile and as gallant as any other like attempt in history on unbroken infantry and guns in position. But it proved to the world that the spirit which inspired the Light Brigade at Balaclava and von Bredow's Todtenritt at Mars-le-Tour was still alive in the cavalry of today.'[39] However, there was to be little role in the war for cavalry and none for heroic charges. By the end of 1914 the combatants were locked in a continuous line of trenches, running from the North Sea to Switzerland. There they stayed for the next four years, moving a mile or two here and there from time to time. As the rain and the shells continued to fall the landscape disintegrated into a waste land of mud, craters, ruins, corpses and barbed wire. Millions of troops lived waterlogged in holes, burrows and ditches, on top of their own dead and filth and squalor which they had created.

There most of them died; and there chivalry died with them. Or at least it received its death-wound. For it is in fact easy enough to find chivalry at work in the years after the war. In fiction, especially, bands of brothers abounded, chivalrously protecting the weak and doing down villains, under the leadership of Bulldog Drummond, Major-General Hannay, Group Captain Bigglesworth and others. Bertie Wooster continued being doggedly and disastrously chivalrous into the 1960s. Evelyn Waugh was fascinated by the images and ideals of chivalry all through his life. But the use of chivalry to provide escapes into fantasy, or portray comic figures, as in Wodehouse, or figures out of gear with their times, as in Waugh, is significant of chivalry's fading powers. As a dominant code of conduct it never recovered from the Great War partly because the war itself was such a shatterer of illusions, partly because it helped produce a world in which the necessary conditions for chivalry were increasingly absent.

To the great majority of the millions fighting in the trenches chivalry meant nothing anyway; it is probably significant that as soon as the Angel of Mons myth got down to a popular level St George and his bowmen vanished, and were replaced by angels. It was the many thousands of upper and middle-class gentlemen (or would-be-gentlemen) to whom chivalry had meant a great deal who had to readjust. The belief that war was glorious and ennobling seldom survived a few months at the front. 'I agree with you about the utter senselessness of war', Raymond Asquith wrote to his wife in July 1916. 'The suggestion that it elevates the character is hideous.'[40] Chivalry, along with patriotism, playing the game, and similar concepts, became not so much devalued as simply irrelevant. It belonged to another world, which seemed infinitely remote from the real world of mud, blood, boredom, fear, endurance, carnage and mutilation in which they now existed.

It was a world in which most soldiers at the front learnt to live and survive under appalling conditions with a mixture of stoicism, bravery and humour much more impressive than the innocent heroics with which the war had started—to survive, that is, until they were killed, wounded or finally cracked up under the strain. Most of them simply accepted this world; but inevitably there were those who reacted more or less violently against it, and against those whom they held accountable for creating it. 'It is vile', Brigadier Philip Howele wrote to his wife in September 1915, 'that all my time should be devoted to killing Germans whom I don't in the least want to kill . . . We are really only fighting just because we are all so ignorant and stupid.'[41] Howele (who was killed in 1916) was a professional soldier, with no ambitions to become a writer. But from the middle of the war onwards a new school of anti-heroic writing got under way, and was to continue to produce into the 1920s and beyond. Knights in armour had no place in it, and Haig, French and their fellow generals were transformed from paladins into ridiculous fools, who lacked the intelligence or the imagination to do anything except order troops to advance and be killed.

At least one image associated with chivalry survived. The image of the waste land became a powerful symbol of what seemed the human predicament. It derived much of its power from the fact that it fitted with the landscape created by the war on the western front; but there had been waste lands in the literature of nineteenth-century chivalry, in Browning's 'Childe Roland', for instance, or Morris's *Well at the World's End*, a romance which was popular reading among soldiers for that reason.[42] But the knights who had ridden through the waste lands faded away; and the more obvious and hackneyed trappings of chivalry, the happy warriors and bands of brothers breaking lances, carrying oriflammes, throwing down gauntlets, or questing for Holy Grails, who still proliferated in a certain style of war poetry, filled the new poets with abhorrence. Herbert Read, writing at the front, used the image of the Happy Warrior somewhat differently from Evan Charteris, writing at home about Julian Grenfell:

Bloody saliva
dribbles down his shapeless jacket.

I saw him stab
and stab again
a well-killed Boche.

This is the happy warrior,
this is he.

The increasing contrast between what was actually happening and how journalists, poets, politicians and clergymen preached or wrote about it at home filled those at the front with derision, amusement or disgust—according to their character. For, although the euphoria of the opening months of the war gradually faded away, those at home still doggedly rolled out the language which depicted the war as glorious, heroic or chivalrous. When it became increasingly hard to apply this kind of language to war in the trenches, they looked for other aspects of fighting which bore (or could be made to bear) more resemblance to war in the story-books. The activities of the Royal Flying Corps were one of them. Inevitably, Henry Newbolt weighed in: 'our airmen are singularly like the knights of the old romances', he wrote in his *Tales of the Great War* (1916); 'they go out day by day, singly or in twos and threes, to hold the field against all comers, and to do battle in defence of those who cannot defend themselves. There is something especially chivalrous about these champions of the air; even the Huns, whose military principles are against chivalry, have shown themselves affected by it.'[43]

Chivalry at home in literature or journalism was combined with chivalry in images. All through the war, and in the years that followed it, St Georges, St Michaels, and knights in armour continue to appear in memorial windows, in cartoons, in statues, in posters and even occasionally on postcards (Plates XXVIII–XXXI).[44] Watts's Sir Galahad was transformed into stained glass in at

least six different places; in Grahamstown in South Africa his Happy Warrior appeared alongside Sir Galahad in the same window.[45]

In retrospect such symbols of chivalry seem a little pathetic, for they were in fact swamped by the mass of other images and mementoes produced by the war, and moreover the values for which they stood were beginning to crumble round them. The sheer weight of numbers involved in the Great War is staggering. It is not the occasional St Georges that move one, or even the memorials to the golden boys of the upper classes so much as the endless rows of headstones in the war

292

178. Adrian Jones's Great War memorial to the Cavalry of the Empire, Hyde Park, London

cemeteries, the long lists of names of ordinary people on memorials in village after village. So many deaths, such vast movements of people, such huge expenditures of money could not but have cataclysmic effects on the structure of society. Among much else, gentlemen were never going to be the same again. Their qualifications to lead had been brought into serious doubt, even if not entirely discredited. Much of their self-confidence had gone. War conditions had brought a new level of wages and independence to the working classes. The absence of so many men at the front had put women in a position of responsibility which made many of them distrust chivalry as a form of concealed slavery.

Eight and a half million people had been killed. The concept of total war had been established. The government of Russia had collapsed, and been replaced by a Bolshevik regime. Germany was left impoverished and resentful, a breeding-ground for future trouble. In the circumstances Newbolt's triumphant celebration of the Armistice, 'Think of the Fleet going up the Dardanelles— Think of the centuries—Think of chivalry victorious', seems inapposite.

293

179. Gertrude Alice Meredith Williams. *Spirit of the Crusaders*. Model for the War Memorial, Paisley, 1921

NOTES TO THE TEXT

NOTES TO CHAPTER I

1. *Where the Rainbow Ends*, by Mrs Clifford Mills and John Ramsey (pseudonym for Reginald Owen). The play was published in 1951; a novel had been based on it in 1912.
2. *Scott's Last Expedition* (ed. Leonard Huxley, 1913) I, p. 592
3. *Ibid.* pp. 597, 600.
4. Sir Clements Markham 'The Field of Geography' *Geographical Journal* XI (1898) p. 6.
5. Logan Marshall *Sinking of the Titanic and Great Sea Disasters* (1912) pp. 59–62, 66, 68 (with illustrations of Butt, etc., see Plates 4–5); Walter Lord *A Night to Remember* (1956) pp. 49–50.
6. Lord *Night* p. 97.
7. *Ibid.* p. 69. In some versions Guggenheim is just described as appearing 'fully dressed'.
8. *Punch*, 24 April 1912; Marshall *Titanic* p. 100.
9. *Times*, 12 July 1912, p. 8; *Graphic*, 13 July 1912, pp. 50–1; *Bystander*, 17 July 1912, pp. 111–12; F. H. Cripps-Day *The Triumph holden at Shakespeare's England* (1912); Diana Cooper *The Rainbow comes and goes* (paperback ed. 1961) p. 87.
10. It subsequently transpired that the knight jousting as Lord Ashby St Legers was in fact his brother, the Hon. F. L. Guest. The cup was accordingly transferred to the Duke of Marlborough (*Times*, 20 July 1912, p. 11).
11. *Times*, 9 April 1852. For the *Birkenhead* see A. C. Addison *The Story of the Birkenhead* (1902). Poems on the wreck were written by Sir Henry Yule, Sir Francis Doyle and J. A. Goodchild. When F. D. Maurice read Doyle's poem to a lecture-room of undergraduates in the late 1860s, they leapt to their feet and burst into cheers (J. F. Maurice *Cornhill Magazine*, February 1897).
12. Sherard Osborn *The Career, Last Voyage and Fate of Captain Sir John Franklin* (1860) pp. v, 26.
13. R. Amundsen *Mitt Liv som Polarforskar* (1927) p. 10; quoted Roland Huntford *Scot and Amundsen* (1979) p. 21.
14. Cooper *Rainbow* p. 87.
15. *Graphic*, 13 July 1912, p. 50.
16. For Parham and Taymouth see p. 206 and M. H. Noel Paton *Tales of a Grand-daughter* (1970). For Budapest see *Daily Mail*, 17 May 1902.
17. The school book is quoted in Addison *Birkenhead* pp. 161–2. Napier Hemy's picture was bought by Messrs Henry Graves & Co. of Pall Mall; I have not traced its present whereabouts.
18. According to Archibald Gracie *The Truth about the Titanic* (1913) pp. 27–8, Major Butt was in the smoking room with three friends while the boats were being lowered: 'neither I nor anyone else, so far as I know, ever saw any of them on the boat deck'. Gracie interviewed a great many survivors, and carefully collated their accounts.

NOTES TO CHAPTER 2

1. Richard Barber *The Knight and Chivalry* (1970) is an excellent contemporary study of chivalry, with a good bibliography.
2. For Elizabethan jousts see Frances A. Yates 'Elizabethan Chivalry: The Romance of the Accession Day Tilts' *Journal of the Warburg and Courtauld Institutes* XIX (1956) pp. 86–103, XX (1957) pp. 4–25; Roy Strong 'The Popular Celebration of the Accession Day of Queen Elizabeth' *ibid.* XXI (1958) pp. 86–103.
3. For a brief account of various aspects of Elizabethan and Jacobean chivalry see Mark Girouard *Robert Smythson and the Architecture of the Elizabethan Era* (1967) pp. 159–74.
4. An Accession Day tilt seems to have been held at Westminster on the anniversary of James I's accession 24 March 1624 (John Nichols *Progresses of King James I* (1828) IV, p. 968). S. Orgel and R. Strong *Inigo Jones: The Theatre of the Stuart Court* (1973) I, pp. 179–80 date the last tournament to 1622.
5. John Cornforth 'Hampton Court' *Country Life* CLIII (22 February and 1 March 1973) pp. 450–3, 518–21.
6. W. H. Pyne *History of the Royal Residences* (1819) I, pp. 177–8.
7. Robert Withington *English Pageantry* (1918–20) II, pp. 26, 80, 90, 97; *London Magazine*, November 1761. The Guildhall Library, City of London, has a collection of prints and cuttings relevant to the Lord Mayor's champions.
8. David Hume *History of England* (1762) I, pp. 209, 211.
9. Edmund Burke *Reflections on the Revolution in France* (Everyman's ed. 1912) p. 73.
10. See Sir Oliver Millar *Later Georgian Pictures in the Collection of Her Majesty the Queen* (1969) I, pp. 132–5, nos. 1158–60; Roy Strong *And when did you last see your father?* (1978) pp. 78–85.
11. For the original appearance of Downton (which was considerably altered in the nineteenth century) see Alistair Rowan 'Downton Castle, Herefordshire' in *The Country Seat* (ed. H. and J. Harris, 1970) pp. 170–3.
12. *Hurd's Letters on Chivalry and Romance with the Third Elizabethan Dialogue* (ed. E. J. Morley, 1911) pp. 51, 58–9.
13. *Ibid.* pp. 98–103, 153–5, etc.
14. *Ibid.* pp. 20–33, 'Dates of some occurrences in my own Life'.
15. Millar, *Later Georgian* I, p. 132; II, pl. 124.
16. *The Later Correspondence of George III* (ed. A. Aspinall, 1968) IV, p. 135.
17. *History of the King's Works* (ed. H. M. Colvin, 1973) VI, p. 376.
18. N. H. Nicolas *History of the Orders of Knighthood of the British Empire* (1842) II, App. pp. xx, xxi.
19. *King's Works* VI, p. 379.
20. *Ibid.* pp. 356–9.
21. Arthur T. Bolton (ed.) *The Portrait of Sir John Soane R.A.* (1927) p. 94.
22. Nathaniel Wraxall *Memoirs* (1884) V, pp. 378–9.
23. Millar *Later Georgian* I, p. 119.
24. The coronation is recorded in two superb folio publications, *Ceremonial of the Coronation of his most sacred majesty George IV* (1823, illustrations by John Whittaker) and Sir George Nayler *The Coronation of his most sacred majesty King George IV* (1st complete ed. 1825–7; 2nd ed. 1839). See also *King's Works* VI, pp. 647–9.
25. A volume of drawings of the costumes, which originally belonged to and appear to have been by Sir George Nayler, is still in existence (information James Miller of Sotheby's). Nayler was Clarenceux King of Arms

at the time of the coronation, and was acting for the Garter King of Arms, who was incapable. For Sir Charles Long's connection with the coronation see *King's Works* VI, p. 647.

26. Nayler *Coronation* (1839 ed.) p. 131, quoting the description by Scott, who was at both coronation and banquet.

27. See *King's Works* VI, pp. 380–92; Derek Linstrum *Sir Jeffrey Wyatville: Architect to the King* (1972) pp. 166–200.

28. George IV's Scottish visit is described in R. Mudie *A Historical Account of His Majesty's Visit to Scotland* (1822).

29. J. G. Lockhart *Life of Sir Walter Scott* (1839) VII, p. 49.

30. Mudie *Historical Account* VII, p. 64.

NOTES TO CHAPTER 3

1. J. G. Lockhart *Life of Sir Walter Scott* (1839) IV, pp. 172–3.

2. L. Simond *Journal of a Tour and Residence in Great Britain during the years 1810–11* (1815) II, p. 115.

3. Eton College, William Johnson MS, 'Notes of his personal possessions', no. 9.

4. S. R. Meyrick *A Critical Enquiry into Antient Armour* (1824) Introduction.

5. Lockhart *Life* (concise version, Everman's ed. 1906) p. 40.

6. *Ibid.* p. 4; and, e.g., p. 47: 'I was a gentleman, and so welcome anywhere.'

7. 'Epistle to His Grace the Duke of Buccleuch' (1814) in *The Poetical Works of Sir Walter Scott* (ed. J. L. Robertson, 1931) p. 719.

8. Lockhart *Concise Life* p. 116.

9. *Ibid.* p. 139.

10. *Ibid.* p. 105.

11. *Ibid.* p. 161.

12. *Ibid.* p. 217.

13. *Ibid.* pp. 219–20.

14. 'Health to Lord Melville' (1806) *Poetical Works* p. 708.

15. Lockhart *Concise Life* p. 280.

16. *Childe Harold's Pilgrimage* 'Addition to the Preface' (1813).

17. The essay was reprinted in Scott's *Miscellaneous Prose Works* (1878 ed.) II, pp. 525–54.

18. Lockhart *Concise Life* p. 226.

19. *The Bridal of Triermain* XIX (*Poetical Works* p. 560).

20. *Ibid.* XI (*Poetical Works* p. 557).

21. *The Lady of the Lake* Canto IV, XXXI (*Poetical Works* p. 250).

22. *Quentin Durward* (1823 ed.) II, pp. 316, 337.

23. Lockhart *Concise Life* p. 51.

24. *Ibid.* p. 186.

25. *Ibid.* p. 212.

NOTES TO CHAPTER 4

1. Carlyle 'Sir Walter Scott' (1838) in *Critical and Miscellaneous Essays* (1857) IV, p. 173.

2. There is a great deal about Abbotsford in Lockhart's *Life*, but a comprehensive modern study remains to be written. Its architectural aspects are discussed in James Macaulay *The Gothic Revival, 1745–1845* (1975) pp. 223–8.

3. Mediaeval baronies by writ could pass through the female line, but, as primogeniture did not apply among women, if a baron had several daughters his barony 'went

into abeyance' because there was no one person to claim it. To call it out of abeyance the descendant of one of the daughters had to prove that the line of all possible co-heirs had died out.

4. Carola Oman *The Portrait of Nelson* (1958) p. 19, n. 1, p. 153.

5.   From high Dunedin's towers we come
        A band of brothers true.

('War song of the Royal Edinburgh Light Dragoons' (1802) *Poetical Works* p. 701.)

6. H. A. Bruce *Life of Sir William Napier* (1864) p. 8; Priscilla Napier *The Sword Dance* (1971) p. 137; L. J. Trotter *The Bayard of India* (1903) p. 109. William Napier's favourite romance, according to Bruce, was *Don Bellamin of Greece*. Charles Napier called Outram 'Bayard' at a dinner given at Sakhar on 4 November 1842.

7. For late eighteenth and early nineteenth-century castles see Christopher Hussey *Country Houses: Late Georgian* (1958); Macaulay *Gothic Revival*.

8. Quoted Hussey *Country Houses* pp. 60–1.

9. P. F. Robinson *Designs for Ornamental Villas* (1827) design VI, p. 1.

10. 'Poems composed or suggested during a tour, in the summer of 1833', XLIV. I owe the reference to Nicholas Penny.

11. Alistair Rowan 'Eastnor Castle' *Country Life* CXLIII (7, 14 and 21 March 1968) pp. 524–7, 606–9, 668–71.

12. Somers *A defence of the Constitution* pp. 42, 93.

13. For Penrhyn see Hussey *Country Houses* pp. 181–92.

14. John Cornforth *English Interiors, 1790–1848: The Quest for Comfort* (1978) pls. 154, 44.

15. F. H. Cripps-Day *A Record of Armour Sales* (1925) pp. xxxiii–xxxvi.

16. *Ibid.* pp. xxxviii, xlviii.

17. In June 1813 he bought a 'splendid lot of ancient armour advertised by Winstanley', a London auctioneer (Lockhart *Concise Life* p. 249).

18. *Dictionary of National Biography*, quoting *Gentleman's Magazine* XCVIII, pt I, p. 463.

19. See pl. 45.

20. Cornforth *English Interiors* pp. 111–12.

21. William White *History and Directory of Staffordshire* (2nd ed. 1851). The arrangement of the armouries at both Goodrich and Alton derived from Meyrick's armour gallery at the Tower of London, which was 149 feet long.

22. Cripps-Day *Armour Sales* pp. 189–90.

23. The collecting and arrangement of armour in England in the nineteenth century is in need of further research; the account of it in the introduction to Cripps-Day's *A Record of Armour Sales* remains the best one available. A London armourer, Charles Marriott, was manufacturing armour from the 1820s, if not earlier (S. H. Pitt *Some Notes on the History of the Worshipful Company of Armourers and Brasiers* (1930); and see Chapter 6, note 2).

NOTES TO CHAPTER 5

1. The details in this paragraph derive from *The Broad Stone of Honour* and Digby's autobiographical poems, but their deployment in a supposed meeting is purely my own fancy.

2. The only biography is Bernard H. Holland's *Memoirs of Kenelm Henry Digby* (1919). Holland was a pupil of William

Johnson and later personal assistant to Alfred Lyttelton (whose contemporary at Eton he had been).

3. *The Broad Stone of Honour* (1823 ed.) p. 419.

4. *Temple of Memory* (1875) p. 23.

5.   He built an abbey four feet high
         In which is pets in coffins lie.
                       Temple of Memory p. 25.

6. *Temple of Memory* Canto III, pp. 55, 57.

7. *Letters and Literary Remains of Edward FitzGerald* (1902–3) VI, p. 185.

8. *Temple of Memory* Canto III.

9. The sketch-books now belong, together with his few surviving papers, to his descendant Michael Dormer.

10. Ehrenbreitstein is in fact a huge Renaissance fortification rather than a mediaeval castle. Digby seems first to have visited it in 1816; but, although he claims that the concept of his book first occurred to him on this visit, his travel journal, which survives, does not comment on the meaning of the name.

11. *Broad Stone* pp. 448–50.

12. *Ibid.* p. 451.

13. *Ibid.*

14. *Ibid.*

15. *Godefridus* (1844) p. 15.

16. *Ibid.* p. 85.

17. *Broad Stone* p. 643.

18. *Godefridus* p. 97.

19. J. S. Mill *Autobiography* (World's Classics ed. 1924) Ch. II, p. 41.

20. *Broad Stone* p. 528.

21. *Broad Stone* p. 516, quoting Lord Shaftesbury.

22. *Broad Stone* Ch. IV *passim*.

23. *Godefridus* p. 251.

24. *Ibid.* p. 50.

25. *Broad Stone* p. 431.

26. *Godefridus* pp. 86–7.

27. Lord Teignmouth *Reminiscences of Many Years* (1878) p. 67. I have not been able to find the reference in Macaulay's own writings.

28. *Selections from the Letters of Robert Southey* (ed. J. W. Warter, 1856) IV, pp. 70, 74.

29. J. C. and A. W. Hare *Guesses at Truth* (1st series 1838) p. 206.

30. 'The Armenian Lady's Love' (composed 1830, published 1835) in *Poems founded on the Affections*.

31. Ruskin *Modern Painters* V. IX. 7. 23n.

32. Letter from Cayley Shadwell to Digby, 25 November 1828 (Dormer papers).

33. Eton College, William Johnson MS. 'Notes of his personal possessions' no. 6: 'Broadstone of Honour. 1 Vol. 8vo morocco. Cost me £6 in 1864. I bought it because it moved me when I was an undergraduate: the spell is lost now.' Georgiana Burne-Jones *Memorials of Edward Burne-Jones* (1904) II, p. 56.

34. See pp. 254–5.

35. *Godefridus* p. 32.

36. *Broad Stone* p. 500.

37. *Ibid.* p. 556.

38. *Ibid.* p. 537.

39. *Orlandus* (1872 ed.) pp. 353, 392.

40. Teignmouth, *Reminiscences* pp. 66–7. And see *Temple of Memory* p. 46.

41. *Temple of Memory* p. 40.

42. *Broad Stone* pp. 16–17.

43. *Ibid.* p. 333.

44. *Godefridus* p. 213.

45. *Ibid.* p. 19.

46. *Broad Stone* pp. 13–14.

47. *Ibid.* p. 575.

48. *Ibid.* p. 604.

49. *Ibid.* Ch. V.

50. *Ibid.* p. 487.

51. *Godefridus* p. 81.

52. *Broad Stone* p. 578.

53. 'Many men, too, are still living who can remember when "The Broad Stone of Honour" was a kind of sacred book to them' (*Daily News*, 25 March 1880). Another longish obituary appeared in the *Spectator*, 27 March.

NOTES TO CHAPTER 6

1. *Morning Herald* and *Morning Chronicle*, 23 January 1821. A printed copy of the address and order of the procession, headed by a splendid coat of arms, is in the Guildhall Library. A less elaborate deputation, with only three knights, had already taken place on 30 October 1820 (Robert Huish *Memoirs of Caroline, Queen Consort of England* (1821) II, pp. 613–15; Guildhall Library print collection). At Alford in Lincolnshire a 'Queen's Champion' on horseback rode through the town championing Caroline's rights (*Stamford News*, 24 November 1820).

2. The early nineteenth-century Company of Brass Founders and Brasiers derived from the Armourers' Company (and is today known as the Company of Armourers and Brasiers). In the eighteenth century it acquired two suits of sixteenth-century armour and provided the knight in armour who rode in the Lord Mayor's Procession. Around 1815 Charles Marriott (who later became Master, and both made armour (see Chapter 4, note 23) and dealt in it) began to provide three knights instead of one; in 1821 he offered to provide five knights, an escort of twenty men, and the use of two new suits of armour, including one 'of a most splendid appearance sent to this country for the use of the Champion at the Coronation, but not used'. He continued to provide knights until at least 1847, and they formed a feature of the procession until about 1880. An especially lavish display is illustrated in *Illustrated Weekly News*, 16 November 1861 (S. H. Pitt *Some Notes on the History of the Worshipful Company of Armourers and Braziers* (1930) *passim*; R. Withington *English Pageantry* (1918–20) II, pp. 104–21; Guildhall Library print collection).

3. Hon. Mrs Hardcastle *Life of Lord Campbell* (1881) II, p. 244, quoting a description of 1848. Brougham's architect was L. N. Cottingham (H. Colvin, *Biographical Dictionary of British Architects*, 1978), but there seems to be no record of the date when Brougham started to rebuild, or to collect armour. The armour was sold at Christie's on 29 June 1933; the sale catalogue of the other contents, sold locally in June 1932, is in the Brougham papers at University College, London.

4. Note in manuscript catalogue of armour at Brancepeth (Russell papers in the possession of Viscount Boyle, Burwarton Park, Shropshire). It is possible that the suit was amongst the armour from the Bullock and Gwennap collection which Tennyson bought for Matthew Russell in February 1821 (see note 15), or that he bought it from Marriott, but if so I have come across no documentation in the Tennyson or Russell papers.

5. For Tennyson d'Eyncourt see Sir Charles Tennyson and Hope Dyson *The Tennysons: Background to Genius* (1974); J. O. Baylen and N. J. Grossman *Biographical Dictionary of Modern British Radicals* (1979) I. There is a large collection of Tennyson d'Eyncourt papers in the County Records Office, Lincoln.

6. Benjamin Disraeli *Lothair* (1st ed. 1870) Ch. XXI.

7. Lt. E. W. Short, D.L.I. *The Story of Brancepeth Castle* (1942).

8. Sir Charles Tennyson *Alfred Tennyson* (1949) pp. 1–5.

9. Boyd Alexander *England's Wealthiest Son: A Study of William Beckford* (1962) pp. 210–25.

10. Tennyson and Dyson *Tennysons* pp. 185–7; d'Eyncourt papers 2 T d'E H 17/45, H 38/42, H 62, T d'E H 8, H 20, H 103.

11. Tennyson and Dyson *Tennysons* p. 186; d'Eyncourt papers T d'E H 4/8, H 56, H 101–15, H 8/43, H 4/8, H 1/34–5.

12. D'Eyncourt papers T d'E H 8/40. One of the French branches has probably been approached; the Order was not refounded in England until 1831, and only became really active in the 1860s (Edwin King and Harry Luke *The Knights of St John in the British Realm*, 1967).

13. There is much about the building of Brancepeth in letters from Russell to Tennyson, d'Eyncourt Papers T d'E H 78, H 86, and in letter from Tennyson and Paterson to Russell in the Russell papers.

14. D'Eyncourt papers T d'E H 86/68, H 86/75 (16 May 1821) refers to 'Collins Puff about the window' in the *Morning Post*. Collins's bill for £1500, dated 24 September 1821, is in the Russell papers.

15. T d'E H 78/22; 2 T d'E H 77; Russell papers. He bought from the Carter (1818, £99.13) Gwennap (27 February 1821, £201.4.6) Bullock (30 February 1821, £67.15) and Cosway (2 June 1821, £93.10) collections.

16. The painting depicting it (plate 45) is now at Burwarton Hall. This and other 'Baron's Halls' were probably inspired by the octagonal Baron's Hall of 1815 at Arundel Castle, built as an anti-Tory anti-Royal-prerogative gesture in celebration of the Magna Carta.

17. D'Eyncourt papers T d'E H 26/19–26.

18. T d'E H 4/8.

19. 2 T d'E H 64/51.

20. Earl of Lytton *Life of Edward Bulwer, First Lord Lytton* (1913) pp. 424–5.

21. *Ibid.* p. 496.

22. S. C. Hall *Retrospect of a Long Life* (1883) I, p. 271.

23. Lytton *Bulwer* p. 416.

24. D'Eyncourt papers 2 T d'E J 7/1.

25. Mark Girouard *The Victorian Country House* (2nd ed. 1979) pp. 103–9.

26. Christopher Hussey 'Lambton Castle' *Country Life* CXXXIX (24 and 31 March 1966) pp. 664–7, 726–9; and see note 3.

27. G. Jackson-Stops 'Newstead Abbey II' *Country Life* CLV (16 May 1974) pp. 1192–3.

28. For *Fraser's Magazine* and Maginn see Miriam Thrall *Rebellious Fraser's* (1934).

29. *Ibid.* p. 126

30. *Ibid.* p. 8.

31. *Ibid.* p. 140.

32. *Ibid.* pp. 155–6.

33. Published *Fraser's Magazine* XI (January 1835) pp. 2–3. The preliminary drawing is at the Victoria and Albert Museum. For it and Maclise generally see *Daniel Maclise,*

1806–1870 (Arts Council Exhibition, 1972, compiled Richard Ormond and John Turpin).

. 34. *Fraser's Magazine* XI (January 1835) pp. 17–18.

35. L. de Sainte-Palaye *Memoirs of Ancient Chivalry* (1784) p. 156. Maclise's friend Laetitia Landon ('L.E.L.') wrote a long poem, 'The Vow of the Peacock' (1835), inspired by the picture.

36. It seems likely that the mediaevalism of the picture derived from a particular event, possibly a fancy-dress ball, but I have not been able to find documentation.

37. *Fraser's Magazine* XVII (May 1838) pp. 635–44.

38. *Fraser's Magazine* XIX (May 1839) pp. 593–603.

39. One of the most interesting examples is Richard Oastler (1789–1861), for whom see C. Driver *Tory Radical: The Life of Richard Oastler* (1946).

40. For Disraeli's Radical-Tory period see W. F. Monypenny and G. E. Buckle *The Life of Benjamin Disraeli, Earl of Beaconsfield* (1910–20) I and II *passim*; Robert Blake *Disraeli* (1966) pp. 84–93, 120–2.

41. Monypenny and Buckle *Disraeli* I, pp. 273–4.

42. *Fraser's Magazine* VII (1833) p. 602.

43. Blake *Disraeli* pp. 136–42; B. R. Jerman *The Young Disraeli* (1960) pp. 280–2.

44. Blake *Disraeli* p. 83.

45. Monypenny and Buckle *Disraeli* II, p. 13.

46. *Maclise* pp. 56, 68.

47. Preface to the collected edition of his early plays (1841); quoted Lytton *Bulwer* I, p. 555.

48. *Maclise* pp. 93–4. The *Combat of Two Knights*, described in *Maclise* (p. 56) as untraced, has since come to light; it was never exhibited and is undated.

49. For John Manners see Charles Whibley *Lord John Manners and his Friends* (1925).

50. *Ibid.* I, p. 66.

51. George Smythe 'Cambridge, 1837' in *Historic Fancies* (1844) p. 151.

52. Whibley *Manners* I, p. 71.

53. James Pope-Hennessy *Monckton Milnes: The Years of Promise* (1949) p. 276.

54. For Digby, Wyndham, Bolingbroke and Filmer see Whibley *Manners* pp. 75, 132–5. Manners's account of his 1839 visit to Spain was published in *Fraser's Magazine* XXI (1840) pp. 573–81 and XXII (1840) pp. 102–12, which suggests that he was a reader.

55. Whibley *Manners* pp. 75–9.

56. *England's Trust* (1841) Stanza IV.

57. For Ferrand see J. T. Ward '"Young England" at Bingley' *Journal of the Bradford Textile Society* (1965–6) pp. 49–59.

58. Disraeli *Coningsby* Bk IX, Ch. I.

59. For Digby and Phillipps de Lisle see B. Holland *Kenelm Henry Digby* (1919) pp. 46–7, 52–3; Edmund Sheridan Purcell *Life and Letters of Ambrose Phillipps de Lisle* (1900) I, pp. 33–5.

60. Purcell *Phillipps de Lisle* II, pp. 284–6. The designs are now in the Drawing Collection of the Royal Institute of British Architects.

61. Girouard *Victorian Country House* pp. 110–19.

62. B. Disraeli *Lord George Bendinck: A Political Biography* (1852).

63. D'Eyncourt papers T d'E H 8/48.

64. *Ibid.* T d'E H 160–28.

65. The architect was H. J. Kendall (inscription on house) but no proper account of the remodelling has been

published. Much of the interior decoration was removed by Lutyens in the 1930s.

66. Lytton *Bulwer* II, p. 161.

NOTES TO CHAPTER 7

1. *Dictionary of National Biography*, under Charles Stanhope, third Earl of Harrington.
2. *Ibid.*, under Maria Foote.
3. W. H. Mallock *Memoirs of Life and Literature* (1920) pp. 116–17.
4. The Elvaston gardens are illustrated and described in E. Adveno Brooke *The Gardens of England* (*c.* 1858). See also William Barron *The British Winter Garden* (1852). Much of the original lay-out has been destroyed since Derbyshire County Council took over the castle in 1969.
5. H. Colvin *Biographical Dictionary of British Architects* (1978). No relevant papers appear to have survived.
6. The lyres and pomegranate suggest that the Harringtons were identifying with Orpheus and Eurydice as well as with a knight or troubadour and his lady.
7. Mallock *Memoirs* p. 117.
8. The original histories are in the possession of Charles Lamb's descendant Mrs Pryce; Ian Anstruther has typescript copies, and photographs of the drawing of guinea-pig castles, etc.
9. Ian Anstruther *The Knight and the Umbrella* (1963) pp. 101–2. This is the only full-length modern account of the tournament.
10. *Ibid.* pp. 122–3.
11. *Ibid.*
12. *Ibid.* pp. 117–18. The opera was published in 1839.
13. *Times*, 1 May 1838, p. 3.
14. *Times*, 16 April 1838. For his catalogues see Victoria and Albert Museum library, Fine Art Pamphlets, 1838, H. 8.
15. In the speech at the banquet in his honour at Irvine, 29 September 1839 (Rev. John Richardson *The Eglinton Tournament* (1843) p. 2).
16. *Ibid.* 'Concluding Remarks', quoting from a 'Morning Journal'.
17. Grantley F. Berkeley *My Life and Recollections* (1865) II, pp. 126–7.
18. Atholl papers; quoted Anstruther *Knight and Umbrella* pp. 159–61.
19. The letters were bound into five volumes, and are now in the possession of Ursula, Countess of Eglinton and Winton.
20. Letters of application, I, p. 35; quoted with others Anstruther *Knight and Umbrella* pp. 168–76.
21. Captain Beresford, who features in some lists as Knight of the Stag's Head, scratched before the day. John Campbell of Saddell was replaced at the last minute as Black Knight by W. L. Gilmour.
22. The story of Charles Lamb and Charlotte Gray is based on family tradition and the unpublished memoirs of his daughter Lady Currie (Violet Singleton). Ian Anstruther and Mrs Pryce have typescript copies of this, both missing the first portion. Charles Lamb's incomplete account of the tournament (quoted Anstruther *Knight and Umbrella* pp. 198–202), illustrated by his own watercolours of himself in armour, his coat of arms. and Eglinton Castle with the procession leaving it, is in the possession of Ian Anstruther.

23. The Ashleys, Grahams and Lord Breadalbane feature in the list of 'those watching mêlée' in Richardson *Eglinton Tournament* XVIII. They are not mentioned in the lists of invited guests and ticket-holders in the stands, belonging to the present Lord Eglinton.
24. J. Macaulay *The Gothic Revival, 1745–1845* (1975) pp. 183–4.
25. Anon. *The Passage of Arms at Eglinton Castle* p. 36; *A Full Report of the Grand Tournament at Eglinton Castle* (newspaper broadsheet, printed Belfast and Edinburgh): 'We overheard a gentleman compare the scene to "a vast herd of young elephants with nothing but their backs seen."'
26. *Passage of Arms* p. 59.
27. Lady Londonderry to Disraeli, 29 August 1859; quoted Anstruther *Knight and Umbrella* pp. 217–18.
28. *Passage of Arms* p. 36.
29. *Ibid.* pp. 40–4.
30. Augustus Hare *The Story of Two Noble Lives* (1893) I, pp. 207–8.
31. *Euphranor* (*Letters and Literary Remains of Edward FitzGerald* (1902–3) VI, p. 187).
32. Digby *The Broad Stone of Honour: Godefridus* (1844) p. 86.
33. A. W. Pugin *True Principles of Christian Architecture* (1844) p. 59.
34. Mark Girouard *The Victorian Country House* (2nd ed. 1979) pp. 154–63.
35. 'The armour had been discarded by a guest, at a fancy dress ball held by the Hollands in February, 1845, and found by the painter' (M. S. Watts *George Frederic Watts* (1912) I, p. 53).
36. The Testimonial is on loan from Lord Eglinton to the Irvine District Council. See *Illustrated London News* II (10 June 1843) p. 404.
37. Ian Anstruther has Eglinton salt-glaze jugs, medals, plates and music sheets; Ursula, Countess of Eglinton and Winton, has an Eglinton scent-bottle, jigsaw and music sheet. Surviving accoutrements of the knights include the following: Lord Gage and Captain D. O. Fairlie have suits of armour; the Duke of Atholl has armour, harness and horse-trappings; Dr Balfour, of Balbirnie (whose ancestor was an esquire to Lord Glenlyon), has the outfit worn in the procession and (probably) the banquet, the former badly rain-stained; Mr and Mrs Lucas (Sharow Hall, Ripon) have tilting lances.
38. For a list see Anstruther *Knight and Umbrella* pp. 261–2.
39. *Full Report* (see note 25). The list does not mention Landseer, who is given by Richardson *Eglinton Tournament* XVIII; possibly it was Edwin Landseer's less well known brother Charles.
40. For Noel Paton and the abortive Taymouth tournament in 1880 see p. 155 and n. 34. Maclise's *Combat of Two Knights* is not dated, but the subject suggests the influence of the tournament.
41. William Vaughan *German Romanticism and English Art* (1979) pp. 168–71.
42. Among them was H. C. Selous, a prolific illustrator in the 'Eglinton' manner, who was the father of F. C. Selous, the African explorer.
43. Macaulay *Gothic Revival* pp. 249–52; Alistair Rowan 'Taymouth Castle, II' *Country Life* CXXXVI (15 October 1964) pp. 978–82; illustrated in colour *Country Life Annual*, 1970, p. 30.
44. Hare *Two Noble Lives* I, pp. 213–29, etc.

45. *Blackwood's Magazine*, November 1861. It is widely believed that the tournament was the financial ruin of Lord Eglinton, but although he seems to have left an embarrassed estate it is unlikely that the tournament was the principal cause of it. The full accounts have disappeared (unless they are among the unsorted Eglinton papers at the Registry House, Edinburgh) but since the costs of the individual knights and their retinues were not borne by Lord Eglinton it seems unlikely that his costs were all that much in excess of those for, for instance, especially lavish coming-of-age festivities—perhaps £10–15,000.

46. Anstruther *Knight and Umbrella* p. 102.

47. The picture, which belongs to Captain J. O. Fairlie, is reproduced as part of a useful account of the tournament in Sara Stevenson and Helen Bennett *Van Dyck in Check Trousers: Fancy Dress in Art and Life* (1978) pp. 105–14.

48. Disraeli MS. Hughenden; quoted Anstruther *Knight and Umbrella* p. 244.

NOTES TO CHAPTER 8

1. Royal Archives, Windsor Castle. The original journals do not survive; up till Queen Victoria's marriage a full transcript was made by the first Lord Esher; the later journals survive in the heavily dated transcript made by Queen Victoria's daughter Princess Beatrice.

2. *Times*, 14 May 1842, pp. 6–7.

3. Royal Archives C6/30.

4. Journal.

5. James Mill *History of Chivalry* (1st ed. 1825) II, p. 2.

6. For Planché see *Dictionary of National Biography* and his own memoirs. His *Costumes of Shakespeare's Historical Tragedy of King John* (1823) and of *King Henry the Fourth* (1824), 'selected and arranged especially for the Proprietors of the Theatre Royal, Covent Garden', represent an early and creditable attempt to design costumes based on mediaeval authorities.

7. J. R. Planché, *Recollections and Reflections* (1872) pp. 56–7.

8. Quoted Charles Whibley *Lord John Manners and his Friends* (1925) I, pp. 152–3.

9. *Times*, 14 May 1842, pp. 6–7.

10. Theodore Martin *Life of the Prince Consort* (1875) I, pp. 212–13.

11. *Sybil* Bk I, Ch. VI.

12. Marcia Pointon *William Dyce, 1806–64* (1979) pp. 97–8, pl. 130.

13. *Journal*, 17 March 1845.

14. It is now on show at Kensington Palace.

15. For the Commission see T. S. R. Boase 'The Decoration of the New Palace of Westminster' *Journal of the Warburg and Courtauld Institutes* XVII (1954) p. 319.

16. See *Works of Art in the House of Lords* (ed. Maurice Bond, 1980).

17. *Letters* (Nonesuch ed.) I, p. 536, 1 September 1843.

18. For the various versions of *The Spirit of Chivalry* see *Daniel Maclise* (Arts Council Exhibition, 1972, compiled Richard Ormond and John Turpin) pp. 92–6.

19. Pointon *Dyce* pp. 104–48 *passim*, 177–8.

20. *Maclise* pp. 107–16.

21. George Rowell *Queen Victoria goes to the Theatre* (1978).

22. Corbould's watercolour is now bound into the 'Theatrical Album' in Windsor Castle library. This contains views of scenes in plays attended by the Queen, mainly depicted in watercolours but including a set of tinted photographs of Charles Kean's *Richard II*.

23. Sketches by Corbould for Kean's productions are in the Prints and Drawings collection, Victoria and Albert Museum.

24. *Dictionary of National Biography*; A. M. W. Stirling *Victorian Sidelights* (1954) pp. 209–13. Apart from ones mentioned in the main text, chivalric pictures painted by Corbould for the Royal Family include *The Contest for the Large Diamond* (from Tennyson's *Enid*), *Joan of Arc*, *The Death of Turgibin at Beverley* and *The Marriage of Nigel Bruce and Agnes of Buchan*, all in the Royal Collection. His *Morte d'Arthur* was given by Queen Victoria to Princess Louise.

25. Martin *Prince Consort* p. 213.

26. The picture is now kept at Frogmore.

27. Journal, 16 February 1864.

28. The original design, dated February 1864, is at Osborne; reproduced John Morley *Death, Heaven and the Victorians* (1971) pl. 36.

29. Unattributed newspaper cutting 'Albert Memorial Chapel at Windsor' dated 23 June 1873 (Royal Archives); Journal, 5 July 1873. Like Corbould's painting and christening gift, the monument is inscribed 'I have fought the good fight', etc.; in a memorandum 'Cenotaphe de Wolsey's Chapel' (Royal Archives, R. 40). Triqueti unjustifiably claimed to have thought up the inscription himself.

30. Gilbert Papers, Royal Archives (Vic. Add. MS., X, f. 200).

31. Charles Wolfe (1791–1823) 'The Burial of Sir John Moore at Corunna'.

32. Isabel McAllister *Alfred Gilbert* (1929) pp. 97–8. For Burne-Jones as model for St George see *ibid.* p. 223.

NOTES TO CHAPTER 9

1. Sermon on 'Faith', preached on 5 December 1865 (C. Kingsley *The Water of Life and other Sermons* (1867) pp. 210–11).

2. T. Carlyle *Past and Present* (1918) Bk III, Ch. I, pp. 124, 129.

3. *Ibid.* III, XI, p. 194.

4. *Ibid.* II, X, p. 171.

5. *Ibid.* III, X, p. 172.

6. *Ibid.*

7. *Ibid.* III, XI, p. 177.

8. *Ibid.* IV, IV, p. 245.

9. *Ibid.* IV, IV *passim*.

10. *Ibid.* II, V, p. 144.

11. C. E. Raven *Christian Socialism, 1848–54* (1920) is the standard monograph on the movement.

12. Susan Chitty *The Beast and the Monk* (1974) p. 109. The publisher was John Parker, who had become the owner of *Fraser's Magazine*.

13. *Ibid.* p. 23.

14. *Ibid.* p. 91.

15. 'Elegiacs' in C. Kingsley *Poems* (1889) p. 254.

16. *Proceedings of the 25th Annual Co-operative Congress* (1895) p. iii; quoted Edward C. Mack and W. H. G. Armytage *Thomas Hughes: The Life of the Author of Tom Brown's Schooldays* (1952) p. 58.

17. J. Llewellyn Davies *The Working Men's College, 1854–1904* (1904) p. 10.

18. Hughes to Marquess of Ripon, 19 May 1881 and 9 March 1883 (British Museum Add. MS. 43, 531).
19. Mack and Armytage *Hughes* p. 57.
20. H. G. Wood *F. D. Maurice* (1950) p. 16.
21. Chitty *Beast and Monk* p. 95.
22. Sir Charles Tennyson *Alfred Tennyson* (1949) p. 260.
23. Raven *Christian Socialism* pp. 378–9.
24. Chitty *Beast and Monk* pp. 144–5.
25. *Yeast* (Macmillan ed. 1908) Ch. XI, p. 152.
26. *Ibid.* p. 248.
27. Raven *Christian Socialism* pp. 127–34, 340–60; Davies *Working Men's College, passim.*
28. In 1905 it moved from Red Lion Square to Crowndale Road, St Pancras.
29. Raven *Christian Socialism* p. 354.
30. Chitty *Beast and Monk* p. 149.
31. *Ibid.* p. 160.
32. *Ibid.* p. 159.
33. Mack and Armytage *Hughes* pp. 62–3.
34. *Ibid.* p. 24.
35. Davies *Working Men's College* p. 74.
36. Mack and Armytage *Hughes* p. 116.
37. Chitty *Beast and Monk* p. 196. When his son Maurice went to preparatory school in 1856 he wrote to him on the correct behaviour for 'a gentleman and an officer' (*ibid.* p. 191).
38. *Westward Ho* (1882 ed.) pp. 8–9.
39. *Ibid.* p. 130.
40. *Two Years Ago*, Ch. XXIII, 'The Broad Stone of Honour'.
41. *Ibid.* pp. 253, 381.
42. *Tom Brown at Oxford* (Macmillan ed. 1880) Ch. XI, 'Muscular Christianity', p. 99.
43. C. Kingsley *David: Four Sermons* (1865).
44. Frances Eliza Kingsley *Charles Kingsley: His Letters and Memories of his Life* (one vol. ed. 1890) p. 267, quoting Evelyn Shuckburgh.
45. Kingsley *David* p. 10.
46. *Two Years Ago* p. 314.
47. E.g., Carlyle *Past and Present* III, XV, p. 210 on the degree of worship in washing: 'this consciousness of perfect outer pureness . . . how it radiates in on thee, with cunning symbolic influences, to thy very soul.' In the late 1850s Kingsley told an audience at a Mechanics' Institute in Bristol: 'If you only wash your bodies, your souls will be all right' (Chitty *Beast and Monk* p. 192).
48. Mack and Armytage *Hughes* pp. 150–1.

NOTES TO CHAPTER 10

1. *The Newcomes* (*Works* (biographical ed. 1900) VIII, p. 73).
2. Christabel Coleridge *Charlotte Mary Yonge* (1903) p. 225.
3. *Ibid.* p. 168.
4. *The Heir of Redclyffe* (Macmillan ed. 1894) Ch. V, pp. 53, 55.
5. *Ibid.* pp. 116–17, 196, 238, 250, 387.
6. *Ibid.* Ch. XXX, p. 314. 'Mr Shene' was probably based on William Dyce, who was a friend of C. M. Yonge's friend Keble and was painting *Sir Galahad adoring the San Greal* for the Queen's Robing Room in 1851, exactly when *The Heir of Redclyffe* was being written.
7. J. W. Mackail *Life of William Morris* (1899) I, p. 41 calls it a book 'which exercised an extraordinary fascination over

the whole group, and in which much of the spiritual history of these years may be found pre-figured'.
8. Coleridge *Yonge* p. 183.
9. *Guy Livingstone* (1857) p. 42.
10. *Ibid.* p. 68.
11. *Ibid.* p. 298.
12. See *Dictionary of National Biography*.
13. G. A. Lawrence *Sword and Gown* (1860) p. 101. The novel is full of chivalric allusion (and has a passage on Muscular Christianity on pp. 262–4).
14. E.g., 'Muscular Christianity' *Marlburian* I (1865–6, reprinted 1867) p. 10; 'Charles Kingsley' *Cliftonian* IV (1874–7) pp. 33–6.
15. For Mrs Craik and her background see Aleyn Lyell Reade *The Mellards and their Descendants* (1915).
16. *John Halifax, Gentleman* Chs. XIV and XXX.
17. *Ibid.* Ch. XXIX.
18. Quoted at the end of the forty-second edition (Hurst and Blackett, London).
19. E.g., W. Holman Hunt *Pre-Raphaelitism and the Pre-Raphaelite Brotherhood* (1905) I, p. 3; Sir George Gilbert Scott *Personal and Professional Recollections* (1879) p. 2; and see p. 263.
20. M. S. Watts *George Frederic Watts* (1912) I, pp. 158, 161–2, 228.
21. The best source for dating Watts's paintings is the MS. catalogue made by Mrs M. S. Watts and now at the Watts Gallery, Compton, near Guildford. A reduced photographic copy is in the Witt Library, Courtauld Institute. The *Eve of Peace* was partly repainted in 1876 (Watts *Watts* I, pp. 287, 289); for Watts's earlier self-portrait in armour (1845) see Chapter VII, note 35.
22. *Ellen Terry's Memoirs* (ed. Edith Craig and Christopher St John, 1933) pp. 44–5.
23. Watts *Watts* I, pp. 171–2.
24. It was especially painted to be engraved as the frontispiece of the 1869 illustrated edition of *Tom Brown's Schooldays*.
25. Watts *Watts* I, pp. 186, 190, 266.
26. *Ibid.* pp. 196–8.
27. Wilfred Blunt, *England's Michelangelo* (1956).
28. Watts *Watts* II, p. 172.
29. 'It should be understood that the vision granted to the happy warrior was an embodiment of the ideal for which he had striven' (M. S. Watts 'Catalogue'). For his comments on Sir Galahad see Chapter XI, note 50.
30. Watts *Watts* III, p. 1888 (written in 1879).
32. *Ibid.* I, pp. 159–60, quoting Lady Constance Leslie.
32. *Ibid.* p. 289.
33. For Paton see *Dictionary of National Biography*; Alfred Thomas Story 'Sir Joseph Noel Paton' *Art Journal*, 1895 (with photographs of interior of his house, see pl. 102); M. H. Noel Paton *Tales of a Grand-daughter* (1970); *Fact and Fancy* (Scottish Arts Council Exhibition, 1967).
34. Paton *Tales*. Paton was asked to be marshal of the lists; Lord Archibald Campbell was among those involved.
35. See R. Scott-Moncrieff 'The late Sir Noel Paton's Collection', antiquarian supplement to *Scottish Art and Letters*, June–August 1903; Malcolm Baker 'A Victorian Collector of Armour' *Country Life* CLVII (25 January 1975) pp. 232–6.
36. The catalogue entry for *Mors Janua Vitae* included a long extract from a poem 'The Good Fight' (Algernon Graves *The Royal Academy of Arts* (1905–6), under Paton).
37. *Sir Galahad's Vision of the Sangreal* (dated 1879; R.S.A.

1880); *Sir Galahad and his Angel* (ex. R.S.A. 1885; it is clearly influenced by Dürer's *Knight, Death and Satan*); *Beate Mundo Corde* (1889–90, based on small oil *How an Angel raised Galahad over the Dern Mere*). Stylistically they all seem to belong more to the 1860s.
38. Description in Story 'Paton'.
39. A. M. W. Stirling *The Richmond Papers* (1926) pp. 136–7.
40. *Ibid.* p. 139.
41. Some pages are illustrated in J. G. Millais *The Life and Letters of Sir John Everett Millais* (1899) I, pp. 31–3.
42. *Ibid.* I, pp. 306–19, with illustration of caricature, p. 321.
43. *Ibid.* II, p. 472.
44. *Ibid.* II, p. 24.
45. Mary Lutyens *Millais and the Ruskins* (1967) p. 34.
46. Mark Girouard *The Victorian Country House* (2nd ed. 1979) pp. 273–90 (Cardiff), 336–45 (Castell Coch), 346–51 (Carlton), 393 (Alnwick), 410 (Horsley). There is no adequate published account of the rebuilding of Arundel. For Burges and Bute see J. Mordaunt Crook *William Burges and the High Victorian Dream* (1981).
47. Girouard *Victorian Country House* p. 393.
48. Alistair Rowan 'Killyleagh Castle' *Country Life* CXLVII (9 and 26 March 1970) pp. 690–3, 774–7.
49. According to a 'memorandum of the circumstances' attached to the 1869 lease. Archibald Rowan Hamilton bought the gatehouse in 1848 for £1000 but 'as it was Lord Dufferin's intention that the Gatehouse and Garden should be a free gift' the £1000 was subsequently repaid and the gatehouse rebuilt. Hamilton's death in 1860 delayed the final drawing up of a formal lease (Dufferin papers).

NOTES TO CHAPTER 11

1. A. P. Stanley *The Life and Correspondence of Thomas Arnold D.D.* (1844) Ch. V, Letter 7.
2. Henry Newbolt *The Book of the Happy Warrior* (1917) p. vii.
3. A. M. Terhune *Life of Edward FitzGerald* (1947) p. 93. He wrote in Browne's own copy of *Euphranor*: 'This little book would never have been written, had I not known my dear friend William Browne, who, unconsciously, supplied the moral' (*ibid.* p. 155).
4. *Euphranor (Letters and Literary Remains of Edward FitzGerald* (1902–3) VI, p. 222 (beefsteak into chivalry), pp. 230–1 (cricket and King Arthur)).
5. A. G. Bradley, etc. *A History of Marlborough College* (1923) pp. 169–70; S. A. Cotton *Memoir of Bishop Cotton* p. 17.
6. C. E. Raven *Christian Socialism, 1848–54* (1920) pp. 378–9; Bradley *Marlborough College* p. 186.
7. *Tom Brown's Schooldays* (small illustrated ed. 1874) p. 282.
8. *Ibid.* p. 338. Confirmation makes one 'a little band of brothers against the whole world'.
9. *Ibid.* p. 73.
10. *Ibid.* p. 123.
11. *Ibid.* p. 255.
12. *Ibid.* p. 122.
13. *Ibid.* pp. 289–90.
14. *Ibid.* pp. 290, 295–6.
15. There is a full list in J. B. Hope Simpson *Rugby since Arnold* (1967) pp. 295–8.

16. G. C. Coulton *Henry Hart of Sedbergh* (1923) p. 121.
17. Quoted Jonathan Gathorne-Hardy *The Public School Phenomenon* (paperback ed. 1979) p. 161.
18. G. St Quintin *The History of Glenalmond: The Story of a Hundred Years* (1956) p. 130. Window in memory of Dr Lowe, the school doctor, *c.* 1890.
19. J. H. Skrine 'The Romance of School' *Contemporary Review* LXXIII (1898) pp. 430–8.
20. *Cliftonian* VI (1880) p. 342; VII (1881–3) p. 406.
21. Perceval *Some Helps for School Life* (1880) p. 2.
22. *Ibid.* p. 258.
23. Sir Charles Tennyson *Alfred Tennyson* (1949) p. 362.
24. He was an intelligent man, but owing to being kicked on the spine during a school game never grew beyond 5 feet 1 inch (Roy Jenkins *Asquith* (1964) p. 14).
25. O. F. Christie *A History of Clifton College, 1860–1934* (1935) pp. 122–3.
26. *Ibid.* p. 360.
27. *Ibid.* p. 78.
28. Henry Newbolt *The World as in my Time* (1932) p. 62.
29. Quoted *ibid.* p. 46.
30. *Clifton College—Endowed Scholarships and Prizes* (ed. G. H. Wollaston, 1914) pp. 18–19.
31. Perceval *Some Helps* p. 223.
32. Christie *Clifton College* p. 46 (Cay), p. 53 (Bartholomew), p. 61 (Grenfell), p. 62 (Moberley).
33. *Cliftonian* XIV (June 1900).
34. Christie *Clifton College* p. 109, n.104.
35. See *Letters of John Addington Symonds* (ed. H. M. Schueller and R. L. Peters, 1967) II, pp. 230–1, 311, 330, 337. For Boyle's relations with Symonds and Dakyns see *Letters* II, pp. 187, 211, 218, etc; Phyllis Grosskurth *John Addington Symonds* (1904).
36. He was killed at Boshof, in the engagement in which the Frenchman Villebois-Mareuil also died (see p. 273).
37. Reprinted *Cliftonian* XIV (June 1900).
38. *Cliftonian* XVII (1903) pp. 348–9, 377–9; XVIII (1904) pp. 190–2, 194.
39. See *Extracts from the Letters and Journals of William Cory* (ed. F. Warre Cornish, 1897); Reginald Viscount Esher *Ionicus* (1923); Faith Compton-Mackenzie *William Cory* (1950).
40. Bernard Holland 'An Eton Master' *National Review*, February 1898, pp. 867–75.
41. See note 6; J. Llewellyn-Davies *The Working Men's College, 1854–1904* (1904) p. 16; *Working Men's College Journal* I (June 1891) p. 259; Cory *Letters and Journals* pp. 57–8; Johnson papers, Eton College, J1/52, 61.
42. Cory *Letters and Journals* pp. 58, 149.
43. *Ibid.* p. 459.
44. *Ibid.* p. 461; and see Chapter V, note 33.
45. *Ibid.* p. 460.
46. Holland 'An Eton Master' p. 874.
47. Gambier Parry *Annals of an Eton House* (1907) p. 143, 'The Revival of Cricket at Eton'; W. Johnson-Cory *Ionica* (1891) p. 114; Cory *Letters and Journals* p. 82.
48. Johnson-Cory *Ionica* pp. 71, 26.
49. See *Letters of H. E. Luxmore* (1929).
50. Quoted in entry on *Sir Galahad* in M. S. Watts's catalogue (see Chapter X, note 21). See also *Eton College Chronicle*, 17 June 1897.
51. Luxmore *Letters* p. 79.
52. C. R. L. Fletcher *Edmund Warre* (1922) p. 134.
53. Gathorne-Hardy *Public School Phenomenon* p. 103.

NOTES TO CHAPTER 12

1. R. F. Brinkley *Arthurian Legend in the Seventeenth Century* (1932) ch. IV, 'Arthur as epic subject'.
2. Chap-books on the story of Arthur were in fact produced well into the eighteenth century.
3. J. G. Lockhart *Life of Sir Walter Scott* (concise version, Everyman's ed. 1906) p. 61.
4. *The Bridal of Triermain* Canto II, XIII.
5. Lockhart *Life* (1839 ed.) V, Ch. XXXIX, p. 252.
6. Sir Charles Tennyson *Alfred Tennyson* (1950) p. 32.
7. *Lady Charlotte Guest: Extracts from her Journal, 1833–1852* (ed. Earl of Bessborough, 1950) pp. 8–9. 63–4, etc.
8. *The Poems of Tennyson* (ed. Christopher Ricks, 1969) p. 582.
9. *Ibid.* p. 185.
10. Earl of Lytton *Life of Edward Bulwer, First Lord Lytton* (1913) pp. 469–73.
11. Newman on Froude *Apologia pro Vita Sua* (new imp. 1913) p. 24.
12. *Poems of Tennyson* pp. 502–5.
13. Dyce to Eastlake (as Secretary) Royal Archives, F 30/61 (copy).
14. Marcia Pointon *William Dyce, 1806–64* (1979) pp. 104–48, 177–8.
15. *Poems of Tennyson* p. 1737 (Guinevere II. 484–8).
16. *Ibid.* p. 1659 (Lancelot and Elaine I. 1358).
17. *Idylls of the King* (ed. Hallam Tennyson, 1908) p. 443.
18. *Poems of Tennyson* pp. 1736–7 (Guinevere II. 464–80).
19. *Poems of Tennyson* p. 1756 ('To the Queen', dedication in 1873 ed. of *Idylls*).
20. *Morte d'Arthur* XVIII. 25 (Guenevere); XX. 9 (Lancelot).
21. Burne-Jones always reproached Tennyson for his unsympathetic treatment of Vivien/Nimue.
22. E.g., *Cliftonian* II, p. 163.
23. Terhune *FitzGerald* p. 309.
24. *Idylls* pp. 445–6.
25. Robert B. Martin *Tennyson: The Unquiet Heart* (1980) pp. 423–4.
26. *Poems of Tennyson* pp. 1627–8 (Lancelot and Elaine II. 244–54).
27. Tristan and Iseult II. 7–8.
28. J. W. Mackail *Life of William Morris* (1899) I, p. 9.
29. G. Burne-Jones *Memorials of Edward Burne-Jones* (1904) I, p. 141.
30. *Ibid.* I, p. 77.
31. Virginia Surtees *The Paintings and Drawings of Dante Gabriel Rossetti* (1971) pp. 36–7.
32. Martin *Tennyson* p. 415.
33. Paul Thompson *The Work of William Morris* (1907) p. 175.
34. *Contemporary Review*, October 1871, pp. 334–50.
35. *Quarterly Review*, 1872; quoted Philip Henderson *William Morris* (paperback ed. 1973) p. 114.
36. Penelope FitzGerald *Edward Burne-Jones: A Biography* (1975) pp. 126–8.
37. H. Quilter *Contemporary Review*, February 1883; quoted R. G. Grylls *Portrait of Rossetti* (1964) pp. 239–40.
38. Reproduced Grylls *Rossetti* p. 160.
39. Quoted *ibid.* p. 240.
40. FitzGerald *Burne-Jones* pp. 130, 146–7, 150–1.
41. E.g., *Sidonia von Bork* (1860); *Merlin and Nimue* (1861); *Morgan le Fay* (1862); *The Wine of Circe* (1863–9); *The Beguiling of Merlin* (1874); *The Sirens* (c. 1875–98); *The Depths of the Sea* (1886).
42. G. G. Cullingham *The Royal Windsor Tapestry Manufactory, 1876–1890* (Royal Borough of Windsor and Maidenhead, Historical Records Publications, IV, 1979). Separate sets of the *Idylls of the King* were designed by Herbert A. Bone in in 1879 and 1881, and woven for Coleridge Kennard and Henry Hucks Gibbs.
43. Cutler, p. xviii. Arthurian tales were also retold for boys by the American Thomas Bulfinch in *The Age of Chivalry* (English eds. 1905 and 1906).
44. *Poems of Tennyson* p. 1596 ('Vivien' II. 11–13).
45. Walter Crane *An Artist's Reminiscences* (1907).

NOTES TO CHAPTER 13

1. *The Poems of Tennyson* (ed. Christopher Ricks, 1969) p. 1738 (Guinevere I. 554).
2. *The Broad Stone of Honour* (1824 ed.) p. 184.
3. E.g., *Temple of Memory* Canto VII, 'Of Travel and Adventures'.
4. *Tom Brown at Oxford* (1889 ed.) p. 389.
5. *Broad Stone* (1824 ed.) p. 389.
6. *Ivanhoe* Ch. IV.
7. *Sesame and Lilies* Lecture II, secs. 64, 66, 90.
8. Augustus Hare *The Story of my Life: The Life and Letters of Frederic Shields* (ed. Ernestine Mills, 1912).
9. Blunt papers, Fitzwilliam Museum, Cambridge, MS. 30–1975, p. 178.
10. R. Blake *Disraeli* (1966) pp. 490–1.
11. Sir George Arthur *Queen Mary* (1934) p. 85.
12. Countess of Antrim *Recollections* (1937) p. 221.
13. Georgina Battiscombe *Queen Alexandra* (1969).
14. Letter from William Johnson, 19 January 1852 (Eton College, Johnson papers, J1/61).
15. Fitzwilliam MS. 42–1975, p. 231.
16. *Ibid.* p. 365.
17. See 'The Four Friends of Baddesley Clinton' *Times*, 13 September 1923, p. 13. The article was called to the attention of Maurice Baring, who used it to provide the plot of his novel *Cat's Cradle*. One would like to have corroboratory evidence in support of its statement that Dering intended to propose to Rebecca Orpen; certainly no correction or protest was published in subsequent issues of *The Times*.
18. *Ibid.* For the 'four friends' see also John Cornforth 'Baddesley Clinton' *Country Life* CLXIII (22 and 29 June 1978) pp. 1802–5, 1866–9.
19. What survives is not usually the original diaries, but Blunt's edited, selected (and, for the earlier years, entirely rewritten) presentation of them, copied and recopied in a number of different versions. For Blunt's life see Elizabeth Longford *Pilgrimage of Passion* (1979).
20. Fitzwilliam MS. 32–1975, p. 116 (6 October 1892).
21. *Ibid.* MS. 31–1975 p. 215 (3 September 1891).
22. *Ibid.* MS. 3–1975 (30 May 1891).
23. *Ibid.* MS. 42–1975, p. 315.
24. *Ibid.* MS. 41–1975, p. 16.
25. *Ibid.* MS. 43–1975, p. 111, etc.
26. *Ibid.* MS. 42–1975, p. 47.
27. *Ibid.* p. 247.
28. *Ibid.* MS. 43–1975, pp. 297–301, etc.

29. *Ibid*. p. 57.
30. *Ibid*. MS. 30–1975, p. 352 (13 September 1890).
31. *Ibid*. MS. 31–1975, p. 272 (4 November 1891).
32. *Ibid*. MS. 364–1975 (16 and 20 September 1899).
33. Blunt disliked the language in which his early diaries were written, burnt the originals, and rewrote their story: 'adventures of the heart . . . need experience to formulate in prose without offence' (MS. 42–1975, p. 253).
34. The classic list of the Souls is in a poem recited by George Curzon at a dinner given on 10 July 1889; quoted Margot Tennant *Autobiography* (Penguin ed. 1936) I, pp. 149–54.
35. Fitzwilliam MS. 31–1975, p. 136 and 31 August 1891.
36. Full accounts in Longford *Pilgrimage* pp. 296–9, 309–14.
37. See Nicholas Mosley *Julian Grenfell* (1976) *passim*.
38. Fitzwilliam MS. 415–1975 (24 June 1913); dedicatory poem in Blunt *Poetical Works* (1914) II.
39. Bound volume of letters to Blunt, in possession of Lord Lytton.
40. Fitzwilliam MS. 36–1975. pp. 76–92.
41. Blunt *Poetical Works* I, 'Later Lyrics'.
42. Longford *Pilgrimage* pp. 332–3.
43. *Poems of Tennyson* p. 596 ('Morte d'Arthur' II. 259–64).
44. Morris to Faulkner, 17 May 1871; quoted Philip Henderson *William Morris: His Life, Work and Friends* (Penguin ed. 1967) p. 147.
45. Fitzwilliam MS. 42–1975. p. 153.
46. Diana Cooper *The Rainbow comes and goes* (1961) p. 63.
47. Information from his granddaughter, Daphne Pollen.
48. Christopher Hussey *The Life of Sir Edwin Lutyens* (1953) pp. 113–17; articles by Lawrence Weaver and Christopher Hussey, *Country Life* XXXI (4 May 1912) pp. 650–9; LXVI (20 and 27 July 1929) pp. 80–96, 120–6.
49. The story is told in Emily Lutyens *A Blessed Girl* (1953).
50. Mary Lutyens *Edwin Lutyens* (1980) pp. 31, 35–9, 43, etc.
51. *Ibid*. pp. 32–8.
52. *Ibid*. p. 49.
53. *Ibid*. pp. 65–6, etc.
54. James Pope-Hennessy *Monckton Milnes: The Years of Promise* (1949) p. 17.
55. *Letters of John Addington Symonds* (ed. H. M. Schueller and R. L. Peters, 1967) II, p. 181.
56. *Ibid*. I, p. 570.
57. *Eric or Little by Little* (1858) Ch. VIII.
58. Quoted Brian Reade *Sexual Heretics: Male Homosexuality in English Literature from 1850 to 1900* (1970) p. 5.
59. Reprinted in full *ibid*. pp. 313–19. See also Timothy D'Arch Smith *Love in Earnest: Some Notes on the Lives and Writings of English 'Uranian' Poets from 1889 to 1930* (1970) pp. 87–8.
60. Review quoted at the back of the book.

NOTES TO CHAPTER 14

1. W. H. Dunn *James Anthony Froude* (1963) II, p. 264.
2. G. N. Curzon *Subjects of the Day* (1915) p. 44.
3. See Chapter 4, note 6.
4. J. A. Froude *The English in the West Indies* (1888) p. 182; R. Faber *The Vision and the Need* (1966) p. 62.
5. C. Kingsley *Miscellanies* (1859) II, pp. 21–2.
6. C. E. Maurice *Life of Octavia Hill* (1913) pp. 148–9.

7. J. H. Skrine 'The Romance of School' *Contemporary Review* LXXIII (1898) p. 438.
8. Ruskin *Works* (ed. E. T. Cook and A. Wedderburn) XX, p. 41. Inaugural Lecture, 8 February 1870. Passage repeated in lecture 'Pleasures of Learning', Oxford, 18 and 20 October 1884 (*Works* XXXIII, p. 422).
9. *Ibid*. XX, p. 240.
10. *Ibid*. XX, p. xlv, etc.; Sir J. Willison *Sir George Parkin* (1929) p. 30; R. H. Sherard *Life of Oscar Wilde* (1906) pp. 127–8.
11. Willison *Parkin* pp. 38, 54, etc.
12. John Flint *Cecil Rhodes* (1976) p. 21 carefully works out his Oxford dates.
13. *Ibid*. pp. 32–3.
14. Little if anything is said in *Round Table* itself or the published writings of its members about the reasons for taking the name; it seems likely that both its Arthurian connotations and the concept of no one country being 'at the head of the table' appealed to them.
15. Kenneth Rose *Superior Person* (1969) p. 179.
16. A. J. Stockwell 'Sir Hugh Clifford's Early Career' *Journal Malaysian Branch Royal Asiatic Society* XLIX (1976) pt 1. See also J. de V. Allen 'Two Imperialists: A Study of Sir Frank Swettenham and Sir Hugh Clifford' *ibid*. XXXVII (1976) pt I, pp. 41–73.
17. J. A. Froude *Oceana* (1886) p. 124.
18. Indirect Rule appealed to the British Government because it seemed a way of running the Empire on the cheap; but there is no doubt that its feudal implications strongly appealed to some members of the Colonial Service.
19. W. H. Dunn *James Anthony Froude* (1963) II, p. 321.
20. *Review of Reviews*, 15 January 1891.
21. Curzon *Subjects* p. 5.
22. A. Duff Cooper *Haig* (1935) I, pp. 90–2.
23. RIBA Drawings Collection, London; Bence-Jones 'The Building Dreams of a Viceroy' *Country Life* CXLVIII (1 and 8 October 1970) pp. 816–19, 900–4.
24. W. S. Blunt *In Vinculis* (1889) Sonnet XIV.
25. Henry Newbolt *The World as in my Time* (1932) p. 162.
26. William A. Shaw *The Knights of England* (1906). The Prince Consort took the greatest interest in the conception, name and insignia of the Order of the Star of India (Royal Archives, N. 23).
27. *Journals of General C. G. Gordon* (ed. A. E. Hake, 1885) p. xliii.
28. Archibald Forbes *Chinese Gordon* (1884) p. 1.
29. Sir W. F. Butler *Charles George Gordon* (1st ed. 1889; 1920 ed. p. 252).
30. Harold Begbie *Albert, Fourth Earl Grey* (1918) pp. 128–9.
31. Begbie *Earl Grey*; Albert, Earl Grey *Memoir of Hubert Hervey* (1899).
32. Begbie *Earl Grey* pp. 32, 127, 177.
33. Grey *Hervey* pp. v and 1.
34. Flint *Rhodes* pp. 217, 238; W. T. Stead (ed.) *Last Will and Testament of Cecil John Rhodes* (1902) pp. 30–45.

NOTES TO CHAPTER 15

1. David Leitch 'Packer's Package' *Sunday Times Magazine*, 19 December 1979, pp. 8–19.
2. W. E. Bowen *Edward Bowen: A Memoir* (1902) pp. 328–35.

3. Frederick Gale *Life of the Hon. Robert Grimston* (1885) p. 308.
4. Inscription in school chapel, Harrow.
5. J. Gathorne-Hardy *The Public School Phenomenon* (Penguin ed. 1979) pp. 158–9.
6. R. Daft *Kings of Cricket* (1893, introduction Lang) p. 14.
7. Baden-Powell *Scouting for Boys* (1908) p. 338. This is followed by a passage on the dangers of professionalism.
8. *Ibid.* pp. 380–1.
9. C. Kingsley *Alton Locke* (1849) Ch. XLI; *Poems* (1889) p. 251.
10. Quoted *I Zingari—Origins, Rise, Progress* (annual club publication, 1924).
11. Attributed to Newbolt in N. L. Jackson *Sporting Days and Sporting Ways* (1932) p. 9.
12. Quoted *ibid.*
13. Quoted Gerald Brodribb (ed.) *The Book of Cricket Verse* (1953).
14. Henry Newbolt *The Book of the Happy Warrior* (1917) p. vii.
15. Lord (G. R.) Harris *A Few Short Runs* (1921) Ch. X, 'The Honour of the Game' p. 265.
16. *Cliftonian* III (1874) pp. 22–3.
17. Lord (E. J.) Hawke *Recollections and Reminiscences* (1924) p. 1.
18. John Cornforth 'Wightwick Manor II' *Country Life* CXXXIII (6 June 1963) p. 1317.
19. Information Lady Mulholland.
20. Gale *Grimston* pp. 171–2; W. A. Bettesworth *The Walkers of Southgate* (1900); *Diary of Lady Frederick Cavendish* (ed. John Bailey, 1927) p. 39.
21. Henry Newbolt *The World as in my Time* (1932) p. 227.
22. E. V. Lucas *Edwin Austen Abbey* (1921) pp. 322–35, photograph of team (reproduced pl. 155) p. 396.
23. *I Zingari.*
24. Edith Lyttelton *Alfred Lyttelton* (1917) p. 229, etc.
25. *Ibid.* p. 379.
26. *Ibid.* p. 409.
27. Such tents had been set up on the edge of cricket fields since at least the late eighteenth century. They seem always to have been referred to as 'tents'; the use of 'pavilion' as a term for permanent cricket structures is perhaps more likely to derive from the eighteenth-century use of the word to describe a pleasure building, than to deliberate mediaevalism.
28. *Recollections of Rugby by an Old Rugbeian* (1848) p. 131.
29. *Ivanhoe* Ch. VIII.
30. *Recollections of Rugby* p. 132.
31. Harris *Short Runs* p. 117.
32. E.g., Queen's Cup, Ascot, 1852, Red Cross Knight (*Illustrated London News*, 12 June 1852; Sotheby's, Mentmore Sale, 23 May 1977, lot 1662); Goodwood Cup, 1864, William the Conqueror; and Chesterfield Cup, 1864, knight rescuing damsel (*Illustrated London News*, 6 August 1864); Croxteth Hunt Steeplechase Trophy, 1868, knights in armour (Sotheby's Belgravia, 21 February 1974, lot 94).
33. J. T. Ward '"Young England" at Bingley' *Journal of the Bradford Textile Society* (1965–6) pp. 49–59.
34. E. C. Mack and W. H. G. Armytage *Thomas Hughes* (1952) pp. 10, 34.
35. A. Gibson and W. Pickford *Association Football and the Men who made it* (1906) I, p. 32.
36. W. T. Dixon *History of Turton Football Club* (1909).
37. Tony Mason *Association Football and English Society* (1980) p. 24.
38. *Ibid.* pp. 22, 51, n.22.
39. *Contemporary Review*, November 1898, pp. 751–60.
40. *Nineteenth Century*, December 1893, pp. 909–10.
41. B. O. Corbett *Annals of the Corinthians* (1906) p. 6.

NOTES TO CHAPTER 16

1. J. Ruskin *Fors Clavigera.*
2. *Ibid.* Letter XXV, p. 28.
3. *Ibid.* Letter LVII, p. 175.
4. J. A. R. Pimlott *Toynbee Hall: Fifty Years of Social Progress, 1884–1934* (1935) Ch. II.
5. A. Toynbee *Lectures on the Industrial Revolution* (5th ed. 1896) p. 318.
6. F. F. Vane *Agin the Government* (1929) p. 55.
7. Pimlott *Toynbee Hall* p. 181.
8. James Springhall, *Youth, Empire and Society* (1977) p. 40.
9. *Ibid.* pp. 41–3.
10. *Ibid.* pp. 72–6.
11. *Ibid.* p. 125.
12. *The Solitary Warrior: New Letters by Ruskin* (ed. J. H. Whitehouse, 1929) pp. 116–17.
13. William Hillcourt and Olave Baden-Powell *The Two Lives of a Hero* (1964) pp. 254–5; Baden-Powell, statement to Supreme Court, New York, 1917, and letter to J. E. West 1915 (kindly communicated by William Hillcourt).
14. E. T. Seton *Trail of an Artist–Naturalist* (1951) pp. 291–301.
15. W. B. Forbush *The Boy Problem* (6th ed. 1907) pp. 100–4.
16. A Centenary Replica edition of the first edition was published in 1957.
17. *Scouting for Boys* (Memorial ed. 1942) p. 223. According to Baden-Powell, King Arthur 'dedicated the Order of St George' and his rules 'were published in the time of Henry VII', but I have not been able to find any such source. Baden-Powell *Aids to Scoutmastership* (1920) pp. 114–15.
18. Digby *The Broad Stone of Honour.*
19. M. S. Watts *George Frederic Watts* (1912) II, p. 301.
20. *Ibid.* p. 135.
21. *The Scout*, 12 September 1908.
22. Mostly in book form not until the 1930s or later, but they may have appeared earlier in *The Scout*, programmes, etc.
23. Pimlott *Toynbee Hall* pp. 179–87.
24. Incomplete runs of its periodicals and other publications are in the British Library.
25. *Record*, April and July 1911, April–June 1913, etc.

NOTES TO CHAPTER 17

1. *King Solomon's Mines* Ch. I; quoted Patrick Howarth *Play up and Play the Game* (1973) p. 112.
2. John Dickson Carr *Sir Arthur Conan Doyle, 1859–1930* (1949) pp. 14–15; Conan Doyle *Memories and Adventures* (1924) pp. 8–9.
3. T. de V. White *The Parents of Oscar Wilde* (1967) p. 21; H. Pearson *Oscar Wilde* (1960 ed.) p. 301, quoting William Wilde: 'Oscar is an Irish gentleman; he will stay to face the music'; *Letters of Oscar Wilde* (ed. R. Hart-Davis, 1962) p. 398: 'I did not want to be called a coward or a deserter.'
4. Viscount Chilston *W. H. Smith* (1965) pp. 1–2.

5. E.g., Emily Lutyens *A Blessed Girl* (1954) p. 183.
6. John Lord *Duty, Honour, Empire* (1971) p. 20.
7. C. R. Attlee *As it Happened* (1954) p. 22.
8. Howarth *Play up* p.119.
9. A. P. Stanley *Life of Doctor Arnold* p. 140
10. Elizabeth Longford *Pilgrimage of Passion* (1979) II, Chs. VII and XIII.
11. Blunt papers, Fitzwilliam Museum, Cambridge, MS. 42–1975, p. 419.
12. Herbert Asquith *Moments of Memory* (1937) pp. 116–17.
13. John Buchan *Greenmantle* (1916) Ch. II.
14. Roger Adelson *Mark Sykes: Portrait of an Amateur* (1975) pp. 75, 101.
15. It is reproduced opposite p. 294 of Shane Leslie *Mark Sykes: His Life and Letters* (1923) but is now too blackened by exposure for a satisfactory photograph.
16. Henry Newbolt *The World as in my Time* (1932) p. 198.
17. *Ibid.* pp. 204–5.
18. Newbolt 'Clifton Chapel'.
19. Newbolt *Book of the Happy Warrior* (1917) p. vii.
20. Carr *Conan Doyle* p. 333.
21. *The Later Life and Letters of Sir Henry Newbolt* (ed. Margaret Newbolt, 1944) p. 7.
22. See *Tyndale-Biscoe of Kashmir: An Autobiography* (1951). It starts with 'A Knight's Prayer'.
23. Roy Macnab *The French Colonel* (1975) pp. 211–12.
24. Isabel McAllister *Alfred Gilbert* (1929) pp. 216–17.
25. Charles T. Gatty *George Wyndham Recognita* (1917) pp. 20–1.
26. Lady (Ethel Priscilla) Desborough *Pages from a Family Journal* (1916) p. 442.

NOTES TO CHAPTER 18

1. *Maud* III, VI, 111
2. *National Observer*, 16 April 1892 (poem by Paul Cushing).
3. *Tom Brown's Schooldays* (illustrated ed. 1872) p. 231.
4. *Ibid.* p. 115.
5. *The Later Life and Letters of Sir Henry Newbolt* (ed. Margaret Newbolt, 1944) p. 7.
6. Foreword to C. de Thierry *Imperialism* (1898).
7. Newbolt *Later Life and Letters* p. 187.
8. E.g., O. F. Christie *Clifton College* (1935) p. 164.
9. *Punch*, 14 November 1914; Clodagh Anson *Victorian Days* (1957) p. 145.
10. Boy Scout's *Headquarters Gazette*, 1914; quoted E. E. Reynolds *Baden-Powell* (1942) p. 180.
11. Article on 'Patriotism', written for Charterhouse Ladies Guild, 1918 (Scout archives, TC/37).
12. Thomas Pakenham *The Boer War* (1979) p. 571.
13. Albert Gray *Patrick Walworth Gray* (1918) p. 118.
14. Pamela Glenconner *Edward Wyndham Tennant* (1920) p. 119.
15. Newbolt *Later Life and Letters* p. 191.
16. *Ibid.* p. 197.
17. Paul Fussell *The Great War and Modern Memory* (1975) p. 21.
18. Typescript memorial volume, now belonging to Nancy Hore-Ruthven.
19. J. S. Arkwright *The Supreme Sacrifice: And other Poems in time of War* (1919, illustrated).
20. Cecil Harcourt Smith (ed.) *Inscriptions suggested for War Memorials* (1919).
21. Arthur Machen *The Bowmen and other Legends of the War* (1915). This includes other chivalric tales, such as 'The Soldier's Rest', and an introduction describing the growth of the legend.
22. *The Love of an Unknown Soldier* (8th ed. 1919) pp. 40, 48, 88, 120.
23. *The Muse in Arms* (ed. E. B. Osborn, 1917) pp. viii–ix
24. Quoted Fussell *Great War* pp. 27–8.
25. A. St John Adcock *For Remembrance: Soldier Poets who have fallen in the War* (1918) p. 150 (on Leslie Coulson); *Philip Howell: A Memoir by his Wife* (1942) p. 247; A. W. Pollard *Two Brothers: Account Rendered* (1917) quotation on last page (on Geoffrey and Roger Pollard).
26. *Frank Maxwell V.C.: A Memoir and some Letters* (ed. by his wife, 1921) p. 10.
27. M. Hastings *The Handsomest Young Man in England* (1967) p. 210.
28. Adcock *For Remembrance* pp. 64, 74, 100, 170.
29. Glenconner *Tennant* pp. 25, 28.
30. *Ibid.* pp. 205, 251, 257.
31. Diana Cooper *The Rainbow comes and goes* (1958) p. 70.
32. Lady (Ethel Priscilla) Desborough *Pages from a Family Journal* (1916) pp. 635, 637–8, 646.
33. *Ibid.* pp. 573, 579, 582.
34. *Ibid.* p. 566.
35. The pictures were used to make up a group photograph, with Lady Desborough seated in the middle; reproduced Nicholas Mosley *Julian Grenfell* (1976) facing p. 183.
36. Newbolt *Later Life and Letters* p. 214.
37. Letter to Angela Manners, 1 August 1915, in possession of Nancy Hore-Ruthven.
38. W. Beach Thomas *Daily Mirror*, 22 November 1916; quoted Fussell *Great War* p. 175.
39. John Buchan *Francis and Riversdale Grenfell: A Memoir* (1920) p. 194. There was another charge at El Mughar, Palestine, on 17 November 1917 (Maj. Gen. Swann, *The Citizen Soldiers of Buckinghamshire, 1795–1926*, 1926).
40. *Raymond Asquith: Life and Letters* (ed. J. Jolliffe, 1980) p. 274.
41. *War Letters of Fallen Englishmen* (ed. Laurence Housman, 1930) p. 143.
42. Fussell *Great War* pp. 135–7.
43. Newbolt *Tales of the Great War* (1916) pp. 248–9; E. C. Middleton *Tails Up* (1918).
44. Among the several hundred Great War postcards in the collection of the late Bill Howell only some half dozen could be described as chivalric.
45. A. C. Sewter *The Stained Glass of William Morris and his Circle: A Catalogue* (1975) p. 295.

INDEX

INDEX

PHOTOGRAPHIC ACKNOWLEDGMENTS

Ian Anstruther 24, 25, 44, 62, 64, 66, 67, 69; Army Museum, London 100; Art Gallery of Western Australia 98; Bayerische Staatsgemäldesammlungen 101; BBC Hulton Picture Library 7; John Bethell XX; Birmingham Museum and Art Gallery 99, 124 and endpaper detail; Viscount Boyne 45, 46, 47; by courtesy of the Trustees of the British Museum 10, 16, 17, 19, 57, 83, 164, VI; Peter Burton XXXI; By permission of the Syndics of Cambridge University Library 6; Cavalry Club 2; David Lytton Cobbold 56; Country Life 11, 29, 109, 111, 133, 134, 135, 136, 137, 142, 144, 145, 146; County Record Office, Lincoln 48; Courtauld Institute of Arts 54, 90, 91, 92, 96, 165; G. C. Cullingham 127; Department of the Environment 53, 87, 119, VIII, XIV; Doncaster Museum and Art Gallery 159; Michael Dormer 37, 38, 39, 40, 41, 42; Dunedin Art Gallery, New Zealand XIX; Ursula, Countess of Eglinton and Winton 68; Captain D. O. Fairlie 79; Miss C. Findlay 103; Fine Art Society 128; Fitzwilliam Museum, Cambridge 1, 125; Fogg Art Museum 126; Viscount Gage 161; Mark Girouard 112, 115, 116, 178; Glasgow Museum and Art Galleries 166, 167; Guildhall Library, City of London 43; Nancy Hore-Ruthven 173; Jill Howell 175, 176, XXVII, XXIX, XXX; Imperial War Museum XXVIII; Laing Art Gallery, Newcastle-upon-Tyne 141; Lucinda Lambton V, IX, X; Earl of Lytton 131; Mander and Mitchenson Theatre Collection 3, 121; Mansell Collection 148; Merseyside County Art Galleries 106, 107, 118, 129, 169; Museum of Fine Arts, Boston XXIII; National Gallery of Ireland 54; National Galleries of Scotland 18, 75, 95; National Library of Scotland 60, 70, 71, 72, XII; National Maritime Museum, Greenwich, 9; National Monuments Record 28, 58, 59; National Museum of Antiquities, Scotland, 73; National Museum of Wales 179; National Portrait Gallery 93; Nottingham City Art Gallery 27; Perth Art Gallery and Museum 78; Edward Piper XXVI; Earl of Plymouth 140; Pre Raphaelite Trust 104 private collections 65, 74, 104, XVIII XXII; Mrs Phyllis Pryce 63; by gracious permission of Her Majesty the Queen 11, 13, 80, 81, 82, 84, 85, 88, 89, 90, 91, 92, 150, XIII, XVI; Lord Revelstoke 143; Patrick Rossmore 108; Royal Academy of Arts, London 86; Royal Botanic Gardens, Kew 14; Royal Commission on the Ancient and Historical Monuments of Scotland 12; Royal Institute of British Architects, London 15, 30, 51; Scout Association 163, XXIX; Trustees of Sir John Soane's Museum 22, II; Society of Antiquaries 130; Sotheby's, Belgravia 55, 160; Reproduced by permission of the Rt. Hon. The Speaker, House of Commons 53, VIII; James Stirling I; F. J. B. Sykes VII; Tate Gallery 123, XVII, XXI; Mrs Veronica Tritton 32, 34, 138, IV; Victoria and Albert Museum 105, 120, 156, 157; Watts Gallery, Compton 132, 139, XXV; Christopher Wood XI; Working Men's College, London 94.

DATE DUE